Cross-Curricular Teaching in the Primary School

How can teaching across the curriculum improve children's learning?
How can you plan meaningful, imaginative topic work?

Cross-Curricular Teaching in the Primary School helps teachers plan a more imaginative, integrated curriculum by presenting in accessible language a rationale and framework for teaching across the subjects. This second edition has been fully updated in light of the new curriculum, illustrated throughout with examples of effective cross-curricular work. With a new structure to emphasise the importance of careful planning and preparation, issues covered include:

- How children learn
- The theory and rationale behind the cross-curricular approach
- Developing the curriculum, and lesson planning
- Teaching and learning in an integrated way at KS1 and KS2
- Cross-curricular approaches for maths
- Whole-school approaches and team teaching for cross-curricular teaching
- The role of support staff in cross-curricular teaching
- Improving children's thinking skills
- Supporting children with special needs
- Using new media and drama to facilitate cross-curricular learning
- Assessing cross-curricular learning.

Cross-Curricular Teaching in the Primary School provides much needed support for busy student and practising teachers. Packed with practical ideas, it offers an accessible guide to all aspects of introducing an integrated curriculum.

Trevor Kerry is the University of Lincoln's first Emeritus Professor, and Visiting Professor at Bishop Grosseteste University.

'This book presents a thorough exploration of the benefits of connecting learning across the curriculum. The mechanics and philosophies of teaching are explored through thought-provoking case studies and accessible analysis of integrated learning in practice. The authors demonstrate the profound value and inherent necessity for discrete and interdisciplinary learning within an effective curriculum. This edition supports reflection, encourages questioning of pedagogical thinking, and suggests ideas which practitioners can use to take their practice forward in an inquiring and progressive way.' – **Yvonne McBlain**, Falkirk Education Services Curriculum Support

'This second edition of *Cross-Curricular Teaching in the Primary School* provides an in-depth insight into the theoretical perspectives underpinning cross-curricular teaching. The practical tasks focus on real teaching contexts shared by a team of authors with a wealth of experience in primary education.' – **Elizabeth Hunt**, Principal, Norland College, UK

Cross-Curricular Teaching in the Primary School

Planning and facilitating imaginative lessons

Second edition

Edited by Trevor Kerry

Routledge
Taylor & Francis Group

LONDON AND NEW YORK

Second edition published 2015
by Routledge
2 Park Square, Milton Park, Abingdon, Oxon OX14 4RN

and by Routledge
711 Third Avenue, New York, NY 10017

Routledge is an imprint of the Taylor & Francis Group, an informa business

First edition published by Routledge 2011

British Library Cataloguing in Publication Data
A catalogue record for this book is available from the British Library

Library of Congress Cataloging in Publication Data
Cross-Curricular Teaching in the Primary School: Planning and facilitating imaginative lessons / edited by Trevor Kerry – 2nd edition.
pages cm
Includes bibliographical references and index.
1. Reading (elementary) 2. Reading. 3. Literacy programmes. 4. Literature – study and teaching (elementary) I. Kerry, Trevor.
LB1573.C69 2015
372.4—dc23
2014033676

ISBN: 978-1-138-78790-2 (hbk)
ISBN: 978-1-138-78791-9 (pbk)
ISBN: 978-1-315-76601-0 (ebk)

Typeset in Galliard
by Swales & Willis Ltd, Exeter, Devon, UK
Printed and bound by CPI Group (UK) Ltd, Croydon, CR0 4YY

Contents

PART 7
Drawing together the threads of cross-curricular thinking   249

Figures

Tables

Case studies

Contributors

Listed in chapter order

Trevor Kerry, contributing editor, is the University of Lincoln's first Emeritus Professor, a Visiting Professor at Bishop Grosseteste University, and the first person to hold professorial status in both of Lincoln's HE institutions. His initial academic career was in theology, specialising in biblical languages; subsequently he pursued higher degrees in teacher education and education leadership. He has taught in primary and secondary schools, spent four periods as a teacher trainer, was a senior manager in FE, a Senior General Adviser for an LEA and an Ofsted Inspector. He was formerly Professor of Education, Senior Vice-President and Dean of the College of Teachers. He is well known for his many authored and edited texts on teaching skills, and on aspects of education management; one of these has been translated into Spanish and one into Chinese; he also has strong links with educationists in Malta. Trevor is a frequent contributor to education journals; he was a governor of two schools and chair of governors of one of them. In addition, he has written an eco-history text about a parson naturalist, has had considerable success in international photographic competitions, and published some papers on natural history and aeronautical topics. For several years he wrote journalistic material about wildlife and political topics (under a pseudonym). A life-long birder (scientific not twitcher!), he has recently completed a set of illustrations for the Lincolnshire Naturalists' Union of specimens from the former Lincoln Museum; he is Treasurer of the Isaac Newton Lecture for Schools at RAF Cranwell, which promotes engineering among young people. Thus he claims to have led an interdisciplinary life.

Elizabeth Wood is Professor of Education at the University of Sheffield. She specialises in early childhood and primary education, and has conducted research into teachers' professional knowledge and beliefs; progression and continuity; gender and underachievement; play and pedagogy; children's choices during free play; critical perspectives on early childhood policy, and equity issues in policy and practice. Elizabeth has an international reputation for her research on play and pedagogy, and has disseminated her work widely at UK and international conferences, as well as providing curriculum guidance and professional development materials in several countries. She has written many articles and books, focusing on contemporary directions in play, learning and pedagogy, curriculum development and policy issues. In a project funded by the Arts and Humanities Research Council, she has been working with

Dr Dylan Yamada-Rice to explore the potential for developing Videogames and Play for Hospitalised Children.

Jane Johnston was Reader in Education at Bishop Grosseteste University, Lincoln, where she coordinated the MA in Education prior to retirement. She works extensively, both nationally and internationally, in three distinct areas: early childhood, primary science education and practitioner research. Formerly she worked as a primary teacher, before moving into higher education, and leading primary science education and early childhood studies. She is the author of many books, chapters and journal articles on early childhood, primary education and science education, including *Early Explorations in Science*, *Enriching Early Scientific Learning*, *Teaching the Primary Curriculum* and *Developing Teaching Skills in the Primary School*, all published by the Open University Press, and *Early Childhood Studies* published by Pearson. She has also contributed to many other publications. In 2006, she was one of the first five teachers to be awarded Chartered Science Teacher status, which recognised the important relationship between research and teaching.

Christine Farmery holds a BEd (Hons) Primary Science, MSc Teaching Science 5 to 18 and EdD. She was head of Anston Brook Primary School in South Yorkshire, a school for 3 to 11 year olds. Christine has been a Visiting Lecturer in Primary Science, and has delivered INSET to schools and groups of teachers in her local authority. Christine is also the author of articles and three books: *Teaching Science 3 to 11*, *Getting the Buggers into Science* and *Successful Subject Coordination*. She and her staff reviewed the curriculum and gained a Leading Aspect Award for their creative and cognitive curriculum.

Peter Ransom is a Past President of the Mathematical Association and a freelance mathematics educator. He taught in state schools from the late 1970s and, since 2010, has done some part-time work with Bath Spa University's PGCE and worked with NQTs as part of the Prince's Teaching Institute. He is on the Education Committee of the London Mathematical Society, membership secretary of the British Society for the History of Mathematics, a Fellow of the Institute of Mathematics and its Applications, and also belongs to the Association of Teachers of Mathematics. He participated in the Bowland Maths initiative as project leader for the sundials case study. Peter has a keen interest in cross-curricular teaching of mathematics as he likes to involve all aspects of general knowledge into his teaching of mathematics. He takes risks. He has enjoyed mathematics all his life and tries to pass on that enjoyment to all he meets.

Carolle Kerry was chair of governors at a Lincolnshire primary school, having served in two schools as a governor, vice-chair and chair over a period of more than fifteen years. Carolle gained her BSc in Social Science and Social Policy with the Open University, and a doctorate in Head Teacher Performance Management at Lincoln University. She also holds a Fellowship of the College of Teachers for a collection of published works on the theme of governorship and able pupil performance. She published on the latter topic over a number of years, was a co-author of the *Blackwell Handbook of Education*, and undertook study visits to schools in Cyprus, Sweden and Portugal. In the last few years she has contributed to books on higher education, looking at issues concerned with effective tutoring and academic freedom. Carolle organised an exchange visit between a Maltese school and a UK school in 2014. In her free time she is Treasurer of the Royal Aeronautical Society RAF Cranwell Branch.

John Richardson is the headteacher at South Hykeham Community Primary School, a small village school with 140 on roll, on the outskirts of Lincoln. He has been head there for ten years. Prior to this he worked in two city-centre schools in Lincoln having started his career in the Peak District. His interests are playing the guitar, playing football and walking.

Sue Lambert is currently an Academic Coordinator for the PGCE Primary programme at Bishop Grosseteste University. Prior to commencing her post in HE, she taught in mainstream primary schools for nineteen years, teaching all ages in the primary phase. She was a SENCo for many years, which included responsibility for the most able children. She was seconded for eighteen months as an advisory teacher for history and was a subject leader for a number of subjects. She completed an MA in Education and her NPQH qualification. Her final post in school was as a deputy headteacher in a large primary school. Since working in HE she has also completed a CPSE and gained fellowship of the HEA.

Pat Foulkes is currently the Assistant Training Manager for the Shire Foundation SCITT. She was previously a Principal Lecturer and Head of Division of Applied Education Studies at the University of Bedfordshire. She has been involved in the training of teaching assistants for many years, particularly in facilitating their progression into a career in teaching. She has carried out research into the training and development of teaching assistants, and has evaluated induction materials for support staff. She has a range of publications relating to support staff development. She is currently a trainer and assessor for higher-level teaching assistants.

Jill Wallis worked for 20 years in the secondary education sector, becoming Head of English, Media and Drama, before moving to the post of Senior Lecturer at the University of Bedfordshire in 2002. She was course leader of the BA (Hons) Applied Education Studies course for five years, and continues to teach the English and research project units of the course – a part-time BA for support staff working in local primary and nursery schools who wish to qualify to become teachers and are completing their degree studies while continuing to work. Jill's research includes a study of the challenges facing mature students returning to HE study, and she has further supported these students during their QTS training following their degree. She is also a published poet and enjoys performance poetry, as well as editing an annual anthology of writing by local writers as a fundraiser for a local charity.

Judith Laurie taught in Lincolnshire and Humberside primary schools, with a period of time as an Advisory Teacher for English, before joining Bishop Grosseteste University in 1995. She became deputy headteacher of a large urban primary school in Humberside and, on behalf of this local authority, coordinated a reading initiative for schools. Judith completed an MA in Primary Education, researching ITE training for teaching reading. She became Programme Leader for the four-year undergraduate ITE programme and later was appointed Head of Department for PGCE and GTP Primary programmes, a post she held until her retirement in August 2009. Since then she has maintained links with schools and ITE by working part-time as a Link Tutor for Bishop Grosseteste, while also continuing in her role as External Examiner for ITE programmes, currently in Sheffield and Bedfordshire.

Kathleen Taylor began her career in education as an Early Years' teacher in primary schools in York, then – on completion of her MEd research into young children's narrative – she joined Bishop Grosseteste University in 1995 as Senior Lecturer for Primary Education and English. In 2001 she became Programme Leader for the BA Hons in Primary Education with QTS leading to Head of Department for undergraduate Primary Initial Teacher Training until her retirement in August 2009. Her work in education and particularly curriculum design led to her involvement in overseas teacher training projects in Macedonia and Bosnia Herzegovina, as well as establishing a teacher training college for women in Northern Pakistan. She continues to work in ITT as a Link Tutor for Bishop Grosseteste University, where she was awarded a Life Fellowship of the University in 2013. Kathleen has co-authored two recent books: *Creative Development: Supporting Development in the Early Years Foundation Stage* and *Values and Vision in Primary Education*. Her PhD research is focused on ethos in teaching and learning interactions in a primary school.

Peter Harrod taught in primary schools before being appointed as a Lecturer in Primary Education at Bishop Grosseteste University College, Lincoln. He gained an MPhil in Education from Nottingham University and an MEd in Educational Psychology and Children's Language Development from Sheffield. His research interests have been in the fields of children's language and reading development and, more recently, in the recruitment and retention of teachers in rural areas. He was an Open University part-time tutor for twenty-two years, and has been a primary school governor for twenty years. Now retired, he spends some of his time as archivist and Foundation Governor at Lincoln Christ's Hospital School. He is an Honorary Fellow of Bishop Grosseteste University.

Acknowledgements

Versions of the paper that underpins Chapter 1 were read and commented upon by Peter Harrod and Dr Carolle Kerry. The author is grateful for their comments and suggestions, but is entirely responsible for any shortcomings. The copyright for the original article is vested in the author, but the item originally appeared in *FORUM for 3–19 Education* 49(1/2), special double issue, 2007. It has, however, been revised, enlarged and updated several times since then. Peter Harrod also read Chapters 12 and 14.

For parts of Chapter 5 the authors would like to thank Mike Russell, the coxswain and crew of the Whitby Lifeboat Station. Readers may like to see the web page at http://homepage.ntlworld.com/dave.brining/welcome.htm. The authors of Chapter 9 are indebted to students on the BA Applied Education Studies degree at the University of Bedfordshire for examples cited.

With respect to Chapter 10, the author would like to express sincere thanks to Kevin Flint, headteacher, and to Alison Navas and Rachel Belk, who were (at the time of writing the case study) respectively deputy headteacher and Key Stage 1 teacher at Dunsville Primary School, Doncaster, for spending time to discuss and share their philosophy and examples of planning. In Chapter 11, thanks are due to: Waddington All Saints Primary School, Lincolnshire; Sir Edmund Hillary Primary School, Worksop; Cranwell Primary School, Lincolnshire; and Prospect Hill Primary School, Worksop.

For Case Study 12.2, the author of the chapter would like to thank Steph Neale, headteacher of Beatrix Potter School, London. Readers may like to follow up the references to Beatrix Potter School at: http://www.beatrixpotterschool.com. For Case Study 12.3, thanks go to Rowena Hill, formerly class teacher at South Hykeham Community Primary School, Lincoln.

In Chapter 13 the authors wish to thank the headteacher and staff of the Priory Witham Academy Primary Section, Lincoln.

A number of items emanated from the children, staff and headteacher of South Hykeham Community Primary School, Lincoln, whose contributions are gratefully acknowledged. In particular, the authors of Chapter 8 acknowledge the help and assistance of Sally Hillier, Deputy Head and art and RE subject leader at South Hykeham, and Nicky Wynne, class teacher Y5, 6.

If any contributor has been inadvertently omitted from this list, please accept our apologies; the mistake will be rectified in any future editions.

The editor would like to put on record thanks to all the authors for their part in seeing this revised edition to fruition in the midst of extremely busy professional lives. Also, his thanks go to Alison Abela, Elaine Scicluna, Kate Spooner, Melanie Ungaro and Geraldine Vella for access to master's work they completed for Leicester University, and for personal communication with Julie Harvie working on a PhD in Scotland.

The greatest vote of thanks goes, as always, to Dr Carolle Kerry for a lifetime of support, affection and hard work.

Foreword to the first edition

Having the opportunity to publish this text on cross-curricular working in primary schools has been a particular joy for three reasons: one related to pupils, one related to the past and one to do with policy. Each of them will be rehearsed here.

With respect to the pupils, while my wife was talking to youngsters in the local primary school as part of her research for this text, she had a conversation with a ten-year-old boy. She asked him why he liked cross-curricular lessons. His reply stopped her in her tracks: 'Well, they're like life; life is cross-curricular.' Out of the mouths . . . as they say.

My second joy relates to a book which I co-wrote twenty-five years ago with a former colleague, Professor Jim Eggleston. Jim and I were engaged at that time with the Schools Council. The Schools Council was government-funded, and what we might now call a quango; but it financed school-based research with a strong emphasis on improving teaching and on using professional wisdom to do this. The Council was disbanded soon after our book came to fruition, to be replaced by more agenda-driven organisations that were concerned with implementing predetermined policy rather than genuinely open-ended research.

But the book – *Topic Work in the Primary School* (1988),[1] also published by Routledge – took what I still believe to be an innovative and entirely correct stance. As well as presenting the reality – good and bad – about cross-curricular topic work in schools across the East Midlands at that time, it looked in detail at lesson sequences. It deconstructed those lessons to look, in depth, a step at a time, at class management, at teachers' skills as explainers, as questioners, as task setters. It looked at children's cognitive skills and how to grow them. The book went on to draw out the lessons that could be learned about the management of curriculum, about objectives, about assessing and recording outcomes, about professional development to support this way of working.

In addition to writing *Topic Work*, Jim and I disseminated the findings around the country in person; and, with others, we compiled a written and audio-visual resource bank for teachers which was put into production as one of the Schools Council's final acts.

The Schools Council did a particular job very well: it gave teachers, with the help of training professionals, the opportunity to apply action research principles to their work and share their practice. For any sceptics out there, the only evidence needed to confirm this view is to look on the one hand at the impressive list of Schools Council publications and projects (which were very influential in schools at the time), and compare these with the trivialised 'case studies' that crop up in government reports over the last decade under the guise of 'research'.

Twenty-five years on from *Topic Work* I suggested to Routledge that a new book about cross-curricular approaches and the integration of knowledge in primary schools might be opportune, and the company had the foresight to agree. The book would not be a retrospective, I suggested, but a new vision of what integrated learning means in the 21st century and why it is even more important now than it was then. I said that I believed we stood at the gate of a new dawn of insight about the nature of learning in primary schools, after several decades straitjacketed by the National Curriculum. I made the point that almost all major advances in thinking over modern times had been made by cross-disciplinary teams. That view is both expanded and tempered in Chapter 1 of this text.

So to revisit cross-curricular themes after twenty-five years was both a challenge and an excitement, plunging me once more into the world of children's thinking and insight, and taking the journey back to some previous roots. To do this I gathered my own cross-curricular team of authors from the UK; with contributions from pupils, teachers, governors, headteachers, and teacher educators and researchers. My hope is that what has resulted is a rounded book, and one which absorbs a variety of perspectives into a coherent whole. In the process, though, a critical aim has been to encourage teachers to develop themselves professionally through these pages: by means of the text, the cases that rehearse real practice in today's schools, and the moments of reflection about one's own practice. In this, the new book will be true to the worthy spirit of the old Schools Council.

So, there was joy in the pupils and joy in the past. My third joy in writing for, and editing, this text relates to a point made a little earlier. There is a wind of change abroad in primary practice. The advent of the Rose Report in May 2009 (Rose 2009) put a whole new spin on curriculum in primary schools. The quotations that follow are short extracts from the summary provided by the following website: http://www.usethekey.org.uk/popular-articles/independent-review-of-the-primary-curriculum-an-overview.

> Subjects will remain but will be complemented by cross-curricular studies.
>
> Subjects remain vital in their own right – cross-curricular teaching works to strengthen them.
>
> The current National Curriculum subjects will sit within six areas of learning. The knowledge, skills and understanding that all primary-aged children need are at the heart of these areas.

The proposed names for the six areas are:

- Understanding English, communication and languages
- Mathematical understanding
- Scientific and technological understanding
- Historical, geographical and social understanding
- Understanding physical development, health and well-being
- Understanding the arts

'Essentials for learning and life' skills run through the curriculum.

There is full scope for teachers to shape how the programmes of learning will be taught. The plan is to give schools much more flexibility to plan a curriculum that meets the national entitlement and greater discretion to select curriculum content according to their local circumstances and resources.

For the first time since 1988 (the year of the National Curriculum) teachers will feel encouraged and empowered, both to teach in an integrated manner and also to loosen the boundaries even of the subject-based work that they do ('areas of learning' having replaced 'subjects'). The view was strengthened by the Cambridge Review, written by Robin Alexander (2009). This is a short extract from the summary of this report:

> The report also rejects the claim that schools can deliver standards in the 'basics', or a broad curriculum, but not both, and argues that in any case the notion of 'basics' should reflect 21st century realities and needs. The report proposes a curriculum which is realised through eight clearly specified domains of knowledge, skill and enquiry, central to which are language, oracy and literacy. It also guarantees entitlement to breadth, balance and quality; combines a national framework with an innovative and locally responsive 'community curriculum'; encourages greater professional flexibility and creativity; demands a more sophisticated debate about subjects and knowledge than currently obtains; and requires a re-think of primary school teaching roles, expertise and training.

Areas of knowledge (Rose) or domains of knowledge (Alexander) – both imply integration and cross-curricular approaches. Both reports seek greater teacher autonomy. Both emphasise the need for schools – not merely governments – to have a steer on the tiller of curriculum.

So why is this book such a joy? Because, at last, there is a public admission that – in primary education at least – subject disciplines are not exclusive and should not be wholly dominant as a way of learning, important though they may be in some respects. We need other layers of understanding, too, to make sense of our rapidly changing world. We always did, of course; which is why schools have often struggled over the last twenty years. But now we can import them openly. This Foreword tells us something else significant regarding this emerging world of cross-curricular approaches: the pupils recognise its importance; the academics and trainers recognise it; and even the government recognises it.

For the first time for a long time it is possible to be optimistic about the shape of primary education.

Trevor Kerry
Lincoln

Note

1 Twenty-five years or more on from this volume's publication, it still breaks new ground in examining systematically a single lesson from a variety of perspectives to take an in-depth look at teaching skills.

References

Alexander, R. (2009) *Children, Their World, Their Education.* London: Routledge.
Kerry, T. and Eggleston, J. (1988) *Topic Work in the Primary School.* London: Routledge.
Rose, Sir Jim (2009) *Independent Review of the Primary Curriculum: Final Report.* London: DCSF.

Foreword and introduction to the second edition

If the reader has perused the Foreword to the first edition, he/she will have noticed that it was a moment of optimism that government would support a less prescribed approach to the National Curriculum and to teaching approaches. The moment passed with the formation of a coalition government composed substantially of former public-school boys, and with the appointment of Michael Gove as Secretary of State for Education: his policies have been described by many educationists (including me) as planning for the future by looking to the past (though, mercifully in the view of many, he was replaced in July 2014). Nonetheless, not all was lost: the National Curriculum 2013 was less content-bound, and provides teachers with greater scope for planning using cross-curricular methods. Children continue, in their wisdom, to enjoy these lessons and see the point of them.

In compiling the second edition of this text, there have been some radical changes, although the reader will recognise also a consistency of message.

The book has been divided into seven parts:

Part 1: Some theoretical issues
Part 2: Cross-curricular learning and teaching in EYFS and Key Stage 1
Part 3: Cross-curricular learning and teaching in Key Stage 2
Part 4: Helping exceptional pupils in cross-curricular lessons
Part 5: Planning and assessing cross-curricular work
Part 6: Some specific techniques for cross-curricular teaching and learning
Part 7: Drawing together the threads of cross-curricular thinking

The purpose of this new organisation of the book was, in part, to meet two criticisms from readers in a text otherwise well received; these will be mentioned *in situ* below.

In Part 1 – which forms the philosophical and theoretical basis for the cross-curricular approach – Chapter 1 has been considerably updated and strengthened to provide an even more robust argument for this way of learning. Chapter 2 sustains this policy.

Part 2 remains very much as in the first edition, with some appropriate updating, presenting the practicalities of teaching in the earlier primary years. In Part 3, Farmery's chapter on KS2 teaching has been retained as an exemplar, but an entirely new chapter has been added to the section. One of the criticisms received in response to the first edition was that, while integration of subject matter may work for 'soft' subjects like drama and art it had little relevance to science or maths. Science is covered intermittently throughout the text, but a specific chapter on integrating mathematics has been provided by Peter Ransom, a respected figure in teaching this area and (as emerges in the chapter) an enthusiast for the integrated approach.

Part 4 contains three chapters. That on inclusion has been substantially rewritten by the editor. The work with more able pupils has been updated and expanded by the authors from South Hykeham Community Primary School. The valuable work of teaching assistants is described by Foulkes and Wallis, with new examples.

The authors in Part 5 have rewritten their chapters on lesson preparation and on assessment from the perspective of the National Curriculum 2013.

Some critics suggested to us that the chapters that form Part 6 looked, in the first edition, like an afterthought. They were never intended to be that. The two themes – education through media, and team teaching – are, in our view, integral to cross-curricular learning and teaching. So the new section clearly explains their purpose as teaching techniques, and provides the reader with an updated review. In Chapter 12 electronic media are added – along with the moral dilemmas that these raise – and in Chapter 13 Peter Harrod follows up the original case study on team teaching three years on.

Part 7 consists of just one chapter, but it is a new addition to the text. It felt appropriate to draw together the thinking, which started from the philosophy of education in Chapter 1 and ranged through a series of practical approaches in Chapters 2–13, into a rebuttal of some of more extreme views of the disciplines-only lobby. This chapter exposes some of the weaknesses of an attitude that considers cross-curricular work as in some sense second-rate and less worthy of consideration.

So the authors hope that the second edition is more rounded, more complete, and more satisfying and useful to the reader than the first. We would like to thank everyone who found the first edition productive in their professional work and encouraged this new edition, not least Routledge staff for having the vision to produce this edition.

Professor Trevor Kerry
Editor

How to use this book

This is a book about the knowledge, understanding and skills required of a teacher in a primary school in order to use cross-curricular approaches to best advantage. The book uses a variety of means through which to set out, examine, and exemplify these skills:

- Text – to provide information, discussion and continuity
- Tables and figures – to convey data quickly or in graphic form
- Lists – to set out key issues or skills
- Reflections – to encourage the reader to apply the text to their own situations
- Case studies – to provide real examples of teaching situations.

The book can be used in a variety of ways.

- It can be read as a textbook.
- It can be used as a source book – you can consult the relevant sections (such as those on assessment or inclusion) as the need arises.
- It can be used as a self-training manual by an individual; in which case you will work through it systematically, pausing to carry out each 'Reflection' as you come to it.

The book is based on the philosophy that teachers need specific skills for the job. These skills can be identified, analysed, refined, broken down into sub-skills, taught, learned and even assessed. We hope that the book will be seen by busy teachers as a kind of *vade mecum* – a source of comfort and inspiration. It would be useful, too, as the basis of a systematic dialogue between a teacher and a mentor.

We trust that this manual of skills, based as it is upon grounded theory and experience, will bridge the gap that often exists for teachers who want to improve their effectiveness.

Part I

Some theoretical issues

Chapter 1

Introducing cross-curricular teaching

The conceptual underpinning

Trevor Kerry

Introduction

This chapter examines the notion of integrated or cross-curricular studies as a way of organising curriculum in schools. Drawing on the insights of educational philosophy, curriculum theory, and learning theory (though see also Chapter 2 for this last), it establishes the soundness of a theoretical case for this approach. It examines what this view means for the art and science of teaching, and notes examples of successful cross-curricular approaches in schools. The chapter identifies the roots of this philosophy in the thinking of the Plowden Report (1967), and suggests that the approach is equally valid today, albeit adapted for today's contexts.

Background

Five decades ago, Plowden (1967) made an important assertion that was later blamed (erroneously, if theorists like Eisner (1996) and practitioners like Campbell and Kerry (2004) are right) for a diminution in children's knowledge. It was this: 'Throughout our discussion of curriculum we stress that children's learning does not fit into subject categories' (Plowden 1967: para. 555).

Throughout a long career in education I have been convinced not only that this assertion is correct but that it applies equally to effective learning in any context. Clearly, I have expressed this view vehemently, as Spooner (2014) notes, referring to the first edition of this book, that, 'most of these themes are further developed by Kerry (2011), an experienced practitioner and researcher renowned for his work in this area, in his armamentarium for an integrated approach'. Clyde (1995: 115) shares my view and talks of children's learning as 'an interpretive network which spreads across domains'. The Trinidadian Minister for Education certainly concurs with this view (www.trinidadianexpress.com/news, accessed January 2014). She notes that, 'according to the academic literature, the more you connect knowledge for a child the better they learn. And this mode enables learners to perceive new relationships, new models and create new systems and structures in their thinking. So it is not limiting the child in any way. It is unleashing the creative potential of the child.' Hus and Grmek (2011: 160) maintain that, 'besides acquiring new knowledge, the emphasis [in what they call project lessons – *ed.*] is also on motivation, acquiring practical knowledge and developing social learning'. Closer to home, Education Scotland (www.educationscotland. gov.uk) is unequivocal.

> Interdisciplinary learning enables teachers and learners to make connections in their learning through exploring clear and relevant links across the curriculum. It supports the use and application of what has been taught and learned in new and different ways and provides opportunities for deepening learning, for example through answering big questions, exploring an issue, solving problems or completing a final project. Learning beyond subject boundaries provides learners with the opportunity to experience deep, challenging and relevant learning.

The vehemence of the 'subject discipline' lobby, however, at least in England, is so assertive and politically aggressive that it is comforting to find others who espouse the integration viewpoint – especially when those others include such intellectual greats as the American scientist Stephen Jay Gould (McGarr and Rose 2007). Gould must have met opposition to his integrationist view, because the chapter he wrote (with Rhonda Shearer, in McGarr and Rose 2007: 59–63) is couched in powerful prose:

> The contingent and largely arbitrary nature of disciplinary boundaries has unfortunately been reinforced, even made to seem 'natural' by our [i.e. human beings' – *ed.*] drive to construct dichotomies – with science versus art as perhaps the most widely accepted of all.
>
> (p. 59)

They go on:

> The worst and deepest stereotypes drive a particularly strong wedge between art (viewed as an ineffably 'creative' activity, based on personal idiosyncrasy and subject only to hermeneutical interpretation) and science (viewed as a universal and rational enterprise based on factual affirmation and analytical coherence) . . . If art and science could join forces by stressing our common methods in critical thinking, our common search for innovation, and our common respect for historical achievement – rather than emphasizing our disparate substrates and trying to profit from the differences in playing a zero-sum game at the other's expense – then we might, in Benjamin Franklin's remarkably relevant pun, truly hang together rather than hang separately.
>
> (p. 60)

This chapter intends to provide a rationale and some conceptual underpinning for this belief in the integrated nature of knowledge and understanding in order that like-minded educators in any context (and indeed, in any phase) may be able to justify their approach on the basis of the best elements in educational thought. It then goes on to explore the implications of cross-curricular content in education. Unlike the deliberately constructed exclusivity of the 'disciplines' lobby, the case for integration embraces both approaches as valuable, as Stephen Jay Gould (above) urges us to. If this chapter succeeds then, at the end of it, only those who feel most threatened by their inability to cope with integration, who line up with the deepest vested interests in ideology, and feel the least appreciation for evidence and reasoned argument, should be able to cling to the 'disciplines' lobby as the sole and exclusive truth.

Analogies are always dangerous, but it is worth risking one at this point. The relationship between 'disciplines' and integration is not unlike that between being a joiner and becoming a master carpenter/cabinet-maker. Both joiners on a building site and cabinet-makers in hand-crafting workshops have to know and understand the medium (wood), the tools (their functions and practical handling), and the processes of carpentry. But only a Chippendale goes on to have the conceptual skills, the design acumen and the aesthetic understanding to create quality products that exceed the disciplines of the trade to become works of art. Chippendale and his like are a million miles away in both levels of skills and, importantly, range of understandings, from making formwork for pouring concrete.

The problem

At the heart of the problem lies what is learned and how it is learned – I shall talk mainly about learning in schools, especially primary schools, but the context is easily widened by the reader, and is widened here from time to time to establish the point of the argument. The root question is, 'Should learning be divided into segments known as "subjects", or would it be better and more effectively acquired in some more homogeneous form?'

Answering this question is difficult, not because the answer is obscure but simply because a complete answer has many strands. Within the compass of this I will attempt to deal, albeit cursorily, with just four of them. If the answer is difficult it is because it defies convention (and people, even teachers, fear change) and because that convention itself supports a structure of vested interests.

The four strands that I will deal with, in turn, are these:

1   The supposed reality of 'subject disciplines'
2   Theories and models of curriculum
3   Theories and models of learning
4   Models of teaching that underpin integrated studies.

For teachers and those in training it is important to note that part of one's professionalism is to be able to justify and articulate the way in which one works; understanding the rationale that under-pins cross-curricular teaching is essential to putting it into action effectively in the classroom.

The supposed reality of 'subject disciplines'

Why do some educators oppose the use of integrated or cross-curricular approaches to learning in schools? Generally, the answer rests with convictions about how knowledge is constructed. The conventional argument goes something like this: *Knowledge falls naturally into 'domains', called subjects, which are bounded by specific kinds of conceptual thinking, specific ways of constructing knowledge that fit the content of the subject, and by procedures that are specific to that content.*

This view, or something approximating to it, has become embedded into educational practice and to depart from it requires a kind of intellectual conversion. But how accurate is it?

The problem is best explored through an example. To avoid becoming mired in controversy and emotional attachment to a subject on the primary timetable, let us take a neutral stance and talk in a detached way about the subject area physics (which appears rarely, if ever, on primary timetables); the principles can then be applied to other areas of learning. Physics is a 'subject discipline' in conventional thought. So what makes a physicist distinctive compared with a chemist or a theologian? First he (or, of course throughout, she) will have a content knowledge that is bounded by 'how the world works', the laws of the universe – at a simple level, the characteristics that define how electric current flows. Our physicist will have a scientific or positivist approach to problem solving: hypothesising, testing and observation, drawing conclusions, constructing a theory or law – and a multiplicity of these will provide a conceptual view of the universe. Then he will use particular conventions to record and communicate his discoveries and other information (symbols, formulae and so on).

So far, so good; every pupil, even in primary school lessons on electric circuits, for example, has experienced this. So then our pupil moves on to a lesson whose focus is rooted more in chemistry (again, I have avoided a subject on the typical primary timetable for the sake of neutralising the example). What changes? Well, not the scientific process and underpinning. Nor the use of particular conventions to record discoveries and information, even though the actual symbols and language may be slightly different – volts and forces may be replaced by valency and states of matter. What has changed fundamentally is not the approach to knowledge but the content of the lesson: the difference between physics and chemistry is in large measure down to content: what is learned, not how it is learned.

But (the reader may be thinking) this example is a poor one because we are comparing two closely allied 'subjects' – they are, after all, both sciences. Fine; then select theology (and again, as noted above, to distance ourselves from personal attachment to the argument and actual primary school timetables we will use this term rather than RE here) instead of chemistry. Theologians have specific subject knowledge (systems, sacred books, rituals); but they too 'solve problems' such as ethical hypotheses, based on observations (of human and divine acts), collect evidence (of good and evil), draw conclusions (moral codes), and speak in symbols (Allah, sacraments). All that has really changed is the content of their studies, not the epistemology that underpins them.

Then, all three of our 'subject specialists' – the physicist, the chemist, the theologian – find themselves moving out of primary school into higher education, teaching their subjects to undergraduates, and behold! Each is trying to offer a rationale for the universe, an explanation for human and material events, and ideas about how people should live within the contexts of the physical, chemical or spiritual universe, and even how their own subjects 'work'. So they all become philosophers!

Their answers and starting points may be different but they are bounded by the same concerns, the same need to establish conceptual structures, the same need to communicate knowledge, and the same requirements to invent symbols and laws to make sense of the universe. Their perspectives may be conditioned more or less by their content concerns, but their knowledge operates quite similarly and to quite similar ends. What distinguishes 'subjects' is not, at root, their 'distinctive disciplines' but rather their 'distinctive content' – and even then that content is, or may be, directed to similar core purposes.

Furthermore, while the physicist, the chemist and the theologian may each have a content-led distinctive contribution to make to human insight, each insight alone is partial, potentially blinkered and ultimately unsatisfying. Only by drawing all the insights – and others – together can the jigsaw puzzle of human life and the universe ever be more than a relatively random and incomplete corner of the real puzzle. Even then, we may need to add some things – from psychology, history or sociology, for example!

Let us advance the argument one stage further and ask, 'What of the "new" subjects so reviled by traditionalists but in which our primary children will, in a few years' time, be seeking university entry – media studies, film studies, American studies, sports studies, forensic or food sciences, and so on? Are these "subject disciplines" in a traditional sense, or are they indeed intellectually undemanding hotchpotches as their detractors claim?' In trying to answer this question I have taken arguments as they commonly emerge in the education press or in discussion.

If we take media studies (which probably started life in the primary school as some element of technology) as an example of a 'new' subject for our future undergraduate, then typically one suspects that it involves its own conceptual structures (e.g. understanding how various media influence the public, principles for judging the validity of information), its own ways to construct knowledge (drawing perhaps on areas like the psychology of perception or the sociology of communication), and its own languages and symbolism (such as headline writing or picture editing). In other words, these new subjects are really just like old subjects except that the content that underlies them is specific to their own area of knowledge and expertise. So we are back to content as the distinguishing feature. Our conclusion is that there are not, as it were, a limited number of pre-existent subject disciplines 'out there' that impose concepts, symbols and procedural processes on their students; we impose those on the material studied. Subjects impose on students only the content that defines them: a piece of knowledge either is, or is not, psychology, or astrophysics, or music. Even that content is to some extent fluid: today's knowledge in media studies is tomorrow's history curriculum.

If this is a fair portrayal, then we have to ask why the 'subject discipline' approach has lingered so long in educational institutions. There are probably a number of reasons (which would each require a longer study than is possible here), so let us merely suggest some indicators. The first is historical: the 'old' subjects, often invented by 'traditional' universities, existed first and so claimed some form of 'precedence'; but actually, if subject disciplines are traced back far enough, only three or four could trace their roots any distance. In the genuinely 'old' universities a would-be graduate had first to achieve his degree in arts (a generalism) before he could proceed to the higher (in the view of the time) 'subject disciplines' such as theology and medicine. But in this context 'disciplines' such as geography, history, Spanish, and so on, would have been considered avant-garde.

Other reasons are just as illogical and even more pragmatic. School-promoted posts may be linked to subjects, and to be a generalist (at least in a post-primary context) is a career disadvantage. People feel more secure if they can label themselves: how often do you hear teachers, on first introduction, announce, for example, 'I'm a historian'? And, since school timetables are subject-based, so parallel pigeonholing of people is convenient. Then there is the simple fear of change: we've always done it this way. And there is arrogance: to be a physicist provides more kudos than to be a geographer or an economist (the argument is circular: it must do, because the promoted post is worth more). In these ways, the vested interests of subject specialists are served, and to adopt another epistemological approach is to abandon one's advantage and launch into a sea of change that both demands thought and provokes insecurity about personal worth.

Those antagonistic towards cross-curricular or interdisciplinary approaches often call on educational philosophers to help them establish a case for discrete 'disciplines'; see especially the work of Hirst (1974). However, this approach is not entirely helpful. Hirst did not establish the discrete nature of 'subjects' in the traditional sense, but of 'forms of knowledge', which he listed as: pure mathematics and logic, empirical sciences, history and human sciences, aesthetics, morals, philosophy, and religion. This list is rather different from a conventional school timetable list consisting of areas like biology, French,

IT, geography, and so on. To qualify as a 'form', the knowledge had to be subject to demonstration as to truth (itself a debatable proposition); but also had to contain key notions or concepts specific to that form of knowing. Thus, while Hirst's classification of forms of knowledge does attempt to define the limits of those forms, the forms are none-theless far broader than traditional 'subjects'. Gardner's (2008) nine 'intelligences' might be considered an updated version of Hirst's propositions – and one that is equally specula-tive, common-sense, non-empirical and broad in its approach. Nor have we proponents of cross-curricular approaches ruled out the existence of concepts, rules, laws or symbols pecu-liar to certain areas of knowledge; we have simply pointed out that all subjects share such (albeit different) codes and procedures, while what they don't share is the subject content. Once again, the key discriminator is content.

In this context, a productive approach was adopted by Lawton (1997), who proposed four principles of change away from content-led curriculum (including specifically the for-mer versions of the National Curriculum, which many educators saw as having more down-sides than advantages to both teachers and teaching), which were:

1 Replacing the thrust of content and objectives, with a concern for skills and processes
2 Moving from subjects and attainment to cross-curricular themes and the affective domain
3 Shifting the emphasis from didactic teaching to self-directed learning
4 Moving from the academic/vocational divide to integration of both aspects.

Lawton, wisely it is suggested, concludes that 'subjects may be useful up to a point' but that 'more pressing problems are not conveniently packaged within a single subject', so there is a need to move 'beyond subjects' (1997: 85). (For devotees of Plowden, let it be said that the report allows for the co-existence of subjects within and alongside thematic approaches (1967: Chapter 17 passim).)

So it is important to say one more thing about this argument. It should not be con-strued as in any way devaluing the worth of any area of knowledge, its content or forms of thinking. Insight, understanding and problem solving can be advanced either by sharing thinking and factual information across areas of knowledge or by pushing back boundaries in some more closely defined corner of learning. Each has its place and its validity. This approach promotes the worth of knowledge as a whole, rather than seeking competition between different forms of knowledge in some kind of possibly spurious hierarchy.

Reflection

Can you think of an instance in your own learning where a problem was solved by using data and skills from across a range of disciplines?

Theories and models of curriculum

But if subject disciplines are redefined as relating more to discrete areas of content than to separate and ring-fenced forms of knowing, then adopting cross-curricular approaches to learning becomes far more respectable and attainable. Indeed, this redefinition forces educa-tional planners not to construct a syllabus based on areas of knowledge *per se* (the very trap into which the former National Curriculum fell, it is suggested) but to construct a curriculum on the basis of what pupils and society need – to begin not from content but from the learner: 'at the heart of the educational process lies the child' (Plowden 1967: para. 9).

I will not rehearse Plowden's arguments (see paras 508–555), but simply summarise a few modern views about curriculum that support and sustain the report's position, and provide some examples of such curricula at work to establish their feasibility and effectiveness.

Eisner (1996), in conclusions not entirely removed from Hirst's, considers curriculum to consist of 'forms of representation': auditory, kinaesthetic, tactile, olfactory, visual, and gustatory . . . which are manifested in art, music, speech, drama, text, mathematics, etc. These forms of representation require an affective context based in social learning and in society. He urges that knowledge ('content' is the label used above) can be understood and appreciated from a variety of perspectives, but that if pupils believe, say, that a 'text possesses a single correct meaning' they will seek only that meaning and will fail to look for other meanings. This attitude, he says, does 'little to promote intellectual values . . . multiple perspectives . . . judgement, risk-taking, speculation and interpretation' (1996: 71). The result of such a paucity of approach is that so-called learning becomes confined to factual material, to what is testable in simplistic ways, and to phenomena such as league tables of achievement that reflect only a fraction of potential intellectual activity – phenomena that resonate with today's educational practices.

In a related critique, Ross (2000: 81, 82) sets out a social transformative theory of curriculum in which 'each individual gets the opportunity to . . . come into a living contact with a broader environment' and to gain 'knowledge as something constructed by the learner as an active experimenter, provoked into enquiry by the teacher'. This theory takes us to a third Plowden principle: that of 'discovery' (1967: para. 549), in contrast with subject-based and content-driven didactic approaches.

Ross (2000) also identifies other metaphors for studying curriculum, among which is his metaphor of the 'natural landscaped curriculum'. In this, 'subjects are . . . highly artificial, dividing forms of knowledge with contrived distinctions . . . of process, knowledge and procedure' (after Rousseau 1913). Plowden had pre-dated this view with the assertion (1967: para. 521) that 'learning takes place through a continuous process of interaction between the learner and the environment'. The report's basic stance on the integration of curriculum is supported by subsequent writers such as Stenhouse (1975), Elliott (1998) and Kelly (1999). Indeed, this brief review leads one to ask whether learning would be subdivided at all, into subject disciplines or otherwise, if it were not for the bureaucratic straitjacket of schooling and timetabling.

Both Eisner and Kelly challenge the exam culture of modern education systems, identifying the failure of content-led teaching in even achieving the declared purpose of communicating the content itself (Kelly 2001), and pointing out the cultures of blame for pupils' failures that are generated among teachers by politicians. The Plowden Report warned against over-prescription (1967: para. 539) of curriculum by individual schools; since that time we have seen prescription by government, championed by Ofsted, and measured by a variety of closed approaches – a far worse scenario than Plowden could have envisaged. Carr (2003: 146) challenges the governmental approach strongly: 'Any philosophy of education that models educational development on the pattern of uniform initiation into a pre-specified range of forms of knowledge and understanding may be dangerously procrustean.'

Later, we shall see that it is not only curriculum theorists who find the Plowden vision liberating, feasible and preferable, but also many influential learning theorists concur. But for the moment the point is made, and it is opportune to ask whether cross-curricular approaches can work even in the inimical context of today's education system. In an article in a secondary school context, Campbell and Kerry (2004) described the construction and implementation of a form of integrated curriculum for 11–14 year olds. Not only was the curriculum remodelled on these lines, but pupils were accelerated through it, taking the appropriate (subject-based) Standard Attainment Tests (SATs), required at the time, a year early. In the first year of operation, therefore, two cohorts of pupils were tested simultaneously, one having moved through the curriculum following conventional studies over three years and one having studied the more integrated curriculum in just two. The results were outstanding, the outcomes of the two cohorts almost identical, and that in one of the country's highest-performing schools.

In another account (Kerry 2005) a further example was outlined, of a comprehensive school that was planning to revert from heavily subject-orientated teaching back to integrated approaches. Cryer School's problem related to providing adequate post-16 opportunities for its academic and less academic pupils; and the solution was seen in a re-examination of both curriculum and learning and teaching methods. Rather less surprisingly, perhaps, the same article describes a similar reversion to integrated approaches in a primary school, Quinnan School; the views of a number of heads are reported to the effect that 'Curriculum has to be more pupil-centred, more integrated, and more demanding [i.e. than the National Curriculum which prevailed at the time]' (Kerry 2005: 17). However, the article also notes a headteacher's view that, of a cohort of teachers trained post-NC:

> Most . . . know how to access lesson notes from the Internet, but they can't devise material for themselves, from the ground up. They don't understand how to lead pupils into high levels of thought because they're fixated on the content. They need some basic help in structuring learning cognitively, and they need teaching skills to draw pupils' thinking out.

This, apparently, is the professional legacy of a generation of educational planners who poured scorn on the Plowden Report. However, Carr (2003: 15) would urge us to define our terms, drawing a distinction between the narrow purposes of schooling (which might include content acquisition for its own sake) and education (which implies that pupils acquire 'an understanding of themselves, the world and their relations with others that enables autonomous recognition and pursuit for their own sake of interests and projects of intrinsic satisfaction').

So how can one sum up the argument of this chapter so far?

First, an attempt has been made to establish that the notion of subject disciplines, if not actually spurious, has at least been overplayed and too restrictively applied in the English education system. Motivation for adhering to this epistemology has been related more to self-interest or convenience, with strong underlying issues of pragmatism, rather than to reality. Second, curriculum theorists, in a respectable line from Rousseau to Ross, have espoused the cause of cross-curricular approaches. Third, it has been demonstrated that integrated curricula work in practice in both secondary and primary schools. Finally, it is suggested that these cross-curricular approaches avoided the worst pitfalls of the National Curriculum (NC) and testing system: limited tests of content-learning reduced to league tables that are de-contextualised to make judgements about schools. Though we have now abandoned the older, more prescriptive National Curriculum, we have not abandoned the narrowly based judgement on outcome tests. But, to do justice to the cause of integration one has to move on two more steps in analysing how best it can be implemented; and first to examine the place of cross-curricular learning in learning theory.

Theories and models of learning

It would be wrong to assume that Plowden represents a merely dated view of the nature of learning; it makes a genuine effort to review the (then) contemporary and progressive theories. The report also anticipates one of the latest and most popular learning theories among modern teachers: Gardner's multiple intelligences (Gardner 1999, updated 2008). Gardner's list of intelligences will rapidly be seen to relate to Eisner's theories about how to classify curriculum. Gardner's learning categories (see also Chapter 2 of this volume) include: linguistic/verbal, logical/mathematical, visual/spatial, kinaesthetic, musical, naturalist, interpersonal, and intra-personal. First, let it be said that this contiguity between curriculum and learning theories is important if one is to construct a sound approach to pupils' educational experiences, and it is exemplified in the Brooke Weston curriculum innovation outlined above. There, Campbell and Kerry describe the new curriculum as underpinned by CELTIC approaches and socially valuable themes (see Campbell and Kerry 2004: 392–396 for a definition of CELTIC). Jarvis, while posing some critical reservations about multiple intelligences, quotes Kornhaber:

> The theory validates educators' everyday experience: students think and learn in many different ways. It also provides educators with a conceptual framework for organising and reflecting on curriculum, assessment and pedagogical practices.
>
> (Jarvis 2005: 53, 54)

This link between learning theory and curriculum design is an important one: indeed it was one drawn to teachers' attention in Kerry and Eggleston (1988), where reflections on learning effectiveness led to the design of a tentative integrated curriculum for able children in schools based on themes rather than subjects (these included scientific studies, literature, aesthetics, thinking skills, technology and computer studies, cultural studies, life skills, and languages). By contrast, the traditional approach began from subject disciplines and projected them on to the learner. Plowden adopted an opposite view and began from the learner. Seen from this end of the telescope the learning picture looks different.

This last was a conclusion born out of my own empirical research in the 1980s, which has been, I believe, under-exploited. Research that was carried out between 1976 and 1981 (for the Department of Education and Science's Teacher Education Project, directed by the late Professor Ted Wragg and managed by the author) explored classroom learning from the perspective of cognitive demand. My work took the Bloomian (1956) categories of cognition (slightly redefined for fieldwork purposes) and explored how much cognitive demand was made by teachers on pupils during lessons through verbal interactions and in the tasks they set in class and for homework. These studies were carried out initially in what are now Year 7 (Y7) classes; the idea was later extended to compare the findings with those in primary schools, and with similar research among older students. The findings were published in a range of journals, but the broad picture is captured in my chapters in Wragg (1984, since reprinted many times). Here only the bare bones of the argument need to be rehearsed.

In the original research, teachers' talk, teachers' questions and classroom tasks set in Y7 classes were assessed for cognitive demand using an adapted Bloomian scale that allowed an overall measure of how many teacher inputs, questions or tasks in a lesson were at a higher level of cognitive demand and how many at a low level (and also the nature of the higher-level demands, but these need not detain us for the present purpose). A very broad conclusion from the wealth of analysis was that fewer than 5 per cent of all verbal transactions and fewer than 15 per cent of tasks were at a higher level. In fact, verbal transactions related to class control occupied between 14.5 per cent and 29.4 per cent of all transactions in the studied schools – much more frequent than higher-order learning activity. This does not bode well for learning.

Within the data it was possible to compare results across subjects, and one of the most surprising and interesting outcomes related to the tasks set in lessons across the schools in the initial study (Table 1.1). Here it can be seen that English and science perform relatively well, but other subjects tail off, with even mathematics performing rather poorly. But, as luck would have it, the organisation of these Y7 classes meant that in some schools there was an element of the timetable taught as integrated studies. In integrated studies lessons, which used cross-curricular approaches, the higher-order task demand rose on average to 41 per cent. In other words, learning was deeper and more effective in lessons where subject content was cross-curricular than in lessons where it was organised simply by subject discipline. So, one might hypothesise, not only is it logically preferable according to the principles of curriculum and learning theory to integrate lesson content, it is actually more effective in producing cognitive outcomes.

Two other findings reinforced the stated conclusion. The first was that, in an accelerated examination group (current Y10), cognitive demand actually fell, because the lesson transactions were related only to the acquisition of content in order to address examination questions. The other was that, when the measures were applied to primary classrooms where work was, without exception, cross-curricular, these lessons scored consistently higher in cognitive demand on pupils than did subject-discipline lessons overall in secondary schools. The clear message from all this research appeared to be: if you want pupils to think, integrate.

These findings might have been the subject of more research and might have resulted in a more widespread adoption of integrated learning but for an unfortunate confluence of factors. The project came to the end of its funded life and so the original team split up (though both Wragg and I continued to make similar informal small-scale measurements, with similar outcomes). No other researchers took up and exploited these indicative findings. The DES itself was in a period of change. Not long afterwards the National Curriculum was initiated, with its bias towards subject disciplines. Interestingly, this had a negative effect in another,

Table 1.1 The levels of higher-order cognitive demand in classroom tasks, by subject, in Teacher Education Project research (%)

English	33.3
Science	23.0
History	11.5
French	11.3
Maths	8.9
Music	6.7
Religious education	5.0
Geography	4.2

unintentional, way. An early version of the assessment by teachers of the newly implemented National Curriculum in 1988 required them to record pupil achievement using a kind of Bloomian system. But the system was bastardised, poorly explained, with teachers untrained in its use, and recording was cumbersome. So, in all later versions of the National Curriculum – which survived until 2013 – this potentially useful approach was quickly abandoned in favour of easier solutions that were administratively less hassle – even if somewhat lacking in meaning.

What, however, is clear is that not only are narrow subject-disciplines not a necessary part of how knowledge is constructed, but school curriculum can be built on a sound body of theory about curriculum and learning that supports an integrated approach. Furthermore, in pedagogical terms, there is research evidence that integration 'works', that it produces good learning and perhaps superior learning. So what are the implications for teachers and teaching?

Reflection

How, and to what extent, do the research findings reported above resonate with your own classroom experiences?

Models of teaching that underpin cross-curricular studies

If we are to move beyond functionality (how much revenue is required to teach ring-fenced content to a given level of acquisition) into a holistic view of curriculum as an approach to the self-development of the learner, then we place not less but more onus on effective teaching. In turn, that teaching has to be redefined. Spooner (2014), in a small-scale study in a Chilean context, made a universal point that change to integration has to be real, and 'warns against falling into the trap of adopting the language connected with integrated curricula without really changing instructional practice'. Teaching in a cross-curricular context makes the place of the learner central, rather than the place of content, and requires a different kind of approach to teaching in order to be effective. Overall didactic approaches won't do, though at times they may have a place.

Though Ofsted has always denied that it favoured didactic teaching, a former Chief Inspector has made it clear that such was his own position (Woodhead 1995); he called papers like this chapter 'pernicious' (Woodhead 2002). Indeed, alternatives to didactic teaching are illogical within a subject-restricted, content-led curriculum; and it was Woodhead who helped establish that curriculum, even though in his 2002 speech he rejected it as ineffectual! For, in this era, it ought to be admitted at the same time that schooling has ceased to be education and has become training. (A parallel process took place in teacher education during the same period.)

The Plowden Report (1967: para. 503) identified a series of 'danger signs' to indicate when effective teaching had collapsed, a list that reads today almost like an indictment of NC as it was taught from its implementation until 2013. In a study of the learning of able pupils after NC implementation, Kerry and Kerry (2000: 38) were given a very similar list of NC failures by teachers. Table 1.2 puts these lists side by side in what is a very telling juxtaposition. They remain relevant today for two reasons: first, because this is the kind of learning many children currently passing through our schools will have experienced for some or the bulk of their school life; and, second, because this reflects the kind of teaching that teachers will have become used to undertaking.

Table 1.2 Comparison of Plowden's indicators of failing lessons with teachers' views of National Curriculum

Plowden's 'danger sign'	Teachers' views of NC
Fragmented knowledge	Prescriptive content
Limited creative work	Lack of creativity
Much time spent on teaching (as opposed to learning)	Restricted teacher initiative in curriculum and teaching
Few questions from the children	Compartmented thinking
Too many exercises	Failures of pace and level
Straitjacketed learning	Narrowed expectations
Concentration on tests	

Plowden, however, is aware that, to be effective, the teaching required by cross-curricular approaches cannot be less well executed than that of didactic approaches. Paras 549–552 assert that words like 'discovery' cannot be used lightly, that teachers must bring to their teaching 'a stringent intellectual scrutiny', that the progress of pupils must be assessed and monitored (in appropriate manners), and that the quality of individual schools must be kept under review. None of this smacks of the 'nambyism' and woolly thinking attributed to the Plowden Report by its detractors (for example, Grossen 1998).

So, given that the Plowden vision of curriculum and of learning is accepted, what are the actual implications for teachers and models of teaching? I would suggest that teaching, while not an easy process, is essentially a simple one. By that is meant that the agenda for teaching skills is clear, even if the skills themselves require to be learned, constantly reflected upon, honed and improved. The complexities of this process of teaching, and of understanding it, are summarised by Bennett (1997: 139–140). To teach an integrated curriculum effectively (in fact, to teach anything effectively) there are some basic essentials in the teacher's armoury, and these can be seen as areas of teaching skill:

- Skills in class management
- Skills in explaining
- Skills in questioning
- Skills in task setting and differentiation and, increasingly
- Skills in assessment.

Within the scope of a short chapter such as this, it is impossible even to outline these skills, but they can be accessed readily in other published work (Kerry 2002a, 2002b; Kerry and Wilding 2004). These skills represent the agenda for teaching competence, and should be high on the priority list of all teacher education establishments. This is not to say that other skills do not exist or are unimportant, but simply to state that these are fundamental – the building blocks of all other classroom teaching and learning. At present, not enough time is spent on them, and too few teachers have genuine command of them. This list evolved from the Teacher Education Project mentioned above, but is slightly extended over the original version; they are not plucked out of the air but based on research and grounded theory. However, many teachers will warm to the version of these events recounted inimitably by Wragg (1984: 8):

> The areas on which we chose to focus, class-management, mixed ability teaching, questioning and explaining, seemed . . . to represent activities which required skill,

intelligence and sensitivity from teachers. They were not so vague as to defy analysis, nor so minute and piddling as to be silly.

It is heartening to discover, as reported earlier, that many schools have recently been reconsidering curriculum approaches and are tending to move closer to an integrated approach with a renewed interest in pupil learning. In the Introduction it was pointed out that there were brief political and 'official' encouragements to take these steps, such as the Rose Report. Curriculum directions for the next few years are, at the time of writing, not entirely clear; and this makes curriculum planning at school level even more crucial. But it is important to stress the need to move in parallel to make teachers' activities and teaching appropriate to the new curriculum and learning intentions. Indeed, where this does not happen, any experimentation may prove at best ineffectual and at worst disastrous; Kerry and Wilding (2000: 259–271) reported just such a case.

Reflection

What do you think will be the skills needed of learners when your pupils are at the peak of their working lives, in twenty or thirty years' time? How will they differ from the ways in which you learned?

The problem with government-led curriculum reform, along with related views about pedagogy and assessment, has been that Britain has been overly prescriptive, as noted by Power, in order to 'position subjects in ways that hark back to some imagined past, rather than forwards into more globalised times' (2002: 103).

In other words, rather than accepting that in an information world knowledge itself will be beyond the capacity of the human brain, and that the important skills will be in evaluating and applying knowledge, successive governments from 1988 sought to narrow views of class and social position through a kind of constrained 'received wisdom' imposed through compulsory curricula and teaching methods. Aldrich, Crook and Watson (2000: 164) call this 'the renewed dominance of the old humanists and of a traditional academic culture'. Yet this position has proved as unsustainable as it is illogical.

The Rose Report (DCSF 2008) is an example of a laudable attempt to fill a gap in curriculum provision that was created by the very government bodies that are now trying to patch up the hole in the ship. Successive governments removed curriculum autonomy and flexible teaching; but let us be grateful for the small mercy that they are now beginning, belatedly, to hand some elements of these things back to the profession.

While much of the rest this book is about teaching and learning strategies as these relate to an integrated approach to curriculum, perhaps it is opportune to summarise some of these, in anticipation of further discussion, by quoting from the Education Scotland website again. Its rather neat summary is reproduced here as Table 1.3.

Summary

This chapter has tried to establish: first, that the Plowden ideals of a cross-curricular approach are relevant (perhaps even more relevant) to schools in the modern world; and, second, that they are soundly based in both the groundwork of research and theory, and in

Table 1.3 Education Scotland's guidance on cross-curricular learning

Learning beyond subject boundaries provides learners with the opportunity to experience deep, challenging and relevant learning.

Practitioners can achieve this by:

- Having a clear focus on a small number of different curriculum areas/aspects of a curriculum area or subjects, for example music and drama;
- Making clear connections with literacy, numeracy and health and well-being across learning;
- Focusing on a few carefully selected and relevant experiences and outcomes;
- Involving learners in in-depth investigation drawing on various sources of information and developing experience and awareness of different curriculum areas in the process;
- Choosing a theme or problem which requires knowledge and skills from different curriculum areas, aspects of curriculum areas or subjects;
- Capitalising on themes for development across learning, including developing global citizenship, financial education and outdoor learning;
- Responding to a significant event;
  and through:
- Stimulating learning and teaching activities which include frequent explicit reference to the knowledge and skills being developed and the connections across and within curriculum areas and subjects;
- Involving learners in:
  - active, collaborative learning;
  - challenging, thought-provoking tasks; and
  - critical thinking.
- Clear planning across curriculum, learning, teaching and assessment which identifies:
  - the specific learning intentions of the interdisciplinary work;
  - the experiences and outcomes from each curriculum area which are being developed.
- How a range of evidence of what has been learned will be gathered; and assessed, including through discussion with the learner.
- Working towards an overall strategy for interdisciplinary learning, which may include consideration of:
  - appropriate balance of disciplinary and interdisciplinary learning;
  - appropriateness of learners' progression;
  - coherence in learners' experiences;
  - effective organisation of learning and/or timetabling;
  - provision of appropriate time and support for teachers' planning; and
  - evaluation of learning.

the pragmatism of teachers' experience and classroom understandings. Much of this experience has to do with cross-curricular approaches in the context of problem-solving, and it is to this we now turn.

Integrated curriculum and problem-solving

It is pertinent for Harvie (2014, pers. comm.) to draw attention to problem solving as a key to understanding the value of interdisciplinary working: 'Research carried out by Hmelo-Silver *et al.* (2009) also showed that students who participated in a problem based interdisciplinary approach were able to construct a deeper understanding of the concept of transfer than students who did not.' Hmelo-Silver (2007), in a small-scale but pertinent study of problem-based learning, had previously concluded:

> Complex learning requires integrated development of knowledge, inquiry practices, reasoning strategies, and lifelong learning skills in a variety of situations. Such learning is hard because complex domains often span a range of subject matter and skills and poses great challenges to cognitive, metacognitive, and social resources. Technology has great power to afford complex learning experiences that would not otherwise be possible as well as providing tools that can help deal with these challenges.

It is also interesting that Humes (2013) implies that the Scottish curriculum, in formulating its cross-curricular plans, does not go far enough philosophically in exploring the concepts underpinning the approach. He suggests that interdisciplinary methods are needed when the issue under scrutiny is 'too broad' for a mono-disciplinary approach. Interdisciplinary working has implications for the kind of curriculum devised and for the purposes that underpin the learning (indeed, that underpin schooling). He calls for support on Repko (2008), and Joyce, Calhoun and Hopkins (1997), but his best ally might be Beane, who says that 'the central focus of curriculum integration is the search for self- and social meaning' (1997: 616).

Similarly, on a more pragmatic level, it could reasonably be argued that science is the most problem-orientated and evidence-based discipline in the primary curriculum. Kelly and Stead (2013) review research into cross-curricular science and conclude:

> In science this view of learning is supported by more than 30 years of research, for example the Children's Learning in Science Project (1984–86) and the SPACE Project (1990–95) (Wellcome Trust 2005), which show that learning in science is most effective when children are able to see the relevance of the science they are learning and when it is meaningful to them. Making science interesting and relevant to children is one of the key features of effective science teaching and learning
> (Harlen 2006: 9; Wellcome Trust 2008)

However, the road is not easy, and it is Beane (1997: 618–619) who once more identifies the pitfalls. In discussing the 'deadening effect of the subject approach', he warns of educational élites 'whose symbiotic relationships are founded upon it' – such as text writers, academics and publishers. He notes that parents are timid because they are always looking for their children to replicate their own school experiences. He notes (as we have elsewhere) that teachers build a professional identity by subject – not a teacher, but a maths teacher. Finally, he warns against the conservative era in society through which we are living (although he speaks of the USA, the same might be said of the current UK government).

Being sceptical about cross-curricular working

It is entirely right to raise issues about cross-curricular working, and to examine its philosophical and practical bases. Every educational system or approach should be rigorously interrogated and subjected to challenge. Challenge is a right and proper academic procedure, but the more dogmatic and ideological assertions of some critics, from the Black

Papers (published by Brian Cox in the *Critical Quarterly*, 1969) down to modern times (Gove, reported by Garner 2014), have hardly been worthy of the descriptor.

Veronica Boix Mansilla and Howard Gardner (2004) collaborated at postgraduate level to examine funded interdisciplinary projects at exemplary interdisciplinary institutes and collect the views of sixty academics about their validity. Though this might seem some way from the primary school, the paper has some useful insights. They concluded that excellent interdisciplinary work involved three key factors: first, the disciplines subsumed within the wider project all individually adhered to the norms of those individual disciplines; second, that the balance between those disciplines was appropriate for the problem being investigated; third, that the project as a whole succeeded in advancing knowledge and understanding. However, the real issues arose not in the execution of the project work, but in its assessment. Usual assessment criteria (somewhat mechanistic ones such as the number of patents generated) often did not apply so easily to the interdisciplinary approach – shades here, perhaps, of government-inspired primary school testing. New criteria, by assessors who understood the cognitive process of interdisciplinary work, were needed, and these they listed (2004: 5) as:

> The relationship between 'inter-disciplinary outcomes and the disciplinary antecedents'
> The adjustments that take place as disciplines are 'intertwined into a well-balanced whole'
> The 'leverage created by the newly-created hybrid insights'.

In much of primary education, too, problems arise because methods of assessment are not adequately married to intentions and pedagogies (see Chapter 10). In the primary school, as in other phases, interdisciplinary work needs to be formulated against rigorous goals and intentions. It probably begins from a problem base. Its assessment needs to ensure that studies remain faithful to the individual disciplines that underpin them, and that those disciplines are used in an insightful and balanced way. Table 1.4 suggests the contrast between a traditional disciplines-bound segment of curriculum and an integrated approach to the same area of learning.

Among the more recent reviewers of the sceptic position with respect to interdisciplinarity is Fuchsman (2009). Succinctly, Fuchsman sums up the sceptics' view thus: 'There are scholars, then, who maintain that integration is a defining component of inter-disciplinarity and those who see conceptual and empirical blocks to integration.' He goes on:

> Interdisciplinary studies is perceived as emerging from the disciplines. There is a 'debt,' philosopher Stephen Toulmin writes, 'that interdisciplinary ideas owe to the very disciplines on which they are parasitic. Only within a world of disciplines can one be interdisciplinary'
>
> (Toulmin, 2001, p. 140)

As has been seen above, this book would not deny a deep and inextricable relationship between disciplines that feed integrated approaches, and the philosophy of cross-curricular studies itself. As has been said here: the strength of the integrated approach to learning is that it *includes* disciplines; while the stumbling block of the exclusive approach through 'disciplines only' is that something vital is lost: a wider understanding and connectiveness.

A whole raft of researchers and thinkers has noted among the failings of the 'disciplines as paramount' lobby that its members become increasingly tightly defined, vested in their

Table 1.4 Survival in nature: an approach from science only and from an integrated perspective

Curriculum element	Subject-specific approach	Some integrated approaches building the science concepts into wider areas	Movement of the subject-only material into cross-subject links
SURVIVAL IN NATURE: BIRDS AS AN EXAMPLE [This Table is an illustration only of how a segment of science curriculum can be located within wider understandings. This is a 'concept-led' piece of curriculum, the concepts being essentially those in bold in the second column. It is not intended to be exhaustive. The reader must provide his/her own additional examples and materials.]	**Habitat:** *Natural requirements and Conservation management*	Personal responsibility; and Ethical aspects of protecting nature: humans as exploiters or custodians of the natural world – debate	PSHE/RE/oral English
	Food: *Availability*	Parallel problems for the human race – e.g. water shortage and starvation in Africa	PSHE, geography, social studies
	Potential for augmentation e.g. winter feeding	Bird table surveys: preferences, frequency, etc. studies; graphical display of data	Mathematics
	Predation: *Source of predation*	Differing perspectives of predator and prey explored through role play and story-telling	Drama & literacy
	Effects of natural predation and Human predation	Cf. slavery ancient and modern	History
	Breeding: *Clutch size* *Second/third clutches – effectiveness*	Newspaper accounts of illegal bird taking	Media studies
	Adaptations: *Specific adaptations considered, e.g.* *Camouflage*	Exploration through visual appreciation of camouflage in the wild, in clothing, in other creatures such as moths or mammals	Art, photography. Printing, dyeing
	Techniques such as flocking	Human group behaviour and its parallels such as football fans, Mexican wave, Red Arrows air displays	Social studies
	Climate: *Adaptations to climate* *Climate change/effects*	Examining the conflicting claims of climate change scientists – notions of propaganda, bias and manipulation	Media studies; social studies

own languages and procedures, detached from the questions that should tax them in common, and prone to in-fighting and vicious competition (Becher and Trowler 2001; Hyland 2004).

Fuchsman (2009: 76, 77) moves to a very important point:

> . . . when a problem or issue cannot be adequately addressed within a single academic discipline and requires concepts and findings from at least one external subject area, a first condition for inter-disciplinarity arises. A second necessary condition for inter-disciplinarity concerns the approach to these complex issues. To be inter-disciplinary, a rigorous attempt to synthesize and integrate the ideas and methods of each pertinent discipline concerning the particular issue must be made. Multidisciplinary, cross-disciplinary, and certain transdisciplinary approaches would not fulfil these criteria.

If one looks at so-called 'topic work' as it was practised in the 1970s and early 1980s in primary schools, Fuchsman's two conditions were often not satisfied. Indeed, those of us working in the field then noted that failure. In an earlier book on the subject (Kerry and Eggleston 1988) we tried to explore the intellectual rigour that underpinned topic work as it was taught in that era (1988, Ch. 7 does this in some detail), and argued for individual subject disciplines to be both taught and assiduously pursued. Looking back, the gradual reduction in the value of topic work may well have been due to facile planning. Teachers too readily took on board the notion that placing a title at the centre of a sheet of paper, and then plotting a series of 'chunks of knowledge' emanating from that title but labelled maths, English or whatever, would sufficiently define intellectual demand and learning.

With this in mind, perhaps, Fuchsman (2009) developed a typology of integration that is instructive (what follows is shortened and adapted from his work).

1   *Full Integration*: Integration of disciplinary insights into a more comprehensive understanding.
2   *Partial Integration*: Some sections of the problem result in integration and a more comprehensive understanding, others remain unresolved.
3   *Incomplete Investigation*: An analysis of the findings and perspectives from various disciplines shows that the evidence presented is not sufficient to resolve the issue.
4   *Insufficient Interdisciplinarity*: The problem is too complex to be dealt with adequately by the multiple disciplines included.
5   *Underdetermination of Theory by Evidence*: When under-determination occurs, any attempt at integration of disciplinary insights can meet an equally good but incompatible integration. In under-determination, there can be more than one comprehensive perspective, but it will not lead to a single coherent entity.
6   *Epistemological Preferences*: A related obstacle to a single, coherent integration is the intellectual orientation of the investigator. As there are divergent standards and perspectives within and between disciplines, some scholars are likely to be committed to certain ideological and epistemological viewpoints; and others to different and competing perspectives. There are times where both disciplinary and interdisciplinary scholars from certain perspectives address the same question but with different intellectual commitments and propose quite different syntheses of them.
7   *Irreconcilable*: The disciplines needed for the intellectual inquiry have such diverging perspectives and methods that integration is difficult to achieve.

8   *Common Ground*: To integrationists, finding the common vocabulary and/or common ground between disciplinary perspectives is a prelude to creating integrative understanding. But, in choosing some common ground over others, there can be competing versions of what is held in common.

What Fuchsman tried to do in his critique and typology is not to sweep aside the notion of interdisciplinarity but to put together new ways of defining it. He makes sound points when he suggests that interdisciplinary studies have to do with the gaps and overlaps between disciplines. But, more importantly, he suggests that it comes into its own when a problem is beyond a single discipline to resolve, or when there are competing discourses emanating from individual disciplines about a problem. But it is instructive to notice once more the centrality of 'problem solving' to the relevance of integrated approaches, and his emphasis on the intellectual demand of this way of working. For, as he concludes (2009: 82), 'Interdisciplinarity examines the fragmentations, interstices and contending discourses within and between disciplines in order to confront epistemological plurality and intellectual complexity.' We would contend that the sooner young people come to terms (at an appropriate level) with the idea that the world is full of plurality and intellectual complexity, and that solutions are often not confined by single, monolithic approaches, the better it will be for their cognitive development.

Cross-curricular approaches in the 'real' world

In our earlier version of this text (Kerry 2011) I used an example from television about the way in which a real-world problem was tackled by academics in an interdisciplinary way. This was about the feasibility of the account of the Ten Plagues referred to in the Bible; and that narrative still has validity for anyone who wishes to look it up. Here, to follow up Fuchsman's points from the previous section, I have used another, more modern, example of a television programme. This is predicated on the strange state of the mummified body of King Tutankhamun (below, we follow the Egyptologists' convention of shortening this to Tut).

The research problem

In a detailed examination televised in 2013 on Channel 4 as *Tutankhamun: Mystery of the Burnt Mummy*, Dr Chris Naunton sets out to answer the research problem from the perspective of history (using the notes of archaeologist Howard Carter, made at the time) and Egyptology. This is what emanates from the notes of Howard Carter:

- Tut's mummy is partially burned; the wrappings are no more than charred powder; the soft tissue of the body carbonised.
- However, the outer coverings are normal.
- The usual embalming cuts are absent, though there are unusual ones.
- There is too much resin in the coffin compared with normal.
- The burial was carried out with unusual haste.
- The tomb is too small for the sarcophagus and grave goods.
- The grave itself is only one of sixty-three to have remained hidden/unplundered.

To solve these problems, Naunton goes on a journey in both space and time, but also across disciplines. This journey demonstrates how complicated problems require interdisciplinary solutions. Each contributor would be considered a specialist in a 'discipline', but none of the individual specialists can solve the problem alone. These were the experts, and the steps, which Naunton took to solve his problem:

- Dr Connelly – anatomist – helps with X-ray pathology and tissue analysis, assisted by Dr Ponting, a forensic anthropologist, for the chemical processing. They conclude that the body has been subject to significant burning – but why?
- Dr Ikram – Egyptologist – is an expert in the process of mummification, who demonstrates the processes through which the body would have (normally) gone, noting the absence of the heart and the misplacement of the embalming cuts.
- Dr Naunton then takes the outcomes to Dr Crowder – a fire investigations expert – who is able to demonstrate that the heavily oiled grave wrappings would have produced their own significant heat from within the wrappings.
- Back, then, to Dr Connelly – anatomist and X-ray pathologist – who finds that, as well as no heart, the breast bone is missing and there are broken ribs on the left-hand side.
- Dr Ikram – Egyptologist – concludes that the heart was too badly damaged at death to be used for the usual embalming purposes. How?
- Dr Anna Williams – forensic anthropologist – sets up an anatomage table at the Cranfield Forensic Institute and carries out a virtual autopsy, which seems to confirm an old but unproven theory that Tut was killed in a chariot accident.
- Mike Brown – crash reconstruction expert – obtains the help of stunt riders and a mock-up of a chariot, and uses laser scanners and digital reconstruction to test various theories of chariot impact. He comes up with a theory . . .
- Dr Horsfall – trauma expert – carries out simulations and concludes that injuries are consistent with Tut kneeling on the ground (having perhaps been thrown from a chariot) and being run over by a following vehicle.
- Dr Zioupous – bioengineering expert – studies the forces in the accident to check trauma patterns. But why did it happen?
- Prof Hardwig – Middle East historian – finds a stone carving of a battle relating to Tut and concludes this is a real battle against the Hittites.

So now we know roughly why, in what circumstances and how Tut dies, and why his corpse has particular traumas and post-mummification issues, but not why he seems to have been buried in haste. However, history tells us that Tut's adviser, Ay (because of a lack of clear succession), claimed the throne briefly. In the process of aggrandisement, Ay rapidly buries Tut in his (Ay's) modest tomb, reserving Tut's for himself – a power-grab – hence Tut's grave goods are cramped into too small a space.

However, this does not tell us how Tut's (new) tomb survived. But:

- Stephen Cross – geologist – comes up with a theory from rock studies: a sediment layer over Tut's tomb at the base of the valley indicates a flash flood after burial, the débris from which would have then been baked hard by the sun, concealing the site from tomb raiders.
- Professor Coulthard then constructs geological models to test and confirm the hypothesis.

So now we have answered all the research problems, thanks to:

- An Egyptologist (historian)
- An X-ray pathologist
- A forensic anthropologist
- Another Egyptologist (mummification specialist)
- A fire investigations expert
- Virtual autopsy
- A crash reconstruction specialist
- Stunt riders
- A bioengineering specialist
- A Middle East historian
- A geologist
- A physical geology specialist and modeller.

The perfect marriage of arts and sciences in academic problem solving.

No one could even remotely claim that the role of disciplines here was irrelevant, nor that the process of problem solving was not interdisciplinary, nor that the solutions that resulted were less credible and elegant than the partial insights from the component parts of the story created by individual disciplines.

The impact on schools, learning and teaching

What is clear, in personal conversation, is the increasing goodwill of a new generation of teachers to rediscover these interdisciplinary ideas and ideals at the school level, too. They are disillusioned with today's prescriptions and yearn for the kind of autonomy that will convert their work back from that of hoop-jumping government technicians to independent-minded professionals. In fact, in this they mirror that other great insight about children's learning (Plowden 1967: para. 1233): 'Finding out has proved better . . . than being told.'

The insight provided by this investigation into the ways subjects work together to stretch perceptions, and disciplines are used as tools to unlock insight, seems to be nicely encapsulated by the aims of the recent Scottish interdisciplinary intentions for its primary school curriculum:

> The curriculum should include space for learning beyond subject boundaries, so that children and young people can make connections between different areas of learning. Interdisciplinary studies, based upon groupings of experiences and outcomes from within and across curriculum areas, can provide relevant, challenging and enjoyable learning experiences and stimulating contexts to meet the varied needs of children and young people. Revisiting a concept or skill from different perspectives deepens understanding and can also make the curriculum more coherent and meaningful from the learner's point of view. Interdisciplinary studies can also take advantage of opportunities to work with partners who are able to offer and support enriched learning experiences and opportunities for young people's wider involvement in society. (Building the Curriculum 3, online at www.LTScotland.org.uk)

References

Aldrich, R., Crook, D. and Watson, D. (2000) *Education and Employment: The DfEE and Its Place in History*. London: London Institute of Education, Bedford Way Papers.

Beane, J. A. (1997) *Curriculum Integration: Designing the Core of Democratic Education*. New York and London: Teachers College Press.

Becher, T. & Trowler, P. R. (2001) *Academic Tribes and Territories* (2nd edn). Philadelphia: Open University Press.

Bennett, N. (1997) 'Voyages of discovery: changing perspectives in research on primary school practice', in Cullingford, C. (ed.) *The Politics of Primary Education*. Buckingham: Open University Press.

Bloom, B. (1956) *Taxonomy of Educational Objectives*. New York: McKay.

Boix Mansilla, V. and Gardner, H. (2004) 'Assessing inter-disciplinary work at the frontier: an empirical exploration of "symptoms of quality"'. Harvard Interdisciplinary Studies Project paper. Available online at: www.interdisciplines.org/interdisciplinarity/papers/6/2/print-able.paper (accessed February 2014).

Campbell, A. and Kerry, T. (2004) 'Constructing a new KS3 curriculum at Brooke Weston CTC: a review and commentary'. *Educational Studies* 30(4): 391–408.

Carr, D. (2003) *Making Sense of Education*. London: Routledge & Kegan Paul.

Clyde, M. (1995) 'Concluding the debate', in Fleer, M. (ed.) *DAP Centrism: Challenging Developmentally Appropriate Practice*. Watson, Australia: Australian Early Childhood Association.

Curriculum for Excellence (2008) Available online at: http://www.educationscotland.gov.uk/thecurriculum/whatiscurriculumforexcellence/index.asp.

Department for Children, Schools and Families (DCSF) (2008) *Independent Review of the Primary Curriculum Interim Report (The Rose Report)*. Nottingham: DCSF.

Docking, J. (2000) *New Labour's Policies for Schools: Raising the Standard?* London: David Fulton.

Eisner, E. (1996) *Cognition and Curriculum Re-considered* (2nd edn). London: PCP.

Elliott, J. (1998) *The Curriculum Experiment: Meeting the Challenge of Social Change*. Buckingham: Open University Press.

Fuchsman, S. (2009) 'Re-thinking integration in integrated studies'. *Issues in Integration Studies* 27: 70–85.

Gardner, H. (1999) *Intelligences Re-framed: Multiple Intelligences for the 21st Century*. New York: Basic Books.

Gardner, H. (2008) 'Multiple lenses on the mind', in Chau, M. H. and Kerry, T. (eds) *International Perspectives on Education*. London: Continuum: 7–27.

Garner, R. (2014) 'Gove's revolution: pupils return to traditional subjects in huge numbers'. *Independent*, 23 January.

Gould, S. J. and Shearer, R. (2007) 'Of two minds and one nature', in McGarr, P. and Rose, S. (eds) *Stephen Jay Gould: The Richness of Life*. London: Vintage Books.

Grossen, B. (1998) *Child-directed Teaching Methods: A Discriminatory Practice of Western Education*. Occasional Paper 1.12.98. Oregon: University of Oregon.

Harlen, W. (2006) *Teaching Learning and Assessing Science 5–12* (4th edn). London: Sage.

Hirst, P. (1974) *Knowledge and the Curriculum*. London: Routledge & Kegan Paul.

Hmelo-Silver, C. E. (2007) 'The power of technology to support complex learning'. Paper delivered at the Network-based Education Conference, 13–15 June, Rovaniemi, Finland.

Hmelo-Silver, C. E., Derry, S. J., Bitterman, A. and Hatrak, F. (2009) *Targeting Transfer in a STELLAR PBL Course for Pre-service Teachers. Interdisciplinary Journal of Problem Based Learning* 2: 24–42.

Humes, W. (2013) 'Curriculum for excellence and interdisciplinary learning'. *Scottish Educational Review* 45(1): 82–93.

Hus, V. and Grmek, M. I. (2011) 'Didactic strategies in early science teaching'. *Educational Studies* 37(2): 159–169.

Hyland, K. (2004) *Disciplinary Discourses: Social Interactions in Academic Writing*. Ann Arbor: University of Michigan Press.

Jarvis, M. (2005) *The Psychology of Effective Learning and Teaching*. Cheltenham: Nelson-Thornes.

Joyce, B., Calhoun, E. & Hopkins, D. (1997) *Models of Learning – Tools for Teaching*. Buckingham: Open University Press.

Kelly, A. V. (1999) *The Curriculum – Theory and Practice* (4th edn). London: PCP.

Kelly, A. V. (2001) 'What did Hitler do in the war, Miss?' *Times Educational Supplement*, 19 January: 12.

Kelly, L. and Stead, D. (2013) *Enhancing Primary Science*. Maidenhead: Open University Press.

Kerry, C. and Kerry, T. (2000) 'The effective use of school time in the education of the most able'. *Australasian Journal of Gifted Education* 9(1): 33–40.

Kerry, T. (2002a) *Explaining and Questioning*. Cheltenham: Nelson-Thornes.

Kerry, T. (2002b) *Learning Objectives, Task Setting and Differentiation*. Cheltenham: Nelson-Thornes.

Kerry, T. (2005) 'Forthcoming success: back to the future?'. *Education Today* 55(1): 14–19.

Kerry, T. (2011) *Cross-curricular Teaching in the Primary School* (1st edn). London: Routledge.

Kerry, T. and Eggleston, J. (1988) *Topic Work in the Primary School*. London: Routledge.

Kerry, T. and Wilding, M. (2000) 'Managing a new teaching space'. *Education Today* 50(2): 8–20.

Kerry, T. and Wilding, M. (2004) *Effective Classroom Teacher: Developing the Skills You Need in Today's Classroom*. London: Pearson.

Lawton, D. (1997) 'Curriculum theory and a curriculum for the 21st century', in Mortimore, P. and Little, V. (eds) *Living Education: Essays in Honour of John Tomlinson*. London: PCP.

McGarr, P. and Rose, S. (2007) *Stephen Jay Gould: The Richness of Life*. London: Vintage Books.

Plowden, Lady Bridget (1967) *Children and Their Primary Schools: A Report of the Central Advisory Council for Education, Volume 1*. London: HMSO.

Power, S. (2002) 'The overt and hidden curricula of quasi-markets', in Whitty, G. (ed.) *Making Sense of Education Policy*. London: PCP.

Repko, A. F. (2008) *Interdisciplinary Research: Process and Theory*. London: Sage.

Ross, A. (2000) *Curriculum: Construction and Critique*. London: Falmer Press.

Rousseau, J.-J. (1913) *Émile*. London: Dent, Everyman Library.

Spooner, K. (2014) 'Leading change from a subject-based to an integrated approach to curriculum management: an examination of Andes View School's readiness for curriculum change'. Leicester: University of Leicester MSc dissertation.

Stenhouse, L. (1975) *An Introduction to Curriculum Research and Development*. London: Heinemann.

Toulmin, S. (2001) *Return to Reason*. Cambridge, MA: Harvard University Press.

Wellcome Trust (2005) *Primary Horizons: Starting Out in Science*. London: Wellcome Trust. Available online at: http://www.wellcome.ac.uk/primaryhorizons.

Wellcome Trust (2008) *Perspectives on Education: Primary Science*. London: Wellcome Trust. Available online at: http://www.wellcome.ac.uk/perspectives.

Woodhead, C. (1995) 'Teaching quality: the issues and the evidence'. *Teaching Quality: The Primary Debate*. London: Office for Standards in Education.

Woodhead, C. (2002) 'The standards of today: and how to raise them to the standards of tomorrow'. Paper presented to the Adam Smith Institute.

Wragg, E. C. (ed.) (1984) *Classroom Teaching Skills*. London: Croom Helm.

Internet sources

www.educationscotland.gov.uk
www.LTScotland.org.uk
www.trinidadianexpress.com/news

Chapter 2

Learning, cognition and cross-curricular teaching

Trevor Kerry

Introduction

This chapter takes a straightforward look at the ways in which theorists view children's thinking. It looks at systems put forward by Bloom, Wallace, Bowring-Carr and West-Burnham, Fisher, Gardner and Wilding to track and build effectively on children's thinking. The practical application of these ideas to a section of the curriculum is explored. It is suggested that there is a need for thinking and higher-order cognition to be made central to curriculum planning, and to classroom learning and teaching.

Background: a Bloomian view

The information age has increased rather than diminished the need for individuals to think. In a world of what seems like infinitely expanding information, the need to process and evaluate all these data becomes not only essential for all of us but the cutting-edge skill of the movers and shakers. Fisher and Scriven (1997: 20) define critical thinking as 'skilled, active, interpretation and evaluation of observations, communications, information, and argumentation'. The more information is directed at us, the more discerning we have to be in processing it. Yet the sad fact is, if you want to find thinking at work, the classroom – whether in primary school or even a university course – is often the last place you might discover it.

This last statement seems like a fairly trenchant judgement, and one that many (teachers and others) might take exception to or require evidence for. But there is evidence – and while things might be changing and it is unfair to tar all institutions with the same brush, you can come to your own judgement by carrying out a fairly simple test using the tools described below.

The guru of thinking was Benjamin Bloom (1956). He established a system for judging what kind of thinking occurs in classrooms. In previous research beginning as long ago as the 1980s (Kerry 1984; etheses.nottingham.ac.uk/2518/1/346624.pdf) I adapted and simplified his system so that it could be applied easily to classrooms. In effect, much of the cognitive life of classrooms can be allocated to one of these categories of thinking (see Table 2.1).

Table 2.2 provides some examples of how the system works for classroom questions. Management questions (category 0) would be things like: 'Jane, will you take this register to the office, please?' or 'Can someone close the door, please?' They may 'oil the wheels' of classroom living but they do not add to its cognitive level. Other categories are exemplified in the table. A simple way of conceptualising the difference between low and higher-order operation is that low-order questions or tasks require a passive reception or

Table 2.1 Categories of thinking adapted from Bloom (1956)

Category (H)	Activity	Low-order (L) or higher-order thinking
0	Management statement, request, task	L
I	Recall	L
2	Simple comprehension	L
3	Application	H
4	Analysis	H
5	Synthesis	H
6	Evaluation	H

Table 2.2 Examples of higher-order questions using the system adapted from Bloom (1956)

Type of task	Examples
I Recall	In your homework reading what did you find out about King Harold?
2 Simple comprehension	Teacher: instead of 'goodbye' a French person might say 'Au Revoir'. What would he or she say?
3 Application	How did Icarus and his father come up with the idea of using wings? How could we try out different kinds of wings to see which shape flies best?
4 Analysis	Why did Jesus concern himself so often with the lives of the poor and the down-and-out? Looking at the map, why do you think Hadrian built his wall in that location?
5 Synthesis	In the first story Tracey behaves meanly to her friend; in the second one she acts differently. What things bring about this change?
6 Evaluation	Looking at this painting, what do think is going through the heads of the people the artist has drawn? In Wind in the Willows, how do you assess the characters of Ratty and Toad?

parrot-like repetition of data, whereas higher-order skill requires pupils to manipulate the data in some way.

In previous publications I have outlined how teachers' questions and explanations or talk can be enhanced to improve cognitive demand on pupils of all abilities (Kerry 2002a), and how the same principles can be applied to task setting in classrooms (Kerry 2002b). These skills manuals coach teachers through the processes of translating research outcomes into effective classroom practice. In this chapter, where the emphasis is more on the principles than on skills' acquisition, it is important to make a further point about outcomes from this work.

One of the most telling points from my own researches on thinking in mixed-ability classrooms using this adapted Bloomian system, and one that was in no way related to mere chance, was concerned with integrating subject matter (see also Chapter 1). In lessons where the subject matter was integrated, as opposed to taught discipline by subject discipline, the cognitive life in the classroom rose by a factor of at least four (Kerry 1984: 177). Several strands of causation probably contributed to this result. First, teaching in an integrated way inevitably involves a lot of synthesis of material across disciplines and sources – and synthesis is, of itself, a higher-order skill. Second, much of this work was rooted more closely to problem solving, so the nature of the tasks set was more cognitively demanding. Third, children of all levels of ability probably become more discerning as a result of the first two factors, and thus begin to make more intellectual responses to material offered and to ask more demanding questions of the teacher. Thus, fourth, learning ceased to be a didactically delivered stream of passively received knowledge data, and became an actively collaborative enterprise between teacher and pupil in investigating issues. Something of this process is described in this book – in Chapters 9 and 13, for example.

Various educationists have championed particular approaches to thinking and to training children to think. What follows is a review of some of these systems, with some assessment of their strengths and weaknesses. It is not the intention to promulgate any particular system but to urge teacher-readers to select among them those facets that hold promise in their own classrooms. What is important to understand are two things: first, that generally these 'thinking skills' are not for able pupils only but for all pupils; second, that they run counter to the view that puts learning facts (usually through single-subject lessons) at the centre of the education process. This stands at the heart of this book: education does not operate on the Skinnerian hoover-bag principle – it is not about children sponging up decontextualised information merely to regurgitate it later with little appreciation of its significance or application. Facts are important; but they are important as the building blocks upon which thinking and insight can be based. Though systems to improve thinking are often developed as a relatively crude response to improving the progression of the most able, their value in motivating and stimulating all children, without exception, quickly becomes apparent.

TASC: Thinking Actively in a Social Context

Thinking Actively in a Social Context is a system developed and used by Belle Wallace (www. nace.co.uk/tasc/tasc_home/htm). Though often used to stimulate able pupils in primary schools, TASC is by no means confined to that context. The broader perspective is reflected in a comment posted on a government website: 'We have used the TASC Framework to lift our school out of "Special Measures". TASC gave us a framework for developing pupils' ownership of their learning. Their motivation and interest soared' (http://www.teachernet. gov.uk/schoolinfocus/ramridgeprimary/). Wallace (2001) claims that her work encourages self-confidence in pupils by allowing them to work independently, discovering research skills. Through their problem solving they gain increased self-confidence, and become active learners capable of working across the curriculum and engaging in self-assessment. These are bold claims, but Wallace has a track record of achieving these aims in schools nationally.

TASC works in a series of stages, often depicted as a wheel. Pupils work around the segments of the wheel:

- To gather and organise information
- To define the task required, using the information available
- To define more ideas around the task
- To select the best of the ideas
- To operationalise the best idea(s)
- To evaluate what they have done
- To tell others what they have done
- To make a final assessment of the experience and learning.

TASC is a form of structured learning where the structure is based not on a series of pieces of information, but on learning to think – creatively, logically, laterally. Part of its success rests on this sequencing process: even when they are at the early, less secure, stages of the process, pupils have a structure to fall back on.

That TASC can work in a wide range of contexts is demonstrated by comments from the school quoted earlier:

> There's been a real improvement in children's thinking skills and greater confidence about tackling problems, verbalising views and finding possible solutions . . . these aren't quantifiable outcomes that you can test, but the children have learned to be more in control of their learning which is highly important as . . . many children have complex needs. The school is in an area of high social deprivation and those identified as having learning difficulties and disabilities are well above the national average, as is mobility.

In following TASC principles teachers have to stand back and surrender some responsibility for learning to pupils – something that many find difficult initially. However, in so doing, they are exercising true professionalism. Users report improved behaviour through increased interest and engagement, the opportunity for pupils to adopt their preferred learning styles, and even that dreaded word – outlawed in the Woodhead era and perhaps in the Govian one – fun!

Reflection

How might you apply the ideas of Bloom, Kerry and Wallace to your classroom?

An approach through philosophy

Another highly effective primary educator, Robert Fisher, prefers to approach thinking through philosophy (Fisher 2003). Teachers might find this a harder system to learn initially as it involves what is often called 'socratic' questioning, but in fact the process is not very different from teaching using questions in the way that is outlined in Kerry (2002a), referred to earlier. Jarvis (2005: 107) sums the method up well: '"Philosophy" is used less in the sense of teaching philosophy as a discipline than in the sense of teaching children to *philosophise*. The aim of this is to develop creative and critical modes of thinking.' The system requires that everyday modes of thinking (guessing, assuming, judging and inferring) are replaced by critical modes (estimating, justifying, analysing and reasoning). Like TASC, the method requires social learning, the establishment of a 'community of enquiry' where freedom of expression and speculation are welcome. In place of the Bloom–Kerry question types, Fisher proposes that thinking can begin from stories about which seven types of question can be asked, as follows:

1   *Contextual*: geographical, historical, cultural, etc.
2   *Establishing the temporal order*: what happened before, after, and its significance.
3   *Particularity*: challenging pupils to say what else might have been done or said in the circumstances.
4   *Intentions*: requiring the analysis of e.g. emotions, motivation.
5   *Choices*: uncovering the moral analysis.

6   *Meanings*: hidden messages behind the overt events.
7   *Telling*: how the telling influences the understanding.

This form of thinking can be applied successfully to current news stories every bit as easily as to ancient myths or novelistic productions. A strong feature of Fisher's approach is the centrality it gives to questioning as a learning and teaching tool.

Shallow and deep learning

By now, the reader will have picked up the message that raising the cognitive stakes in lessons is about trying to find effective systems for analysing the thinking that happens in classrooms and to establish better ways to harness its power for all pupils. It is a very different process from simply scoring the number of facts learned or the conformity of pupils to reiterating received mantras of information, things these writers maintain impinge on us 'not one whit' (Bowring-Carr and West-Burnham 1997: 77). Bowring-Carr and West-Burnham are less concerned with the 'how' and more concerned with the 'what' of thinking – with trying to establish what is, and what is not, useful learning. As a result they develop a theory of shallow and deep learning, which is important and persuasive. In doing so they quote Willis (1993): 'Quality learning is about conceptual change – seeing the world differently is an essential outcome.' Once again, they are forced back into identifying those verbs that epitomise the kind of learning they see as achieving the desired ends: explaining, giving examples, applying, justifying, comparing, contrasting, contextualising, generalising, selecting the appropriate medium for communication of the idea. They advocate the use of mind-maps to track the changes in pupils' understandings – a kind of metacognitive process (see below).

Thus it is possible to progress from surface to deep, or profound, learning. This learning has certain essential characteristics. Beginning from the pupil's initial mind-map the teacher and pupil proceed with the learning in a context where the learning process is itself the subject of discussion. The assessment procedures, too, will reflect the profound learning required. Pupil and teacher explore and agree the ways in which learning is best demonstrated. Over time the kinds of intelligences required (these are discussed in the next section) will all be involved. The approach to learner and learning will be holistic, and the intention will be to explore material in depth rather than cover a syllabus superficially. Curiosity will trigger and promote the learning, and is not confined to the school context or day. The purpose of the learning is to 'enable the individual to change, grow and become autonomous' (Bowring-Carr and West-Burnham 1997: 83).

So what are these 'intelligences' that need to be explored and educated? The classic answer to this question has been provided over many years by the work of Howard Gardner in an evolving theory. It is to this that we now turn.

Multiple intelligences: the work of Gardner

A recent exposition of Gardner's theory is to be found in Chau and Kerry (2008). Here Gardner extends his theory of multiple intelligences from his previous seven or eight intelligences theory into a theory of nine intelligences. So we should begin by establishing what these are, and in so doing I have used a shortened version of his own words from the text cited above.

1   *Linguistic intelligence*: the intelligence of a writer, orator, journalist.
2   *Logical mathematical intelligence*: the intelligence of a logician, mathematician, scientist.
3   *Musical intelligence*: the capacity to create, perform and appreciate music.
4   *Spatial intelligence*: the capacity to form mental imagery of the world – the large world of the aviator or navigator, or the more local world of the chess player or the surgeon – and to manipulate those mental images.
5   *Bodily-kinaesthetic intelligence*: the capacity to solve problems or fashion products using your whole body, or parts of your body, like your hands or mouth. This intelligence is exhibited by athletes, dancers, actors, craft people and, again, surgeons.
6   *Interpersonal intelligence*: involves the understanding of other persons – how to interact with them, how to motivate them, how to understand their personalities, etc.
7   *Intrapersonal intelligence*: is the capacity to understand oneself – one's strengths, weaknesses, desires, fears.
8   *Naturalist intelligence*: involves the capacity to make consequential distinctions in nature – between one plant and another, among animals, clouds, mountains, and the like. The scientist Charles Darwin had naturalist intelligence in abundance.
9   *The 'intelligence of big question'*: when children ask about the size of the universe, when adults ponder death, love, conflict, the future of the planet, they are engaging in existential issues.

These intelligences are largely self-explanatory, and they are an attempt to define more closely the areas of understanding that teachers need to encourage their pupils to develop. Once more, they do not challenge the necessity for factual information, but they do transcend data to look at the thinking processes from a number of perspectives. Gardner is constantly moving on this theory, and he emphasises that – allied with his theory of intelligences – there is need to recognise what he calls 'kinds of mind'.

The minds that teachers need to develop include the cognitive: the disciplined mind that is concerned with knowledge and skill, the synthesising mind that orders knowledge in useful ways, and the creative mind that moves beyond the current boundaries. But, he suggests, our success as human beings depends on more than even these: on the respectful mind that is about tolerance and working together, and the ethical mind that weighs the effects and motivations for our actions. What Gardner has done – and it is an insight born out of a current socio-political worldview – is to extend his theory into the realm of behaviour and the rationales that govern it. This is an extension of the Bowring-Carr and West-Burnham position, and represents an important insight. But we need to return to the classroom, and to ask how all this learning can be tracked by the teacher within the realities of the busy social relationships that are current class sizes. To this end we turn to the concept of metacognition which, until this point, has been mentioned only in passing.

Reflection

Gardner's work is well respected and well received around the world. To what extent and in what ways does it influence your own thinking about your work?

Metacognition

A clumsy word for a useful concept, metacognition is the process of reflecting on one's own learning, and it is a process as applicable to pupils as to learning adults. In the drive to listen to pupils' voices, one of the areas of hearing must be about how pupils learn. Stoll, Fink and Earl have a useful definition:

> Human beings can reflect on their own thinking processes. Experts describe their thinking as an internal conversation – monitoring their own understanding, predicting their performance, deciding what else they need to know, organising and re-organising ideas, checking for consistency between different pieces of information and drawing analogies that help them advance their understanding.
>
> (2003: 26)

While Stoll *et al.* (2003: 70) note that using metacognitive processes in the classroom is an advanced teaching skill, Wilding (1997) suggests that pupils will learn more effectively if they understand their own learning processes. In an interesting article describing work with younger primary children, she argues that almost every pupil can be helped to learn by using this process. She introduced 'learning diaries' into her primary school with children as young as 6, to great effect. Her conclusion about using this method is optimistic. So let us consider metacognition as a tool for teachers in helping children to learn and reflect on their own thinking processes and their efficacy.

Having experimented with various approaches to children recording what they had learned, including one-to-one discussions with the teacher, Wilding (1997: 20) concluded that a number of problems beset these approaches:

- The reviews were extremely time-consuming.
- Children generally only remembered and referred to very recent activities; also they used very general labels and imprecise language, such as 'My maths was best 'cause it was good'.
- I found myself constantly drawn towards 'putting words in their mouths' as they struggled with the language.
- There was a wide spectrum in the level of sophistication in the responses of different children.

The issue of language is picked up by Loughran (2002), who describes a metacognitive approach to teaching in an Australian setting, where learning the 'language of learning' was an important prerequisite in order to enable students and teachers to communicate about the processes of learning. Wilding decided that a solution to achieving metacognitive practice was to put aside some timetabled time on a regular and fairly frequent basis for the compilation of learning logs:

> I anticipated that, once the children were familiar with the task, it would only take up about 30–40 minutes . . . I felt there was time available during Friday morning . . . It could be justified in terms of the English National Curriculum as providing a meaningful purpose for Speaking and Listening, and Writing . . . the majority of the children had the necessary writing skills (Y2/3 class) . . . in the case of the four children who might struggle my ancillary or myself should be able to give extra support.
>
> (Wilding 1997: 20)

Each child was issued with an exercise book in which to write the log, and some prompt questions were added to the front page:

- What have I enjoyed most during this week? Why?
- What have I done best during this week? Why?
- What have I found difficult during this week? Why?
- What am I going to try harder at next week? Why?

The sophistication of the children's learning diaries increased rapidly – the rather bald statements of the kind quoted earlier soon turned into:

> I have enjoyed writing on the computer. Why – because it is good but I did make some mistakes. I have been best at my stamp ready reckoner. Why – because it is a bit hard but I got used to it. I have found it difficult doing my Ancient Greece research. Why – because it is hard to get information. I am going to try harder not to shout. Why – because it is hard to keep it under control.

It is important to remember here that metacognition is not only about supporting the learning of the less able (Lovey 2002), useful though this is; it is a tool for all pupils, including the very able. Wilding, in fact, went on to give a number of other examples of how the learning diary had not only helped the pupils understand their own learning processes – their strengths, weaknesses and distractions – but also had helped the teacher.

- *Example 1*: 'I have done my best at pot drawing this week because it is the only time you have said "Well done".' (This shows how important the teacher's response can be to children, and reminds us of the importance of being positive.)
- *Example 2*: 'I have found reading difficult because I am guessing the words.' (The teacher followed this up with the child and found that he was feeling very unsuccessful with his reading book; the book was changed to one he understood and enjoyed. It was also possible to explain that careful 'guessing' can be a very useful and appropriate strategy in reading.)

Wilding goes on to conclude that the aim of this process is to raise the pupil's stake in the learning process – to put the pupil at the centre of learning (see Chapter 4). To do this it is important to show that what pupils say has an effect on what happens in the classroom: they need to 'see the point' of the activity, and see it expressed in action. The learning diary – the metacognitive process – was subsequently introduced throughout the school: in an oral version with the youngest pupils.

Reflection

How might metacognition help your work and the pupils in your classes?

Thinking and creativity

This survey of ways of thinking about thinking in classrooms is not exhaustive. No mention has been made, for example, of De Bono's work (2000) or of the Activating Children's

Thinking Skills (ACTS) project in Northern Ireland (which was more orientated towards the secondary sector) (McGuiness 2000). Nor have I included the work of Fuerstein, which, though interesting, may seem somewhat impenetrable at times. Nonetheless, the survey has demonstrated several insights.

Though differing in detail, each system has attempted to explore what might be called 'learning beyond the facts'. All are agreed that this kind of learning is of a higher order of cognition. All imply that, to achieve these ends, teachers need to operate at an advanced skill level and also, by implication, that teachers need training in these skills. All the systems identify improved learning performance, and some improved behaviour, in pupils as a result of the provision of more meaningful learning tasks. The systems are more important for their similarities than for their differences. Individually, each system has strengths and drawbacks. TASC has a proven track record, but may appear a touch mechanistic. Fisher's philosophical approach is very logical but may be off-putting to some teachers at first encounter. Bowring-Carr and West-Burnham's work is more theoretical than practical but involves good insights. By contrast, most educators are familiar with Gardner's approach; if it has a weakness it is that it is sometimes employed too simplistically by those who do not delve adequately into it, and serves only to justify a range of curriculum knowledge and skills rather than to reach into the more obscure 'minds' that are so essential. Metacognition is valuable, and features as a part of most of the systems, but can be time consuming and requires some effort to train pupils to use it. The Bloomian-based approach can work very successfully, making teachers very self-aware of the performance, but it is demanding on teachers' willingness to be self-analytical.

The problem with this whole topic is that it is easier to find rhetoric than reality. The Qualifications and Curriculum Authority (QCA) attempted to formulate some intentions about teaching thinking. They are couched in the now familiar platitudes of government-driven initiatives, and they contain the inevitable agendas about citizens as economic units, which are often traced back as far as Callaghan's Ruskin College speech in 1976 (Docking 2000: 4, 158). The following short extract is typical:

> Creativity and critical thinking develop young people's capacity for original ideas and purposeful action. Experiencing the wonder and inspiration of human ingenuity and achievement, whether artistic, scientific or technological, can spark individual enthusiasms that contribute to personal fulfilment. Creativity can be an individual or collaborative activity. By engaging in creative activities, young people can develop the capacity to influence and shape their own lives and wider society. Everyone has the potential for creative activity and it can have a positive impact on self-esteem, emotional well-being and overall achievement. Creative activity is essential for the future well-being of society and the economy.
>
> (http://curriculum.qca.org.uk/key-stages-3-and-4/
> cross-curriculum-dimensions/creativitycriticalthinking/index.aspx).

Creativity is discussed in more detail in Chapter 8 of this volume. In the meantime, the QCA also expressed a keenness to add on (the 'afterthought' semantics of its statement are significant) critical thinking to its knowledge content. To encourage imagination, the generation of ideas and connections between them, to explore the links between subjects, to give pupils' ideas audience and for them to pursue their individual interests are not rocket science and they are belated – but they are steps in the right direction. But thinking is not an add-on. Its omission as an integral part of learning is an indictment. One problem for teachers is that are exhorted about what to do, but less often given the tools about how to do it. So how can we do better than this, where it matters – in our schools?

A thinking lesson

In this section I want to move from the theory of higher-order thinking and learning to a brief, and albeit far too short, exposition of its nature: an example in miniature. So what follows is an attempt to give a flavour of a piece of primary curriculum seen from the perspective of a teacher who wants to achieve both higher-order thinking and, through it, pupil engagement. Table 2.3, then, is an outline of a cross-curricular lesson series on the Second World War, giving something of the process and outcomes of the work. It is based on real lessons in real classrooms, and the principles are easily adaptable.

So, what characterises this process? It is, of course, a voyage of discovery. It involves what teachers love to call 'research' – though I prefer the concept of investigation, which is similar but does not imply originality. The structure of the series of lessons is not far from the TASC principles rehearsed earlier. The teacher's questions and tasks move into the higher-order realms as measured by the Kerry–Bloom categories. The work is high on involvement. It rests within the community. It generates knowledge, but knowledge contextualised. And it ends by making the knowledge each child's, not the teacher's – indeed, they are the teachers. So it is deep or profound knowledge. In the process, it addresses Gardner's ethical mind; and the teacher can now ask the children to reflect on what and how they have learned – metacognition.

Alternatively . . .

Alternatively, I could sit you down in rows and, with voice well modulated and interesting, I could entrance you with the data that you need to know about the Second World War. I could explain how the German empire under its somewhat unlikely leader began a series of annexations (look, here on the map, this is Austria; and this is Czechoslovakia, which does not exist as such any more); and I could show you a picture of a grey-haired man waving a piece of paper, and tell you how empty the promise on it had been. I could tell you about the precautions that were taken for the population: gas masks, shelters, 'digging for victory', and eventually evacuation of the children. I could enliven this bit by showing you a picture of kids, labelled and suitcased, bidding a tearful farewell . . .

. . . and I could feel you slipping away already, entranced by Wayne's five-legged spider in a matchbox under the desk. Only another three weeks to go but distraction is setting in. So you could be told to read about it instead so you didn't get fidgety. And if I were very lucky you'd remember enough to write something sensible in the assessment, and all the world would be happy.

Except you. For you would have been reinforced in your belief that school was boring, that learning was of little relevance, and that only the score counted. And you would be able to remember the dates but have absolutely no idea about the fear, the desolation, the destruction, the legacy of poverty, the joy, the hope, the anticipation of a brave new world, or the big questions about humanity, mortality and morality.

Table 2.3 Cross-curricular lesson series on the Second World War

Lesson series	Activities	Outcomes
Find out what the pupils know	**Question and answer session**	
	Establish key facts – dates, names, local events of the period	
	One or two have memorabilia at home	
	Some have watched TV programmes	
	One has read a story about the evacuation.	
	Most have seen *Dad's Army* – discuss role of fiction – what's real what's not Fashion, rather different, why?	Enough basic knowledge established to get everyone thinking, and to ensure that all the pupils have at least a grain of empathy with the topic even if their real knowledge is minimal
	Shortages – why?	
	Why didn't the Germans roll in and invade us like they did Poland?	
	Look at a map – 'island race'	
What do they want to know	**Collect a fairly random list of ideas or interests**	
	Rations, ration cards, what could you buy to eat?	Several pupils think they have old ration books and similar artefacts available from grandparents
	Could we try some	
And explore?	What was the real Dad's Army like?	
	Luke's family has some medals	Luke says his dad would lend the medals
	Jane likes the maps, chronology – Where? When? Why?	
	Life as an evacuee	Resource collection available from Library service
	Tanks	
	War planes – Spitfire. Jake has a book about planes	
	What was it like to be bombed?	Teacher has had the foresight to collect resources on DVD and in pictures
	What makes people do terrible things to other people?	
	What was it like to walk or drive around in the dark with no signposts?	Pupils want to send off for copies of newspapers of the time
	Churchill	
	What happened to schools in the war?	Tracey says she'll ask her great-gran about how she went to school in the war
	Who else was involved besides us and the Germans?	

Finding out

How could we get to know more?

Books, the collected materials in the classroom and from the Films (probably now on DVD?)

Old newspapers

People – who was there?

('Were you, Miss?' 'No, I'm not that old.')

Look around – any buildings that might have been destroyed or rebuilt?

Family photos?

Local army base?

The early lessons are devoted to some 'research' using sources identified above

Deciding what to do

The pupils decide among themselves what their interests are

Planning session, vetted by the teacher, to see what each group has decided and its overall direction and value

Decision is for groups to work on agreed topics, and for some whole-class activities a bar that says 'Eighth Army'

The outcome of this are several pieces of group – research:

Luke's group is going to begin from the medals and look at some of the famous battles – one of the medals has

Jane's group is going to draw maps of the countries involved and how the battles moved to and fro

Donna's group wants to get the mums together to put on a wartime austerity meal using things like spam and powdered egg

– Will and Samantha have seen pictures of the day the war ended, with people dancing in the streets; they want to gather some of the others to produce a VE Day newspaper, with stories about wartime experience and plans for a new and happy life

[And so on]

(continued)

Table 2.3 Continued

Lesson series	Activities	Outcomes
	Also, there will be several whole-class activities spread over the study period, led by the teacher: – Tracey's great-gran and several other relatives are coming to spend an hour reminiscing – The groups are going to take it in turns to sit in the sport store with the light off and play DVDs of the sirens, the bombing, and the all-clear – The teacher is going to give everyone a token for a piece of cake (a rare treat for which mum would have queued for hours) – but if you lose the token you don't get the cake! – All the pupils have a 'WW2 art afternoon' where they convey their impressions in paint, collage, and other media	The work has taken in literacy (reading, writing); historical knowledge and understanding; some geography to support the historical data; time management, to produce the newspaper on time; aesthetics through artistic expression; emotional intelligence; communication skills; science of flight, etc.
Relaying what is done		
To each other	**The project draws to a close with each group presenting their findings to the rest, including their drawings, maps, newspaper, etc.**	
To others	**The teacher arranges for them to visit the school in the next village to share their new-found knowledge at a special assembly**	Pupils have dealt in concepts such as fear, uncertainty, pride, aerodynamics, editorial truth, resilience, teamwork – and so on

Revisiting the implications of learning theory for curriculum and teaching

In this chapter we have looked at learning theories and how they might be applied in primary classrooms; the emphasis has been on various modes of thinking. But these theories, however refined and attractive, are meant to be pragmatic: to work in practice, as we have tried to show. They drive us back to reconsider our philosophy of education. This is no bad thing – it should be under continuous review.

The predominant curriculum approach adopted over the decades for primary education has been pedagogy, more or less defined as learners dependent on educators who decide what, where and when the pupil will learn. The same approach permeates secondary schools; a case can be made that it tightens its grip of the education system through the periods when public examinations are prevalent.

At some time late in the secondary phase of education, or in the post-16 sector, there tends to be a shift of philosophy towards andragogy. This moves the focus away from content to some extent, and on to process: how the learner learns. In this approach the curriculum is given less direction and more relevance to the learner's own situation. Modes of teaching may promote a degree of personal discovery and exploration, and the work may be partly individualised to take account of where the student has reached in his/her learning.

But there is another way that has developed in higher education, and that can be applied to primary learners, too. This is known by the rather ugly title 'heutagogy'. It may be better described as self-directed learning. The principles of it are outlined in Table 2.4.

Self-directed learning does not imply that there are no boundaries: that there is no syllabus, that there are no objectives for courses of study. What is does, rather, is to give the pupil discretion about routes through that learning to achieve the desired ends. Clearly, some pupils will require very little teacher support to do this, others considerably more. But what the approach does is to rid teaching of the constraints of narrowly conceived content communicated through mechanistic teaching procedures to hit incremental and sometimes

Table 2.4 Principles of heutagogy

There are four key principles:

1. *Learning when the learner is ready*: the learner has a role in controlling the process of learning, making their own decisions about pace and activity according to need and interest
2. *Learning is seen as a complex process* requiring the learner to move beyond knowledge and skills – it is not regurgitation, copying, modelling (though these things may happen); it requires new connections and more inventive insights to be made
3. *Learner does not depend solely on the teacher* and can be triggered by an experience beyond the control of the teacher
4. *Learning is focused on the student not on a syllabus*: it is about what the pupil needs to know and chooses to explore to advance their learning

These elements of the approach lead in turn to:
* *Self-sufficiency in learning* – having the confidence to explore new avenues
* *Reflexivity* – the ability to take on board the implications of learning and to change ways of thinking and acting as a result
* *Application of what is learnt* – so that connections are made beyond content/theory alone
* *Positive learning values* – learning becomes a pleasurable experience indulged in for its own sake

Source: Hase and Kenyon (2013: 72, 73)

fairly meaningless targets. It is as far away as possible from the stultifying approach of: I am going to tell you something, you are going to write it down and remember it, and later on I will test how well you have remembered it and rank order you on the result – indeed your whole future might depend on this mind-numbing process. It does not denigrate high-quality didactic lessons, but it contextualises them.

We give enough examples in the rest of the book to demonstrate that this kind of approach is practical and does not tax teachers' abilities beyond what it is professionally exciting and interesting. The reader will be able to trace in Parts 2 and 3 some phase-related examples. Part 4 will indicate how learning can cater for individual needs and be aided by a variety of adults. In Part 5 we discuss some useful tools with which to plan, keep track of and promote learning, while Part 6 deals with aspects of teaching skill. The final chapter then returns to the themes of Chapters 1 and 2, drawing together the threads into both a defence and a polemic for a change of direction in primary education.

References

Bloom, B. (1956) *Taxonomy of Educational Objectives*. London: Longman.
Bowring-Carr, C. and West-Burnham, J. (1997) *Effective Learning in Schools*. London: Pearson.
Chau, M. H. and Kerry, T. (eds) (2008) *International Perspectives on Education*. London: Continuum.
De Bono, E. (2000) *Six Thinking Hats*. Harmondsworth: Penguin.
Docking, J. (2000) *New Labour's Policies for Schools: Raising the Standard?* London: David Fulton.
Fisher, A. and Scriven, M. (1997) 'Critical thinking: its definition and assessment'. *Argumentation* 16(2): 247–251.
Fisher, R. (2003) *Teaching Thinking*. London: Continuum.
Hase, S. and Kenyon, C. (2013) *Self-determined Learning*. London: Bloomsbury.
Jarvis, M. (2005) *The Psychology of Effective Learning and Teaching*. Cheltenham: Nelson-Thornes.
Kerry, T. (1984) 'Analysing the cognitive demand made by classroom tasks in mixed ability classes', in Wragg, E. C. (ed.) *Classroom Teaching Skills*. London: Croom Helm.
Kerry, T. (2002a) *Explaining and Questioning*. Cheltenham: Nelson-Thornes.
Kerry, T. (2002b) *Learning Objectives, Task Setting and Differentiation*. Cheltenham: Nelson-Thornes.
Loughran, J. (2002) 'Understanding and articulating teacher knowledge', in Sugrue, C. and Day, C. (eds) *Developing Teachers and Teaching Practice*. London: Routledge Falmer.
Lovey, J. (2002) *Supporting Special Educational Needs in Secondary Classrooms* (2nd edn). London: David Fulton.
McGuiness, C. (2000) 'ACTS: a methodology for enhancing children's thinking skills'. Paper presented at the ESRC TLRP First Programme Conference, Leicester University, November.
Stoll, L., Fink, D. and Earl, L. (2003) *It's About Learning (and It's About Time)*. London: Routledge Falmer.
Wallace, B. (2001) *Teaching Thinking Skills across the Primary Curriculum*. London: NACE Fulton.
Wilding, M. (1997) 'Taking control: from theory into practice'. *Education Today* 47(3): 17–23.
Willis, D. (1993) 'Learning and assessment: exposing the inconsistencies of theory and practice'. *Oxford Review of Education* 19(3): 383–402.
Wragg, E. C. (1984) *Classroom Teaching Skills*. London: Croom Helm.

Internet source

etheses.nottingham.ac.uk/2518/1/346624.pdf

Part 2

Cross-curricular learning and teaching in EYFS and Key Stage 1

Chapter 3

Cross-curricular teaching to support child-initiated learning in EYFS and Key Stage 1

Elizabeth Wood

Introduction

This chapter focuses on the ways in which teachers can support child-initiated learning, by developing integrated pedagogical approaches in the Early Years Foundation Stage (EYFS) and into Y1 and Y2. The version of this chapter that appeared in the first edition of this book was composed at a time of optimism. Outcomes of the Independent Review of the Primary Curriculum (DCSF 2009) and the Cambridge Primary Review (Alexander 2009) had proposed a number of challenges for teachers in England in how they reconceptualise learning, curriculum and pedagogy. Though these were not adopted as policy following the 2010 election, a change of climate in primary education appeared to pertain. As has been described in the Foreword to this edition, however, the optimism was relatively short-lived: under Michael Gove, Secretary of State for Education until July 2014, the emphasis was on formal adult-led activities, teaching phonics and ensuring good behaviour, to create the 'school ready' child. Literacy and numeracy were emphasised, and there was a return to the traditional doctrine of subject-led learning in Key Stage 1. In the process, cross-curricular approaches, while achieving some lip-service, fell off the agenda and those espousing this cause were once again relegated to a quiet minority.

In that context, the present chapter intends to help teachers meet these challenges, and looks at contemporary socio-cultural theories that align with these directions: integrating child-initiated and adult-initiated learning activities is central to high-quality education. However, developing cross-curricular approaches involves the teacher in challenging traditional notions of education and rethinking adults' roles and responsibilities. To meet the challenges, I will argue that teachers need a deep and sophisticated understanding of learning, and a wide pedagogical repertoire, in order to develop the curriculum in ways that combine structure and flexibility, and support play and playfulness. Examples are used to link theory and practice, and illustrate integrated pedagogical approaches.

Background

The Independent Review of the Primary Curriculum (Rose Review) (DCSF 2009) recommended an upward extension of the pedagogical approaches in the Early Years Foundation Stage (EYFS) (DCSF 2009) into Y1 and Y2. The Independent Review also recommended extending and building on active, play-based learning across the transition from the EYFS to Y1 and Y2, in order to improve continuity of pedagogical approaches. However, the review was less clear about how teachers can develop challenge and extension in play in order to sustain progression.

As a result of the Cambridge Review, Alexander (2009) argued that teachers needed to move towards 'repertoires rather than recipes', with greater emphasis on professional knowledge and decision making than has been possible under former versions of the EYFS and the National Curriculum. The content and recommendations of both these reviews urged teachers to undertake a reconceptualisation of traditional notions of child-centred education. Teachers, it was suggested, would need to develop a more critical focus on cross-curricular work, and on their own roles. I argue that, by developing their repertoires of teaching, teachers can extend children's repertoires of participation and learning, and that this can be achieved via cross-curricular pedagogical approaches.

While the recommendations of the Independent Review were welcomed (and long over-due), there remain a number of challenges for teachers in supporting the upward extension of integrated pedagogical approaches. In the first section of this chapter, therefore, I examine the case for a reconceptualisation of established theories that have underpinned child-centred education in the light of current directions towards cross-curricular pedagogical approaches, and contemporary socio-cultural theories. In the second section the intention is to develop the concept of child-initiated learning in the light of changes in policy directions and theo-retical perspectives. To do this, it is important for teachers to take into account the complexity and diversity of children's socio-cultural life-worlds and experiences. Examples from classroom practice and empirical research provide illustrations of cross-curricular pedagogical approaches, and the ways in which teachers might anticipate and implement curriculum change. In the final section of the chapter I look at how these trends for improving pedagogical and curriculum continuity from the Foundation Stage to Key Stages 1 and 2 can be implemented in practice.

Before proceeding to undertake these two tasks, however, it might be useful to reflect on attitudes towards play, and then to examine the latest government position on EYFS. On the first issue, Chazan's (2002:198) definition remains useful:

> Playing and growing are synonymous with life itself. Playfulness bespeaks creativity and action, change and possibility of transformation. Play activity thus reflects the very existence of self, that part of the organism that exists both independently and inter-dependently, that can reflect upon itself and be aware of its own existence. In being playful the child attains a degree of autonomy sustained by representations of his (sic) inner and outer worlds.

Although few would deny the importance of play in young animals, some seem to want to do away with it, or at least relegate it to a minor role, in the development of the young human animal. As a result, 'play can be regarded as deeply serious and purposeful. It can be characterized by high levels of motivation, creativity and learning, or perceived as aimless messing about' (Wood 2013a). These tensions are evident in the guidance (issued in late 2013) about the EYFS (https://www.gov.uk/early-years-foundation-stage), which minimises any mention of play. This guidance is far less explicit than the Rose Report was, for example, in either ruling in, or ruling out, cross-curricular approaches to learning, as can be seen:

> Early years learning concentrates on 7 areas split between prime and specific areas of learning. The prime areas of learning are:
>
> communication and language
> physical development
> personal, social and emotional development

The specific areas of learning are:

literacy
mathematics
understanding the world
expressive arts and design

Teaching is often done through play, where the child learns about subjects and other people through games.

Clearly educational and purposeful play is the dominant message in the EYFS. The guidance introduces the notion of testing, beginning with a developmental health check at the age of two years, and culminating in a baseline assessment at the point of school entry. It is somewhat disingenuous in suggesting that this is not 'testing of pupils', but assessments made through the observations of pupils by the teacher. In a document emanating from the National College of School Leadership (2013: 4, 5), which had effect from September of that year, the skills required of teachers are identified in sections 4 and 5, and include the following:

4. Plan education and care taking account of the needs of all children.

4.1 Observe and assess children's development and learning, using this to plan next steps.

4.2 Plan balanced and flexible activities and educational programmes that take into account the stage of development, circumstances and interests of children.

4.3 Promote a love of learning and stimulate children's intellectual curiosity in partnership with parents and/or carers.

4.4 Use a variety of teaching approaches to lead group activities appropriate to the age range and ability of children.

4.5 Reflect on the effectiveness of teaching activities and educational programmes to support the continuous improvement of provision.

5. Adapt education and care to respond to the strengths and needs of all children.

5.1 Have a secure understanding of how a range of factors can inhibit children's learning and development and how best to address these.

5.2 Demonstrate an awareness of the physical, emotional, social, intellectual development and communication needs of babies and children, and know how to adapt education and care to support children at different stages of development.

5.3 Demonstrate a clear understanding of the needs of all children, including those with special educational needs and disabilities, and be able to use and evaluate distinctive approaches to engage and support them.

5.4 Support children through a range of transitions.

5.5 Know when a child is in need of additional support and how this can be accessed, working in partnership with parents and/or carers and other professionals.

The document then goes on, once more, to talk about assessment processes. None of these requirements, of itself, makes any value judgement on (or indeed, provides any guidance about) the 'packaging' of the curriculum. Therefore, cross-curricular approaches would appear, at least in theory, to be as valid as any other, as long as children are achieving the learning outcomes at the transition to Key Stage 1. However, the debate continues as to whether children learn through subject disciplines that are taught through integrated or discrete approaches.

Child-centred education: change and challenge

Early childhood education (defined here as birth to seven) has been based on a strong ideological commitment to child-centred approaches, which embrace child-initiated learning through free play and free choice, discovery and exploration, and 'hands on' experiential activities. Child-initiated learning, it is argued, provides the foundations for building meaning and understanding from experience.

In order to support these approaches to learning, teachers are expected to provide richly resourced learning environments (both indoors and outdoors), and to support children's choices, which lead to autonomy and ownership and control of their learning. By observing and interacting with children, it is claimed that teachers can build the curriculum around children's emerging developmental needs and interests, and stimulate further learning through adult-initiated as well as child-initiated activities. The concept of child-initiated learning is grounded in the assumption that children intuitively know what they want and need to do, and can follow their own interests through free choice and free play (Wood 2009).

Moreover, many teachers of this age range would see children as being developmentally 'primed' to learn from their self-initiated activities because they are intrinsically motivated, and have natural inclinations for curiosity, investigation, discovery and playfulness. Play has always enjoyed a high status within this ideology, again on the assumption that, when children are playing, they are more engaged, more motivated and more likely to learn than in adult-initiated activities. These claims are central to the 'play ethos', in which play has been given a privileged position in early learning and development (Smith 2009). There is, though, a danger here: play is often used as an umbrella term to include all child-initiated activities. However, an uncritical devotion to the play ethos masks the reality that children-initiated learning is not always play based, and that play does not consistently offer the best or most effective ways of learning (Wood 2010).

The commitment to child-initiated learning has been incorrectly interpreted as a 'laissez-faire' approach, in which adults did not take proactive roles in supporting children's learning and development. Because of this, teachers have come under fire from the press and politicians – and, sometimes, even from parents who are anxious to accelerate their children's progress. Thus, there have been long-standing debates about play versus work, processes versus outcomes, freedom versus structure, child-initiated versus teacher-directed learning, which have tended to polarise rather than synthesise pedagogical approaches. This lack of consensus about the values of child-initiated learning made early childhood education vulnerable to the downward pressures of the National Curriculum and National Strategies.

So, while the principles of child-initiated learning are ideologically seductive, they have not provided a universally agreed underpinning for educational practice. This is because these principles are based on a range of theories about the different ways in which young children learn and develop, and have produced contrasting views about pedagogy, and the content and organisation of the early childhood curriculum.

There have always been varied, and sometimes contradictory, views about the pedagogical models that adults should use with young children, from predominantly non-interventionist (laissez-faire), to mixed child-initiated and adult-initiated activities, and to highly interventionist, in which adult-planned activities are prioritised, with little time for children's free choice (other than in dedicated 'choosing time' on a Friday afternoon). Where teachers do mix child-initiated and adult-initiated activities it is not always the case that these are actually integrated.

Child-initiated activities are sometimes planned as preparatory curriculum-based skills training (Fassler and Levin 2008), or to keep children occupied while adults are engaged in more formal activities that are related to curriculum goals (Rogers and Evans 2008) – for example, where a teacher allows some pupils to 'choose' an activity while she deals with the more formal process of listening to other children read. It follows that, if teachers have little involvement in child-initiated activities (through observation and interaction), then they are not able to plan in ways that are responsive to children's interests or that extend children's play. Another assumption is that, beyond the pre-school years, children can tolerate more sedentary and formal activities that are predominantly teacher-directed, and focus on specific learning outcomes. This means that, beyond the preschool phase, children typically experience reduced opportunities for child-initiated activities and play, even though they have developed considerable expertise as players and learners, and are more able to benefit from such activities (Wood 2013b).

Diversity and complexity

Some of the principles stated above carry implicit assumptions that all children benefit from self-initiated activities, and that all children can direct their own learning through free play and free choice. Teachers will be aware that there are always dangers in making universal assumptions about children's learning and needs. We need to be aware, too, that our assumptions may be based on ethnocentric assertions of predominantly Western child development theories, which are not universally applicable in diverse and complex societies (Genishi and Goodwin 2008).

In contrast, contemporary theories of child-initiated learning acknowledge the role of culture as a dynamic and complex process that both influences and is influenced by people's everyday lives and experiences in different communities. Culture is not expressed merely in everyday artefacts and images (such as having chopsticks and saris in the role-play area), but is expressed as ways of living and being that reflect traditions, values, beliefs, customs and child-rearing practices. These in turn profoundly influence children's ways of learning, perceiving, thinking and experiencing the world. So the interests that children express, and the ways in which they are able to learn through self-initiated activities, vary widely according to social and cultural diversity, which take into account the dimensions of diversity identified by Genishi and Goodwin (2008): gender, race, ethnicity, religious affiliation, ability or disability, sexuality, social class and language.

Teachers may have very different perceptions of this issue of culture according to their school contexts – for example, a school where more than forty languages are spoken by pupils will inevitably be different from a small, isolated school where there is perhaps one pupil whose origin is not within the local community. Thus, when rethinking 'child-centred' education, it is important to consider what is at the centre of the child in terms of identity and cultural diversity, what personal meanings the children hold, and the ways in which these shape children's interests and orientations to schooling.

The influences of identity and cultural diversity are exemplified in research by Levinson (2005, 2008) and Brooker (2002, 2010). This research is important to teachers because it highlights the tensions that can arise for a child as a result of two different sets of expectations and experiences. Levinson has carried out ethnographic studies of children and their families in Gypsy and traveller communities, and has provided some striking contrasts between the range of child-initiated activities that children experience in their home settings and their experiences in schools. He argues that children's orientations to learning in school and home contexts are divergent, for a number of reasons:

> Apart from the skills that are acquired at home, less tangible learning is also occurring – the acquisition of wider social skills, the ability to adapt quickly between tasks, the growth of self-confidence, independence and group identity. To some degree, such learning might be expected to complement that acquired in formal schooling, but there are certain tensions that make this less likely. In both content and style, learning is divergent from that encountered at school; of still greater significance, from an early age, children are part of an adult world. Already socialized into such a world, the hierarchical divisions at school are likely to strike the Gypsy child as being neither natural nor logical.
>
> (Levinson 2008: 74)

Levinson also juxtaposes the concept of learner autonomy in home and school contexts:

> At home, they were often expected to work on their own initiative, and this brought status. J.R. (aged 20s) was proud that his 7 year old son, Billy, could be left to change spark-plugs on a car, a skill acquired through observation then encouragement. In contrast, it is argued that school education does not permit children to 'learn at their own speed' or 'to pick things up on their own'. Such remarks are revealing in their implication of: (a) undue pressure on the learner at school, and (b) a substantial degree of autonomy granted to the learner at home. This entails both the (spatial) freedom to move around during learning, and the (temporal) freedom to decide when to stop, start and take breaks in learning.
>
> (Levinson 2008: 75)

This is an interesting juxtaposition, because it alerts teachers to the fact that concepts such as choice, freedom and autonomy have contrasting meanings in home and school contexts. The interests that children develop at home may not easily be expressed or accommodated in school contexts, especially if teachers have little knowledge or understanding of children's home cultures and experiences. Therefore it may be difficult for children to initiate learning if they cannot make meaningful connections.

Similarly, research by Brooker (2002) on young children's transition to a reception class highlights cultural differences between the participants (working-class Anglo and Bangladeshi families) that influenced children's orientations to school and their expectations of appropriate behaviours and activities in the classroom. The established pedagogic discourse of free play and free choice made it difficult for the children from Bangladeshi homes to adjust to the culture of the classroom. In their home environments, they had not been prepared for these approaches to learning, and the concept of children being independent and autonomous was unfamiliar to parents. Brooker's research also highlights some of the tensions in the traditional child-centred pedagogic discourse: children are required to show compliance with the rules of the setting, but at the same time are expected to direct their own learning through choosing their own activities (both individually and with others). The studies by Levinson and Brooker ask teachers to raise some challenging questions about an uncritical commitment to child-centred education, and to child-initiated learning, particularly in relation to the skills and interests children develop at home, whether these can be transferred into school contexts, and even whether they are recognised by teachers as valued forms of learning. Teachers themselves, or schools, may be sources of tension for children's self-initiation. For example, certain types of interests and activities may be banned if they do not meet with the teacher's approval, or if there are health and safety implications. Such activities include rough-and-tumble play, superhero play, and war or weapons play (Holland 2003; Jarvis 2010). In addition, children's interests that are based on popular culture may be sidelined in favour of interests that are approved by teachers.

It follows that, if certain interests are banned, then certain areas of learning may also be denied to children. For example, in her research on young children's self-initiated activities during playtimes, Jarvis (2010) identifies many complex skills and routines that children develop to initiate and maintain play. These include older children mentoring the younger ones into the complex rule construction that frames their games of football, modelling the negotiation of rules, communicating playground rituals and customs, and developing social networks. The research by Jarvis reveals that child-initiated learning activities may incorporate levels of complexity that are not accessible to teachers unless they take the time to understand the ways in which children's interests are the driving force for forms of learning that are intrinsically meaningful for them. Therefore a key pedagogical challenge is to consider how the levels of motivation and engagement that children demonstrate in their self-initiated activities could be harnessed during teacher-initiated activities.

> **Reflection**
>
> How would you analyse and define the culture of your school? How does that culture affect your planning in terms of the curriculum you teach and the learning/teaching methods you use?

Child-initiated learning: new directions

One of the key principles of the Independent Review was that planning the curriculum around 'a carefully constructed amalgam of areas of learning and subjects' deepens children's interests and understanding as they use and apply the knowledge and skills gained in one subject, or area of learning, in another (DCSF 2008: 34). The Independent Review opened the door to more cross-curricular approaches, but nonetheless explicitly rejected the more open-ended kind of 'laissez-faire' approaches:

> Good primary teaching involves far more than waiting for children to develop by following their every whim. It deliberately deepens and widens children's understanding by firing their imagination and interest and paving the way to higher achievement

through 'scaffolding' learning in a community of learners. As envisaged by Vygotsky and other well-respected cognitive researchers, good teaching means that 'what children can do with adult support today they can do unaided tomorrow'.

(DCSF 2009: 56, para. 3.6)

The rejection of laissez-faire approaches reflects the long-standing tensions in teachers' pedagogical roles, particularly regarding the extent to which teachers should respond to or provoke children's interests as a means of supporting child-initiated learning. Imagine a line, or continuum, with teacher-controlled learning at one end of it and laissez-faire approaches at the other. Most of us would feature at a point along the line rather than at one extreme or the other. We take a pragmatic view that this is not an 'either/or' choice, because cross-curricular pedagogical approaches should enable teachers to do both.

As De Vries (1997) argues, the provision of activities that appeal to children's interests shows respect for the child's point of view, and for how they learn and develop. She also distinguishes between general interests and specific purposes: general interest in an activity gives the teacher an opportunity to challenge children to pursue a specific purpose, and to find their own purposes in an activity. But it should also be remembered that children's interests can be content rich, in that those interests typically form the springboard for developing their knowledge, skills, understanding and areas of specialist expertise, as demonstrated by Jarvis (2010) and Levinson (2008). In addition, shared or group interests (especially in play activities) support social affiliation, friendship skills, empathy and collaborative learning.

Responding to children's interests therefore implies reciprocal engagement between adults and children, in ways that challenge and extend children's knowledge. In addition, children should develop 'mastery orientations' to learning, which involves taking risks, making mistakes, using enquiry and problem-solving capabilities, and developing meta-cognitive awareness of their own learning capabilities. The concept of reciprocal engagement is fundamental to cross-curricular pedagogical approaches. Teachers inevitably tune in to the many different ways in which children learn, in order to understand their interests and motivations, and how these can be supported through responsive curriculum planning. This concept is illustrated in an example (Case Study 3.1) from a Year 1 class.

Case Study 3.1 Integrated pedagogical approaches: learning outdoors

A primary school had recently invested in developing the outdoor learning environment, which included a vegetable garden, spaces for play and den building, a fire circle, and a wild area with a pond. A group of four boys developed an interest in 'bugs', which was provoked by finding a large colony of woodlice under some rotting logs. This was developed by the teacher as a group interest, to include learning about respect for the environment, and finding ways of investigating insects and other creatures without harming them or their natural habitats. As the children's interests developed, their purposes became more refined: they used a range of equipment to investigate living things in the environment, including binoculars, digital cameras (still and video images), and magnifying glasses. They recorded their investigations in different ways, including drawings, classification charts and ICT equipment.

Their interest in classification was supported by the teacher through guided use of books, websites, and understanding how entomologists study and classify insects. As a result of their observations, the children were highly motivated to learn how to use the electronic microscope, and to upload and record the images on the computer. Some children pursued related activities at home, such as visiting museums and creating small wild areas in their own gardens. Artistic responses included making large sculptures and models of some of the creatures from natural materials, which were placed in the outdoor area, and doing detailed observational drawings based on the enlarged computer images.

The initial interests of the four boys became shared interests across the whole class as new investigations were planned. The teacher continued to challenge their thinking, add new areas of knowledge and understanding, and suggest further areas for investigation. This combined responsive planning (building on what emerged from the children's activities and interests) with her own planning (making decisions about what areas of knowledge and understanding to add, or what investigations to provoke with the children). She responded to their affective as well as cognitive engagement in the project, and made sure that the indoor and outdoor learning environments were well equipped to support the development of the topic. In these ways, the children's interests became the focus for shared and purposeful modes of enquiry, where they were engaged in creating and solving problems, and gaining new knowledge and skills. Moreover, the teacher and children co-constructed contexts for using and applying cross-curricular knowledge and skills, which is a key recommendation in the Independent Review of the Primary Curriculum (DCSF 2009). The integrated pedagogical model used here is based on theories of guided participation and co-construction, where differently knowledgeable people support each other's learning, drawing on the tools, knowledges and resources of the community (Plowman and Stephen 2007).

This vignette demonstrates what experienced teachers already know: that children's interests by themselves do not constitute the basis for successful learning. Rather it is the ability of the teacher that helps children to make connections across areas of learning and experience, by integrating subject content knowledge as well as real-life experiences, and making creative use of indoor and outdoor learning environments. Children's interests are often driven by their fascination with the world, and their motivation to become more knowledgeable, more competent, and more confident in using and applying their skills in different contexts. In other words, their interests are dynamic and not static. Children's interests are also linked to the diverse ways in which they develop and express personal identities, and the extent to which they feel included, respected and valued in a learning community. If children are surrounded by discrimination and conflict, they will learn that their interests are not valued, which may lead to feelings of exclusion and disaffection. Therefore, contemporary versions of child-centred education must see learning as a multidimensional process whereby children's interests arise and can be extended in diverse home and school contexts.

Developing cross-curricular pedagogical approaches

There is clear theoretical justification for supporting teachers and headteachers in developing cross-curricular pedagogical approaches in schools in order to incorporate new approaches to learning through information and communication technologies (ICT), to integrate formal and informal approaches to learning, and to build on children's interests in ways that provoke further challenge and extension. From a theoretical perspective, the latest theories suggest that children's learning, development and identity formation are socially and culturally situated – that is, they cannot be divorced from their social contexts. Children are an integral part of, not separate from, complex cultural belief systems and practices. They are bound up in complex relationships between the home and community, educational institutions and wider society (Hedeggard and Fleer 2008). As teachers, we need not simply to appreciate this theoretical standpoint but to apply that knowledge to our understanding of our own pupils' learning and learning experiences.

New interpretations of child-initiated learning rest on a number of theoretical assumptions. Important among these are the following:

- Children are not just 'active learners' but are active agents in their own learning and development, and active participants in cultural communities.
- Children's repertoires of activity and participation are culturally shaped with adults and peers, and with cultural tools, resources and symbol systems.
- Thus different social practices provoke qualitatively different changes in children's learning and development, as documented by Levinson (2008) and Brooker (2002).
- It follows that children's repertoires of participation provoke different forms of activities, based on their motivation and interests.
- Participation also provokes situated agency – children actively engage in the social construction of their own identities and subjectivities (how they see themselves as individuals, and how they see themselves in relation to others).

Children's interests derive from many different sources, including shared childhood cultures and popular culture. Childhood cultures involve shared meanings and experiences, and opportunities for building peer relationships, all of which contribute to shared interests and identities. Children are also fascinated by the world of adults, but their interests are driven not merely by wanting to be adults, but by wanting to experience what they perceive as adult control, autonomy and decision making. These processes are often visible in children's imaginative play activities when they act out adults' roles, particularly when they exaggerate power and control, or create roles that disrupt adults' power, such as being wild animals, destructive monsters and naughty pets, or taking on magical powers as fairies, witches and wizards (Wood and Cook 2009).

From children's perspectives, play is also about subversion and inversion, order and disorder, chaos and stability, inclusion and marginalisation, which is where issues of power, agency and control are played out. Therefore the interests that children pursue in their play tend to have personal relevance for their social, affective and cognitive development. Anyone who has watched children at play can see these processes at work – for example, in the child who knocks over the brick tower he and others have been building with great care, in the comings and goings of friendships and alliances, and in attachment to some traditional (if not politically correct) entertainments, such as Punch and Judy.

A key to successful learning lies in the teacher's awareness of children's play activities and the learning that is associated with it. In order for teachers to achieve a successful upward extension of the EYFS pedagogies into Key Stage 1, much greater attention needs to be paid to how children's play changes and develops, and the ways in which school provision can support challenge and extension.

Learning takes place in many different contexts – in homes, schools, communities, and in virtual and online worlds. Traditional boundaries between these different learning contexts are dissolving, and the increasing use of electronic media is merging the personal, the local and the global in terms of the knowledge that can be accessed, and the ways in which it can be used. Therefore child-initiated learning is increasingly taking place not just in new technological spaces but in much wider spheres. In developing cross-curricular pedagogical approaches, teachers need to utilise ICT and new media technologies in creative ways, because they are helping to break down hierarchical barriers between 'teachers' and 'learners', and to create contexts for collaborative learning where risk taking, creative problem solving and creativity are encouraged (Yelland *et al.* 2008).

But a key issue for education – that is, for teachers and heads – is whether policy frameworks are keeping pace with these changes, and whether school-based practices are reflecting the complexities and diversities of children's everyday interests, knowledge and experiences. Children's opportunities for successful self-initiated learning depend on flexible learning environments in which they can draw on their own funds of knowledge and experience, and incorporate them in to school experiences, in traditional face-to-face and virtual contexts.

Cross-curricular pedagogical approaches create opportunities for co-construction and engagement between adults and children, and between peers, which contribute not just to achieving defined learning outcomes but also to children's identities, self-image and self-esteem. In pursuing their own interests, children generate and test out their own ideas, build personal (and sometimes idiosyncratic) theories about their social and cultural worlds, and often build identity markers, such as developing expertise in using computers, being an expert footballer or being a good co-player. Contemporary research (especially in the field of ICT) indicates that peer learning can be productively co-constructive within integrated approaches (Plowman and Stephen 2007; Yelland *et al.* 2008).

In summary, as teachers explore their new curriculum freedoms in a changing climate of increased teacher autonomy, the concept of 'repertoires not recipes' is central to the kinds of changes that need to come about in terms of repertoires of teaching, and in the repertoires of learning activities that are available to children. By using cross-curricular pedagogical approaches, teachers can plan in proactive and responsive ways. Proactive planning involves identifying intentional learning outcomes, and designing activities that will lead to those outcomes. Responsive planning includes observing and responding to the ways in which children develop the teacher's planned activities, as well as initiating their own activities.

An integrated model of planning (see Chapter 10) is likely to be quite demanding of teachers' time, skills and expertise. In addition, it may mean that schools review their adherence to fixed planning cycles centred on specific themes or topics (if it's autumn term in Year 1 then it's 'People Who Help Us'). Letting go of the recipes may prove to be a challenging and potentially difficult process, which does not mean 'going back' to outdated models of planning themes and topics. Developing cross-curricular pedagogical approaches is challenging but much more rewarding than the command-and-control models of the past twenty years. Teachers will be able to use their pedagogical repertoires in creative and innovative ways, but will need to develop a much more critical understanding of child-initiated learning.

Reflection

How can you find out about the diversity and complexity of children's knowledge and interests, based on their home and community cultures?

In what ways can ICT be used to support children's choices, and to enhance their learning?

To what extent does your provision enable children to choose how they communicate in multimodal ways?

What resources would enable you to create multiliterate and multimodal means of enhancing children's learning, thinking and communicating?

Analysing learning in a classroom setting

It is usually the case that the youngest learners in educational settings have the most freedom to choose and initiate their own activities. But how do we come to understand the value of those activities in terms of what the children choose to do, how the activity developed, what actually happened and how we plan further activities? Read the observation in Case Study 3.2. You should reflect on your own responses to the observation, in terms of how you read and interpret what is happening, before you read the accompanying notes that follow. This case study indicates the importance of adult observations of children's activities, and how these can inform integrated pedagogical approaches.

Reflection

How do you think the children are interpreting what is happening in Case Study 3.2? How would you plan responsively to support the children's learning and development? What does this episode reveal about child-initiated learning?

Case Study 3.2 Learning in progress

Foundation Stage setting (children are all aged 3–4), Listening corner, 15.7.09, 9.45am (CD player with six headphones which the children are able to manage themselves).

Leanne, Jed, Joseph and Alfie are wearing headphones and using the leads as microphones. They are singing and dancing along to the music. Jed, Joseph and Alfie are wearing capes. Gail and Owen try to join.

Leanne (to Gail and Owen):	You two aren't allowed in here. Go away, you haven't got these on (points to headphones) so you aren't allowed.
Gail:	I'm allowed cos I'm the policeman. (She is wearing the police tabard and cap)

Owen leaves the area and returns wearing headphones. He plugs them in and starts dancing along with the others, with obvious enjoyment.

Leanne: Look, Owen's allowed cos he's got these on, same as me (points to headphones).

Jed: You can't come in here if you're not a bat cos we're all bats.

Jed, Joseph and Alfie are trying to negotiate some rules about imaginative play involving bats. They leave the area. Gail has tried to take the earphones from Leanne, who immediately goes into high-pitched crying and sobbing. The teacher persuades her to give her headphones to another child, and Leanne leaves the area. Close by, two younger girls are absorbed in playing with a large doll's house. Leanne stands close by, absolutely still. She drops her head and looks sad, but at the same time glances sideways at the doll's house activity. I ask her what she wants to do.

Leanne: There's two girls and they don't want another girl to play with them.

I suggest that Leanne asks the girls if she can join, which she does. Henry has already joined without asking permission, and takes a place in front of the doll's house. The two girls walk away without saying anything.

Leanne: Henry, Henry, Henry, Henry, Henry.

Henry ignores her.

Leanne: Henry can I play? Can I play with you?

EW: Henry, Leanne is asking you a question. I think she would like to play with you.

Henry looks at Leanne.

Leanne: Can I play, Henry?

Henry nods. They play in parallel, with some self-speech and some interaction. Faye joins in, but is not interacting with Henry and Leanne.

Leanne: Here's the baby, Henry. Look at the baby.

Henry looks in her direction but offers no response. Leanne places her pony and play people very precisely in two rooms. There is some brief interaction between Henry and Faye but mostly about which rooms they can play in. They are each sticking to their own spaces, even though there has been no negotiation of which space 'belongs' to each child. Parallel play continues to 10.35 (snack time), with little engagement between the children.

Some reflections on Case Study 3.2

Once you have read Case Study 3.2 and carried out the Reflection associated with it, read on to compare your views with my own as I analyse this sequence. In the paragraphs that follow, I reflect on this episode and suggest some ways in which it may have contributed to children's learning.

The six children at the listening corner were clearly enjoying the experience, so it could be claimed that they were learning to use the technology and to enjoy shared participation in a very lively activity (dancing, singing along, laughing). However, negotiating access and inclusion was, for these young children, more problematic, which makes me think more carefully about the ways in which children might be interpreting these events. They had some understanding of how the 'rules' of access sometimes work in child-initiated activities – having the right props, being a member of an established friendship group or being seen as a play leader. Jed, Joseph and Alfie left the activity because they seemed to be more engaged in their ongoing 'bat' play. Leanne left because she knew the rules about taking turns, but seemed unable to cope with this at an emotional level.

It could be argued that Leanne needs further support with her social skills in terms of accessing an activity and taking turns, both of which require some degree of empathy and altruism – seeing another person's perspective and giving up one's own place willingly to someone else. In the house play the children have chosen the same activity, but their actions and perspectives are not aligned, and there is little interaction between them. As there is little language or social interaction, it is difficult to determine the content or focus of their individual activities, or what they might be learning. From a pedagogical perspective, it might be useful to consider what other experiences could be planned to develop the children's social skills and play skills, and to enhance the learning potential of their self-initiated activities. However, at a deeper level, I am left pondering the personal meaning of these activities to the children, and the social and relational complexities involved in self-initiated activities.

Conclusion

Teachers continue to be tossed on the storm waves of trends at work within the EYFS and the Primary Curriculum. However, as is always the case, teachers need to be proactive (rather than merely reactive) in how policies are implemented in practice. In order to develop cross-curricular pedagogical approaches, teachers need detailed understanding of children's funds of knowledge, and the ways in which these can be connected and extended across adult-initiated and child-initiated activities. It is also important for teachers to take into account children's diverse backgrounds, and the ways in which they can use their interests as the springboard for further learning, so that children can develop as master players and master learners.

References

Alexander, R. (2009) *Children, Their World, Their Education*. London: Routledge.
Brooker, L. (2002) *Starting School – Young Children Learning Cultures*. Buckingham: Open University Press.
Brooker, L. (2010) 'Learning to play in cultural context', in Broadhead, P., Howard, J. and Wood, E. (eds) *Play and Learning in Early Childhood Settings*. London: Sage.
Chazan, S. E. (2002) *Assessing and Observing Structure and Process in Play Therapy*. London: Jessica Kingsley.
Department for Children, Schools and Families (DCSF) (2008) *The Interim Report of the Independent Review of the Primary Curriculum*. Available online at: http://publications.teachernet.gov.uk (accessed June 2009).
Department for Children, Schools and Families (DCSF) (2009) *Independent Review of the Primary Curriculum*. Available online at: http://publications.teachernet.gov.uk (accessed October 2009).
DeVries, R. (1997) 'Piaget's social theory'. *Educational Researcher* 26(2): 4–17.
Fassler, R. and Levin, D. (2008) 'Envisioning and supporting the play of preschoolers', in Genishi, C. and Goodwin, A. L. (eds) *Diversities in Early Childhood Education – Rethinking and Doing*. New York: Routledge.

Genishi, C. and Goodwin, A. L. (2008) *Diversities in Early Childhood Education – Rethinking and Doing.* New York: Routledge.

Hedeggard, M. and Fleer, M. (2008) *Studying Children: A Cultural-historical Approach.* Maidenhead: McGraw-Hill.

Holland, P. (2003) *We Don't Play With Guns Here: War, Weapon and Superhero Play in the Early Years.* Maidenhead: Open University Press.

Jarvis, P. (2010) '"Born to play": the biocultural roots of "rough and tumble" play, and its impact upon young children's learning and development', in Broadhead, P., Howard, J. and Wood, E. (eds) *Play and Learning in Education Settings.* London: Sage.

Levinson, M. P. (2005) 'The role of play in the formation and maintenance of cultural identity: gypsy children in home and school contexts'. *Journal of Contemporary Ethnography* 34(5): 499–532.

Levinson, M. P. (2008) 'Issues of empowerment and disempowerment: gypsy children at home and school'. *International Journal of Citizenship Education* 4(2): 70–77.

National College for School Leadership (2013) *Teachers' Standard (Early Years).* London: NCSL.

Plowman, L. and Stephen, C. (2007) 'Guided interaction in pre-school settings'. *Journal of Computer Assisted Learning* 23: 14–26.

Rogers, S. and Evans, J. (2008) *Inside Role Play in Early Childhood Education: Researching Young Children's Perspectives.* London: Routledge.

Smith, P. (2009) *Children and Play.* Oxford: Wiley-Blackwell.

Wood, E. (2009) 'Conceptualising a pedagogy of play: international perspectives from theory, policy and practice', in Kuschner, D. (ed.) *From Children to Red Hatters®: Diverse Images and Issues of Play. Play and Culture Studies, Vol. 8.* Lanham, Maryland: University Press of America.

Wood, E. (2010) 'Challenging play', in Edwards, S. and Brooker, L. (eds) *Engaging Play.* Maidenhead: Open University Press.

Wood, E. (2013a) 'Free play and free choice in early childhood education – troubling the discourse'. *International Journal of Early Years Education*, DOI:10.1080/09669760.2013.830562.

Wood, E. (2013b) *Play, Learning and the Early Childhood Curriculum* (3rd edn). London: Sage.

Wood, E. and Cook, J. (2009) 'Gendered discourses and practices in role play activities: a case study of young children in the English Foundation Stage'. *Journal of Educational and Child Psychology* 26(2): 19–30.

Yelland, N., Lee, L., O'Rourke, M. and Harrison, C. (2008) *Rethinking Learning in Early Childhood Education.* Maidenhead: Open University Press.

Internet sources

Department for Education and Skills (DfES) (2008) *The Early Years Foundation Stage*: http://www.standards.dfes.gov.uk/primary/foundation_stage/eyfs/

https://www.gov.uk/early-years-foundation-stage

Chapter 4

The cross-curricular approach in Key Stage 1

Jane Johnston

Introduction

This chapter is based on a case study example of good cross-curricular practice in Y1 and Y2 of the primary school, which illustrates the following principles of effective KS1 practice:

- Learning is child-centred
- Learning is practical and exploratory
- Learning is best acquired through motivating experiences
- Learning is enhanced through effective peer interaction
- Learning requires effective adult support and interaction
- Learning is most effective in cross-curricular contexts.

It also considers how children move from the Early Years Foundation Stage (EYFS) and into Y1 and Y2.

Background: thematic teaching in Y1 and Y2

Childhood today is significantly different from other generations. For example, children are rich in electronic stimuli, but poor in the quality of relationships (Bowlby 2006). Children have more pressures on them to grow up and yet have less freedom in which to develop (Palmer 2006). Education is more formalised than in the 1960s and 1970s, and yet educational performance is considered to be less good. While teaching, particularly in the early years, we have to accommodate not only social changes but also the conflicting pedagogical advice and changes to the curriculum. As teachers, we have to navigate our way through the expectations and demands placed upon us, and still provide motivating and relevant experiences for children, which are manageable in the school context and have clear learning outcomes.

An integrated approach to learning popular in the 1960s was weakened by the introduction in 1988 of a National Curriculum with discrete subjects, in turn questioned by the Alexander, Rose and Woodhead (1992) discussion paper, and further weakened by subsequent national strategies (DfEE 1998, 1999). When most primary teachers had adapted their practice or left the classroom, and new teachers had no real experience of integrated, thematic approaches, it was realised that the curriculum lacked relevance and pedagogical approaches stifled creativity. The introduction of a skills-based and more thematic early years' curriculum (QCA 2000; DCSF 2008a) has had a positive impact on learning and teaching. The Rose Review (Rose 2009) advocated a cross-curricular approach to learning and teaching, identifying that it strengthens subjects and supports understandings. But, as so often happens with political intervention, the wheel is now turning against integrated approaches to learning once more (Garner 2014), and the picture remains unclear at present. All the more reason, then, to hold on to these traditional and proven values.

Planning for cross-curricular or topic work

Cross-curricular topic work has some distinct advantages over teaching discrete subjects or concepts. It makes learning relevant and motivating for children, and enables children to see the relationships between different subjects. It also enables larger areas of the curriculum to be covered, as one activity can address objectives in a number of areas. For example, when baking (see example below) children can be developing aspects of speaking and listening (English), measurements (mathematics), how materials change (science) and evaluation skills (design technology). The groupings of subjects proposed in the Rose Review (2009) were these:

- Understanding English, communication, and languages
- Mathematical understanding
- Scientific and technological understanding
- Historical, geographical, and social understanding
- Understanding physical development, health and well-being
- Understanding the arts.

This suggested grouping went some way to support more thematic approaches to development and learning. Working to these principles is still possible within the current curriculum formats though some thought and imagination is needed on the part of schools and teachers to marry the two. While this sounds daunting in reality, well-planned topics take into account individual needs by:

- Identifying clear learning outcomes across two or more subject areas
- Being open-ended enough to allow individual children to develop at their own rate (see Kerry 2002a; Johnston, Halocha and Chater 2007)
- Using assessment for learning (Black and Wiliam 2004) to inform on individual children – this last is different from the Assessing Pupils' Progress initiative (DCFS 2009), which conflicts with the principles of personalised learning and assessment for learning.

Planning (see Chapter 10) should also consider the learning environment, as this supports development in a whole range of ways. The classroom environment should be such as to encourage and motivate children, through interactive displays and motivating resources that encourage children to be curious, to want to learn and to feel safe to learn. A questioning environment is one that encourages curiosity, interest and enquiry.

Planning for the learning environment includes taking account of the opportunities for using the outside environment. Even urban schools set in concrete and brick playgrounds provide a multitude of learning opportunities. Exploration of the school grounds and pavements in the surrounding area will identify evidence of life, such as plants growing in cracks in the paving (science). Patterns can be seen in grates, brickwork and roof tiles (art). Local shops can be visited so that children can map the variety of community services (geography), customers can be interviewed to see how they rate the services (English and geography), and a tally of the number of customers can be made and later plotted on a graph (mathematics). A local general store can lead to consideration of the origin of different products (geography), how goods are packaged (design and technology), and value for money (mathematics). Observing the buildings in the street can produce evidence of the ages of the buildings through different brickwork, windows, front doors and general construction (history, design and technology). Visiting the local church, mosque or temple can lead to understanding of the local community and different religions (religious education, citizenship) and their musical traditions (music). Some local industries will be happy to allow the children to visit them and set some community or personal tasks for the children. For example, rubbish collectors could set 'green' targets for children to recycle or compost waste; the local park can give children seeds to grow, which can later be planted in the park or window boxes, giving children pride and ownership over their local community; a community dentist may encourage children to improve their dental hygiene.

Reflection

Look at your classroom environment and local community, and consider opportunities for integrated work.

How could you change the classroom environment to make it more encouraging for cross-curricular work?

How could you make better use of the local environment to develop opportunities for work across the curriculum?

Recent visits to Key Stage 1 classes have identified a variety of different practices in planning. Some schools and teachers advocate detailed weekly plans that have clear learning outcomes and map out ideas for activities and resources. Others provide more detailed daily plans, which identify specifically what children and adults will do throughout the session, differentiated tasks and outcomes, and questions to focus on the learning outcomes. In many ways it does not matter which type of planning is used, but what is important is that planning is effective and focused on the identified learning outcomes, and that the teacher is well prepared for any eventuality. The worst scenario is where teachers spend lengths of time planning but it is wasted time; in reality the teachers are not well prepared, with the result that the activities do not match the learning outcomes, they are not well differentiated for individual learners, they do not challenge, question or support individual children, and the pace of the activity is too fast or too slow, leading to frustration or boredom.

Case Study 4.1 Mr Bembleman's Bakery

Our case study involves a topic stimulated by the story of Mr Bembleman's Bakery (Green 1978), which offers a rich opportunity for looking at a range of curriculum areas in a holistic way, through:

• reading and deconstructing the story (En2 Reading)
• understanding the need for standard measures (Ma3 Shape, Space and Measures)

- exploring materials, and how they change when mixed and baked (Sc3 Materials and their Properties; En1 Speaking and Listening)
- writing recipes for bread (En3 Writing)
- making bread using different recipes and evaluating the product (D&T)
- understanding different family and community traditions (Citizenship).

Though dated, this way of proceeding is in fact a classic in the sense that it contains the basic procedures for all work of this kind. Specific learning outcomes should be tailored to your own context and children.

The topic starts with the story of Mr Bembleman's Bakery. Activities focus on the book, its structure, vocabulary, grammar, tense, and sentence construction. This was planned as a whole-class activity with follow-up activities carried out in small groups of about six children throughout a week. These included the following:

- The setting up, with the children, of a bakery play area with a range of resources such as balances, oven, tables, playdough, trays, cutters, bowls, spoons, aprons and bakers' hats. If this can be set up near a sink, the children can also be responsible for ensuring their hands are clean when they make and play with dough, and for washing up tools used at the end of a session. The children can suggest and collect the resources to go into the bakery. This can also include a range of different breads (fajita, pita, chapatti, sourdough, brioche, ciabatta, etc.).
- Semi-structured play where children can play in and explore the bakery with support, where needed. Children decide what to do and how to do it, and usually will start from their own level of learning and decide where they should go next. This approach provides an element of self-differentiation, which is motivating and supports both learning and behaviour.
- Adult-led making of playdough for bakery play area and bread for baking.

Differentiation by support, questioning and outcome can all be planned for. Support is needed while making playdough and bread to ensure safety and to achieve learning outcomes by challenging the more able and supporting the less able children. Likewise, planned questions will be varied to support, challenge and extend. For example, when looking at the use of measures, questions include: *Why do we not measure the ingredients with our hands? Why should we not use handfuls and spoonfuls when measuring?* When focusing on the way materials change when mixed or baked, questions include: *What does this feel like? What do you think will happen if we cook this?* Questions that focus on vocabulary and speaking and listening include: *Can you think of another way to describe this? How did you make the bread?*

Differentiation by outcome involves clearly planned expectations for children at different levels. During and after the activity, these can aid assessment (of children) and evaluation (of teaching). For example, in this case study differentiated expectations are as follows.

High achievers should:

- Be able to describe the similarities and differences between materials in their own words and using some scientific vocabulary
- Be able to predict what will happen when materials are mixed, heated and cooled.

Middle achievers should:

- Be able to describe the similarities and differences between materials in own words
- Be able to suggest what will happen when materials are mixed, heated or cooled.

Low achievers should be able to:

- describe materials (with support if necessary) in their own words
- make a simple suggestion as to what will happen to the materials.

Using differentiated expected outcomes allows the teacher to identify whether the expected learning is at the correct level for the children; if most children achieve the expectations for higher-ability children, then the expectations were too low, and if most children needed support to achieve the outcomes, then the expected outcomes were too high. Individual children can be assessed using the expected outcomes and their next step of learning can be planned appropriately.

Reflection

Consider your current planning format and reflect on its effectiveness for:

- motivating children
- meeting individual needs through challenge, support and appropriate questioning
- achieving the learning outcomes in a number of curriculum areas
- incorporating assessment for learning.

How can you develop your planning to be more effective in the future?

Individualising cross-curricular topic work

Research tells us, rightly, that learning in the early years should be child-centred and personalised as identified and advocated through many policy documents and initiatives, such as the primary strategy (DfES 2003a), *Every Child Matters* (DfES 2003b), *2020 Vision* (DfES 2006) and *Personalised Learning – A Practical Approach* (DCFS 2008b).

A major aim in education should be to encourage children to take ownership of and responsibility for their own learning: a feature of the High/Scope Cognitively Orientated Curriculum (Hohmann and Weikart 2002). Although this curriculum was designed for children in the Early Years, some aspects appear relevant for older children. For example, encouraging child autonomy and independence should be a universal goal. Discovery is not the dirty word it is sometimes held to be. Too often curriculum is structured (often under government-led guidance) in such a way that whole-class interactive formats initiated by the introduction of these national strategies, embedded in whole-class teaching approaches with minimal personalisation and very little real engagement, are paramount.

From observations of early years lessons it seems that most tend to have the whole-class introduction, individual written tasks (maybe grouped through ability), and a whole-class plenary, even when this format is inappropriate for the task. For example, if the learning objectives involve the development of individual skills, whole-class approaches are less likely to be effective. Children are often passive: sitting and listening for long periods of time. My own analysis of the actual learning or time on task by children in an hour's literacy or numeracy lesson can be very depressing, with individual children learning for less than 25 per cent of the lesson.

The High/Scope approach (Hohmann and Weikart 2002) involves children planning their activities before carrying them out and then reviewing them afterwards, in a child-centred, reflective cycle of plan–do–review. This captures the twin requirements of effective teaching: curiosity (Taylor 2013) and creativity (Compton 2013).

Involving children in their topic has advantages in motivating children, which in turn maximises learning and supports good behaviour. Children are an indispensible resource for identifying their own current abilities and can be involved in identifying what their next learning needs are. As teachers, we can elicit knowledge, understanding and skills in a variety of ways, such as group concept maps, a simple interactive activity, use of a puppet in a discussion, and use of a concept cartoon. Effective teacher questioning (see Kerry 2002b; Johnston *et al.* 2007) can lead to developed questioning skills for both children and teachers, and lead to improved understanding of learning needs as well as raising new questions for exploration, which is the next step of learning.

For children to be fully involved in their own learning, it is important that they have clear understandings of their learning expectations and that these are not changed. All too often one sees a child who had been undertaking enthusiastically the work set for him or her, but when he or she has completed the work early, the teacher sets more work to do. This not only demotivates the child, but creates behavioural problems that can even lead to disruption.

Case Study 4.2 A class discussion

In our topic on Mr Bembleman's Bakery (Green 1978), the adult-led baking provides an opportunity to focus on volume and measurement. While making some bread rolls, the adult asked the children why they thought they needed to measure out the ingredients and why they could not just use their hands (as in the book). This led to an interesting dialogue:

Kelly: My hands are smaller than yours, Miss.
Adult: Do you think that will make a difference when we make our bread?
Joe: We could all put a handful in like in the story.
Kyle: But, but . . . if we did that . . .
Kelly: It would not work right.
Adult: Why?
Kyle: Our hands are different.
Kelly: . . . and the bread would not work properly.
Siobhain: Should we use a spoon?
Joe: The weights!
Adult: Yes, that is right, we should measure the flour and make sure we have the right amount.
Adult (a little later): What should we use to measure the water?
Joe: A cup?
Adult: A good idea. Which cup would be best?
Simon (picking up a measuring beaker): This one with numbers on it.
Adult (asking the other children): What do you think?
All: Yes, Yes.

Later, in the role-play bakery area, Kyle spent a long time pouring water from one short and fat measuring beaker into another taller and thinner (but which held the same volume), and then pouring it back again. He repeated the action over and over again, muttering to himself, '*But that one's bigger*', before he announced to the teacher, '*They are BOTH the same!*'

Reflection

Consider the interactions above.
How did the two different interactions help Kyle to understand the conservation of volume?
How could Kyle's understanding be further supported?
How was Kyle taking ownership over his own learning?

Consider your own teaching.
How do you provide opportunities for children to take ownership over their own learning?
What steps can you take to provide more opportunities for children to make their own learning decisions?

Creative interdisciplinary work

Creativity is a complex concept that has numerous and seemingly diverse definitions, from making or creating in both the arts and science (Prentice 2000; Compton 2013), making connections (Duffy 1998), thinking and problem solving (De Bono 1992; Beetlestone 1998; Hutchinson 2013), and risk taking, as well as discovery (Johnston 2004) and innovation. The importance of creative teaching and learning is now well recognised (e.g. DfES 2003a; QCA 2003) and creative topic work is endorsed through recent curricular changes (Rose 2009) (see also Chapter 8). Creative integrated work is likely to:

- Be planned by teachers who are creative risk takers and will not just follow imposed pedagogical approaches, and who are knowledgeable about the subjects and pedagogical approaches;
- Make the links between the different areas of the curriculum in a meaningful and relevant way (Duffy 1998; Rose 2009);
- Allow children to make decisions for themselves, plan their own learning with support and discover things for themselves (DfES 2003a; DCSF 2008a);
- Include learning that is practical and exploratory, with motivating experiences, so that they develop understandings, skills and important attitudes (Johnston and Nahmad-Williams 2008; Bruce 2009).

There are different ways in which creative cross-curricular topic work can be included in the curriculum. Some schools use the curriculum guidance documents prevailing at the time. Some provide relevant play areas in all classrooms, so that a history topic on the Second World War may have an air raid shelter, or a geography topic comparing the local environment with a more tropical environment may have half the classroom set up as a school room in a tropical area and the computer corner as the 'School of the Air' school room. Other schools have topics that bridge the transition from one key stage to another, and link different aspects of the curriculum and the key stage. Some schools abandon the normal curriculum for a week when the whole school focuses on some thematic work (see Chapter 8).

In one school, a teacher had planned a topic week involving the children in exploring other countries, and learning about their geography, history and nature. The topic started with the children making passports (English, ICT) so that they could travel by air to their chosen destinations. The first destination was Brazil and the children visited a travel agent (geography), decided on their exact destination within Brazil, looked up Brazil on the internet (ICT) and packed their bags ready to go (geography, science). The chairs in the classroom were set out in front of an interactive whiteboard in rows to represent the inside of an aircraft. The teacher acted the role of the air steward, and gave them the safety notices and told them to fasten their seatbelts. She then put on the screen pictures of Brazil and played some Brazilian music. Finally the pictures change to aerial views of Brazilian landscapes as though they were looking out of an aeroplane window. The final part of the lesson concerned where Brazil was on the map (and colouring it in) and copying the Brazilian flag (geography), and unfortunately did not follow the creative lead of the first part.

An alternative and more creative follow-up would have been to analyse the Brazilian flag (Figure 4.1), which is full of symbolism: the green background represents the forests, the yellow rhombus the mineral wealth of Brazil, the blue circle shows the sky over Rio de Janeiro on the day Brazil was declared a republic (15 November 1889), and each star group represents the Brazilian states (the number changes when new states are created – originally it was 21 stars, now it is 27). The band represents the Equator, which crosses Brazil, and the motto *Ordem e Progresso* ('Order and Progress') is inspired by a motto by Auguste Comte, *L'amour pour principe et l'ordre pour base; le progrès pour but*: 'Love as a principle and order as the basis; progress as the goal' (Wikipedia 2009).

Analysis of the flag could lead to children designing their own flag to go on their passports with symbols that represent their lives (design technology). Visits to other countries could also look at their flags and the symbolism of each (geography). There are, of course, plenty of other creative ways to follow up such a lesson, such as focusing on the animals of the Amazon (science), and looking at weird or amazing facts about the animals. They could then apply them to themselves (if I had the strength of a soldier ant I could lift . . . , or if I could move as slowly as a sloth, it would take me . . . long to get to school). They could also create a fictional animal using a number of weird and amazing facts about different animals. Another follow-up could include using some of the songs from *Yanamamo*, a musical written by Peter Rose and Anne Conlon (2006) that is very suitable for young children (music).

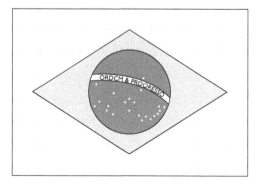

Figure 4.1 The flag of Brazil

Case Study 4.3 Creativity

In our case study exemplar of Mr Bembleman's Bakery (above), the role-play area provides opportunities for children to be creative by making their own decisions. The children decide whether to make pizzas, bread, cakes and for what purpose. They create new pizza toppings, design advertising leaflets, sales lists or packaging for the products they make. They design and change the layout of the bakery so that it runs efficiently, and decide the roles and responsibilities of the different people working there.

Rajat and Hafiza decided to turn the bakery into a cake shop, making sweets for the festival of Diwali. They found a recipe for Sohan papdi (a square sweet made with sugar, gram flour, flour, ghee, milk and cardamom) on the internet and printed it out.

Ingredients
1¼ cup gram flour
1¼ cup plain flour (maida)
250g ghee (clarified butter)
2½ cups sugar
1 cup water
2½ tbsp milk
½ tsp cardamom seeds

Instructions
1   Sift both flours together. Then heat ghee (clarified butter) in a pan.
2   Add flour mixture and roast on low heat until light golden. Keep aside to cool a little, stirring occasionally.
3   Now make syrup out of sugar. Bring syrup to 2½ thread consistency. Pour at once into the flour mixture.
4   Beat well with a large fork until the mixture forms thread-like flakes. Pour on to a greased surface or thali, and roll to 1 inch thickness lightly.
5   Sprinkle the elaichi (cardamom) seeds and gently press down with palm.
6   Cool, cut into squares, store in airtight container.

The teacher purchased the ingredients and the children in the class all made some sweets for their Diwali celebrations. While they were doing this, Rajat and Hafiza decorated the bakery role-play area and dressed themselves in their best clothes. They explained the festival of Diwali to the rest of the children and then all the class joined in the Diwali celebrations using the role-play area.

Reflection

How do your plans for cross-curricular work provide opportunities for creativity?
How can you develop your plans to increase opportunities for children to be creative?
Try out some of your ideas and reflect on the learning outcomes.
How did the creative aspects aid the learning outcomes for the children?

Interactive learning through cross-curricular approaches

A key feature of topic work involves children in learning with others in an interactive way. In learning in the early years, children should not only be independent learners, who develop through solitary play and activities, but should also learn through peer interaction. Rogoff (1995: 139) has identified three 'inseparable, mutually constituting (sociocultural) planes': the personal, interpersonal and community/contextual, which together aid learning. Children learn as much, if not more, from the social interaction they have with their peers and so topics that take this into account and maximise the opportunities for interaction are likely to be the most effective. However, the importance of effective adult support and interaction cannot be overestimated, and have been recognised since Vygotsky (1962). This interaction should challenge all children, advancing them cognitively (see Shayer and Adey 2002; Dahlberg, Moss and Pence 2007), and supports individuals appropriately by scaffolding learning, and modelling learning and behaviours as appropriate.

Case Study 4.4 Increasing vocabulary

In our case study exemplar of Mr Bembleman's Bakery (above), the adult-led activity of baking encourages children to describe the material ingredients in their own words and introduce new words as appropriate to develop scientific vocabulary. Children are encouraged to predict what will happen when the materials are mixed, heated or cooled, and to describe changes in their own words, with the adult modelling predictions and making their own suggestions that the children can discuss.

In the bakery role-play area, the children weigh, measure and play with dough, using the words used in the adult-led area, thus internalising the words into their own vocabulary, and gaining a better understanding of them.

Reflection

Set up an interactive topic activity so that children can interact with one another during their learning. Observe their interaction; you could try videoing them and make notes on the interactions you observe.

How does the interaction affect the children's learning?
What parts of the interaction are the most effective? Why do you think this is?
Video your own interaction with a child or group of children. This could follow on from the peer interaction or precede the peer interaction. This can be a bit scary, but can be very helpful in improving your own practice.
How does your interaction support the children's learning?
What else could you do to facilitate the children's learning through your interaction?

Conclusion

There is increasing pressure for children to be put into learning environments at ever earlier ages. Baroness Sally Morgan claims (Paton 2013) – in that enlightened denizen of humanitarian philosophy, the *Telegraph* – that it would be appropriate to deliver children to schooling at two years old with the intention of raising allegedly 'dire' standards of education at later stages of schooling. On the one hand, it is important to stress that there is little credible evidence that this position is tenable: one could debate if later standards are indeed dire; whether two is an appropriate age for schooling; what kind of schooling is envisaged; why other countries tend not to suffer problems from admitting children later rather than earlier; and, above all, if the intended outcome is a necessary and logical conclusion from the putative solution. On the other hand, any trend to earlier schooling must take account of the kinds of learning which might work effectively with young children (surely not more targets and testing?) and which would not (see above, and Chapter 3).

References

Alexander, R., Rose, J. and Woodhead, C. (1992) *Curriculum Organisation and Classroom Practice in Primary Schools: A Discussion Paper*. London: Department for Education and Science.

Beetlestone, F. (1998) *Creative Children, Imaginative Teaching*. Buckingham: Open University Press.

Black, P. and Wiliam, D. (2004) *Working Inside the Black Box: Assessment for Learning in the Classroom*. London: Nelson.

Bowlby, R. (2006) *The Need for Secondary Attachment Figures in Childcare*. Available online at: www.telegraph.co.uk/opinion/main.jhtml?xml=/opinion/2006/10/21/nosplit/dt2101.xml#head5Childcareproblems.

Bruce, T. (2009) *Early Childhood* (2nd edn). London: Sage.

Compton, A. (2013) 'Creativity', in Taylor, K. and Woolley, R. (2013) *Values and Vision in Primary Education*. Maidenhead: Open University Press: 33–49.

Dahlberg, G., Moss, P. and Pence, A. (2007) *Beyond Quality in Early Childhood Education and Care: Language of Evaluation* (2nd edn). London: Falmer Press.

DCSF (2008a) *The Early Years Foundation Stage: Setting the Standard for Learning, Development and Care for Children from Birth to Five: Practice Guidance*. London: DCSF.

DCFS (2008b) *Personalised Learning – A Practical Approach*. Nottingham: DCFS.

DCFS (2009) *The National Strategy – Assessing Pupils' Progress (APP)*. Available online at: http://national strategies.standards.dcsf.gov.uk/primary/assessment/assessingpupilsprogressapp.

De Bono, E. (1992) *Serious Creativity* London: HarperCollins.

DfEE (1998) *The National Literacy Strategy*. London: DFEE.

DfEE (1999) *The National Numeracy Strategy*. London: DFEE.

DfES (2003a) *Excellence and Enjoyment: A Strategy for Primary Schools*. London: DfES.

DfES (2003b) *Every Child Matters*. London: DfES.

DfES (2006) *2020 Vision: Report of the Teaching and Learning in 2020 Review Group*. London: DfES.

Duffy, B. (1998) *Supporting Creativity and Imagination in the Early Years*. Buckingham: Open University Press.

Garner, R. (2014) 'Gove's revolution: pupils return to traditional subjects in huge numbers'. *Independent*, 23 January.

Green, M. (1978) *Mr Bembleman's Bakery*. New York: Parents Magazine Press.

Hohmann, M. and Weikart, D. P. (2002) *Educating Young Children* (2nd edn). Ypsilanti, Michigan: High/Scope Press.

Hutchinson, N. (2013) Taylor, K and Woolley, R. (2013) *Values and Vision in Primary Education*. Maidenhead: Open University Press, 79–90.

Johnston, J. (2004) 'The value of exploration and discovery'. *Primary Science Review* 85 (November/December): 21–23.

Johnston, J. and Nahmad-Williams, L. (2008) *Early Childhood Studies*. Harlow: Pearson.

Johnston, J., Halocha, J. and Chater, M. (2007) *Developing Teaching Skills in the Primary School*. Maidenhead: Open University Press.

Kerry, T. (2002a) *Learning Objectives, Task Setting and Differentiation*. Cheltenham: Nelson-Thornes.

Kerry, T. (2002b) *Explaining and Questioning*. Mastering Teaching Skills Series. Cheltenham: Nelson-Thornes.

Palmer, S. (2006) *Toxic Childhood: How the Modern World is Damaging Our Children and What We Can Do About It*. London: Orion.

Paton, G. (2013) 'Schools should admit children at two, says Ofsted chief'. *Telegraph*, 4 November.

Prentice, R. (2000) 'Creativity: a reaffirmation of its place in early childhood education'. *Curriculum Journal* 11(2): 145–158.

QCA (2000) *Curriculum Guidance for the Foundation Stage*. London: DFEE.

QCA (2003) *Creativity: Find It Promote It*. London: QCA/DFEE.

Rogoff, B. (1995) 'Observing sociocultural activity on three planes: participatory appropriation, guided participation, and apprenticeship', in Wertsch, J. V., Del Rio, P. and Alvarex, A. (eds) *Sociocultural Studies of Mind*. Cambridge: Cambridge University Press: 139–164.

Rose, J. (2009) *Independent Review of the Primary Curriculum: Final Report*. Nottingham: DCFS.

Rose, P. and Conlon, A. (2006) *Yanamamo: An Ecological Musical for Soloists, Chorus, Narrato and Stage Band, Commissioned by the Education Department, World Wide Fund for Nature*. London: Josef Weinberger.

Shayer, M. and Adey, P. (eds) (2002) *Learning Intelligence: Cognitive Acceleration Across the Curriculum from 5 to 15 Years*. Buckingham: Open University Press.

Taylor, K. (2013) 'Curiosity', in Taylor, K. and Woolley, R. (eds) *Values and Vision in Primary Education*. Maidenhead: Open University Press: 1–17.

Vygotsky, L. (1962) *Thought and Language*. Cambridge, MA: MIT Press.

Wikipedia (2009) Flag of Brazil. Available online at: http://en.wikipedia.org/wiki/Flag_of_Brazil#Symbolism.

Part 3

Cross-curricular learning and teaching in Key Stage 2

Chapter 5

The cross-curricular approach in Key Stage 2

Christine Farmery

Introduction

This chapter draws together much of the content presented in this book, illustrating the theory in practice within Key Stage 2. It mirrors the preceding chapter, which provided a living example of the integrated approach to the curriculum in YR to Y2, and leads on to a consideration of the whole-school focus. The chapter thus builds on the theoretical framework set out in Chapter 1, and demonstrates the use of the teaching skills outlined in other chapters, specifically with regard to how effective planning is essential to the success of the approach. A current example of work in progress in Y3–Y6 is set out here in order to provide a critical and analytical commentary of the approach in practice.

Background

This chapter is a personal story. It is not intended as a polemic or even as a mission statement – i.e. follow me, it's the only good way. But it is the story of a conviction: of what works, of why it works, and how others may benefit from its advantages.

As a class teacher I was fortunate to work for many years with a headteacher who believed very strongly that an integrated curriculum was the most effective and successful teaching approach at the primary level. Consequently, as a new headteacher, I took this philosophy into my headship as I had seen for myself how effective it is for engaging children in their learning, and for providing both the links that enable them to make sense of new knowledge and a meaningful context for developing skills and understandings. My own view was then strengthened by the introduction of *Excellence and Enjoyment* (DfES 2003), and was further validated by both the Cambridge Review (Alexander 2009) and the Rose Review (DCSF 2009).

Getting started

On taking up my headship I was presented with a curriculum delivery that was not grounded within the philosophy I was committed to, and therefore I started to introduce the ways of working I wished to see in the school. Previously, the curriculum was addressed through lessons that were mostly subject-exclusive and based firmly on schemes of work. My view was that what was important was not *what* to teach but *how* to teach it. This familiarisation started quite a journey towards the cross-curricular approach that became embedded across the school. Whatever curriculum content needs to be delivered (and these are important decisions) requires interpretation towards a cross-curricular way of working.

> **Reflection**
>
> Think about your own personal story of how your teaching and your pupils' learning have developed or are developing. What are the key influences? How is this text beginning to guide or change your thinking?

The cross-curricular approach in practice

The integrated approach to the curriculum we use has evolved and changed since it was first outlined by Plowden (1967); it is continuing to evolve as new research provides further theoretical understanding of how the approach can be effective in bringing about deep learning. Although it remains child-centred, as in 1967, it is now much more rigorous at the planning stage (see also Chapter 11). Whereas previously it was acceptable that topics were identified by their title, with the teacher then engaged in considering what activities would 'fit' with the topic title, the teaching and learning are now objective-led and it is this that determines the activities to be undertaken. Using objective-led planning thus ensures that each activity within the topic has a specific purpose, that of a vehicle for the planned learning to take place. Assessment is ongoing and used to identify what the child needs to experience next, thus leading to the identification of the objectives for the next stage of learning and, in turn, to progression in learning. This is illustrated in Figure 5.1.

Planning cycle for the cross-curricular approach

Using the process outlined in Figure 5.1, the class teacher will begin by reviewing the prior learning of the children, initially through previous assessments and later through a simple activity to elicit the children's current knowledge of the topic, to determine the learning needs of the children. The assessments consulted will have been made the previous term; they may therefore have been made the previous academic year. The learning will therefore be identified in terms of the knowledge, skills and understandings the children need at their next stage of learning. School and national requirements will then be considered. The objectives to be covered during the full academic year are listed and so the teacher will identify which of the objectives fall naturally into each of the topics they have named for the coming year. However, where objectives to be covered do not naturally fit into a topic, tenuous links are never made, and so some discrete lessons and/or mini-topics of a week or two may also be planned.

Other learning needs are then considered, including skills development and the opportunities afforded by the topic to cover the current requirement of government. Through this process, the cross-curricular topic is ensured to be relevant, interesting, motivational and meaningful to the children, and will provide the learning opportunities needed to allow for the coverage of the learning identified thus far; the next stage is therefore to devise a range of activities within which each objective will be covered.

In order to further illustrate in practice the process outlined in Figure 5.1, an aspect of the current Year 5 spring term topic in my school will be outlined here. The full topic centres on Whitby, a small fishing port and popular holiday resort in North Yorkshire that is a two- to three-hour journey from the school and so makes an ideal destination for a short residential visit. It is a traditional seaside resort that is compact and provides many

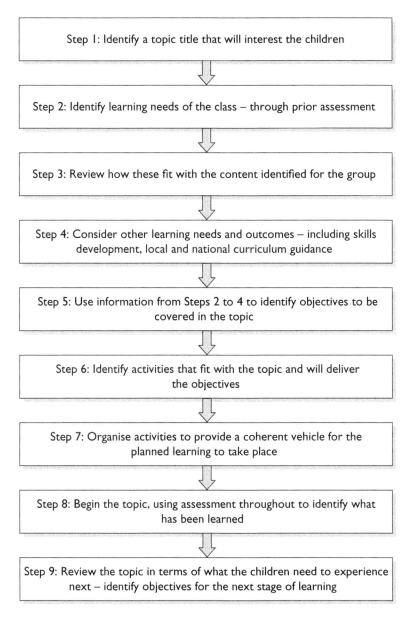

Step 1: Identify a topic title that will interest the children

Step 2: Identify learning needs of the class – through prior assessment

Step 3: Review how these fit with the content identified for the group

Step 4: Consider other learning needs and outcomes – including skills development, local and national curriculum guidance

Step 5: Use information from Steps 2 to 4 to identify objectives to be covered in the topic

Step 6: Identify activities that fit with the topic and will deliver the objectives

Step 7: Organise activities to provide a coherent vehicle for the planned learning to take place

Step 8: Begin the topic, using assessment throughout to identify what has been learned

Step 9: Review the topic in terms of what the children need to experience next – identify objectives for the next stage of learning

Figure 5.1 Planning cycle for the cross-curricular approach

opportunities for educational study, including the first-hand experience that is essential to the cross-curricular approach to curriculum delivery. Thus, when planning the topic, the learning opportunities to take place before, during and after the residential visit are explored in order to ensure that the topic presents a coherent package of learning. It is this level of thought and planning that brings necessary rigour to the cross-curricular topic and ensures that learning is both meaningful and set in the context of the 'real world'. It is through this that the children are able to develop skills and understandings that are common to different subject areas and to have opportunities presented for making sense of their learning.

Reflection

Taking the topic title of a nearby coastal resort, what areas of learning can you identify that you could cover with a Y3 to Y6 class during a half-term of six weeks?

Planning the cross-curricular topic

Using the process outlined in Figure 5.1, when Steps 1 to 7 have been completed, a topic plan is written but not yet finalised, as it is necessary to elicit the children's current knowledge of the topic to be studied. Thus each topic begins with a simple exercise to determine the children's knowledge and to enable them to initiate their own learning. The exercise requires the teacher to introduce the topic and an overview of the learning opportunities they have identified. The teacher will then ask the children to work in pairs or groups to record both the knowledge they already hold and what they would like to find out about the topic. This, too, is an essential aspect of the approach we have adopted as it ensures that the children's interests are built upon, previous assessments are brought up to date and the children are starting to take responsibility for their own learning. Therefore, it is following this exercise that the medium-term plan for the topic can be fully completed, although it is still subject to change if appropriate alterations are identified as the topic proceeds. However, it is at this stage that any learning that has been identified by the teacher but demonstrated by the children can be removed from the plan and the children's ideas for learning can be added.

The class teacher then provides an overview of the topic, setting out the activities to be carried out each week; this is known as the 'curriculum balance matrix' for the topic. The matrix is thus used to ensure there is a logical progression to the activities presented through which the learning needs will be addressed; the learning needs are identified as the learning objectives that appear on the medium-term plan. A brief extract from the matrix for the Whitby topic appears in Table 5.1, showing various activities that were identified within the topic; however, it is the study of a lifeboatman – Henry Freeman – that will be discussed in detail. The discussion of this one aspect only is for clarity as the learning taking place through the full topic is quite extensive; indeed, the discussion will illustrate the learning across a range of subject areas, where there are clear links and common skills to be used and developed. Also, for convenience here, the activities are listed under five headings only – those of the core subjects of English (literacy), maths (numeracy) and science; a foundation subjects heading and PSHE/RE heading (personal, social and health education/religious education).

The curriculum balance matrix extract therefore sets out a number of learning opportunities presented through the study of Whitby, with the life of Henry Freeman as a main focus. However, there were other facets to the topic but, as noted earlier, where natural links between the topic and objectives to be covered are not identified, they do not feature in the full curriculum balance matrix but are listed on the topic plan. For example, during the term that the topic of Whitby was being studied, the focus for PE was coaching by the

Table 5.1 Curriculum balance matrix: extract from the Year 5 Whitby topic

	Literacy	Numeracy	Science	Foundation subjects	PSHE/RE
Week 1	Introduction to topic Henry Freeman biography	Coordinates (link to atlas work/ location of Whitby)	Investigation into floating and sinking	Location of Whitby (geography) History of RNLI Seascapes (art)	Parts of a church (RE)
Week 2	Write a newspaper article about Henry Freeman	Data handling – in preparation for shopper questionnaires	Coastal erosion	Water pollution (geography) Review water safety leaflet (D&T) Seascapes (art)	Feelings of Henry Freeman (PSHE)
Week 3 In Whitby	Talk by RNLI Visit local museum – includes a Henry Freeman display Visit Whitby church Field sketches Shopper questionnaires Produce a film documentary and podcast Collate a Whitby fact file				
Week 4 Back in school	Recount of Whitby visit	Data handling – of results of shopper questionnaires	Introduction to habitats and food chains	Comparison of local area to coastal area (geography) Review of museum exhibits (history) Development of field sketches (art)	Would you volunteer to be a lifeboatman? (PSHE)

local rugby team, in preparation for an interschool rugby tournament; it was accepted that this did not in any way link to the topic and so tenuous links were not made.

Henry Freeman

Henry Freeman is somewhat of a local hero in the resort; a brief biography is presented in Table 5.2. Although not born in Whitby he later became a resident of the town and is highly acclaimed for his achievements. Such is his standing that a bronze plaque of him hangs on the wall of the modern Whitby Lifeboat Station, having been chosen to represent the many lifeboatmen who have served locals and visitors to the area, and their long history of saving lives at sea. In addition to this tribute at the lifeboat station, there is also a small display at the local museum, there is a written account of his life (Shill and Minter 1991), and various references to him are to be found on the internet.

The story of Henry Freeman is therefore 'real' and readily accessible, both in the resort and using published material. It is of particular interest to boys, thus making his study an excellent motivator for them, with girls also enjoying the story of his heroism. It is this that makes the study of Henry Freeman a meaningful context for the children and leads to many learning opportunities, only some of which are explored here in order to enable the reader to understand how an integrated topic can be planned and effectively delivered. It is therefore the learning that it yields, and how such learning takes place across traditional subject boundaries, that is considered here.

Introducing the cross-curricular topic

As noted in Table 5.1, following the introduction of the topic and the exercise to elicit both the children's current knowledge and their desired learning, the life of Henry Freeman is used to provide a context for the learning to take place. It can already be appreciated from the brief biography in Table 5.2 that the study of Henry Freeman readily lends itself to developing enquiry skills in history, for using and developing reading comprehension skills, and for considering a moral dilemma within PSHE. It also provides a real-life purpose for investigating floating and sinking in science.

In literacy teaching the features of a biography are considered: comprehension skills are needed to look beyond the literal retelling of his life; this leads on naturally to a discussion about the character of this important man. Such questions as why he became a fisherman and why he decided to join the lifeboat service are thus explored. This yields many theories that further research may answer, and lends itself to drama and role play to investigate these and other questions raised by the children, thereby developing their speaking, listening and reasoning skills. It is particularly interesting to consider his feelings at being asked to try out the experimental cork life jacket and his subsequent feelings when he knew he was the only survivor of the 1861 disaster, and that this survival was attributed to the jacket. Was he worried about the jacket? Did he feel guilt and/or relief to have survived? These are questions that require the children to empathise with Henry Freeman, to explore how they might feel if presented with the dilemma he had been presented with, and their feelings following the disaster. The children are required to articulate their thoughts and to justify them; these are

Table 5.2 Henry Freeman (1835–1904)

Henry Freeman was born in Bridlington, North Yorkshire. As a young man, Henry was a brick maker; later in life he became a manager at the brick works where he worked.

Later, when the brick making trade declined, Henry turned to the sea and fishing. He moved to Whitby, and became both a fisherman and a lifeboatman. In 1861 Henry was the sole survivor of a lifeboat disaster when a freak wave drowned all his companions. His survival was credited to the newly developed cork life jacket that only he was wearing.

The disaster occurred during Henry's first mission as a lifeboatman and made him a local hero. Henry went on to serve the RNLI for forty years, saving many lives at sea. He remains a hero to many and is remembered in Whitby to this day.

high-order skills for children aged nine but they are able to demonstrate them because they are discussing a real-life issue.

Already subject boundaries are being crossed as the above topic relates to the subjects of English through the use of a biography to introduce the story of Henry Freeman; history through the use of a story of a tragedy and how this impacted on the local area; and PSHE through the discussion of moral dilemmas. In addition, an understanding of floating and sinking is needed to appreciate how the life jacket that is integral to the story worked, and so the subject area of science is added to the list, followed by design and technology. The children are therefore provided with a meaningful context for investigating the properties of materials that float and sink, and for researching the developments in buoyancy aids, leading naturally on to designing 'a life jacket of the future'. The learning is already being presented as a coherent package, and children are using and developing knowledge, skills and understandings that are necessary for the topic being studied but not in isolation within subject areas. The approach also ensures that there are opportunities for the children to apply newly acquired skills where they are needed – for example, enquiry skills in both history and science.

The children are asked to use their knowledge and understanding thus gained to write a newspaper article about Henry. To do this they need to know the features of a newspaper article, and understand the audience and purpose for which they are writing. They may also use ICT skills both to carry out further research into the life of Henry, the RNLI (Royal National Lifeboat Institution) and Whitby itself, and also to present their work. All ability levels are catered for here as the focus of the article is chosen by the individual child. The focus may be a simple retelling of the disaster, an investigative piece about the development of the experimental life jacket, or an in-depth interview with Henry Freeman – survivor of an incident at sea. It can be appreciated that each focus identified here requires understandings and skills at different levels to be used by the children.

The residential visit is then carried out; this is an essential part of the integrated learning as it provides the first-hand experience that really brings the topic *alive*. After being introduced to the story of Henry Freeman and carrying out the activities already noted, the children are able to find out further information for themselves and understand the context of his life. This first-hand exploration is therefore motivating and makes the learning relevant for the children. It also provides a vehicle for them to practise their speaking and listening skills, through a talk at the RNLI station and talking to adults in various situations. The visit requires the use of a range of observational skills, in order to identify the many references to Henry Freeman around Whitby and the legacy he has left the town. The visit thus enables the children to deepen their understanding of an influential character in history and his effect on his surroundings, specifically within the local lifeboat service and the area as a tourist destination.

The focus of the residential visit thus easily leads on to an exploration of the resort, necessitating the use of an atlas to identify its location, the use of coordinates in map work, and planning routes to (and around) the town. Again this crosses subject boundaries and brings in knowledge, skills and understanding from the subject areas of history, maths and geography. The list of other activities that could be carried out here is vast but is narrowed down to the learning identified by the children and that which is indicated through prior assessment. The Year 5 children attending this residential wished to know more about Whitby as a holiday destination, and assessment had indicated that they needed to increase their use and understanding of data handling. The vehicle for addressing both of these needs was easily identified as a visitor questionnaire, asking passers-by if they were residents or visitors, and the purpose of their walk in the town, and asking about their knowledge of the work of the RNLI in Whitby. The skills needed for this activity were introduced in school, prior to the visit, with the questionnaire administered during the visit and the results handled and presented back in school. Again the topic provided a *real* reason to develop and use data handling skills, thus providing meaning for the children, and built on their own interests in the learning. Other purposeful and necessary learning opportunities contributed to the topic as it developed. These included an understanding of coastal erosion and the effects of water pollution, using primary sources of information in preference to secondary sources such as pictures or an internet simulation. The visit would be incomplete without carrying out field sketches, leading to artwork based on Henry Freeman and the coastal town itself. Following the visit, learning obviously continued by building on the experiences the children had while being immersed in life in modern-day Whitby.

Learning within the integrated topic

The short example detailed here demonstrates well that the integrated approach links together related work and so learning is not fragmented by being divided into subject lessons. For example, in a non-integrated curriculum, the features of a biography could be taught discretely and then practised by writing a biography of a known person, either a friend or a famous person. The features of a newspaper article could then be taught and practised by writing about a local event. The two literacy objectives will have been fulfilled – to know, understand and use the features of a biography and a newspaper article – albeit discretely. It is not guaranteed that all children will have understood the features or their practical application using the discrete activities: however, by providing meaningful links through the use of a real-life context that is readily accessible and both well-known and renowned within a town to be visited, the children have more reason to understand the usage. This provision of a meaningful context for learning, and the blurring of subject boundaries, is evident throughout the example presented here. It has demonstrated how history, English, geography, maths and science can be studied concurrently to provide an in-depth investigation into an influential character from the past and the town in which he lived. It cannot be overstated how motivational this is for the children. It provides a purpose for their development of knowledge, skills and understandings that they will use throughout their educational career and beyond. This is of significant importance for the more reluctant learners as they can see the purpose of the learning opportunities and have input into this themselves.

The integrated approach also caters for all learning styles; this obviously includes the visual, auditory and kinaesthetic learners (see the discussion in Jarvis 2005). Such activities as the use of pictures and the visits to the lifeboat station and museum cater for the visual learner; the use of 'experts' to talk about Henry Freeman and Whitby itself caters for the auditory learner; and both the scientific investigations and the hands-on museum visit cater for the kinaesthetic learners. Although these activities could be experienced discretely, the integrated approach ensures that individual learning styles are addressed together and the need for learners to make connections in their learning is met.

In addition, the approach encourages the development of skills that are transferable – for example, the skill of recording observations is essential in all subject areas, but, if it is taught only in the context of one subject, many learners will have difficulty using the skill in another subject as it will be internalised as relating only to the subject in which it is taught. Within this example of integrated learning, observations were recorded (in many forms) and used to provide reports that could be categorised as English, science, history and geography, in addition to art and design. The records include biographies, newspaper articles, reports and subject-specific records, e.g. investigation reports, field sketches and questionnaires. The residential visit itself provided the perfect opportunity to use ICT in the form of photographs, to make film documentaries and podcasts, and to collect ideas in the form of a fact file or scrapbooks. All these were included as natural aspects of the learning but required knowledge, skills and understandings across a range of subject areas to be both used and developed.

It is important to note that this way of working also develops the skill of working with others, both peers and adults; this accords with Kerry's (2002) work on setting learning objectives, in which he argues for five domains of objective that include the affective. The children are encouraged to work together throughout the topic, to share ideas and their developing knowledge, skills and understandings. The adults with whom the children work include not only the class teacher but support staff, experts consulted on the visit, and visitors to the town being studied. The adults thus support the learning of the children, facilitating opportunities that are relevant to the children rather than delivering a prescribed curriculum through the provision of a ready-made series of lesson plans. Again this makes the learning meaningful and relevant to the child.

Reflection

It is essential in this way of working that you are able to identify the learning that is taking place. Try to list all skills that will have been used/developed in this short example of an integrated theme.

Conclusion

This chapter has presented a living example of the cross-curricular approach to learning in Key Stage 2. It has demonstrated that the cross-curricular approach is based on making meaningful links between subject areas in order to make the learning coherent and to be motivational, relevant and real for the children. The example has set out how knowledge, skills and understandings that cross subject boundaries are developed; it can be appreciated how this forms an excellent basis for the next stage of learning where subjects are taught discretely but shared skills need to be applied. An exciting element of the approach is that the learning is beginning to be initiated by the children, and provides for both formal and informal learning to be recognised, again leading to relevance and ensuring deep learning by the children. The topic planning and delivery outlined within the chapter has also fully demonstrated that the approach is grounded within the ten key principles for effective teaching and learning identified by TLRP (Teaching and Learning Research Programme 2007). These principles are detailed in Table 5.3 and matched with their interpretation within the topic presented in this chapter.

This way of working is not a new, and it reflects soundly argued research from the Cambridge Review (Alexander 2009) and the Rose Review (DCSF 2009). These reviews have a common theme: that the curriculum is to be learner focused, should build on learner capacities and on prior knowledge, and link together the learning from different subject areas. The illustrative topic here demonstrates these common themes in practice.

Table 5.3 Teaching and learning principles into practice

TLRP (Teaching and Learning Research Programme 2007) Teaching and Learning Principles	Principles in Practice
Equips learners for life in the broadest sense	Sets learning in the 'real world'
Engages with valued forms of knowledge	Learning grounded in the requirements of the National Curriculum
Recognises the importance of prior experience and learning	Uses prior experience and learning, through assessment and using children's own interests
Requires the teacher to scaffold learning	Scaffolding is considered and provided throughout
Needs assessment to be congruent with learning	Assessment continued throughout the topic, leading to adjustments to the learning opportunities provided
Promotes the active engagement of the learner	The topic was chosen to provide a meaningful context for learning, to be motivational and to engage the children
Fosters both individual and social processes and outcomes	Throughout individual, paired and group work was planned for, in addition to engaging with adults during the residential visit
Recognises the significance of informal learning	Opportunities for informal learning to be shared are provided, for example within the fact files and filming documentaries
Depends on teacher learning	Teacher knowledge is essential for identifying relevant learning opportunities within a topic
Demands consistent policy frameworks with support for teaching and learning as their primary focus	The use of the National Curriculum orders and the Literacy and Numeracy frameworks are integral to the planning of the topic

References

Alexander, R. (ed.) (2009) *Children, Their World, Their Education: Final Report and Recommendations of the Cambridge Primary Review*. London: Routledge.

DCSF (2009) *Independent Review of the Primary Curriculum: Final Report*. Nottingham: DCSF.

DfES (2003) *Excellence and Enjoyment*. London: HMSO.

Jarvis, M. (2005) *The Psychology of Effective Learning and Teaching*. Cheltenham: Nelson-Thornes.

Kerry, T. (2002) *Learning Objectives, Task Setting and Differentiation*. Cheltenham: Nelson-Thornes.

Plowden, Lady Bridget (1967) *Children and Their Primary Schools: A Report of the Central Advisory Council for Education, Volume 1*. London: HMSO.

Shill, R. and Minter, I. (1991) *Storm Warrior*. Birmingham: Heartland Press.

Teaching and Learning Research Programme (2007) *Teaching and Learning Principles into Practice*. DVD, Available Light.

Chapter 6

Mainly mathematics: cross-curricular activities in Key Stage 2

Peter Ransom

Introduction

This chapter looks at integrated approaches in the teaching of mathematics. Some critics of integration maintain that, while the approach can be used with 'soft' subjects such as drama and the humanities, it is inappropriate for science and mathematics. Abela (pers. comm. to editor), by contrast, draws attention to Root-Bernstein and Root-Bernstein's limitless examples of exceptional professionals in art or science who succeed by transferring ideas between domains, and notes that 'What the scientist perceives as common problem solving, the artist understands as shared inspiration – but the answer springs from the same creative act' (Root-Bernstein and Root-Bernstein 1999: 11). Throughout this book there are many mentions of the use of integrated approaches related to science teaching, but here we look specifically at KS2 mathematics in the light of the National Curriculum. The chapter explodes the myth, and provides a plethora of ways in which mathematics can be used in interdisciplinary contexts.

Background

Motivating mathematical work tends to get harder towards the end of Key Stage 2, probably because mathematics starts to get more theoretical in preparation for Key Stage 3, and less arithmetical. To counter this, a number of case studies using mathematics in a historical context are given, describing both the mathematics involved and the integration of other subjects. The national curriculum for mathematics (2013) states:

> Mathematics is a creative and highly interconnected discipline that has been developed over centuries, providing the solution to some of history's most intriguing problems. It is essential to everyday life, critical to science, technology and engineering, and necessary for financial literacy and most forms of employment. A high-quality mathematics education therefore provides a foundation for understanding the world, the ability to reason mathematically, an appreciation of the beauty and power of mathematics, and a sense of enjoyment and curiosity about the subject.

It is with great hope that these case studies give some ideas as to how the above statement can be met.

These case studies started life in the secondary school back in 2003 at the 60th anniversary of the Dambusters' raid (16 May 1943) when I finished working with a Year 11 group before their GCSE exams. This final lesson with them was meant to bring together a number of mathematical topics in a different scenario. At the time my daughter was doing a BEd in primary education and we developed the work for Year 5 pupils and both of us, in 1940s RAF uniform, delivered some Year 5 masterclasses on a Saturday, each lasting two hours. This went well and we developed similar masterclasses (delivered in period costume) centred on the battle of Trafalgar (21 October 1805) to celebrate the 200th anniversary in 2005. Other primary cross-curricular work has since been developed on sundials (as John Blagrave (1558?–1611), a gentleman of Reading) and fortifications (as Vauban (1633–1707), the French engineer during the reign of Louis XIV (see LePrestre de Vauban n.d.). These lessons in period costume were meant to inspire pupils by showing how mathematics was used at these periods in time, and to help them realise that mathematics, science, technology, geography, history, English and music are all intertwined. It was intended that the mathematics covered should develop what they knew already and that they should sometimes be working at the frontiers of their knowledge when it came to applying that mathematics to different situations.

Sundials

The STEM subjects – science, technology, engineering and mathematics – are essential to the future economic growth of the UK, and interest in those subjects begins when children start school. Working with sundials, observing how the shadow of the gnomon (the past of a sundial that casts a shadow) changes throughout the day, is perhaps the first evidence we have of the fact that the Earth rotates on its axis. Early humans would have noticed that the shadows of trees changed both length and direction during the day and that this varied throughout the year.

A preliminary activity to making a sundial is to make a pointer (a pencil stuck on a piece of blu-tack, a bent piece of card, etc.), and place it on a piece of paper in a sunny position (see Figure 6.1). Now mark where the tip of the shadow lies. Pupils should put a mark where they think the tip of the shadow will be an hour later. Most pupils are quite surprised

x

Figure 6.1 Pencil sundial

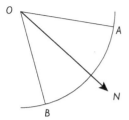

Figure 6.2 Finding north

when they see how far the shadow has rotated. You can make it into a competition by see-ing who is closest at the end of a given period.

Use this idea to find due north, as follows (see Figure 6.2).

1   At some point in the morning (a couple of hours before noon) mark the tip of the shadow on the paper at *A*, say.
2   Draw an arc, centre *O*, at the base of the pointer, radius *OA*.
3   Later in the day, mark where the shadow next meets this arc. Call this point *B*.
4   Measure the angle *AOB* using a protractor (angle measurer). Draw the line *ON* that bisects the angle *AOB* and then the line *ON* points to the north.

In the Earth and Space part of the National Curriculum it mentions in the non-statutory guidance that:

> Pupils might work scientifically by: comparing the time of day at different places on the Earth through internet links and direct communication; creating simple models of the solar system; constructing simple shadow clocks and sundials, calibrated to show midday and the start and end of the school day; finding out why some people think that structures such as Stonehenge might have been used as astronomical clocks.

Of course pupils can calibrate the sundials to mark certain points in the day, but they can take this a lot further. A simple sundial template is shown here as Figure 6.3. Print the horizontal sundial template on to A4 card so learners can make something robust.

They can label the lines with 6, 7, 8, 9, etc., until they reach 6 pm at the other side. Round the edge are some numbers to help them. Since learners need to cut out the square it is important they write the numbers *inside* the square.

If learners wish to decorate the sundial, they should do it before they do any cutting. Cut up the thick black line where 12 noon is – stop when the line goes thin. Cut out the gnomon along the thick lines and score on the dotted line. Fix it to the dial plate as shown in Figures 6.4 and 6.5.

Cut out the dial plate and gnomon. Cut a slit in the noon line equal to the total tab length.

Attach the gnomon along the noon line as shown.

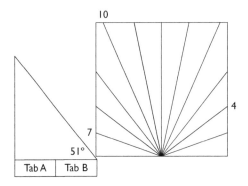

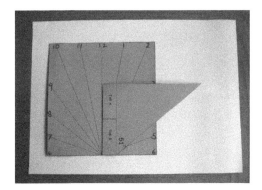

Figure 6.3 Calibrating sundials

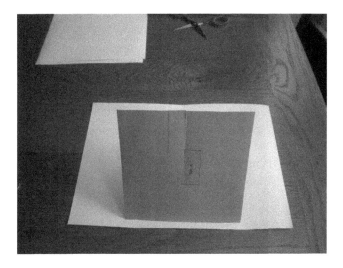

Figure 6.4 Dial plate

Figure 6.5 Gnomon

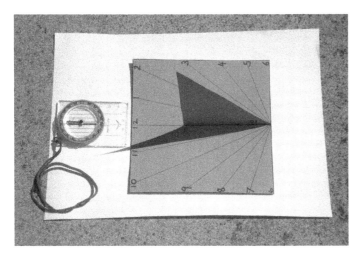

Figure 6.6 Finished sundial

Reflection

Consider how much of the National Curriculum for science and mathematics has been covered in the activity so far.

As the sundial is orientated in a true north/south direction, orientate it using the north line obtained by the earlier shadow observation (a magnetic compass will give a close enough approximation to true north/south; see Figure 6.6).

Pupils enjoy playing games and I have used a set of 30 sundial 'cards' (three of which are shown here as Figure 6.7) to encourage their number skills. They share out the cards and then play like the Top Trumps game, looking at their top card and comparing to see who has, for example, the oldest card, the highest latitude, the maximum dimension. Since the older dials used imperial units the pupils have to do some conversion as well as comparing numbers!

Older pupils can go on to make a sundial from an empty clear plastic bottle (good recycling!) and lots of information on sundials can be found at the website of the British Sundial Society (http://www.sundialsoc.org.uk/). The society celebrated its 25th anniversary in 2014.

Work on sundials with one local primary school's Year 3 and 4 pupils included a lot of technology as the half-term holiday project was to design and make a sundial. The results (Figure 6.8) were magnificent, with materials used varying from Jurassic limestone to wood, ceramics and plastic. Talking with the pupils about what they have achieved is enlightening: in my opinion their verbal reasoning and oral communication skills show far more understanding of mathematics and science than can be evidenced by any written test.

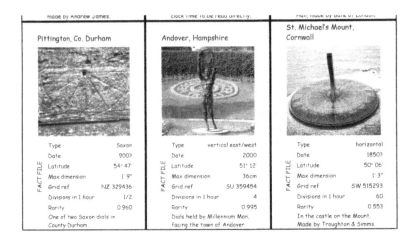

	Pittington, Co. Durham	Andover, Hampshire	St. Michael's Mount, Cornwall
Type	Saxon	vertical east/west	horizontal
Date	900?	2000	1850?
Latitude	54° 47'	51° 12'	50° 06'
Max dimension	1' 9"	36cm	1' 3"
Grid ref	NZ 329436	SU 359454	SW 515293
Divisions in 1 hour	1/2	4	60
Rarity	0.960	0.995	0.553
	One of two Saxon dials in County Durham.	Dials held by Millennium Man, facing the town of Andover.	In the castle on the Mount. Made by Troughton & Simms.

Figure 6.7 Sundial cards

Figure 6.8 Pupils' display

Reflection

Think about how much explanation occurs between pupils, between children and adults, and between adults. What similarities and differences occur in each of these groups? Is verbal or written communication the most successful way of passing on information in the classroom?

Fortification

Incorporating events from history into mathematics lessons allows pupils to see the practical applications of mathematics set into the period when it was used. This episode allows the teacher more STEM opportunities as well as the chance to do some modern language work, bringing in some French vocabulary. Although mathematics is the main thrust of the work, there are many opportunities for history and geography by examining where in France the Vauban fortifications occur (around the boundaries with other countries) and why they are at those places.

Using Jankvist's and Grattan-Guiness's previous works (Grattan-Guiness 2004; Jankvist 2009), Tzanakis and Thomaidis (2011) classify the arguments and methodological schemes for integrating history in mathematics education, and this episode on fortification fits in to the two-way table mainly as *History-as-a-tool* and *Heritage* – though there are overlaps into the *History-as-a-tool* and *History* cell (2011: section 4, Table 1). The overriding concept in this episode is *History-as-a-tool*.

The reliability of my work in the sense of reproducibility by someone else is impossible to quantify, since teachers use such episodes in different ways with different students and probably not in costume! Every session I do with students is different according to local conditions and the knowledge students bring to the sessions, so any classroom outcomes will, of course, vary.

Vauban and his fortifications

French fortification is an incredibly rich area for geometry. Marshal Sébastien le Prestre de Vauban, or Vauban (1633–1707) as he is better known, spent years under Louis XIV, the Sun King, fortifying towns and cities in France. He rose to prominence as an engineer during campaigns of the 1650s then set to work to reconnoitre the defences of France. After the War of Devolution (1667–68) he took the lead in planning the sieges and fortress building on the Belgian frontier. I was fortunate to acquire an old mathematics text (Du Chatelard 1749) that contained a treatise on fortification (as well as gnomoniques (sundials) – another interest of mine) and the plates intrigued me so much I developed a series of lessons based on them.

The number of fortresses that Vauban designed is unknown. Estimates vary between 60 and 330 – it all depends on how much work Vauban put in to the fortresses before one counts them. There are considerable differences between the number of complete new fortresses built from scratch such as Neuf Brisach (normally quoted as eight or nine), the number of improvements to existing fortresses, and the number of ideas for future work that he laid out for others to build.

The plate with which I start the work is shown here (Figure 6.9).

I use this plate with pupils, asking them about the symmetries of the shapes and how they would draw them accurately. I give the following information to students about the plate shown in Figure 6.9. It refers to campaign forts that are used when armies are on the move. I ask them to describe the symmetries of shapes f.23 to f.30. There is a short discussion about f.25 and we realise that the printer has probably deliberately omitted part of the fort at corner b to get the whole plate on to one page. The construction marks on one side of f.28 allow pupils to see how each side is divided to obtain the bastions. Pupils are asked to describe how this fort is constructed since mathematical communication is important.

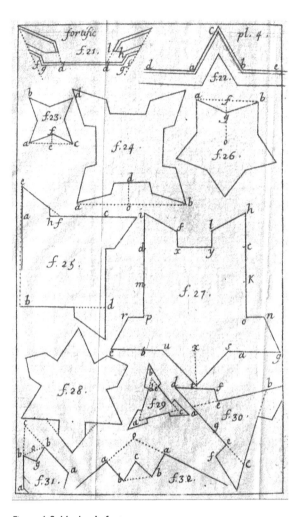

Figure 6.9 Vauban's fortresses

I ask students to draw the 'four star' fort of f.23, given that *ac* is 12 centimetres, and *ef* is 2 centimetres (Vauban's work states that the indent should be one-sixth of the side length), then to calculate both the perimeter and the area of the fort.

Developing mental geometry

This is a neglected part of all school mathematics. To encourage pupils to develop their mental geometrical skills I show them a simple figure based on a 5 x 5 square array of dots, drawn large enough for the whole class to see (Figure 6.10).

I hold the board at B and F and give it a half-turn so that the class now sees the back of the board. They then have to draw *exactly* what I can see. Students draw the result on a piece of dotty paper. After they have drawn their attempt, I turn round so that they can see the result. This is repeated with hands at HD, then at CG. For a challenge, rotate the board

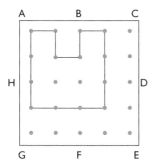

Figure 6.10 Mental geometry

180° with hands at AE then follow this immediately by a 90° rotation with the picture still facing you.

Initial success with this task is rare – however, repeating it every month or so soon sees increasing success with mental geometry and students need to appreciate that, since we live in a 3D world, things can appear differently depending on our viewpoint.

Proportional dividers, enlargement and ratio

Few mathematics teachers have heard of proportional dividers (and even fewer have used them), yet they date back many years. Heron of Alexandria (1st century AD) has been credited with a device that was probably an early version of a fixed proportional compass. In 1565 Jacques Besson in Lyons describes and illustrates a slotted variety with legs engraved with linear scales.

The proportional dividers have four scales: *lines* that enlarge lines with a given factor; *circles* that divide circles into a given number of equal parts; *planes* that enlarge areas with a given factor; and *solids* that enlarge volumes with a given factor (Figure 6.11).

Pupils make their own pair of proportional dividers for enlarging lines from a sheet of A4 card. This introduces the concepts of dividing a scale in a given ratio and similar triangles. To get the proportional dividers to enlarge with a factor of 2, the scale needs to be divided in the ratio 1:2. Since the scale divides the length into 60 parts it is equivalent to dividing 60 in the ratio of 1:2 and so students add the ratio parts and divide 60 by that sum, and so can pin the two legs at either 20 or 40 to give the desired enlargement. They then work out where to put the pin to enlarge with a factor of 3, 4, 5, etc., and as an extension with a factor of 1½. There is the 'wow!' factor when they check that it actually does work with the scale factor of 2 – the number of times one hears students say 'It works!' never ceases to please me. Part of the fact that it does work is that it does not matter how accurately the student cuts out the pieces because the central scale is not affected – the other reason it works is because it is mathematics!

Reflection

How often do your pupils take home something mathematical that they have made in the classroom? As well as the proportional dividers, consider letting the pupils fortify your school, and make a plan and a model.

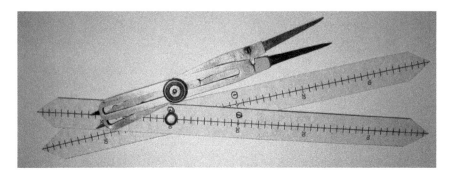

Figure 6.11 Proportional dividers

Trafalgar

This section is based on mathematics masterclasses with eight and nine year olds, which subsequently have been taught in one-hour lessons to a variety of schools and classes. It covers the history of the battle of Trafalgar (21 October 1805), and how Lord Nelson may have used mathematics in a variety of situations. My daughter and I did the work in the period costumes of an able seaman and powder monkey of 1805, explaining the social conditions and mathematics of the time, though that is not necessary!

The mathematics includes:

- Mental geometry, visualising ships from different positions
- Links between algebra and geometry in the piling of cannonballs
- Using a mathematical text of the time to calculate the number of cannonballs in a pile
- Comparing two data sets using statistics.

The work also shows how historical incidents can be used to motivate learners.

The work that follows was set up to be both cross-curricular in nature as well as being functional and covering all areas of mathematics. It was also fun to develop! It is a source of motivation for learners to see how mathematics has been/is used and applied. Sometimes it is used to teach new topics, but mainly it reminds learners about techniques taught in previous lessons as well as taking them forward with new learning.

This work is tackled by learners across the whole attainment range by carefully selecting the materials to use and going as far as is appropriate with their learning. Recently developments with this work include more attention paid to citizenship issues such as the improvement of conditions on board ship, the importance of morale and working as a team and the reduction in corporal punishment.

In 2004, we acquired some old cannon balls. With the approach of the 200th anniversary of the battle of Trafalgar, we decided to incorporate these cannon balls into a mathematics lesson to explore how they are piled and the destructive effect they had on ships. The objective was to look at the resulting number sequence and use concrete materials to see how the patterns arose, using plastic play balls.

The pupils deal with some geography by looking at where Trafalgar is on two different scale maps. One shows England, France and Spain, the other deals with the area around Cadiz that shows Cape Trafalgar.

Reflection

Think about how you can use maps to develop pupils' use of ratio and proportion. How would you get from your school to Trafalgar? How long would it take?

We have always used government guidance with 'a light touch', following it in the spirit in which we believe it was written and in what we believe to be the fun of learning – enjoyment, motivation, interest and application. We know that if we get this right then learners are involved in their learning and do not forget what they have learned.

To start the work, learners are given an introductory explanation to how Nelson split his fleet of 27 ships into two columns to divide the French and Spanish fleet of 33 ships into three sections. Then the plan was for each group of 13 or 14 to engage an enemy group of 11 while the first 11 enemy ships had to sail round to rejoin the battle. This is an example of game theory (divide, defeat, regroup), which they meet in certain board games. Like the sundial cards mentioned earlier, we made a set of cards featuring all the 27 ships and each containing seven items of data that can be compared in various ways.

They then work in groups of three and name their group after one of the ships at Trafalgar. In the first lesson they work with cannon balls (plastic play balls), piling them into square-based pyramids and filling in the first worksheet that looks at the number pattern that emerges. The use of concrete materials helps the abstract thought processes needed to extend the pattern. High attainers go on to find the formula that gives the number of cannon balls in a pyramid.

Proto-algebra features highly in this work as pupils explore number patterns, starting with the square numbers, which they add up to give the pyramidal numbers. Depending on how the cannonballs are packed, they can work with square-based or triangular-based pyramids.

The pupils handle coins of the time (Figure 6.12). The ones featured here are those I have in my collection, but I also distribute similar copper coins of the period for good work (having bought them on eBay in bulk lots they are in very poor condition, but George III's head can be made out).

Learners have a table of some of their values and complete the missing values, reasoning them from other parts of the table. This brings together direct and inverse proportion in an informal way. Low attainers contribute to the group work by finding out how old the coins are from their dates.

There is more arithmetic to be done and this is used in conjunction with handling data. The number of guns and men on each of the ships is given and students compare the two databases using measures of location and spread. A template allows students to compare the two data sets visually using a pyramid diagram, and learners write a report comparing the two fleets for King George III. Some learners did this by making a replica scrolled document. This way pupils develop their creative writing. Further information gives the numbers of casualties (wounded and killed) on each ship and this allows further comparison of data sets. As expected, those ships near the front of the column have more casualties than those further back.

The work appeals to the visual, auditory and kinaesthetic learner. In my opinion it is far better done with a class of learners split into small groups rather than have them work individually since the discussion is essential for learners to voice and refine their ideas.

Figure 6.12 Coins

Benefits of the work

The following comments come from feedback sheets from students who have encountered the work. They were asked 'What have you learnt?' The spelling remains the way it was written.

> *I learned a lot about Trafalgar and battleships. I also learned lots about mathematics. How much money was worth. Very fun.*

> *I learnt that when a cannonball is dropped from a certain height it can go 5 metres per second.*

> *About the battle of Trafalgar, how they stored cannonballs and how much damage they can cause.*

> *It was brilliant, not only did I learn about (maths) But I learned some history too. If I could I would do it again. I think the cannon balls were my favourite.*

> *At school I find history dull but this was really interesting.*

> *I learnt about Trafalgar and the battle and ratio.*

> *I learned a lot about history and maths.*

> *Today I learnt a lot about cannons. I also made some new friends.*

> *I learnt a lot more about olden day money and I think I am doing better at multiplication and division.*

> *I learned so much that I can't write it all down.*

> *Much about cannons, splinters, balls, boats and numbers.*

> *I learned lots about Maths and Trafalgar.*

> *I learnt a lot about Trafalgar and maths that I didn't know.*

I learnt about the battle of Trafalgar and how you can use Mathematics. If you put your brain to you can always do it.

Talking about the composition of the ship's crew as a complete cross-section of society, from gallows cheaters to the landed gentry, showed learners how people from different backgrounds operated as a team. That and the fact that the British Navy had good morale, made people believe in themselves. Other citizenship issues covered the harsh punishment at the time and how forward-thinkers like Nelson reformed the Navy by reducing punishment and encouraging the crew.

This work has proved popular with all learners because they see a purpose to the mathematics – it is not just number crunching or pattern spotting for its own end. Linking it to a historical event holds the learner's attention. Working in small groups encourages learners to communicate with others. Pupils summarised their work on posters, which allowed the others in the class to see what the different groups had done and how they could improve their work.

Victory, a book written by Susan Cooper (2006), is an extraordinary time-shifting adventure tale that tells the interwoven stories of Molly (a modern-day English girl forced to emigrate) and Sam (a kidnapped farm boy forced to serve aboard HMS *Victory*), and should be read by all teachers (on their own or, better still, to their classes) to help everyone appreciate the historical context.

The development of this work has involved much risk taking, but that is all part of the enjoyment of teaching mathematics! Activities such as this and the visual and kinaesthetic links help consolidate learners' mathematical knowledge. The time invested in the use of these materials did in fact, gain time.

Reflection

Are there any local naval resources that you can use to help with this topic? Do any of the pupils' parents have any naval connections?

Dambusters

This is a popular session with primary schools and I have worked with various schools on this topic when they have been studying the Second World War. In fact the pupils at one school had all taken the time to be dressed in the fashion of the 1940s, and had made imitation gas masks from card and bubble plastic. Using (Airfix) scale models of the Lancasters (the planes used to carry the 'bouncing bomb' to the dams of the Ruhr Valley) allows pupils the opportunity to do some measuring work and then pace out the length of the planes in the school yard. They are given a sheet with a side view of the Lancaster, and they use the scale to develop the concepts of ratio and proportion.

Other work deals with measuring angles and distances: they are given a map and a description of the route taken by the Lancasters and have to plot that route on the map, then describe the route in terms of the bearings and distances travelled. As with the Trafalgar work they have a sheet on the coins and the notes of the period, and compare that to our present decimal currency. I give them a farthing, a penny and a brass dodecagonal threepenny bit, and we do some fraction work with them. Some language work is covered by looking at the words on the coins as well as the dates: again these coins are cheaply obtained in bulk lots on eBay.

In Hampshire the 'bouncing bomb' and later developments were tested in the New Forest, and so this fits in well with the history National Curriculum non-statutory guidance, which mentions under the local history study 'a study of an aspect of history or a site dating from a period beyond 1066 that is significant in the locality'.

After seeing a clip from the film that shows how the aircrew managed to fly at a steady height just above the water, the pupils realised that the angle at which the lights were mounted was important and, on a side view of the Lancaster, they drew lines converging on a point. This allowed them to do some more angle measurement from various points that helped them orientate the protractor correctly.

After seeing another film clip of how the bomb aimer knew when to release the bomb, higher-achieving pupils went on to make a bomb-aiming device from basic materials that allowed them to fix a position a given distance from two objects in the playground. This meant that some technology work was incorporated into this episode.

To finish up the work, pupils were shown the Dambusters badge, which features three forks of lightning hitting a breached dam. They then did some artwork by designing a new badge based on what they had learned about the Dambusters.

Reflection

What historical events are significant in your locality? How do/could you utilise this within your classroom?

Summary

One question I often get asked is how do I manage to get through the scheme of work when I sometimes spend two or three weeks on a topic. This is where flexibility comes in to play. There is not enough time to do something on top of a scheme of work, so the cross-curricular work must include some of the topics in that scheme, though not necessarily from textbooks that might have otherwise been used.

There is much benefit in planning cross-curricular work with a colleague. Not only does it share the workload, but many useful ideas arise when there are two or more people thinking about what the work could encompass and how to bring in a range of subjects.

For cross-curricular work to have an impact in the classroom, it must be of some significant interest to the teacher who delivers it. Then the enthusiasm of the work comes over to the pupils in the classroom and they realise why they are learning certain skills and how these have been applied in the past. If the work has local interest then relatives of the pupils are sometimes keen to get involved, and can be a great source of information and artefacts relevant to the work. In particular, cross-curricular work shows pupils the interconnectedness of subjects and that mathematics plays a major part in our lives.

Reflection

What interests do you or your pupils have? How could you plan some cross-curricular work around these interests?

If you have not done any cross-curricular work before, is there any small-scale project that you could try?

Who might have similar interests at school? Can you plan something with someone else?

References and further reading

Adkin, M. (2003) *The Sharpe Companion: The Early Years.* London: HarperCollins.

Bekken, O. B. and Mosvold, M. (eds) (2003) *Study the Masters.* Göteborg: NCM.

Cooper, S. (2006) *Victory.* London: The Bodley Head.

Dixon, L., Brown, M. and Gibson, O. (1984) *Children Learning Mathematics.* Oxford: Cassell.

Du Chatelard, P. (1749) *Recueil de traités de mathématique ... tome quatriéme.* Toulon: Mallard.

Fauvel, J. and van Maanen, J. (eds) (2000) *History in Mathematics Education: The ICMI Study.* Dordrecht/Boston/London: Kluwer.

Grattan-Guiness, I. (2004) 'History or heritage? An important distinction in mathematics for mathematics education', in van Brummelen, G. and Kinyon, M. (eds) *Mathematics and the Historian's Craft.* Springer: 7–21. Also published in *American Mathematical Monthly,* 111(1): 1–12.

Griffith, P. (2006) *The Vauban Fortifications of France.* Oxford: Osprey.

Hambly, M. (1982) *Drawing Instruments: Their History, Purpose and Use for Architectural Drawings.* London: RIBA Drawings Collection.

Hogben, L. (1960) *Mathematics in the Making.* London: Macdonald & Co.

Jankvist, U. T. (2009) 'A categorization of the "whys" and "hows" of using history in mathematics education'. *Educational Studies in Mathematics* 71(3): 235–261.

Lambert, A. (2004) *Nelson: Britannia's God of War.* London: Faber & Faber.

LePrestre de Vauban, S. (n.d.) *A Manual of Siegecraft and Fortification* (trans. Rothrock, G. A.). Ann Arbor, MI: University of Michigan Press.

Root-Bernstein, R. S. and Root-Bernstein, M. (1999) *Sparks of Genius: The Thirteen Thinking Tools of the World's Most Creative People.* New York: Houghton Mifflin.

Tzanakis, C. and Thomaidis, T. (2011) 'Classifying the arguments and methodological schemes for integrating history in mathematics education'. *CERME7 Proceedings.*

Internet source

The Mathematics National Curriculum (2013) can be found at:
https://www.gov.uk/governmentpublications/national-curriculum-in-england-mathematics-programmes-of-study

Part 4

Helping exceptional pupils in cross-curricular lessons

Chapter 7

Inclusion in cross-curricular context[1]

Trevor Kerry

Introduction

This chapter looks at some issues concerned with special educational needs in the context of cross-curricular working. Specifically, it explores the issue of inclusion: its definitions, theoretical underpinning, and the pros and cons of implementation. It sets out why inclusion is an important element in the education of all children and how achieving inclusion should affect the life of the school. The chapter draws a distinction between inclusion, on the one hand, and meeting special educational needs, on the other. The relevance of working across the curriculum is considered as an integral part of this approach. The chapter provides a case study of an 'inclusive' lesson, identifying how individual needs are met in the context of cross-curricular learning.

Background

The landscape of special needs education has changed in recent times. Increasingly the needs of a wide range of pupils – those with learning difficulties, physical disabilities, emotional and behavioural problems – are being met within a mainstream school environment. At the time of the first edition of this book it seemed fair to argue that government policy seemed to be moving away from a notion of special schools and towards the idea of specialist education within all schools. Cynics might say that such a move was funding driven, but that is a debate beyond the scope of this book. The move towards inclusion was well illustrated by the following extract from one local authority policy statement:

> All children within Wrexham County Borough have equal rights to the opportunities offered by education. The Authority is committed to supporting children with special needs within mainstream provision wherever possible, with appropriate support. They are also entitled to an education which ensures continuity and progression from pre-school to post-16. Wherever possible, we shall seek to meet the needs of children and young people within Wrexham schools and residential school placements will only be used where there is no suitable local provision.
> (http://www.wrexham.gov.uk/assets/pdfs/education/senpolicy241007.pdf)

However, the case remains contested, and its validity needs to be debated. Before that can happen, though, it is important to try to define what exactly is meant by inclusion, and the limitations implied by the phrase 'wherever possible' in the quotation above.

Definitions

This chapter looks at the issue of inclusion – that is, at the right of all children, regardless of ability, to be educated in the same schools and in the same classes. Inclusion is more than catering for special educational need – it is a recognition that all children should learn alongside one another. It is a topic that gains emotional commitment, but simultaneous scepticism about its practicality. As the Centre for Studies on Inclusive Education put it, as long ago as 1997:

> There is a growing consensus throughout the world that all children have the right to be educated together. In the last six years a number of major international statements have appeared, affirming the principle of inclusive education and the importance of 'working towards *schools for all* – institutions which include everybody, celebrate differences, support learning and respond to individual needs' (World Conference on Special Needs Education 1994).
> (http://www.leeds.ac.uk/disabilitystudies/archiveuk/CSIE/inclusive%20ed.pdf)

But the issue is far from unproblematic, and is open to some debate. This debate is reflected in Rose's work (http://www.isec2000.org.uk/abstracts/papers_r/rose_1.htm), and he is right to draw our attention not just to the philosophical issues that underpin that debate but to the practicalities of classroom teaching:

> It is evident that whereas much has been written about inclusion from a socio-political or human rights perspective, less attention has been afforded to developing a greater understanding of what works in inclusive classrooms. Dyson (1999) has described inclusion in terms of an issue of two discourses; the first of these, a discourse of ethics and rights, concerned to gain an understanding of pupils' rights and how they may best be addressed within the education system, is one which has received considerable attention within the inclusion debate. Dyson's second category, the discourse of efficacy, with a focus upon gaining a greater understanding of what might work in an inclusive school, has received less attention. Teachers faced with an overload of work resulting from a plethora of educational legislation express apprehension with regard to their ability to adequately meet the needs of an increasingly complex school population.
> (http://www.isec2000.org.uk/abstracts/papers_r/rose_1.htm)

Around the nation, and around the world, the emotional pull of the topic provokes statements of laudable intent, such as this from Scotland (Her Majesty's Inspectorate 2002):
An inclusive approach to education involves:

- Creating an ethos of achievement for all pupils within a climate of high expectation;
- Valuing a broad range of talents, abilities and achievements;
- Promoting success and self-esteem by taking action to remove barriers to learning;
- Countering conscious and unconscious discrimination that may prevent individuals, or pupils from any particular groups, from thriving in the school; and
- Actively promoting understanding and a positive appreciation of the diversity of individuals and groups within society.

Dame Mary Warnock (Warnock Report 1978) was a pioneer in the rights of, and provision for, children with special educational needs. After nearly three decades of reflection and change, however, she herself (Warnock 2005) suggests problems that have arisen, in part because of her own report. She had begun to question the label Special Educational Needs (SEN) and concluded that:

> the idea of transforming talk of disability into talk of what children need has turned out to be a baneful one. If children's needs are to be assessed by public discussion and met by public expenditure it is absolutely necessary to have ways of identifying not only what is needed but also why (by virtue of what condition or disability) it is needed . . . the failure to distinguish various kinds of need has been disastrous for many children.

> (2005: 20)

But what Warnock calls 'possibly the most disastrous legacy' of the original Committee was the advocacy of an 'integrationist' approach within the framework laid down by the government of the day. The committee was told they should not count children whose mother tongue was not English or those living in particularly deprived circumstances among those having 'special needs'. In both cases the reason was that language provision and family support was channelled through the Home Office and the Social Services, respectively, and the Department of Education did not wish to be saddled with this expenditure. As a result the committee was not able to stress the links between social deprivation and learning disability, nor to advocate additional resources for schools that found themselves having to cope with a sizeable proportion of such pupils with this double disadvantage.

Definition, then, is critical to the approach to, and the solution of, the problem of inclusion. To this end, Crowley (in Irish National Teachers' Organization 2004) offers some useful, if not exhaustive, insights: 'Inclusion at its most basic level is about the presence in the school of pupils from across the nine grounds. It focuses attention on admission and intake. It reflects the importance of matching the diversity of the local population, both transient and permanent, in the pupil population of the school. This matching is necessary if the school is to serve all sections of the local population' (2004: 12). The nine grounds (not all of which apply at primary school level) are defined as:

1   Gender
2   Marital status
3   Family status
4   Sexual orientation
5   Religion
6   Age
7   Disability
8   Race
9   Membership of the traveller community.

But Crowley goes on to argue that this is only the first level of definition. At another level, it is 'about participation by all pupils within this diversity in all areas of school life'. Participation by all is required in: the full range of learning experiences available in the school; the various sets of relationships that make up and drive school life; decision making;

and cultural initiatives that seek to shape and define the ethos, norms and values of the school. Crowley adds (2004: 13): 'participation goes beyond presence', i.e. extends to full participation.

So, the issue of definition is not clear and the parameters are not fixed; and Glazzard (2011) warns: 'practitioners have different interpretations of inclusion and this interpretation affects how inclusion is performed'. Ungaro (2013) is similarly cautious (and draws attention to the importance of differentiation in this process – a point to which we shall return later). She suggests that inclusion:

> Implies 'the progressive extension of the capacity of mainstream schools to provide for children with a wide range of needs' (DfEE 1997: 44). One principle is that all students should be valued for their abilities and included as individual members of the school community (Obiakor *et al.* 2012). Children learn in different ways (Baldwin & Sabry 2003) and seem to profit most when instruction is differentiated in some manner to accommodate these differences (Sternberg & Zhang 2005).

It can reasonably be argued that the world around us is constantly changing. Society expects people with a range of special needs to be able to be increasingly independent, self-sufficient and successful. As teachers, we have the responsibility for providing children with an education in tune with the world, and one that can support them with skills to succeed and flourish in their future, as Cline and Frederickson (2009) point out:

> All the books that we read about special educational needs (SEN) and inclusion did not seem to us to reflect adequately the rapidly changing, increasingly diverse nature of the society we live in. What was once a relatively homogeneous and stable population has been transformed. Every aspect of society that affects the treatment of disabilities and learning difficulties has changed radically and continues to evolve – the cultural, ethnic and religious profile, patterns of family organisation, economic and occupational structures, the relative status of men and women, and the perception of human rights and social responsibilities.

Pupils need to develop skills that allow them to be lifelong learners: to have the enthusiasm and ability to question and pursue lines of enquiry that interest and fascinate them. Social justice demands that these aspirations should not be limited to those deemed to be in the higher percentiles of achievement. Nonetheless, inclusion comes at a cost, and the cost has to be weighed.

The cost of inclusion

A significant study by MacBeath *et al.* (2007) spelled out a number of factors that weighed against inclusion. There are two important caveats to add about this study, however. The first (and this is certainly not to call into question the quality of the scholars involved) is that it was undertaken on behalf of a trades union, and all research supported in this way has to be viewed with its commissioning body in mind. The second observation relates to the fact that the researchers do not conclude against the principle of inclusion, only against its blanket application: they ask that cases of individual children be carefully reviewed to ensure that a mainstream provision really does meet their needs.

MacBeath *et al.* do, though, do the right thing in illuminating the downsides to the debate. Inclusion, pursued rigorously, has considerable implications for teacher professional development. Curriculum strictures that tend to apply more generally in schools do not, or cannot, apply in the inclusive school. There are fiscal and financial implications for staff ratios – not just teachers but teaching assistants (see Chapter 9). Having children with extreme forms of behaviour present in regular classes can create imbalances in the targeting of teachers' time and energies. Schools that develop a good reputation for inclusion often become highly sought after by parents of children with special needs, creating an admissions crisis. Government league tables make no allowance for the presence of pupils with learning difficulties or social and mental problems. The statementing procedures, which underpin both the inclusion process and its funding, are ineffectual.

This study arose from a study of teachers' workloads; some would object that this was not the right starting place. The researchers suggested that there were three areas of educational practice that needed to be scrutinised. The first of these – policy making, usually at national government level – was often out of line with hard realities, something noted also in an international context by Rashid and Tikly (2010: 12). At a policy level, MacBeath *et al.* (2007) argued, inclusion:

> . . . ought, in principle, to demand a shift in pedagogy, less teacher direction, more self-assessment, and more peer-tutoring, and imply a less impatient need to dutifully cover the curriculum . . .

The second area of concern was that of aspirational classroom practice, which the report's authors thought should be characterised by a more open curriculum, increased choice and more group work. Third, the report noted the necessity for teachers to be better trained to deal with pupils' individual needs so that they were able to develop an increased range of pedagogical strategies.

On the basis of the evidence in the report, the authors concluded that the day of the special school had not passed: specialist organisations served an important role for some pupils, and they might also act as a reservoir of expertise and training for mainstream teachers. But they did favour inclusion as a principle provided this embraced the notion that inclusion implies 'the right to be taught by a suitably qualified teacher' (2007: 65).

In many ways, MacBeath *et al.*, while guarded in their approach, combine supportiveness of the principle of inclusion with reservations about its implementation in practice; and in this they are not far removed from Glazzard (2011). Glazzard's study was limited to one school, so its generalisability has to remain in question. Nevertheless, it seems likely that it threw up some fundamental issues: notably (again) the basic commitment of teachers to the inclusive principle, but also reservations about lack of funds, human resources and training, parental resistance, and issues arising out of the government's standards agenda.

This same ambivalence was present in the detailed Irish study, by the Irish National Teachers' Organization (2004), which, while fully endorsing the principle of inclusion and actively seeking to implement it, remarked:

> The daily and mounting pressure on principals and class teachers to include children who simply cannot participate fully in the mainstream class, without proper diagnosis, and appropriate teaching and back-up, is intolerable.
>
> (Irish National Teachers' Organization 2004: 9)

Inclusion, then, is a concept that needs careful and detached appraisal. It is, though, becoming a reality for many pupils who would, formerly, have been excluded from the mainstream – and this is to be welcomed. In what follows, an attempt is made to describe how inclusion might work, and what effects and emendations it may imply or impose on the process of education in mainstream schools. The relevance of cross-curricular approaches to inclusion are regarded as particularly relevant in this context.

Inclusion and cross-curricular learning

Experience suggests that the cross-curricular approach to learning and teaching allows learners to be taught together; the gap between the abilities is narrowed and the opportunities it provides are so significant for pupils that it is hard to see why many schools still opt only for a traditional subject-based approach. Indeed, when the author taught in a class made up of the full range of ability, and that included pupils from four primary years (Y3–Y6), no other approach seemed even remotely feasible. Elsewhere in this chapter and through the book we have argued that this is a Plowdenesque ideal, and in the context of inclusion it is repeated by the Irish National Teachers' Organization, which sees a building block of this approach as 'a commitment to a child-centred concept of education' (2004: 22). Throughout life we group our skills and abilities without differentiation or deliberate exclusion. We use geographical and scientific skills with literacy, all immersed in the skills of enquiry. Cross-curricular learning allows learners to practise and mirror these life skills – a fact that is recognised by the Ministry of Education of British Columbia (Canada):

Educators can assist in creating more inclusive learning environments by attending to the following:

- Activities that focus on development and mastery of foundational skills (basic literacy);
- A range of co-operative learning activities and experiences in the school and community, and application of practical, hands-on skills in a variety of settings;
- References to specialised learning resources, equipment, and technology;
- Examples of ways to accommodate for special needs (e.g., incorporating adaptations/ extensions to content, process, product, pacing, and learning environment; suggesting alternate methodologies or strategies; making references to special services);
- A variety of ways for students to demonstrate learning, not just through paper and pencil tasks (e.g., dramatising events to demonstrate understanding of a poem, recording observations in science by drawing, composing/performing a music piece);
- Promotion of the capabilities and contributions of children and adults with special needs;
- Participation in physical activity.

(This summary is provided by the Province of British Columbia Ministry of Education derived from the *Handbook for Curriculum Developers* (Ministry of Education for British Columbia, February 1994) and *Special Education Services – A Manual of Policies, Procedures and Guidelines* (Ministry of Education for British Columbia, Response Draft, December 1994). It resonates with the themes of a number of chapters in this text.)

Inclusive means all

Ofsted (2001) defines an educationally inclusive school as 'one in which the teaching and learning, achievements, attitudes and well-being of every young person matters'. It is important to remain open-minded about all learners in the school, but perhaps it is also important that we remember to take account of those learners who are considered to be able, gifted or talented (the government-preferred labels shift in the breeze (see Chapter 8), or those with dual or multiple exceptionalities. These learners, too, may be vulnerable, or may not be recognised as especially able because their difficulty masks their true talents. A recent estimate suggests that 5–10 per cent of more able pupils could have a learning difficulty and that 2–5 per cent of pupils with disabilities may also be highly able (one might think, for example, of Stephen Hawking) (http://www. teachingexpertise. com/e-bulletins/links-between-sen-and-gifted-and-talented-6636).

Thus, inclusion is a cultural and pedagogical stance, demanding high-quality experiences, achievement, and collegiality for all learners throughout the entire school and community. It is an entitlement for everyone who learns, works and is influenced by the school. But it is not necessarily about identical experiences for all – something that is recognised by HMI in Scotland (Her Majesty's Inspectorate 2002: 32), who recommend that inclusion is:

> . . . the antithesis of the 'one-size-fits-all' approach to education. It requires schools to be able to offer a wide range of different learning opportunities, which are adapted and tailored to meet the needs of particular individuals in ways which engage and motivate them.

Alexander (2009: 140), too, speaking of the pre-2013 National Curriculum, identifies the need for consistency within our schools, urging that there is:

> Evidence that the current curriculum – in terms of balance, content and progression – does not suit all children equally well, even though it is presented as an entitlement for all. The absence or marginalization of some activities and subjects raises the likelihood that some children will fall behind, misunderstand or opt out completely.

Consistency is defined by our relationships and values, enabling a shift from our historically driven desire to have a detailed constraining system into which to fit learners, to a set of reasoned approaches. Inclusive approaches fit learning *and* may be applied humanely, with care, consistency and professional judgements as the driving force.

Inclusion has implications for the ways in which schools are organised and staffed. Effective and well-trained Learning Support Assistants are undoubtedly one of the best resources to support learners with additional needs (see Chapter 9). It is important to ensure that they are supporting the learner by encouraging independence, communicating skills that will come into their own when the learners move to a different class or school. It is also important to build in familiar 'unfamiliarity' and ensure that different adults are deployed to support the learners so, if their particular adult is away, the learner is able to cope with that change and be supported by somebody else.

Inclusive strategies are formulated around high-quality pedagogical approaches, not distinct from, but akin to, mainstream strategies, engaging learning in a meaningful and social context. What is apparent is that the deployment of staff and the skills needed are complex, specific and sometimes time-bound. To include learners with significant difficulties the school may need to draw on all the resources in the local community to work collaboratively in order to meet the needs of children. Inclusion is not an add-on, it is part of professional responsibility to build a more empathetic community that cares for its families.

Developing the inclusive school

How does inclusion, as a philosophy and approach, meet with social and moral expectations and stereotypes? Generally, young learners are very supportive of those with specific difficulties. By giving more able pupils an opportunity to work alongside others it is possible to create an atmosphere of acceptance, one in which learners can take their experiences of school to the outside world, too, and share with society. Equally, it enables those learners with learning needs to access an ethos and environment where they can share social and emotional behaviours in a safe and secure place, alongside the quality of experiences to which all human beings are entitled.

Where it is possible to do so, developing a wholly inclusive school is not some kind of self-contained task that requires a member of the team to take a specific responsibility and to report on progress occasionally to the governing body. It is an integral way of working. It answers Claxton's (2008: xii) question: 'How do we organise schools so everyone will feel that they are there to improve something, and are able to do so, and not that they are constantly being reminded how "bright" or "weak" they are?' Developing successful inclusive practices means developing a whole-school approach to learning. With success at being inclusive, it could be argued that the impact on a learner's attitudes, achievements and life chances substantially improves, as does the pedagogy. Teachers' professional development becomes focused on achieving the desired intentions of this philosophy. Inclusion needs a serious and articulated focus underpinned by common sense. However, inclusion should be challenged and be subjected to review like all innovation in order to discover how individual teachers and teams are facilitating learning. Daniels and Porter (2007) refer to overarching pedagogical approaches, rather than separate strategies focused on special needs, as being the key building block in achieving inclusion. Davis and Florian (2004) agree:

> We found that there is a great deal of literature that might be construed as special education knowledge, but that the teaching approaches and strategies themselves were not sufficiently differentiated from those which are used to teach all children to justify the term SEN pedagogy. Our analysis found that sound practices in teaching and learning in mainstream and special education literatures were often informed by the same basic research.
>
> (Davis and Florian 2004: 33–34)

Case Study 7.1 looks at the process that Bedford and Parsons (see the first edition of this book) went through at Abbots Green Primary School from 2005 to 2009 in order to make the transition from traditional approaches to special educational needs teaching to an inclusive philosophy that embraced all learning for all pupils.

Case Study 7.1 Making the transition to inclusiveness at Abbots Green

Abbots Green School, Suffolk, was built between 2004 and 2005. It opened in September 2005 to serve a growing and diverse population. Within the mainstream school nested a Specialist Support Centre for moderate and complex learning difficulties. Children between the ages of four and nine were supported at the school.

An inclusive journey began well before the school opened. Engagement with the community was a priority. Supported by local businesses and community establishments, the school was able to communicate its inclusive message. Maslow's (1970) hierarchy served as the guiding principle above all others – that physical and emotional needs were met first in order to secure effective learning. This was embodied in the practice of the staff and a set of expectations:

- Developing open, secure, and respectful relationships with children and their families by all staff at all levels.
- Acknowledging that all children have a right to learning.
- Teaching that learning alongside children with significant differences is empowering and a privilege.
- Breaking down prejudice and misunderstanding. We know this is a crucial balanced life skill because parents and learners cited it as a positive experience in their time at the school.
- Acknowledging that we learn from each other. The empowerment children and parents felt through learning Makaton sign language to communicate with a wide range of learners highlighted the power of inclusive strategies.
- Accepting that children are developmentally at different stages and have different interests, just like adults.
- Acknowledging that teachers and Learning Support Assistants are skilled in ensuring that learning across ages is effective.

Inclusive strategies are effective for all learners and not exclusive to children on the 'SEN register'. They should be seen as tools within the teacher's learning repertoire, deployed to maximise achievement. This is once again highlighted by Davis and Florian (2004: 33–34) with respect to a specific SEN pedagogy.

Over a period of five years, Abbots Green was recognised as a leading school for inclusive practice. The school had no choice but to be inclusive, with 86 per cent of learners in 2005 being categorised as 'hard pressed' according to Acorn data. (Acorn data are a measure of social deprivation – a standard measure of family income, etc.) There are five categories and 'hard pressed' is one of the most deprived. The school had an unprecedented level of children with significant special educational needs in the mainstream, coupled with a Specialist Support Centre at the heart of the school.

Staff skills were significantly developed over a period of time through focused CPD, performance management, and the expectation of living and breathing inclusion. The school became very effective in supporting a wide range of learners.

In 2009 the leadership of the school changed; the headteacher and deputy head took new roles within the local authority.

The school supported children and families in the local community and opened its specialist resources, such as sensory rooms, used by preschool children with multiple and profound difficulties.

In 2008–2009, the school employed a Cognitive Behavioural Therapist with the brief to support families and learners from the immediate and wider community. To complement this strategy a Learning Support Assistant was deployed to be not the interface but the 'human face' between children, families and staff. The barriers were well and truly being broken down as the school opened its facilities for wider uses.

Year-on-year parents told us that some of the most important experiences they and their children had were from being able to learn and socialise with children who had difficulties.

Some of the most challenging experiences at Abbots Green were with children who presented extreme behavioural, social and emotional difficulties. Relationships, environments and strategies were developed specifically to meet the needs of these 'exceptional' pupils.

To complement the journey a bespoke nursery was designed using Dr Kenn Fisher's principles of the pedagogy of space and built (opening in 2010) to ensure a smooth pathway from three years onwards. This facility ensures that high-quality early years learning is accessible to local families, and also to young children with specific moderate and complex learning difficulties within a wider geographical area.

How ready is your school for inclusive practice?

Given this outline of the development of the inclusive philosophy between 2005 and 2009 at Abbots Green, you might find it helpful to look at practice in your own school situation. Initiating an inclusive philosophy in the primary school introduces into the learning debate many interrelated and complex factors. We are in a climate where mainstream schools are being called upon to take greater accountability for children with both specific and generalised, social and emotional, communication, physical, behavioural and learning difficulties. As a result of this, schools have responded in a variety of ways. Positive approaches have enabled schools to learn a great deal and to apply their insights successfully to the whole school community – in other words, to practise inclusiveness. This process involves several interrelated factors, as shown in Figure 7.1.

Every school is unique in having its own staff, its own traditions and its own ways of working, i.e. its own culture, people and processes – or, to put it another way, we are dealing very much with the way we do things, the people who do it and the systems that support them. These elements form the start of a working model. All these links are connected historically, systemically, emotionally and physically. A good place to begin in examining your own school's inclusiveness is with the elements in this model. Successful schools that engage with effective inclusive practice have reviewed the impact that their culture, their people and their systems have on their learners and wider community.

Reflection

Look at Figure 7.1. What can you say about your school under each of the headings? How do these elements work towards inclusiveness, or hinder it? How does your school compare to the elements described in Case Study 7.1?

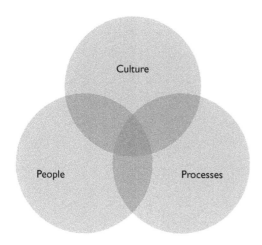

Figure 7.1 Culture–people–processes

It can be a challenge for school professionals and governors to analyse and align their school's culture, people and process to improve learning outcomes. But consider the wider implications when this model is applied to groups of schools in a community cluster. How do the culture, people and processes of disparate groups merge successfully without the uniqueness being diluted, compromised or stifled? Change for the collective good of a community will happen only when the barriers of traditional thinking are removed, and schools, along with their children, are recognised as being part of a living community.

So far in this chapter we have looked at the development of the philosophy of the inclusive school, and have indicated that cross-curricular learning and teaching have a logical place within that development. In the rest of the chapter the intention is to revisit these two themes to add a little more substance to the arguments outlined above. First, we will look at the theory of inclusion and then examine a practical example of cross-curricular learning in an inclusive setting.

Readiness for inclusive practice

To throw some further useful light on the process of change to inclusiveness we suggest another model – the so-called 7S Model of Peters and Waterman (http://www.jiscinfonet.ac.uk/tools/seven-s-model). Though the model is now quite dated it contains within it enduring insights. We can use this reflective tool (Figure 7.2) to analyse the complex links and interdependent factors within a school and its community to bring about change.

Here, the core item, Shared Values, must be realised every day in the school to ensure inclusiveness. These central values consist of: attitudes and relationships, a shared understanding of learning, and openness to accountability.

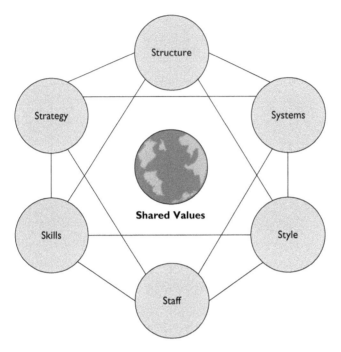

Figure 7.2 The 7S model

Reflection

What are the inclusive values your school holds? Why?
How strong are these values? What needs to be done to build upon them?
What is the culture of the school? How do you know this?

Attitudes and relationships

Crozier has emphasised that, while everyone has a view about how education should be, it is a rapidly changing phenomenon, in which teachers – as professionals – need to keep parents on-side: to give them 'a sense of agency' (2000: 73). Teachers need to be the intermediaries who explain the learning process to other stakeholders. Watkins and Lodge (2007: 15) believe that there are three different models of learning in the modern classroom: reception, construction and co-construction.

- *Reception*: effectively, the didactic mode.
- *Construction*: individual sense making – where learning is more open ended, and pupils are encouraged to make sense of learning through discussion and discovery.
- *Co-construction*: building knowledge with others – here pupils find themselves learning through dialogue and collaboration with others with the teacher acting as facilitator.

Stakeholders need to understand, and share, the values of the classroom. Over the years other scholars, too, have put forward similar models of learning (some of these were rehearsed in Chapter 2; see also Jarvis 2005). How do these models impact on inclusive cross-curricular learning? The theory of the three models of learning could be very closely linked with the attitudes and beliefs of staff and, most importantly, parents. There is a danger that people expect children to be taught as they themselves were taught. Parents need to have an understanding of the benefits of constructionist and co-constructionist learning, and how they go hand in hand with cross-curricular teaching, to enable schools to have confidence and belief in these techniques with their pupils. Given the importance of parental support, it is vital that we consider the skills that learners need to access this style and to ensure that their learning is as effective as possible. Watkins and Lodge's study (2007), supported by many others since, concluded that children learn best when:

- They take responsibility for their own learning
- They are actively engaged in their learning
- Learning is interactive
- They see themselves as successful learners.

This approach not only complements cross-curricular learning but defines it pedagogically. It demonstrates the importance of children understanding their own learning – a metacognitive process (Wilding 1997).

Shared understanding of learning

The ideal of the previous section is clearly supported in Alexander's work (2009: 282), which clearly articulates the need for a national change in teaching and learning approaches: 'The common strand, and it should be closely heeded, is that children want and need to know what they are doing and why, to be brought inside the thinking that informs the teacher's decisions on their behalf. Children, too, are interested in pedagogy.'

Building on Alexander's thinking, that children 'are interested in pedagogy', we can review our teaching practices to engage them earlier and make more sense of the journey (see also the material on heutagogy in Chapter 2). Hart *et al.* (2004), in looking to engage learners and secure their involvement, define this transformability as a 'joint enterprise', but engaging learners, especially those who are 'turned off' and present what could be described as learning difficulties, is a high priority for schools. Successful and inclusive strategies make learning irresistible and hook those children who are not engaging and are therefore placing themselves at risk, their well-being at risk, their learning at risk, and ultimately their futures at risk. Consider the model below for engaging learning.

Reflection: a possible model for engaging pupils in learning

Identify learning focus; children involved at this stage – existing understanding shared and questions raised.
    Construct planning around enquiry and needs.
    Apply experiences directly to learning.
    Ensure learning is validated, valued and communicated.
    Plan next steps collaboratively.

> Plan with children, listen to their interests and build meaningful, authentic experiences with them.
>
> Teach and explore with them, refer back to their enquiries, make the reasons for learning explicit – give them a cause.

Accountability

Everyone who has a role within an inclusive school is accountable for making inclusion work. But inclusion may demand a shift in public perspective concerning schools and their purposes. Standards are important in the learning process. The level at which these are achieved will affect learners' life chances and personal success. But translating Ofsted categories into crude accountability measures for schools does nothing to improve outcomes for pupils. Inclusion demands that we have to ensure that standards are aspirational, that all learners have realistic targets, and that all learners can be supported within this system. If learners have support and resources within the classroom we can create a cross-curricular learning environment, such as the one described in Case Study 7.2, that inspires learners and captures their specific needs.

One of the problems with the current approach to accountability is that measures are crude, and they are crudely applied. The mechanistic system of measurement through testing assumes that all pupils are the same and have the same potential, and that they can all reach the same levels of achievement. This cannot, logically, be true; no allowance is made for this in applying the accountability measures. Effectiveness is much more than being able to deliver learning targets to pupils; it is an awareness of the bigger picture that enables learners to have a personalised and individualised curriculum and learning journey: a journey of knowledge and skills. This is embodied by Watkins, who boldly stated at Suffolk's Primary Curriculum Conference in 2010 that 'Coverage is the enemy of learning.'

Having examined the nature of Shared Values in the 7S Model in Figure 7.2, we can move on to look briefly at the other six components of the model. In effect, these build towards answering the question 'What are the factors that are prerequisite for operating inclusive learning policies and practices in a school?' Table 7.1 draws the insights of these components together into a series of questions that challenge educators – heads, teachers, administrators, governors, support personnel – to examine their own practice.

Table 7.1 An analysis of some components for ensuring readiness for inclusion

Systems

What demands does inclusive practice make on factors such as finance, professional training, staff, or parental commitment?
Do all staff, including administrative and school business managers, share the underpinning values? How do the ways they conduct themselves, their systems and their activities show this?
What are the appropriate measures of success for this way of working?
How are these monitored, evaluated and built upon?
What aspirations and markers does the school use to keep learning for all at the forefront?

Structure

How is the school organised to achieve the inclusive goals it aspires to?
Who leads? What is the structure of responsibility within the school?
In practice, what model of management predominates: e.g. collegial, distributed, the heroic?
How do different subgroups form teams?
How do those teams communicate effectively, with common goals and through efficient processes?
Who makes the ultimate decisions and at what level are these shared?
Does every participant feel a part of the whole, and how well are they integrated into the
    communication structure?

Staff

What roles within the school are needed to achieve positive outcomes for learners?
What positions need to be filled?
What kinds of people, with what range of skills, are needed to fill them?
Are there gaps in the skills staff need to meet the learners' needs?
What skills audits have been undertaken to drive this process?

Skills

Where are the school's strengths?
Are these shared professionally with others?
Are there skills gaps?
Who can support or reduce these gaps – e.g. by better use of existing staff or by bringing in
    outside assistance?
What is the school known for doing well? What evidence is there?
Are there any obvious weaknesses?
What is the evidence for these, and how can improvement be effected?
How are staff skills acknowledged, monitored, assessed and celebrated?
What impact does monitoring and appraisal have, e.g. are identified needs genuinely met?
These and similar issues need to be examined and re-examined; and, of course, this process should
    be part of the regular updating of the school's Self-Evaluation Form and the headteacher's
    discussion with the School Improvement Partner.

Style

How do stakeholders see the physical environment of the school? Within the building, and outside?
How safe is the environment?
Does it present a climate that reflects psychological security and safety?
Is the school well and appropriately resourced?
Is learning collaborative?
Are the ethos and climate marked out by positive values?

Strategies

What is the school's inclusion strategy? Can everyone in the school community articulate it?
Is everyone committed to the strategy as a broad principle and as the beacon that guides day-to-
    day decisions and behaviours?
What can be done to make it come alive and be real for all the learners?
How does the school deal with parental, local authority and government pressure that conflicts
    with the strategy?
How is the strategy communicated and celebrated within and beyond the school?

Pulling the threads together: an example in practice

So far this chapter has attempted a definition of inclusion. It has set out how inclusion can be an important element in the education of all children and how achieving inclusion may affect the life of the school. In Case Study 7.1 we looked at the effect that introducing an inclusive philosophy had on the functioning of one school. The chapter has also considered the topic from a range of theoretical perspectives. The relevance of working across the curriculum is considered as an integral part of the inclusive approach.

The intention is to draw the chapter towards its end by looking at how inclusion works in the context of a single lesson. To this end, Case Study 7.2 describes a 'typical' lesson, making explicit how the needs of all children, regardless of ability, are catered for in a cross-curricular context.

Case Study 7.2 Some elements in cross-curricular, inclusive learning

High-quality learning is naturally inclusive. To enable this, it is worth paying close attention to several key principles.

First, a rigorous and secure *assessment procedure* is embedded in the pedagogy of the teacher and school. This assessment allows the teacher to plan and teach at the appropriate pace, with challenge and level of achievement. One strand of this assessment is the use of the KWFL approach – what the children *Know*; what the children *Want* to investigate; how they will *Find* it; what they have *Learned* – which gives a clear picture of where the children are from a skills, knowledge and understanding perspective.

Second, *communication*: once the *Know* and *Want* have been explored, the class engages with the planning and teaching phase. The aim is that learners must be prepared for their learning to start. Useful resources like whole-class visual timetables support learners and focus them to become more aware of what they will be learning next, and give them a broader understanding of the wider learning agenda. For SEN learners with specific difficulties, resources such as an individual visual timetable and a discussion before the learning commences give them an opportunity to question and prepare.

Third, capturing and linking the interests and *imagination*: the wow, the awe and the wonder.

There are a myriad ways to inspire learners – for example, dilemmas, problems and enquiry approaches. One might begin by telling the children: 'An Anglo-Saxon letter has been found and a local museum is organising an archaeological dig to gather information . . . '. The right stimuli and context will have all learners enthusiastic, willing and keen to take part. What is important here is to consider how the stimulus fits with the learning, providing a context for the children that allows them to have a purpose.

Children need ownership over their learning; they must feel that it is valued and they must feel confident to share their ideas. Giving them a range of ways to communicate their ideas independently (see Chapter 13) will enable the teacher and adults to make clear evaluations about those learners who need more input and those learners who are ready for a challenge. Learning Support Assistants (see Chapter 9) are vital in encouraging positive talk and questions, and in helping to correct any misconceptions in a supportive manner.

Mixed class of Y5/6 in an urban primary school – afternoon lesson in December for two and a half hours

Class 5UR is a fantastic class with a wide range of abilities, attitudes and talents. They present a wide social spectrum and a range of learners with social, emotional, behavioural and communication difficulties. Learning for these children has to have meaning, be in context and stay active. Writing reluctance is common for many of these young people. The class teacher and I have been empowering their skills as learners using a model of high-quality communication, capitalising on respectful listening, engagement, and active learning built around trust and relationships that are intrinsically valued.

The skills of listening, empathy, interdependence and collaboration are significantly challenged through the learning experiences extended by questions from their friends and adults.

One small example of this has been captured in what follows. Each learner has a single strip of plasticine. They are encouraged to play with it and mould it. The story, 'The Tunnel' by Anthony Browne, is read and reread with the class, and they are asked to shape the plasticine into anything that captures their imagination or feelings in the story. Learners have the choice of who they sit with and whereabouts in the class they do this, but the expectation is that if they make this choice then their learning reflects it.

Adults discuss and model the skill of interdependence (knowing when it is best to learn with others and when by yourself) and learners choose to create their model individually. They are naturally curious about one another's ideas and they talk with one another, asking increasingly deep questions about one another's creations. This is a routine within the class and has been made a natural part of the learning repertoire. Questions and observation lead to revisions to their own models; children have the opportunity and permission to broadcast these and share their learning with the class. Resources are an integral part of learning. Children know where the available resources are to capitalise and build upon their imagination. They use IT independently, capturing the design phases with digital cameras as a record for their synthesis and evaluation of the learning. Individual work, pairs and small groups develop as each learner makes the personal decision about how they want to improve and build upon their learning. Some work collaboratively, others cooperatively and some individually.

The story continues with learners using everyday class resources including books, textures, coloured papers, words to represent feelings, and 'what ifs' to inform the reader. This is personalised through the children's perspective of what's at the end of their own tunnel . . . what's it like?

All adults are briefed to extend the thinking by encouraging questioning, reflection that can lead to intuition. Children are required to challenge themselves and not rely on external motivation, but move towards the inner want and desire to succeed.

Outcomes are differentiated by adult support and questioning, but the key driver here is that the learning is led by the children.

Outcomes focus on the most able, including linking moral dilemmas and engaging in profound learning.

The quality of language, imagination, social skills and constructive learning is assessed, and linked to the 'traditional' subjects of English and maths.

A clear strength of this inclusive practice is that the teacher is responsible for English and maths with the class. The adults have a personal, clear and focused understanding of where to support, extend and challenge pupils across the areas of learning.

Differentiation

In Case Study 7.2 differentiation was picked up on as a key skill in inclusive teaching. This view is shared by Ungaro (2013: 10), who concludes as follows:

> Responding to pupil differences is not just good teaching, because what works for most might not work for some. Differentiation is good practice for all students as it allows students from all backgrounds and with all abilities to demonstrate what they know, understand and are capable of doing (Fenech Adami 2004: 91). Thus it is not only for the education of marginal students. Children learn well in different ways and 'seem to profit most when instruction is differentiated in some manner to accommodate these differences' (Sternberg & Zhang 2005: 245).

Ungaro (2013: 35) further suggests:

> Differentiation in the classroom is based on the assumption that learners differ in the way they acquire knowledge. For all students to succeed there has to be an efficient system of inclusion, a system that caters for individual needs. Students will then be motivated to learn.

This insight should be a *sine qua non* of all teaching in all phases.

Conclusion

What can be said, in conclusion, about inclusion?

Clearly, social justice demands that the education of all pupils, and of all pupils as individuals, should address their needs in a ways that are, and are seen to be, equitable. Inclusion offers a route towards meeting that intention – albeit, not in every single case. In a sense, in the lifetime of many of us, we have seen moves towards social justice in our schools through the demise of single-gender schools (in which girls particularly were disadvantaged), through comprehensive education (which did away with life-long labelling at eleven years old), and now progressively through attitudes to special needs education.

Inclusion has costs; these are real but often not insurmountable. Teachers are well disposed to the principle of inclusion, but the governmental systems within which they work are often inimical to implementation.

Curriculum and pedagogy have to move in time to the music of systemic change. Systems are often tardy.

As indicated in this chapter, cross-curricular approaches are particularly suitable for learning and teaching in inclusive contexts.

If there is a key skill to be extracted from cross-curricular approaches it is probably the skill of differentiation; but that is not much different from the teaching of the more able, too.

Note

1 This chapter is based on the original, by Bedford and Parsons, in the first edition of the book, but it has been extensively remodelled and altered in line with developments in the field; the original authors are not responsible for any changes of emphasis that result – *ed.*

References

Alexander, R. (2009) *Children, Their World, Their Education*. London: Routledge.

Baldwin, L. & Sabry, K. (2003) 'Learning styles for interactive learning systems'. *Innovations in Education and Teaching International* 40(4): 325–340.

Claxton, G. (2008) *What's the Point of School?* Oxford: One World Publications.

Cline, T. and Frederickson, N. (2009) *Special Educational Needs, Inclusion and Diversity*. Milton Keynes: Open University.

Crozier, J. (2000) *Parents and Schools: Partners or Protagonists?* Stoke on Trent: Trentham Books.

Daniels, H. and Porter, J. (2007) *Learning Needs and Difficulties Among Children of Primary School Age: Definition, Identification, Provision and Issue*. Cambridge: Primary Review.

Davis, P. and Florian, L. (2004) *Teaching Strategies and Approaches for Pupils with Special Educational Needs: A Scoping Study*. London: DfES.

DfEE (1997) *Green Paper: Excellence for All Children, Meeting Special Educational Needs*. London: Department for Education and Employment.

Dyson, A. (1999) 'Inclusion and inclusions: theories and discourses in inclusive education', in Daniels, H. and Garner, P. (eds) *World Yearbook of Education: Inclusive Education*. London: Kogan Page.

Fenech Adami, A. (2004) 'Enhancing students' learning through differentiated approaches to teaching and learning: a Maltese perspective'. *Journal of Research in Special Educational Needs* 4(2): 91–97.

Glazzard, J. (2011) 'Perceptions of the barriers to effective inclusion in one primary school: voices of teachers and teaching assistances'. *Support for Learning* 26(2): 56–63.

Hart, S., Dixon, A., Drummond, M. and McIntyre, D. (2004) *Learning Without Limits*. Maidenhead: Open University Press.

Her Majesty's Inspectorate (2002) *Count Us In: Achieving Inclusion in Scottish Schools*. HMI Report.

Irish National Teachers' Organization (2004) *Proceedings of the Joint Conference of the INTO*, Limerick: 27 March.

Jarvis, M. (2005) *The Psychology of Effective Teaching and Learning*. Cheltenham: Nelson-Thornes.

MacBeath, J., Galton, M., Steward, S., MacBeath, A. and Page, C. (2007) *The Cost of Inclusion*. Cambridge: University of Cambridge Faculty of Education.

Maslow, A. (1970) *Motivation and Personality*. New York: Harper & Row.

Ministry of Education for British Columbia (1994) *Handbook for Curriculum Developers* (February 1994) and *Special Education Services – A Manual of Policies, Procedures and Guidelines* (Response Draft, December 1994).

Obiakor, F. E. *et al.* (2012) 'Making inclusion work in general education classrooms'. *Education and Treatment of Children* 35(3): 477–490.

Ofsted (2001) *Evaluating Educational Inclusion – Guidance for Inspectors and Schools*. Available online at: http://wsgfl.westsussex.gov.uk/ccm/content/curriculum/inclusion-and-equalities/educational-inclusion-general-issues/statements-about-educational-inclusion.en?/page=3.

Peters, T. and Waterman, R. (1982) *In Search of Excellence*. London: Profile Books.

Rashid, N. and Tikly, L. (2010) *Inclusion and Diversity in Education: Guidelines for Inclusion and Diversity in Schools*. London: British Council.

Sternberg, R. J. & Zhang, L.-f. (2005) 'Styles of thinking as a basis of differentiated instruction'. *Theory into Practice* 44(3): 245–253.

Ungaro, M. (2013) Managing differentiation and inclusion: a case study to explore the implementation of the Let Me Learn model at St Lea's Secondary School. Unpublished MSc dissertation. Leicester: University of Leicester.

Warnock Report (1978) *Special Educational Needs: Report of the Committee of Enquiry into the Education of Handicapped Children and Young People.* London: HMSO.

Warnock, M. (2005) *Special Educational Needs: A New Look.* London: Philosophy of Education Society of Great Britain.

Watkins, C. and Lodge, C. (2007) *Effective Learning in Classrooms.* London: Paul Chapman.

Wilding, M. (1997) 'Taking control: from theory into practice'. *Education Today* 47(3): 17–23.

World Conference on Special Needs Education (1994) *The Salamanca Statement and Framework for Action on Special Needs Education* Salamanca, Spain, 7–10 June. Available online at: http://www. unesco.org/education/pdf/SALAMA_E.PDF.

Internet sources

http://www.isec2000.org.uk/abstracts/papers_r/rose_1.htm

http://www.jiscinfonet.ac.uk/tools/seven-s-model

http://www.leeds.ac.uk/disabilitystudies/archiveuk/CSIE/inclusive%20ed.pdf

http://www.teachingexpertise.com/e-bulletins/links-between-sen-and-gifted-and-talented-6636

http://www.wrexham.gov.uk/assets/pdfs/education/senpolicy_241007.pdf

Chapter 8

The most able within an integrated curriculum at Key Stage 2

Carolle Kerry, John Richardson and Sue Lambert

Introduction

This chapter examines the way in which schools educate the most able pupils. There is a problem from the outset with the changing nomenclature adopted by successive governments and this is outlined in what follows along with some reflections on identification and definitions. The practical approach taken by the chapter to the education of the more able is that of creativity. Examples of this approach are rehearsed and discussed. The chapter evaluates the role of cross-curricular working in the education of this group of children, partly through the use of pupil voice, noting that there are resonances with the previous chapter on children with special needs. Assessment of cross-curricular sessions is considered, before the chapter embarks on discussing in detail the way in which one school has approached the issue of teaching and learning creatively.

Issues associated with changes in terminology

To begin, it is pertinent to think about and discuss the thorny issue of terminology as it relates to the more able child. Within the English system, the education of the more able child has long been something of a challenge for educators and governments. Legislation is in place (Special Educational Needs and Disability Act 2001) to ensure that those children with an educational or physical disability receive an education appropriate to their need; the more recent Children and Families Act (2014) sought to give greater protection to vulnerable children. In a government press release on the day of The Royal Assent to the Act, Edward Timpson, Children and Families Minister, noted:

> The Children and Families Act is all about reforming services for vulnerable children – reflecting this government's deep determination to give every child, whatever their start in life, an equal chance to make the best of themselves.
>
> (Timpson 2014)

Despite such ministerial assertion that 'every child . . . has an equal chance to make the best of themselves', it is important to note that no such legislation exists specifically for the child of higher ability.

The Chief Inspector of Schools, Sir Michael Wilshaw, drew attention in 2013 to what he perceived to be a problem, and ordered 'an urgent "rapid response survey" of how state schools teach the most able children' (Henry 2013). Although his remarks on this occasion were directed at secondary schools, it is worth pausing to consider the way in which primary school pupils are taught, the way that encourages and enables the more able child to achieve high grades in Year 6.

One of the difficulties, of course, is that currently many of the earlier descriptors for the able pupil are out of fashion. In the 1970s 'bright pupils' was the tag afforded the top 20% of school pupils; at the turn of the new century, 'gifted and talented pupils' became the buzz-word of New Labour. Arguably, this improved definition at least had the impact of widening the boundaries from the earlier 'bright pupils' nomenclature with its focus on academic ability, to include children whose talents lay outside conventional, examinable, subjects – for example, in music, sport, dance, drama or the arts generally. But with the passage of time and different emphases being placed by Ofsted on school inspections, definitions have again narrowed and those young people whose talents lie outside achievement in literacy and mathematics are in danger of finding them going unrecognised and, ultimately, not nurtured. And so, as we enter the first half of the second decade of the 21st century, having learned nothing from history, the focus shifts again to '*academically* more able pupils' replacing the term 'gifted and talented youth' DfE (2013a). As if to reaffirm the change in terminology, future Ofsted inspections will, in the words of the Chief Inspector, 'look more closely at the progress of the most able and disadvantaged pupils before judging achievement to be good' (Wilshaw 2013).

Though some of the definitions favoured in the 1990s and 2000s contained loop-holes through which gifted or talented pupils might slip, they did at least provide a degree of national consistency and a more systematic approach to identification by individual schools. A good example of this was the self-evaluation and planning tool for schools, the Quality Standard for Gifted and Talented Education, jointly developed by the then DfES and the National Association for Gifted and Talented Youth (NAGTY) (DfES 2005). School leaders and teaching staff assessed their school's provision for gifted and talented pupils through a series of statements indicating whether, in their perception, the school was at 'entry', 'developing' or 'exemplary' level. This systematic approach meant that, once the level of provision had been established, the tool supported improvement by identifying the next phase for development and appropriate provision could be made for the individual child. Now that the criteria have narrowed, and the Quality Standard is no longer mandatory, it has taken the strain/accountability from schools to deliver according to identifiable and thus assessable criteria.

Challenges faced by teachers in the identification of the able pupil

Given that there is no single test to help teachers identify whether a young person is at the top end of the ability range, individual schools, within the parameters and boundaries of current legislation, have been given the opportunity to devise systems of their own (HMI Wales 2011) with all the attendant dangers of inconsistency and error.

Generally, mathematics, literacy and science form the basis of *formal* assessment for identifying children through testing, but if the definition of intelligence is narrow, or indeed narrowed further still, then it follows that high attainment in other areas of the curriculum or areas such as inter- and intra-personal skills will not 'fit' easily the prescribed indicators or measures. Children who are highly able in sport or music can often be more easily identified through their performance, but those whose ability to work collaboratively, demonstrate leadership skills or perceptive appreciation of music, for example, may be less obvious. This makes identifying such children and providing appropriate challenge, extension and support difficult, given there is little specific guidance and information about how to identify, monitor and assess children who are high attaining in non-core curriculum areas. In essence there has been no specific government guidance since the DCSF publication, '*Effective Provision for Gifted and Talented Children in Primary Schools*' (2008a), which indicated that it is schools themselves that have the discretion to decide how best to identify these pupils.

Means of identification

A challenge here is that one of the criteria in identifying children is ability rather than achievement (DCSF 2008b), and many characteristics of the children who are higher attaining in other areas are not easily measured with reliability and validity (Sousa 2003). The ability may be skills based, linked to particular intelligences (Gardner 1993) that transfer across subjects rather than being subject specific, or may be in areas where quantifying the ability is difficult and arguably not applicable. Although multiple intelligence is a matter for debate it does highlight the need to consider the range of activities in which pupils can show their abilities but, as Sousa (2003: 36) suggests, multiple intelligence is not a panacea for education, and focusing on particular intelligences disproportionately could be counter-productive.

Emotional intelligence across groups

It is important to recognise that emotional intelligence has a strong influence on how well high-attaining children progress and that able children from vulnerable groups are more likely to underachieve (Goleman 1996; DCSF 2008a; Alexander 2010). Frustration, low self-esteem, lack of challenge, physical well-being and the expectations of others can all impact on the achievements of the most able children from vulnerable groups and hide their abilities (Headington 2003). Furthermore, narrowing the focus to more academic areas may increase frustration for those children with abilities that are not recognised as easily or given as high a priority.

Issues in the intelligence debate

The debate within research about whether intelligence is fixed or changeable, and what it actually is, varies, but contemporary research findings seem to indicate that intelligence can be taught, learned, developed and enhanced, so fixed identification is perhaps inappropriate or at best unhelpful (Hymer 2002; Lazear 2004; DCSF 2008a) – in short, an outdated concept.

Given that more able pupils have diverse needs and that 'ability' itself may develop over time, testing and classifying at an early age may be inappropriate (*pace* the 11+ debate). This insight impacts on approaches to teaching and learning: whether it is seen as a linear or cyclical process (Smith 2005). If intelligence is changeable and can be developed, then more weight should be given to continuous process-based identification of children rather than reliance on point-in-time tests or exams (Hymer 2002). Learning needs to be more interactive: less about right answers and more about collaborative work. Identification of the able is better achieved by multiple criteria so teachers do not become too reliant on uni-dimensional methods (Hymer 2002; Smith 2005). Pressures within schools to meet targets and the judgements about schools based on attainment within a narrow band of subjects can put undue strain on headteachers and teachers, and may mean that there is an imbalance in subjects and areas of the curriculum given priority in school. This may become better or worse with the introduction of the new national curriculum for England (DfE 2013b), with guidance being given to encourage schools to develop the curriculum to meet the needs of their area and community. Although the document states clearly that the national curriculum forms only 'part' of a *broad and balanced curriculum*, schools may still prioritise core subjects unduly as these remain the subjects by which they are judged in terms of Ofsted judgements and school improvement.

Teachers' roles in identification

DCSF (2008b) notes the essential part that teacher observation and informal assessment play in identification, monitoring and assessment of highly able children, but again professional development in the skills to do this effectively and consistently is very much reliant on initiatives and competence in individual schools. It is through a skilled teacher developing a pupil's thinking by asking high-level searching questions that demonstration of different levels of learning can often be assessed (Headington 2003). Although it could be argued that experienced class teachers are good at using ongoing assessment and observation to address learners' needs and plan next steps in learning, this may not be specific to meeting the needs of the higher-attaining children, particularly in mixed-ability classes, or identifying children whose abilities develop as they mature.

Clearly, then, teachers can play an integral part in the development of learning and skills within the classroom and, increasingly, beyond. Before going on to describe the ways in which South Hykeham teachers develop the thinking skills of their pupils, it is worth pausing for a moment to consider teachers' attitudes to highly able pupils and the way in which these attitudes may impinge upon their teaching.

'High attaining' and 'high attainment'

In the current climate the emphasis has shifted from process to outcome: governments show less concern for developmental learning, and more about measurable attainment and achievement. It is interesting to note the inclusion section in the new national curriculum for England (DfE 2013b), which comments only broadly that teachers should plan stretching work for pupils whose attainment is significantly above the expected level. However, the sentence that follows in the document is phrased in such a way as to suggest that prioritising the needs of other learners over those of the most able is expected.

The use of the wording 'having an even greater obligation to plan lessons for pupils who have low levels of prior attainment or come from disadvantaged backgrounds' (DfE 2013b: 8) could suggest greater priority and monitoring being expected for these children than for the most able, although there are able children within the vulnerable groups and from disadvantaged backgrounds. It is also well established that pupils of high ability often underperform and therefore underachieve. On this regime their needs would be significantly neglected. *2020 Vision: Report of the Teaching and Learning in 2020 Review Group* (DfES 2006), commenting on underachievement, noted that gaps persist in achievement, and factors that contribute are complex and interrelated; but they include individual attitudes, beliefs and expectations of pupils, parents and teachers.

For teachers it is useful to be aware of individual views about expectations, values and beliefs: how far we are willing or able to be flexible and open to ideas in our responses to children or their alternative ways of working and learning when they may not be what we planned for, expected or understood. Sousa (2003: 7) suggests that teachers may need training to recognise any stereotypical views they may hold, and it has been argued that some teachers' concern is often for rewarding conventional behaviour and task completion rather than encouraging less obviously talented children who may work in very different but equally valid ways (Winstanley 2006).

Pollard (2008) urges that reflective teaching is important for developing skills through a cyclical process in which teachers monitor, evaluate and revise their own practice continuously. Teachers do well to help learners to invest in the learning, know the purpose of the learning and have ownership of it. Research led by Rudduck and Flutter (2004) shows that consulting pupils, and involving them in teaching and learning approaches leads to higher pupil engagement and attainment, particularly through Assessment for Learning strategies, which enable all children, but particularly the most able children, to have ownership of learning, engage in self-reflection and target setting, evaluate and check work, negotiate with staff, use their own initiative, and attribute success or failure to their own decision making rather than the teacher or curriculum (Wallace *et al.* 2007). Hymer (2002: 29) suggests the teacher needs to create an enriching and stimulating environment in which children have opportunities to reveal the abilities they have, though the same observation would apply to the teaching of all children. Pupils need to be actively engaged in the process so targets can be set for future learning to aid motivation (Headington 2003; Smith 2005). Training for teachers and support staff is important to help provide the skills and expertise to recognise a range of abilities and identify potential, as well as recognise those pupils already achieving. Sousa (2003) acknowledged that there is still a need for more research on the practicalities of able pupils' needs. Often, even when potential is recognised, there is little practical guidance available about how to address the needs of these learners.

Reflection

To what extent do you think that making special provision for able pupils is élitist? How does this square with the provision you make for children with special needs? Dealing with and even defining able pupils is, as we have seen, not simple. With this in mind, the chapter now considers the way in which one primary school attempts to create a situation that is both creative and stimulating, where, for one week, subject disciplines *per se* are put aside and absorbed into cross-curricular working in what is known both to staff and pupils as 'the themed week'.

Context

South Hykeham School opened in 1871 as a one-room building. The original red-brick Victorian classroom remains today. In 1958 an extension to the school took place and the main building was considerably enlarged; this was followed in 1989 by the addition of a mobile classroom. The school was further extended in 1993 to provide two extra purpose-built infant classrooms; a new hall and ICT room were built in 2003, and administrative facilities in 2010. The school has five teaching staff and a non-teaching head, all of whom are supported by well-qualified teaching assistants and governors.

In what follows we attempt to bring four distinct approaches to the issue of teaching the more able pupil in primary schools using a creative approach and to do this in the context of our school setting. Earlier in the chapter we looked briefly at the theory that underpins the nomenclature, identification and teaching of the able pupil within a mixed-ability context. Second, we illustrate current practice by looking at South Hykeham's cross-curricular 'themed weeks', which bring learning together across subject areas. We then scrutinise our own assessment practice in order to discover the effectiveness or otherwise of our teaching strategies during these themed weeks and how this has impinged upon our able pupils, and lastly we pursue our normal policy of listening to the pupils' voice. By talking directly with the pupils we are enabled to discover how the young people themselves view the cross-curricular approach and the ways in which it helps them to understand the links between subjects.

'Themed weeks' have been ongoing for five years now. During that time we have researched and designed pro formas that enable us to audit the progress of the more able pupils' learning within a cross-curricular environment, and link the processes to, particularly, the nature of knowledge. The original thinking behind the creation of the themed weeks was, in part, to enable staff to discover any hidden talents a child may have (particularly within the social or affective domains). It was felt that, once discovered, these could be drawn out in subsequent lessons, and thus help provide a better educational experience for our able pupils *as well as all other pupils* in the class or school.

Creativity in teaching and learning thematically

The importance of teaching creatively and teaching for creativity is at the forefront of current issues in primary education (NSEAD, undated). Creativity should be an integral part of every primary classroom. But, as with any initiative that involves the participation of the children in their own learning, introducing an appropriate environment requires teachers to reflect upon and evaluate new and different approaches to their teaching and, consequently, their pupils' learning. Handy's (1997: 55) pertinent warning should be heeded: 'creativity needs a bit of untidiness', though Duffy (2006: 25) defines creativity as being 'about connecting the previously unconnected in ways that are new and meaningful to the individual'. Abela (2014) notes that: 'While creating what he calls the "creative thinking spiral", Resnick (2007) debates that for children to succeed in today's creative society, they need to become creative thinkers. Resnick also refers to early childhood curricula that have creativity as a central pedagogical concept . . . and notes that they have frequently been related to notions of childhood as a developmental phase of inherent creativity.'

In order for these visions to become reality, teachers need to become creative thinkers themselves. They need to define their own attitudes towards creativity, and to understand that the outcomes of their teaching depend, in part, upon variables, variables that may change year-on-year, e.g. relationships between teacher and pupils; pupils and pupils; class ethos. What does not change, however, is that creative teaching, of necessity, requires the provision of quality material, material that is designed to extend the pupils' lateral thinking as well as vertical. De Bono (1970 p. 34) highlighted the differences over four decades ago:

> With vertical thinking one uses information for its own sake in order to move forward to a solution. With lateral thinking one uses information not for its own sake but provocatively in order to bring about re-patterning.

Grainger and Barnes (2006) do not see the issue of creativity in teaching as necessarily straightforward and offer words of caution:

> The distinction between creative teachers and teaching for creativity is a helpful one in that it is possible to imagine a creative teacher who personally enters creatively into the classroom context, yet fails to provide for children's creative learning.
>
> (2006: 4)

Having thought in small measure through some pros and cons of creative teaching, we now consider the role of the themed week in the cycle of school life.

The use of cross-curricular themed weeks in meeting the needs of able pupils

Five years ago the senior management team at South Hykeham Community Primary School developed the strategy of dis-applying the then National Curriculum for one week every term. In its place they envisaged whole-school teaching, across the curriculum on a predetermined topic chosen for its ability to appeal to children across the range of Y1–Y6. Thus the themed weeks were born.

The initial philosophy behind the strategy was primarily to enhance the curriculum, to provide increased breadth and enrichment for the children and to provide opportunities for staff to confirm or challenge their understanding of pupils' ability. Within the context of multi-subject teaching it was hypothesised that new talents might emerge, talents that were less likely to be identified in single-subject teaching and within the context of objective-driven focused lessons.

To ensure that meaningful time is given over to each curriculum area, core subjects are a focus for one half-term each year. Non-core subjects are focused in a three-year cycle.

The cross-curricular themed weeks do not only support identification of needs, however, nor do they benefit the able pupils alone. They are also a powerful tool for the development of gifts and talents for all children. One such example was our original art and RE week in which we observed children developing abilities within a variety of media very quickly. As a result they were able to have a greater choice over which media would best illustrate the week's work. The ability to link concepts from different curriculum areas also allowed for enhanced learning, and an outcome of the art and RE week is developed below.

Themed weeks are being implemented across the curriculum primarily to enhance learning for all students, but the intensity of focus lends itself to clearer assessment by staff of what individual children can achieve. From this, provision at other times during the school year can be more closely linked to individual children's needs, catering again for both able pupils as well other children. This supports our philosophy that enhancing learning for the most able enhances it, too, for all students (Kerry and Kerry 2000). Examples of work carried out in themed weeks follow appearing as Case Study 8.1 and Case Study 8.2.

Case Study 8.1 describes, first, the content of the week; interviews with the subject leader and with a pupil, Jonathan, are then described, and subsequently an analysis of Jonathan's interview draws out aspects of the learning that has taken place.

Case Study 8.1 A themed approach: art and RE

Art and religious education were the subjects of exploration by pupils during a themed week in which they studied 'Creation'. The art and RE subject leader described the week as 'a purposeful cross-curricular learning opportunity' engaging the whole school. Normal lessons were set aside, and all staff were involved in the planning and execution of the week's activities. Staff had previously attended a painting workshop at a local secondary school, in which they learned first-hand about progression in painting skills and what they could expect from their children. During the RE sessions the children learned about and from the story of Creation from a Christian perspective and that of other faiths and cultures, and, through the medium of art, applied this learning. They learned first-hand from visitors, and second-hand through stories and myths. Throughout the week the subject leader monitored the children's work to ensure that each child worked purposefully and that differentiation, where applied, was appropriate. Observer governors noted the enjoyment and engagement of the children, and the subsequent artistic outcomes were displayed throughout the school.

Within these parameters it is pertinent to ask, 'What evidence does the school have that this method of cross-curricular learning develops the skills and understanding of the able pupil, and, second, how can this learning be assessed?'

To try to ascertain the levels of learning, it was necessary to understand the planning, execution and reflection processes that took place. A semi-structured interview with the subject leader was undertaken (extracts below), and to triangulate this process the authors had access to taped interviews between her and pupils that took place within a few days of the art/RE themed week.

Interview with the subject leader

The subject leader was asked about the motivation and planning behind the cross-curricular art/RE themed week:

> We are continually looking for purposeful cross-curricular learning opportunities throughout the school. To ensure that we can monitor progression and continuity throughout the school we try to adopt whole school approaches where relevant. The motivation was based on looking at the two subjects that I coordinate, asking how we measured progress in the two subjects, knowing where the school was at in RE and art, knowing what we were doing on a daily basis and asking: 'Where do we go from here?' . . . Our planning for the themed week revolved around a document which shows the basic skills in art . . . We all work on a basic skill at one time . . . so all of the teachers were teaching painting at the same time. The document breaks up where the children should be at in each year group . . . We know where the children should be at, where they are supposed to be and we know the next step and the one below.

But how did this work in practice? The subject leader's interview with a nine-year-old Y4 pupil – Jonathan – provided clues.

Jonathan's understanding of creation

Jonathan was asked to look at a selection of photographs and artwork and asked whether, by looking at the pictures, he could make any link between the Christian story of creation and the aboriginal story of creation:

> Well, we say that God created the sun, moon, and the stars, and it is sort of the same for the aboriginals because they thought it was, they thought it was the ancestors who created the sun, moon and stars . . . Christians think that there was one person who created all of it whereas some other religions believe there are a series of different people or things who created different things and like, for example, with the aborigines, they had like ancestors, they could be snake, they could be human, they could be emu, they could be whatever animals that are in Australia. Well, we say that God then rested but they say that they just turn themselves into something different, and they slept. And they also think that dream time is for ever, and they don't think, whereas we think that Creation ended once God created the earth, the sun, and the moon and the stars and the planets, they don't. They think dream time is still happening and that it is always happening just like trees grow, that's their explanation . . .

Jonathan was then asked whether he believed God created the world in six days:

> I personally think, I believe He created the world of course. I personally think it might have taken Him a bit longer than six days. Perhaps instead of six days, there might have been six weeks, six months or six years. One year for each of them, 'cos God is eternal living, so days to Him are different from days to us. Like a day to Him would be like a second. To us, a day is 24 hours, hours to Him are weeks or months . . .

He then returns to the Aboriginal creation story:

> I would like to have found out exactly why they believe there were ancestors, though I respect other people's religions . . . I'd like to know how they believe that ancestors had magic . . .

He ponders further about Aboriginal magic in the story:

> And also I do find that having a sacred digging stick which made things appear would be a bit dramatic, perhaps where they dug they just dropped seeds in. But I do find that a bit, well, how exactly would that just spring up?

Analysing the learning in a cross-curricular themed week activity

In a follow-up interview, the subject leader saw Jonathan as 'using higher-order thinking skills . . . that he had the ability to compare and contrast two differing cultures and he was able to give his own opinion about them'. But in order to confirm or refute the teacher's assessment, and to try to understand in greater depth the thinking that Jonathan was undertaking, it was necessary to conduct a small-scale content analysis deconstruction of his conversation.

Content analysis determines the presence of certain words or concepts within, in this instance, language. Researchers quantify and analyse the presence, meaning and relationships of the words or concepts, and then make inferences about the messages that the conversation conveys.

From the outset Jonathan's ability to make comparison across cultures was apparent: '*We say that God created the sun, moon and the stars . . . the aboriginals . . . thought it was the ancestors who created the sun, moon and stars*'. He compares and contrasts: '*Christians think . . . one person created all of it . . . with the aboriginals they had ancestors . . . snake . . . human . . . emu. We say that God then rested but they say . . . [the ancestors] slept*'. He muses that for aboriginals '*dream time is for ever . . . we think that Creation ended once God created the earth, the sun . . .*'.

Within this paragraph Jonathan rehearses in great detail the knowledge he acquired during the lesson. But his knowledge is not just repetition of fact, i.e. data recall: he evaluates and applies the knowledge: '*We say . . . but the aboriginals thought . . .*'.

Jonathan then turns to the abstract and discusses Creation, both Christian and Aboriginal. He analyses what he has learned: '*I personally . . . believe He created the world*', but within that belief there is a dimension that causes him reflection: '*. . . it might have taken Him a bit longer than six days*'. Speculation creeps in: '*. . . it might have been six weeks, six months or six years*'. He evaluates and makes judgements about the Creation story suggesting that '*God is eternal living, so days to Him are different from days to us.*'

Jonathan's account of the Aboriginal story of creation causes him to think deeply – he wants to know answers to questions: why Aboriginals believe in ancestors, why these ancestors had magical powers. The '*sacred digging stick*' causes him problems and he tries to solve this issue with a rational explanation: '*Perhaps where they dug, they just dropped seeds in.*'

Case Study 8.1 focuses on the perception of one child, a highly able pupil able to disseminate the learning and to rationalise his thinking in areas that cause him concern, i.e. 'the sacred digging stick'.

Case study 8.2 focuses more on the whole-school approach; this case is described below and some of the learning processes identified.

Case study 8.2 The Viking invasion

Clad in tunics of linen and wool, hair akimbo and wild, three Vikings invaded South Hykeham, Lincolnshire, one fine, sunny spring day. It is 2014 and this time the Vikings come in peace, a friendly invasion.

Their presence is greeted with enthusiasm by the pupils of South Hykeham Community Primary School. During the previous term the youngsters studied the ways of the original invaders and now was the chance for the children to experience something of what life would have been like had they lived and been part of an original 'invasion'. But first the invasion was put into context via a timeline from the start of the Common Era until the present: 22 children represented the turn of each century with some – the arrival of the Vikings and the Normans, invaders each – highlighted by way of questions from the present-day Vikings and answers from the 'Viking children'.

Authenticity and participation were the watchwords. The majority of the one-hundred or so children had taken to heart their Easter homework – to make, or get help with making, a suitable Viking costume with, of course, a little help from the local market stall selling a variety of weird and wonderful costumes and helmets.

Introductions over, the children returned to their classrooms which, during assembly, had miraculously been transformed into mini-Viking settlements.

And so the children were transported back to an age known to them only through the previous term's work, in effect the theory of the Viking Age. The practising new-age Vikings talked about their home life, their living spaces and food preparation, and made contrasts between the school children's lives and the way in which Viking children lived, who worked in the home from the earliest age, on the land from seven years old and marrying at thirteen.

Having thought about the Vikings' home life it was time to move on to the 'how' and 'where' of everyday living: How do you keep the home dry? How do you cook? Where do you cook? Where do you get your water? Where do you sleep? How do you keep warm? And, of course: How and where do you go to the toilet?

It was clear from the ensuing dialogue that the youngsters were drawing on previously learned work, and thus both the questions and answers consolidated their learning in a practical way.

As a diversion from listening and handling the artefacts it was time to engage the empathetic brain and make the leap from the present day to the past, from the known Roman alphabet to the mysteries of the Runes, still to be found on monuments – the rune stones – in Scandinavia.

In Old Norse the word 'rune' means 'letter', 'text' or 'inscription'; the challenge for the children was to 'read' the runic alphabet (conveniently written on the whiteboard by the resident Viking) and to translate their own name into Runic. Once translated, another challenge awaited – to make a rune stone upon which to inscribe their name for all time.

Modern-day material (clay) provided the basis of the activity; with great care the clay was moulded into a free-standing circular (or in some cases triangular) rune stone and finished with the chosen inscription. As well as being immense fun, this and the other activities that preceded and followed it, needed empathetic connections with a bygone era and unknown peoples.

The children had learned that the Viking families lived very different lives from their own – harsh lives in a very harsh climate where, in winter, the sun never rose above the horizon. So how, they asked, did they spend their short days and long nights? The Vikings explained that the longhouse was cosy, made more so in winter by sharing it with their animals. The smoke from the fire drifted out through the roof and it was here, sitting on benches, that games were played and tales told. And thus the children played their final part in their 'day in the life of a Viking'.

Groups of four children settled down to play a board game involving brown counters (the marauding invaders set to capture the king); a silver counter (the king) and white counters (the king's bodyguard). By a series of moves and counter-moves the king's bodyguards had to deliver the king to the safety of an exit point at each corner of the board, all the time evading the marauders. This involved deep concentration on the part of the children and analysis of the danger of any potential move, an understanding that any move had implications for future strategy; one child commented: 'I have a plan but I'm not going to say what it is just at this moment.' Unfortunately, the plan was never divulged – the modern world intruded and the constraints of the end of the school day meant that it was time to retire to the 'longhouse' (school hall) for the final act of the day, the Viking Saga, brilliantly enacted by the Vikings themselves with the help of some very enthusiastic children.

The learning outcomes

This day-long activity brought out the key factor in interdisciplinary learning – pupils being challenged by 'problems' or puzzles to solve using knowledge drawn from a range of 'subject' areas. As well as identifying (empathetic learning) with the subject matter, the children were 'transported' into the historical situations. They were challenged by the direct questions posed by the Viking team. They engaged at various cognitive levels (in Bloomian terms), e.g. from 'How and where do you go to the toilet' (lower order) to 'I have a plan but I'm not going to say what it is just at this moment.' (Note: from observation, and discreet attention to the conversation between this one boy and the other children, it was clear that ideas were forming in his head that would have fallen into one or other categories of Bloom's higher-order thinking skills. Time precluded from categorising further.) This last example highlights the constant need for children to articulate the learning; and this process helps to make learning their own so that they assimilate what they know. Yet all of this happens within a context of fun, enjoyment and the generation of positive attitudes to the learning process. Both in class and during the lunchtime, the children acquired and practised new social skills drawn from the affective domain.

Reflection

How might you use the idea of a cross-curricular themed week in your own situation to help meet the needs of all children, and specifically those of able pupils?

How could you use Bloom's taxonomy, as described in Chapter 2, to help you understand the levels of thinking in your own classes?

Think about ways in which a teacher might develop a child's talents outside the academic curriculum.

Tracking progress using a cross-curricular approach

Typically at South Hykeham, non-core subjects such as art have been assessed using expectations of achievement at the end of a unit of work. Each unit of work has a designated series of learning outcomes. Where children have exceeded or not met these outcomes this is recorded. Children who are consistently recorded as exceeding expectations may be considered as able or talented within that subject area, and their needs may not be met by differentiation alone.

This approach to assessment can be used when adopting a more themed approach to curriculum planning as long as all relevant outcomes are identified and, importantly, children are assessed accurately. Themed approaches of themselves do not cause assessment and tracking difficulties. It is the need to provide a curriculum framework with a high regard for continuity and progression that allows for accurate assessment to ensure that future learning builds on prior skills and knowledge. Children who are able or have specific talent may best exhibit these within the context of integrated learning and indeed may learn best within such a framework, but it is also necessary to assess and track progress by subject in order to tailor provision to needs. With the advent of more sophisticated assessment systems several years ago (e.g. APP), assessment of pupils, within the core subject of the National Curriculum at least, is changing. If its principles were extended to other aspects of the curriculum, it would support the assessment and tracking of progress of talented children further.

Perceived benefits of teaching and learning during themed weeks

The use of themed weeks has a number of advantages for both teacher and learner, and some of these are of particular benefit to the more able pupil. From discussion with pupils and staff at South Hykeham Community Primary School there was a consistency in outlook from children and adults interviewed regarding the perceived benefits of themed weeks:

> The context is memorable for children – it is an approach that sits outside traditional models of curriculum delivery and allows for children to make conceptual links more easily due to the rapid succession of lessons with a similar context. This allows children to make strong links between areas of learning and increases the opportunity to use higher order thinking skills and anecdotally, supported retention of learning.

> It allows for the study areas that don't fit with the planned curriculum – offering more opportunity to learn about what children can excel at. Improving identification of more able pupils in this way allows for better provision on an ongoing basis when talents have been recognised.

Themed weeks can allow for specialist teachers to work with children – this has a double advantage – the learner is being taught by someone with excellent subject knowledge, and the class teacher, in their role as observer, is able to use the opportunity to assess understanding more fully than if they were the facilitator for learning.

The change in routine allows for learning opportunities to change, lessons that would be started and finished to a fairly rigid timetable could be lengthened or shortened depending on need and children's interest. Diversions from plans are more acceptable in a week that would have a more fluid learning model than a typical primary school week.

Assessment of learning using a cross-curricular approach to teaching: the headteacher voice

The headteacher contributed the following insights into assessment for learning in this context:

> Opportunities for assessment can be seen as twofold – within the week and afterwards; the former allows the teacher to understand what the learner has absorbed into their existing understanding and the skills they have demonstrated or developed, whilst the latter is a consideration of the depth of learning from the week's outcomes. Almost all assessment will be formative in the sense that because learning is fluid in themed weeks it is the teacher's quality of questioning and observation that will inform them of what the learner can do, has achieved and has synthesised. This stresses the importance of good-quality teaching and assessment skills from the teacher.

An example of 'in week' assessment would be the application of learning from one session to another. In a dance and music week children were able to use evaluation skills developed in early sessions to compare dances that they were learning about; this skill was supported by the close succession of lessons, which in the planned curriculum would be at least a week apart in most non-core subjects.

Teachers were also able to identify skills that may be more difficult to identify or assess in the typical curriculum, e.g. where particular children demonstrated leadership skills evident because of the time allowed for projects to develop.

The use of specialist teachers during some themed weeks particularly supported class teachers who felt that they were able to take a step back from facilitating learning and observe their children in activities and when learning directly from the specialist. Formative assessment was aided by these opportunities, which are difficult to replicate when one becomes part of the teaching and learning.

Teachers felt more empowered to follow the interests of their children and in so doing were better able to assess their understanding and skills set. In addition they felt that the greater opportunity to set learning activities for mixed-ability groups developed the more able child's social and emotional skill set, and allowed the teacher to take a more holistic view of the child's development. More able children had opportunities to teach other pupils and also to not always be right and placed in situations where they had to persevere to succeed to a greater extent than at other times in the school year. Both the teaching of others and seeing where children have difficulties in their learning are key tools for assessment.

Teachers also identified skills and knowledge used after the themed weeks, which had been applied from learning within the themed week. An example from our music and drama week was that children are now able to create their own warm-ups and cool-downs based on what they had learned in themed weeks. Being aware of how children have learned from themed weeks gives teachers the opportunity to plan more effectively for their future learning needs.

A third, but no less important, feature of assessment opportunities in themed weeks is the opportunity for children to use and apply prior learning to different contexts. Where children are able to apply their knowledge and skills, learning becomes deeper. More able pupils were able, for example, to use their understanding of story settings in activities during a themed week. Understanding of how and where existing knowledge comes from again comes from a skilled teacher probing and questioning within the context of themed week activities.

Developing the concept

Themed weeks have enriched the curriculum at South Hykeham for a number of years now but are limited, through curriculum constraints, to three per year. We are starting to make more use of themed days, which have similar benefits to those outlined above and serve a particular purpose. An eco week, where each class had a day to focus on activities, was followed up by a whole-school celebration event and the Viking day (see above) consolidated learning from the previous term's topic. Both activities provided rich assessment opportunities. This shorter time commitment allows for more frequent opportunities to use the themed week model and retains a lot of the benefits outlined above.

Cross-curricular learning experiences: the pupil voice

Having discussed in some depth the way the curriculum for able and talented pupils is constructed both from the perspective of government policy and from the school's interpretation of that policy, it is pertinent to pause and ask: 'Is what we present to the children as a way of learning something that they can own and enjoy?'

A distinctive feature at South Hykeham is its readiness to hear the pupils' voices. We have a long tradition of school council activity, and a strong commitment to meeting pupils' own expressed needs. In order to discover the answer to the question posed above, the authors met originally with Y5/6 pupils in 2010 and replicated the discussion with a different set of Y5/6 pupils in 2014. A synopsis from both discussions is presented as Case Study 8.3, although the printed word hardly does justice to the way in which they articulated 'fun', 'exciting' and 'enjoyable'.

Case Study 8.3 The pupil voice in cross-curricular working

The children were invited to consider what they learned during the cross-curricular, themed weeks and how that was different from normal lessons:

> We learned things that we wouldn't have learned during ordinary lessons, because you didn't have time to go on to them, . . . take for example during the Money week, if we had not had a themed week we would probably have brushed on the currencies, we would have had say a single lesson [on currency] but during the themed week we had a whole time to study the currencies, so we were able to look at lots of currencies, not just one. (Michael)

> It helped build my confidence and it made me enjoy it a little bit more and with the art, it made me better at colouring inside the lines. It made me more careful. (Harry)

> A bit like Harry, because we had more time to focus on what we do, because if we have art we have like the afternoon but because time flies a lot and we don't get a lot done and we rush a lot and we don't get things finished and we have to carry over to the next day but because we have nearly the whole day to do it we have time to focus a bit more. (Bethany)

They then thought back to the most recent themed week: music and dance around the world. The authors had access to the coordinator's notes (see Figure 8.1–8.3), which indicated that she expected cross-curricular links to be made with:

- Art (mood paintings to music; portraits of composers)
- Geography (country/continent studied linked with around the world work)
- History (history of music/dance through the ages)
- Literacy (poetry inspired by music, research/reports linked with dance/music around the world)
- Maths (link with rhythms in songs/dances, graphs, e.g. favourite music/ musicians)
- Science (link with sound, e.g. pitch, making vegetable instruments).

Both in 2010 and 2014, the authors' conversation with the pupils took place some eight weeks after the event. The children were asked about skills they had learned to use during a themed week – first when they worked on their own, and second when they worked in groups:

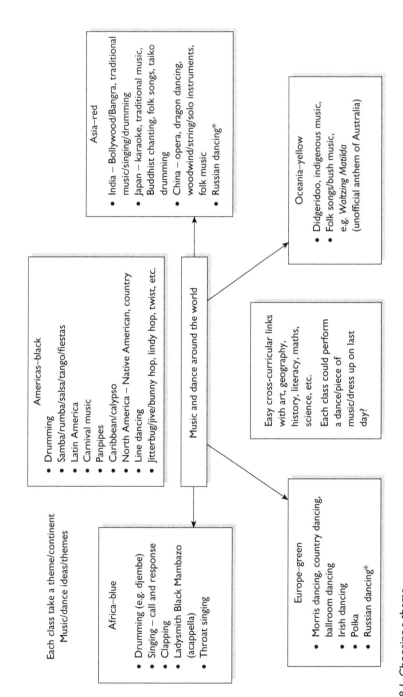

Each class take a theme/continent
Music/dance ideas/themes

Americas–black

- Drumming
- Samba/rumba/salsa/tango/fiestas
- Latin America
- Carnival music
- Panpipes
- Caribbean/calypso
- North America – Native American, country
- Line dancing
- Jitterbug/jive/bunny hop, lindy hop, twist, etc.

Asia–red

- India – Bollywood/Bangra, traditional music/singing/drumming
- Japan – karaoke, traditional music, Buddhist chanting, folk songs, taiko drumming
- China – opera, dragon dancing, woodwind/string/solo instruments, folk music
- Russian dancing*

Africa–blue

- Drumming (e.g. djembe)
- Singing – call and response
- Clapping
- Ladysmith Black Mambazo (acappella)
- Throat singing

Music and dance around the world

Easy cross-curricular links with art, geography, history, literacy, maths, science, etc.

Each class could perform a dance/piece of music/dress up on last day?

Europe–green

- Morris dancing, country dancing, ballroom dancing
- Irish dancing
- Polka
- Russian dancing*

Oceania–yellow

- Didgeridoo, indigenous music,
- Folk songs/bush music, e.g. *Waltzing Matilda* (unofficial anthem of Australia)

Figure 8.1 Choosing a theme

Music
Quizzes, classical music, games, songs, music from a certain era, making instruments, introduce children to a new piece of music a day, karaoke competition, composing own music/song, music from around the world

Literacy
Biographies of composers/pop stars, etc., poetry inspired by music, books you can sing along to, research/reports linked with dance/music around the world, 'wordles', instructions (i.e. for making instruments), film-based work linked with country/continent

History
History of music/dance around world/through ages

Maths
Link with rhythms in songs/dances, graphs, e.g. favourite music/musicians

Science
Link with sound, e.g. pitch, making vegetable instruments, animals/habitats around the world

Art
Mood paintings to music, portraits of composers, art from the continent/countries studied

PE
Dance through the ages/around the world, use of wii Zumba/wii fit/daily activate, dancing/exercising with guests

RE
Music/dance linked with certain religions, beliefs and practices linked with country/continent studied

Geography
Map work, country/continent study linked with around the world work

Figure 8.2 Subject dimensions

MON	TUES	WED	THURS
A.M.	A.M.	A.M.	A.M.
Zumba – Marissa Murray Reception, Y1/2, Y2/3	African dancing Reception, Y1/2, Y2/3	HALL FREE FOR PRACTISING DANCE/MUSIC READY FOR THURSDAY AFTERNOON	Tim Brain Brazilian Samba Drumming Short sessions with Reception and Y1/2 Longer sessions with Y2/3, Y4/5, Y5/6
P.M.	P.M.	P.M.	P.M.
Zumba – Marissa Murray Y4/5, Y5/6	African dancing Y4/5, Y5/6	Street Dance – 3 sessions Y1/2 children together Y3/4 children together Y5/6 children together	Hall free for end of week celebration

Figure 8.3 Timetable

> You use your heads instead of your mouth because you keep your ideas to your-self because you don't want people to take your ideas. On your own you are thinking of every possibility. It's harder on your own than in a group because you have to think of every possibility, the answer to the question, you've got to kind of rocket your brain about.
>
> (Michael)

Ben took the opposing view:

> Before we do anything we have to get everyone's ideas in the group.
>
> (Ben)

Eve provided clues to the way in which the children worked whether in a group or on their own:

> Miss Wynne always gives us little tips about what we could do, so that it makes our minds think.
>
> (Eve)

The pupils were asked, 'Do themed weeks excite you as a way of learning?'

> You get to do different things; you get to build up your confidence and it's like really, really fun. You get to work with your friends and if you don't know one idea you can get to ask your friends and they would like help you.
>
> (Ben)

And subsequently, 'Which themes would you like to investigate in the future?' The children thought long and hard about this, and their thinking progressed from the single strand of:

> I know that the children in reception are very young but it would be nice to look back over the year . . . to look at the moments with friends and see what they did . . . to look back at the teachers since you were in reception and see what they did . . . to thinking about the wider horizon and the part their school has played since it was opened in 1871.

> We could look at the different classes from when the school was built in 1871; look at the classes then . . .

The children were asked whether they knew of the existence of the school's log book.

> Yes. The headmaster's notebook where he says who arrived late today. We looked at it before . . .

> . . . with the name of the headmaster, the founder who built the school . . .

> . . . there was just our Victorian classroom, then there's the expansion and the names of the other classrooms like the mobile.
>
> (Bethany)

Suddenly, the switch was thrown and ideas came tumbling out, making the links with the present-day curriculum:

> You could look at the school 50 years ago and then from the year you started and you compare what the school was and the school now.
>
> (Bethany)

> You know the Victorian classroom has little marks saying that it is a Victorian classroom, you could look for other things that might show you signs of the school then.
>
> (Eve)

> Yes, it could be like history . . .

From a historical perspective, the children looked to the future:

> We could look to the future and design a new classroom . . . We could design the classroom of the future.
>
> (Eve)

Summing up the discussion, the author agreed that history, literacy and art could feature in their topic on the school's history, but asked 'What is the role of numeracy in this topic?'

> We could look at the numbers of children, measurement of physical well-being, a time-line over 10 years

> See how the teachers have changed

> Interview the different generations who have been here.

Mrs Read, the teaching assistant, suggested that children could follow the family tree of the generations who had attended the school. Some of the children were clearly enthused by this idea because their own parents had previously attended South Hykeham School. Carefully monitored, this would give the children a unique opportunity to pursue the 'Living Voice' philosophy and build a library of pupils' past and present experiences.

Conclusion

For young people growing up and entering the workplace in the late 2020s the need now is for teachers and educators to teach in such a way as to enable the next generation to adapt to changing situations in a rapidly changing world. Fostering creative thinking will allow them to root themselves in the future and, in order for them to be able to do this, they need to be taught creatively and across the spectrum of subjects. Their education needs to enable them to generate ideas, be inventive, imaginative, ingenious and innovative, and not to be afraid of the occasional error. No longer should their education be rooted in the 19th century, when children sat in rows and were fed upon a diet of 'facts' (see Chapter 14).

Einstein pre-dates the move towards creative teaching and teaching children to think rather than just listen; his understanding of knowledge is perhaps more pertinent today given that children leaving school now will still be shaping the world in 2050:

> Imagination is more important than knowledge. For knowledge is limited to all we now know and understand, while imagination embraces the entire world, and all there ever will be to know and understand.
>
> (http://www.goodreads.com/quotes)

References

Abela, A. (2014) 'Creativity in the primary classroom – teachers' responses to the use of children's creative ideas in classrooms'. Assignment in partial fulfilment of the MSc Education Leadership (Distance Learning) Regulations. Leicester: University of Leicester.

Alexander, R. (ed.) (2010) *Children, Their World, Their Education. Final Report and Recommendations of the Cambridge Primary Review*. Abingdon: Routledge.

Children and Families Act (2014) Available online at: http://www.legislation.gov.uk/ukpga/2014/6/contents/enacted (accessed 10 June 2014).

DCSF (2008a) *Effective Provision for Gifted and Talented Children in Primary Schools*. Nottingham: DCSF.

DCSF (2008b) *Identifying Gifted and Talented Learners – Getting Started*. Nottingham: DCSF.

De Bono, E. (1970) *Lateral Thinking. A Text Book of Creativity*. Harmondsworth: Penguin.

DfE (2013a) Available online at: http://www.education.gov.uk/vocabularies/educationtermsandtags/35 (accessed 7 February 2014).

DfE (2013b) *The National Curriculum in England. Key Stages 1 and 2 Framework Document*. London: DfE.

DfES (Department for Education and Science) (2005) *National Quality Standards for Gifted and Talented*. Nottingham: DfES.

DfES (Department for Education and Science) (2006) *2020 Vision Report of the Teaching and Learning in 2020 Review Group*. Nottingham: DfES Publications.

Duffy, B. (2006) *Supporting Creativity and Imagination in the Early Years*. Maidenhead: Open University Press.

Gardner, H. (1993) *Frames of Mind: The Theory of Multiple Intelligences* (2nd edn). London: Fontana.

Goleman, D. (1996) *Emotional Intelligence: Why It Can Matter More Than IQ*. London: Bloomsbury Publishing.

Grainger, T. and Barnes, J. (2006) 'Creativity in the primary curriculum', in Arthur, J. and Grainger, T. (eds) *Learning to Teach in the Primary School*. London: Routledge: 209–225.

Handy, C. (1997) *The Hungry Spirit*. London: Hutchinson.

Headington, R. (2003) *Monitoring, Assessment, Recording, Reporting and Accountability: Meeting the Standards* (2nd edn). London: David Fulton.

Henry, J. (2013) 'Brightest pupils failed by state schools, chief inspector warns'. *Daily Telegraph Online*, 25 January. Available online at: http://www.telegraph.co.uk/news/9828734/Brightest-pupils-failed-by-state-schools-chief-inspector-warns (accessed 10 February 2014).

HMI Wales (2011) *Supporting the More Able and Talented Pupils in Primary Schools*. Her Majesty's Inspectorate for Education and Training in Wales.

Hymer, B. with Michel, D. (2002) *Gifted and Talented Learners: Creating a Policy for Inclusion*. London: David Fulton.

Kerry, T. and Kerry, C. (2000) 'The centrality of teaching skills in improving able pupil education'. *Education Able Children* (Autumn): 13–19.

Lazear, D. (2004) *Multiple Intelligences Approach to Assessment*. Carmarthen: Crown House Publishing Ltd.

Pollard, A. (ed.) (2008) *Reflective Teaching – Evidence Informed Professional Practice*. London: Continuum.

Resnick, M. (2007) 'All I really need to know (about creative thinking) I learned (by studying how children learn) in kindergarten'. *Proceedings of the SIGCHI Conference on Creativity and Cognition*, Washington, DC.

Rudduck, J. and Flutter, J. (2004) *How to Improve Your School*. London: Continuum.

Smith, C. (2005) *Teaching Gifted and Talented Children in the Primary School: A Practical Guide*. London: Paul Chapman Publishing.

Sousa, D. A. (2003) *How the Gifted Brain Learns*. Ventura, CA: Corwin Press, Inc.

Timpson, E. (2014) Available online at: https://www.gov.uk/government/news/landmark-children-and-families-act-2014-gains-royal-assent.

Wallace, B., Fritton, S., Leyden, S., Montgomery, D., Pomerantz, M. and Winstanley, C. (2007) *Raising the Achievement of Gifted and Talented Pupils within an Inclusive School Framework*. Oxford: NACE/London: Gifted and Talented.

Wilshaw, Sir Michael (2013) Her Majesty's Chief Inspector, Letter to Schools, July.

Winstanley, C. (2006) *Inequity in Equity. Tackling the Excellence–Equality Conundrum*, in Smith, C. M. M. (ed.) *Including the Gifted and Talented. Making Inclusion Work for More Gifted and Able Learners*. Abingdon: Routledge: Ch. 2.

Internet sources

Children and Families Act 2014: http://www.legislations.gov.uk/ukpga/2014/6/contents/enacted (accessed 10 June 2014)

NSAED: http://www.nsaed.org/primary/national/research.aspx (accessed 8 February 2014)

Special Educational Needs and Disability Act 2001: http://www.legislation.gov.uk/ukpga/2001/10/pdfs_20010010_en.pdf (accessed 10 June 2014)

Chapter 9

The contribution of teaching assistants to cross-curricular learning

Strengths and issues

Pat Foulkes and Jill Wallis

Introduction

This chapter argues that the role of teaching assistants in schools' delivery of cross-curricular learning must be continuously monitored to ensure that their contribution is effective. Teaching assistants have a range of areas of strength in a cross-curricular approach and some exemplary case studies are used to illustrate these. However, the chapter also warns that key issues recurring in the management and deployment of teaching assistants must be addressed if their contribution in advancing pupils' learning is to be fully effective.

Background

There has been a dramatic rise in the number of teaching assistants working in English schools in recent years. Statistics from the Department for Education (2013a: 2) demonstrate that the number of full-time teaching assistants in publicly funded schools in England has risen substantially, from 79,000 in 2000 to 232,300 in November 2012. This represents a threefold increase and compares with an increase of only 8.9 per cent in teacher numbers over the same period. More recent figures (Department for Education 2014: 4) confirm this continuing upward trend with a 4.9 per cent increase in teaching assistants in the year November 2012–November 2013, noting that 'increases in the size of the school workforce are driven by increasing numbers of teaching assistants and school support staff'.

Much of this significant increase in numbers followed the Workforce Reform agreement in 2003: *Raising Standards and Tackling Workload*, which was largely designed to free teachers from more routine administrative tasks by transferring some areas of responsibility to support staff. As a result, teaching assistants became more involved in providing intervention support and focused learning support for small groups in class. The role has thus become increasingly more educational and more embedded in classrooms as an integral part of the teaching and learning support team: the 'partner paraprofessionals' foreseen by Kerry (2001: 35).

Increased training and career progression opportunities were subsequently introduced for those teaching assistants working directly to advance pupils' learning, including, in 2003, that of Higher Level Teaching Assistant (HLTA). The NFER research survey (Wilson *et al.* 2007: 91) concluded that the HLTA role was having a positive effect on pupil performance 'with almost three quarters of senior leaders identifying *supporting pupil learning* as the most significant impact of HLTAs in schools'.

However, the increase in numbers of teaching assistants also brought some areas of concern. A later report by Ofsted (2010: 10) recognised that the quality of the support for teaching and learning depended very much on class teachers' ability to manage teaching assistants effectively, and concluded 'It is a considerable challenge for teachers to direct the work of additional adults in the classroom.' Another issue noted by the Inspectors was that 'in nearly all the sessions of general support observed during the survey, teaching assistants worked with lower-attaining pupils or those most likely to disrupt the lesson', and that these pupils were more likely to be withdrawn from lessons and, as a consequence, 'they spent considerably less time than other pupils being taught by qualified teachers' (Ofsted 2010: 17). Similar findings were reported in the very influential, larger-scale research carried out by Blatchford *et al.* (2009a, 2009b), which reinforces the view of support staff deployment as consisting routinely of work with lower-attaining pupils and pupils with SENs, often removing pupils from the classroom for intervention support. Significantly their findings indicate 'a negative relationship between the amount of additional support provided by support staff and the academic progress of pupils' (Blatchford *et al.* 2009a: 129) with the key finding of the effect of support staff on pupils' academic progress as 'the more support pupils received, the less progress they made' (2009a: 34).

Such a conclusion raises considerable concerns, and Blatchford *et al.* consider some possible explanations, including the teaching assistants' lack of 'preparedness' (2009a: 138) because of problems in ensuring sufficient time for planning with the teacher and gaps in the teaching assistants' subject and pedagogic knowledge. They conclude by stating that 'we do not want to give the impression that support staff do not have an important role to play', but feel that 'problems may have arisen from assuming that extra support will lead to positive outcomes for pupils without first establishing a clear understanding and view of the role of support staff' (2009a: 140). The assumption that the mere presence of an extra adult working with one pupil or a small group will automatically advance learning has thus been challenged and has resulted in some schools taking a more critical review of their deployment of teaching assistants, in part further fuelled by the controversial report published by the 'Think Tank' *Reform* (Thorpe, Trewhitt and Zuccollo 2013), one of whose recommendations is that 'Ministers should support schools that reduce numbers of teaching assistants' (2013: 17). Partly based on evidence from the report by Blatchford *et al.*, the *Reform* authors justify the recommendation for a reduction in numbers of teaching assistants on the conclusion of their 'negligible impact on pupil progress, though some impact on teacher productivity' (2013: 16). The effect of such a recommendation was considerable and resulted in national newspaper headlines such as that in the *Daily Mail* (3 June 3013): 'Army of teaching assistants faces the axe as Education department attempts to save some of the £4billion they cost each year', and a subsequent internet campaign to resist cuts in teaching assistant numbers.

A follow-up study by Blatchford, Webster and Russell (2012), designed to address some of the issues identified in their earlier report about teaching assistants' wider pedagogical role, found that, by working in collaboration with target schools, they were able to develop and evaluate alternative strategies for teaching assistant deployment that resulted in 'marked and productive changes to the deployment of TAs at the classroom level'. They noted that 'perhaps for the first time TAs were encouraged to adopt the pedagogical goal that interactions with pupils should be about understanding, *not* task completion' (2012: 3) and that, particularly in primary schools, there was a shift so that teaching assistants were spending more time working with middle and high-attaining pupils (2012: 36). This study demonstrates that, by taking a more strategic view of school policy in the deployment of teaching assistants, schools could 'challenge entrenched, unhelpful mindsets towards the use of TAs' (2012: 3).

The debate about the effectiveness of teaching assistant support may continue, but there is general underlying consensus with the research studies reiterating the same key recommendations: that teaching assistants need appropriate training and continuing professional development for their enhanced wider pedagogical role; that teachers need to be trained to manage the deployment of teaching assistants so that the teacher maintains responsibility for all pupils in their class; that schools must review their deployment policies for teaching assistants, and ensure time is scheduled for teachers and teaching assistants to prepare together.

It is therefore imperative, when reviewing the role of teaching assistants in supporting all aspects of the curriculum, that the contribution they offer should be continuously re-examined and their role in the process of a cross-curricular approach should be carefully managed for that contribution to be fully effective.

In Special Schools there is already evidence of good practice both in valuing and managing learning support assistants (LSAs), and also in maximising productive learning time through a personalised and often thematic approach. As Halliwell (2003: 36) found, in Special Schools 'assistants are often the persons most frequently involved in the daily implementation of a programme or in the use of specific resources'. The potential contribution of teaching assistants and learning support assistants to an innovative cross-curricular approach is wide ranging and multifaceted. They can bring a wide range of personal skills and enthusiasms to the planning and delivery of integrated and thematic learning, building on and complementing the skills of teachers, and can foster positive attitudes to learning. With many having followed a different career path to that of qualified teachers, teaching assistants often have a different perspective and life experience to those of the class teacher, which may open up new ideas and possibilities. Simply having another adult involved in the planning process can generate ideas and encourage creativity. The workload in preparation and planning is also shared and can be distributed according to particular areas of interest. Kerry (2001: 75) highlights the fact that a teaching assistant in the classroom provides 'not just another pair of hands, but another pair of eyes, ears and an informed brain', which can be harnessed to advance learning.

Greater opportunities for interactive learning and activities such as role-play and practical experiments can be offered through the teamwork of teacher and teaching assistant. Mindham (2004) has identified the positive impact of the wider range of experiences these approaches may offer: 'By involving a variety of tasks and valuing skills beyond those associated only with the core curriculum we enable all children to feel a sense of pride in their achievements.'

During the learning activities the presence of another supporting adult also helps with behaviour management if an excitingly different activity is planned; and it allows the exploration of more potentially 'risky' activities, resources and environments. In identifying the positive aspects of teaching assistant support, Blatchford et al. (2009a: 2) found that, for less able pupils in particular, 'the more support received, the lower their distractibility and disruption and the better their relationships with peers, being independent and following instructions'.

Teaching assistants may also have a wide range of links with the local community and may be able to draw on a network of local support for visits or they may have an awareness of key personnel locally who could be approached for their involvement. 'The local community directly influences the pupils' lives and there is much to be gained from furthering closer interaction, links and liaison between school and community. The community is also a rich resource for support staff with valuable local knowledge' (Campbell 2005: 131).

Case Study 9.1 A history theme

When involved in planning a thematic approach in history through the Great Fire of London, the teaching assistant had the exciting idea that a real fire would really engage the pupils' interest and she suggested creating a London street (D&T) and then setting fire to it (science). She was able to enlist the support of the local fire brigade for safety (her brother-in-law was a local fire officer) and thus the learning was extended to links to 'People who help us'. Learning objectives in art (painting the frieze of houses to be burned), literacy (writing newspaper reports), and ICT for historical research and presentation of the newspaper account were all developed. There was a key focus on involving all year groups in the themed project as part of vertical grouping, and pupils from Year 1 helped in the production of 'houses' while Year 6 interviewed and were interviewed through role-play as house owners and newspaper reporters. Parents were kept informed of the school 'fire' and were invited to attend. They were also canvassed for props and materials for D&T.

Kirtlan (in Walton and Goddard 2009: 129) recognises the importance of teaching assistant support in a creative curriculum and the guidance they provide for pupils to 'begin their learning journey'. However, she cites Watkinson's warning that teaching assistants must 'provide the scaffolding, not build the complete tower'.

Teaching assistants often have more opportunity to personalise learning by getting to know each pupil's interests and being aware of potential barriers to their engagement in learning. A child may well have more opportunity to confide in a teaching assistant who works more regularly with them or provides individual support so the teaching assistant can plan ahead to remove any possible barriers to inclusion in integrated learning. Their awareness of the quiet, 'invisible' child can ensure an appropriate strategy is planned to provide them with equality of access to learning experiences and to enable them to demonstrate skills in a range of learning. A teaching assistant's potentially greater awareness of a pupil's home background can also minimise potential barriers to an interactive learning experience.

Case Study 9.2 Inclusion

The school was planning a book week with themed characters involved in drama, in literacy (by developing the characters and story lines), and in art through display work. The first day in Reception Class was planned for pupils to dress up as characters from *Peter Pan* and talk about them, and then enact the story for the rest of the school. The teaching assistant was aware that some pupils might not have support at home for creating the costumes and so she produced a spare set of basic costumes (pirates and fairies) that could be offered to any pupils who arrived without their own costumes, enabling them to be fully included in the learning activities.

Teaching assistants can themselves be a valuable resource of unexpected skills and interests. A passion for music, art or cookery can be exploited to support a range of integrated learning opportunities. Teaching assistants may also be more representative of the local community than many of the teaching staff in terms of their ethnic and cultural backgrounds. Thus they may be more aware of cultural issues and become a valuable source of advice.

Case Study 9.3 Multiculturalism

A teaching assistant who was originally from Poland was working in a multicultural urban primary school and she suggested that, as part of an integrated approach, the school should plan a year-long celebration of languages represented by the school community. She offered to plan a calendar so that each week represented a different global or community language, and she involved any pupils fluent in that language to teach the rest of the school basic greetings for registration, polite exchanges and the numbers 1–5 which were to be used throughout the school for that week. The teaching assistant researched key phrases on the internet and produced displays that were changed weekly to reinforce the vocabulary. She also copied photographs and taped music from the part of the world represented, to be played in the school entrance.

Case Study 9.4 Bilingual teaching assistants

In a large primary in an inner-city area, with a multi-ethnic student intake, bilingual teaching assistants were deployed to work with recent arrivals and those with significant vocabulary issues as a result of having English as an additional language (EAL). In one unit, the book *The Mousehole Cat* was being used as the basis of a range of cross-curricular lessons. These included drawing maps of the area in the story, with accurate placing and labelling of key places; measuring distances between some of these features; writing diary entries for key characters; and writing recipes for characters' favourite foods.

One teaching assistant involved in this series of lessons was bilingual and was allocated to a group of pupils whose mother tongue she spoke. In addition, she and the teacher had designed a range of visual aids to assist pupils. For example, illustrations from the book were copied and laminated, with labels, for key features in the story such as the harbour, various characters' houses, and key geographical features. These were always available as props on the table, and the teaching assistant also asked or answered questions in the mother tongue to ensure pupils could understand the tasks. Thus the key learning objectives could be met by students provided they understood the vocabulary being used. The use of teaching assistant language support and the visual prompts made the lesson accessible to them.

Teaching assistants may be creative and skilled in producing learning materials or displays to celebrate pupils' work. They may have more time available than teachers for designing and producing interactive displays throughout the school to support school themes. They can help in the production of props and costumes. A teaching assistant, trained in ICT skills in previous employment and aware of the wide range of resources available to support learning, can become a real enthusiast and may choose to explore school themes in integrated learning for personal development and understanding.

When considering the contribution that can be made to teaching and learning by teaching assistants and other support staff, the greater focus of the new National Curriculum on subject knowledge may cause concern, given that teaching assistants historically have tended to have lower levels of qualification than teachers and are not required to be qualified to graduate level.

However, new curriculum demands, such as the requirement for Modern Foreign Languages (MFL) teaching in primary schools from 2014 (DfE 2013b), can be equally challenging for fully qualified teaching staff, whose training or previous qualifications often did not include such subjects.

Under these circumstances, schools may wish to look closely at the qualifications and life experiences of their support staff. As previously mentioned, in many schools with high populations of children with EAL, teaching assistants may well have been employed as second-language support staff, and may have a range of language skills not shared by teaching staff. In some cases support staff may also have formal language qualifications higher than existing staff, even if not as qualified teachers.

Case Study 9.5 Learning languages

A student completing a BA (Hons) in Educational Practice, focusing her research project on Action Research into her experience in one Bedfordshire primary school, researched and evaluated an initiative to introduce several languages to children in both Key Stages 1 and 2, which involved several teaching assistants and an HLTA (herself) who had first language knowledge, or had completed qualifications in a MFL, which equalled or exceeded the expertise available in the full-time teaching team. In the case of the student involved, this included a degree in European Business Studies and A-levels in French and Spanish. This allowed a very successful programme to be instigated, which her research showed was warmly received by staff, pupils and parents. Teaching assistants drawn from the local community may also be more likely to share the first languages of others coming from overseas to live in the area, especially in the case of recent and locally grouped arrivals, and this may not only allow a wider range of languages to be offered, but also give status to the first language(s) of recently arriving pupils and families with EAL. In the example quoted above, those interviewed reported a strong sense that learning had been a two-way process, with children being able to contribute on occasion as the experts.

Potential pitfalls to be managed for effective deployment of teaching assistants

While earlier examples highlight a range of ways teaching assistants can contribute to the effectiveness of integrated learning, their role in the process needs to be carefully managed.

Planning

It is even more essential in the potentially more complex creative curriculum sessions that teaching assistants are fully involved in planning processes for integrated learning. They may be able to cope with individual discrete lessons in particular subjects without being involved in the planning but merely being told their role in a brief aside prior to the lesson, although this should not happen in a professional relationship. As mentioned earlier, Blatchford *et al.* (2009a: 133) identify a lack of *preparedness* as one of the key facets in limiting teaching assistant effectiveness in advancing pupils' learning: 'a lack of meaningful time for joint planning and preparation before, and for feedback and reflection after, lessons . . . means the potential for effective pedagogical involvement reduced'. Moreover, the complexity of the learning objectives in integrated learning means that a teaching assistant who has not been part of the planning cannot be expected to support the learning to greatest effect. Teaching assistants need to understand the underpinning skills and range of learning objectives in order to support pupils in developing those skills.

There could be a danger that the teaching assistant has a rather superficial view of an integrated learning activity and, in some instances, may lack the necessary breadth of subject knowledge and pedagogic understanding of the key aspects on which pupils need to build. It is the role of the class teacher to make the learning explicit for the teaching assistant and in doing so to facilitate pupil learning.

Subject knowledge

It is important to recognise that entry qualifications for teaching assistants are not the same as those of qualified teachers who must be graduates and must have completed teacher training to be awarded Qualified Teacher Status. Blatchford *et al.* (2009a: 134) make the point that, since teaching assistants are likely to have a less advanced subject knowledge in comparison to teachers, 'it seems commonsensical for them to be deployed with the lower attaining pupils, where the level of work is at a more rudimentary level'. However, they then highlight the consequence that 'the pupils in most need are often supported by staff with lower levels of subject knowledge, compared to teachers'.

Lack of subject specific knowledge might perhaps be considered to be less of a problem for teaching assistants working in the primary and early years sectors. However, this assumption can be dangerous if teachers expect that their teaching assistant, albeit with a good general educational background (perhaps from schooling completed some years ago), is automatically able to cope with the concepts and vocabulary required for the range of subjects in the primary curriculum of today and particularly with a cross-curricular approach.

Case Study 9.6 Resources to support subject knowledge

One primary class teacher demonstrated good practice in ensuring that her teaching assistant was enabled to effectively support the learning of the more able group she was working with by her careful advance planning. She became aware that the teaching assistant, as a mature adult, was unfamiliar with some of the more recent changes in the primary curriculum (phonics, grammar, new mathematical vocabulary and operations, etc.) but she was sensitive to raising this concern directly with the teaching assistant. The class teacher was a Newly Qualified Teacher and she used her own recent experience of training for teaching areas of the curriculum that were new to her in order to support her teaching assistant. So she introduced a series of key concept guides and glossary cards, initially for English and mathematics and intended primarily to allow the more able children to work independently and to reinforce key learning across curriculum areas. The joint production of the cards facilitated a discussion with the teaching assistant and the assistant was encouraged to suggest any additions she felt would also be useful, so this provided the opportunity for clarification in a professional way. The cards were then laminated and made available in class as an immediate and easy aide-memoire.

As referred to earlier, the new National Curriculum was introduced by the Prime Minister as 'tough and rigorous' (2013: online). Largely this has meant a greater focus on facts and retention. This has raised concerns with some teachers, both in terms of the speed of introduction and the overlap of the old and new curricula, while existing examination schedules run their course, and the greater demands on both pupils and teachers. This may cause particular concern for schools depending heavily on teaching assistants, who may not be reasonably expected to have the same level of subject knowledge as qualified teachers. In some areas, such as the increased focus on grammar teaching or the introduction of MFL, even well-qualified teachers may find themselves teaching content they are not comfortable with or fully qualified in. The clash between the requirement for primary teachers to be both generalists covering a wide range of subjects and, increasingly, experts in many of them is challenging for individuals and schools. However schools tackle this, whether by increased delivery of subjects by specialists, at ever lower age groups, the use of peripatetic staff, the sharing of expertise with secondary schools they may be teamed with, or use of both internal and external training courses, the fact remains that maximising the expertise of each member of staff is likely to be crucial.

Training and development

The Ofsted report (2010: 5) found there was 'a huge variation in the knowledge, expertise and abilities of support staff'. Senior managers must therefore ensure that they are aware of all their staff's expertise in order to most effectively utilise that expertise for pupils' benefit. It is becoming more routine for support staff to be involved in school staff appraisal procedures and this process can form the basis for a staff database of subject knowledge and experiences, as well as identifying key areas for professional development and training.

It is interesting that immediately after Workforce Reform the training of support staff (including initiatives for formal induction programmes for all teaching assistants and Higher Level Teaching Assistant training and assessment) was promoted and relatively generously funded by central government. However, this funding ceased following the change of government in 2010. The HLTA National Partnership (2012), which assumed responsibility for the continuation of HLTA assessment in 2012, estimates that nearly 50,000 teaching assistants have attained the status since 2003, which clearly demonstrates the commitment of such staff in working to gain the status, their desire for career progression and the experience they have in meeting the HLTA professional standards.

Schools are now expected to arrange for and to fund their own support staff training as part of good management in schools, but the national impetus in leading this development is no longer seen as a funded priority in raising standards in schools.

Resources preparation

An enthusiastic teaching assistant, particularly one who has contributed a key idea to the planning, may go to extremes in researching and preparing materials: enthusiasm needs to be tempered with a realistic view of the impact on learning. A teaching assistant may not share the teacher's professional training, experience and judgement in such matters. In addition, a teaching assistant may feel partly responsible for the success of such a planned activity and may focus heavily on the stimulus and excitement rather than the learning outcomes. Thus, discussions of assessment criteria and learning outcomes should also be part of the initial shared planning. Furthermore, one activity, even one in which a period of integrated lessons has culminated, should not require an unrealistic amount of advance preparation and should be balanced against the other curriculum needs of the school.

Similarly, a teaching assistant may volunteer to be involved in arranging trips and recruiting visitors to support an area of integrated learning such as a museum trip or a geography field trip, or inviting a visitor to school to talk about their occupation. The administration and organisation of such visits can be onerous, and occasionally the learning intention can be lost in the search for an exciting out-of-school experience. Pupils may remember the drama of the event, or sometimes even the gift shop, rather than the intended learning. Again it is important for the manager of the teaching assistants to remind them of the need to keep the focus on the learning intention, which can sometimes be met more effectively by a simple activity.

Case Study 9.7 Parity of access

As part of her final-year degree project, one teaching assistant in a school for pupils with profound and multiple learning difficulties (PMLD) chose to investigate the parity of access of pupils in the school to outside trips and visits, and the potential value of such trips for all. It was her perception that those in wheelchairs in particular were often excluded, and also that there was inconsistent use of such visits across the age range. Through questionnaires she gathered staff perceptions of the value and practicality of trips into the local community and to settings such as parks and zoos. Staff were overwhelmingly positive about the range of benefits offered by such outings, but also expressed concerns, particularly about staffing such trips safely and accessing appropriate transport. She gained permission to take out one trip a week for two terms with her class of eight pupils, who had a range of severe disabilities and included several wheelchair-bound pupils. Her research showed that issues affecting the success of the trips were almost entirely practical – mainly linked to the time taken to load and disembark students, which then cut in to the relatively short total time available for the trips. However, she also found that when she was allowed to use the same two staff for each trip, and undertook some specific training with them in managing wheelchair handling, working with the minibus used for the trips, the time taken to embark and disembark was significantly reduced and the trips began to gain in visible results. She was able to show that staff concerns regarding pupils' ability to cope with the different environments and stimuli were almost entirely unfounded and that, during a range of trips by bus or walking, to places including local lakes, garden centres, farms, museums and parks, no significant issues or problems were experienced.

In addition, pupils with severe physical and cognitive impairment experienced a wider range of activities and experiences than would otherwise be the case, and some demonstrated improvements in engagement, behaviour and achievement of P-level targets. For one pupil, the difference in her confidence and attitude was marked. For all pupils the project allowed them access to a range of experiences previously denied them, with the attendant benefits well evidenced in research (Fox and Avramidis 2003; Ofsted 2008; Skates 2013), and ensured greater parity of provision with other, less disabled, pupils. The success of the intervention depended heavily on a high staff-to-pupil ratio and on the same, increasingly experienced and confident, group of teaching assistants undertaking the trips, and building their own and their pupils' confidence and expertise in managing the practical challenges of such a venture. The results of the project enabled the teaching assistant to approach the headteacher to recommend an extension of the trip provision across the setting.

TA strengths, skills and enthusiasms

Campbell (2005: 128) highlights the importance of playing to everyone's strengths in school and the value of flexibility. She quotes one headteacher:

> You can't afford for teachers not to have strengths in core areas of maths and literacy but with support workers like Miss X you can use her expertise in sport and community work almost exclusively. You have a lot more flexibility about using the expertise of support workers.

A teaching assistant can gain considerable job satisfaction from the feeling of contributing expertise to a topic and from recognition of that expertise by professional colleagues. The HMI report (2002: 18) reviewing the impact of the work of teaching assistants concludes 'making the most of [teaching assistants'] abilities should certainly not threaten the professionalism of teachers; rather it should be encouraged and developed to the full'.

Case Study 9.8 Using teaching assistants' skills effectively

In an average-sized urban primary school, a Year 4 group experienced a cross-curricular week in which teachers and teaching assistants worked together to provide a range of experiences with a new school garden as a central resource. One teaching assistant who was a keen gardener brought in a range of plants for a science session, demonstrating directly the key aspects of plant biology by allowing children to remove plants from their pots and examine in detail their parts, matching these with the diagrams they had been given. The plants were later planted out in the garden and monitored, to extend pupils' knowledge of the cycle of growth and life cycles.

While an enthusiastic teaching assistant with a passion for creativity and a desire to be involved in resource preparation can be a much appreciated asset, occasionally enthusiasms need to be curbed and this has to be managed sensitively by the class teacher, otherwise it will place a strain on this important relationship. A careful teacher overview is needed to rein in enthusiasm and keep the focus on learning though experience, rather than just the experience.

Special Schools and the integrated curriculum

One setting where the creative curriculum, topic-based learning and extensive integration of support staff can often be seen at its best is in the Special School. There are a number of reasons for this.

First, most, if not all, pupils have Individual Education Plans, and very fully defined needs and targets. Inevitably, the range of their skills and academic achievement is narrower, and progress is much slower and more precisely defined, and thus, perhaps, easier for staff to monitor. For less academically qualified staff, as many teaching assistants are, curriculum subject knowledge is less likely to be a stumbling block than in mainstream classes, although this is more than balanced by the medical and SEN understanding and expertise they may need to have. However, the severity of those very needs often means that teaching assistants in Special Schools are more likely to have had specific training for working with the pupils for whom they are responsible and are often working more closely with teaching colleagues. As Murray (2009: 14) comments, teaching assistants' work in Special Schools 'can require in-depth knowledge and understanding of a wide range of learning and physical disabilities'. She points out that such teaching assistants are also more likely than mainstream teaching assistant colleagues to have teaching responsibilities.

Second, because pupils' learning is so often severely constrained by their needs and difficulties, considerable ingenuity is needed to design activities that meet the curriculum requirements yet are accessible to the pupils.

Third, short concentration spans and significant loss of teaching time for medical or toileting interventions mean a need to be creative about using activities not necessarily obviously academic in focus for curriculum delivery.

Fourth, pupil targets are often focused on personal development and early communication or engagement skills at the bottom or middle of P-levels, and these tend to lend themselves to a wider range of activities than more curriculum-specific learning objectives.

Finally, in some settings, the needs of the children can lead to there being one member of staff for every child in a group, with those staff members, be they teacher or teaching assistant, taking significant responsibility for their pupil during the lesson as the teachers cannot leave their own charge unsupervised to monitor all the other pupils and staff. This also means teaching assistants are more closely involved in training, planning and curriculum and assessment meetings, decisions and implementation than is the norm in mainstream settings. Murray quotes a Special School teaching assistant who comments, 'You're part of a classroom team where everyone has specific skills to offer' (2009: 14).

All of these factors lead to lessons where many curriculum areas and skills may be covered, albeit at a limited level, and where consolidation may occur even when the intended activity breaks down or is suspended to allow for pastoral or medical care to be administered. Special School staff in the observed setting had often developed, or even planned, excellent spur-of-the-moment adaptations to the original plan to maximise learning when things change.

In addition, because of the need to capture small achievements and keep close records of these, and because the one-to-one work makes this possible, Special Schools often have well-developed informal as well as formal assessment methods. These may include photographs (as some skills being recorded may be physical or related to facial expression), post-it notes quickly written and later attached to pupil records, and shared achievement feedback during plenaries. These are often the only ways in which such students can have some experience of self-assessment – or at least of assessment in which they can take some part, as the comments are usually made by the teaching assistant, referring to what the child has done – for example, 'Tim managed to do all the actions for that song, didn't you, Tim?' Also, during activities, teachers and teaching assistants frequently make very specific assessment for learning and give formative feedback directly to students, such as 'Good signing, Abdul', 'Good watching, Louise.' Halliwell emphasises the need for teaching assistants in Special Schools to be trained to support, differentiate, assess and record progress, and indeed suggests that experienced teaching assistants may well be used to 'model how to deliver an intervention programme or use a specific resource' (2003: 15).

In each of the following case studies, some at least of the elements above were in evidence.

Case Study 9.9 Maximising learning experiences

In School A, a student also studying for a part-time degree completed her research project into the time 'lost' to curriculum delivery because of breaks for medical or toileting care. She found that those staff who felt most satisfied with their ability to deliver the curriculum were those who had developed strategies to extend learning into those areas – for example, by counting the tiles in the toilet area to continue a mathematics session, or identifying colours of clothes, or continuing to sing the songs being used in the main lesson, or practising fastening clothing. As it was often teaching assistants who did toileting tasks, this had become a well-developed skill in those whose teachers had seen the advantage of working in this way, or who had themselves seen the opportunities. The research recommendation was that the school should formalise this by identifying explicitly in planning ways in which such intervals in the school day could be used, and linking key skills to specific activities.

Case Study 9.10 Capturing teaching assistants' expertise

In the same school, a teaching assistant with musical skills was invited to attend a session in Foundation Stage to play songs for the children to engage in. Songs with interactive components and repetitive refrains were used to maximise pupils' engagement and to assess their ability to predict, to make deliberate movements and choices, and to engage with others. Pupils were also encouraged to take turns to communicate, in some cases using electronic methods, or signing whether they wanted the songs to be loud or quiet, or to be fast or slow. Teaching assistants worked with each child, in some cases holding them on their laps to assist or control movement, and ensured that each was encouraged and supported to take part. Further skills, such as turn-taking and listening to others, were also developed. It would not have been possible for the children to be engaged and enabled in this way without the one-to-one support of the class teaching assistants or the musical skills of the visiting teaching assistant. Very specific assessment was also possible because of the close observation, including of small voluntary movements, each could make of their pupil.

Case Study 9.11 Personalised learning and assessment

In a lesson with a focus on 'pushing and pulling', a group of Key Stage 1 children functioning at low P-levels was enabled to take part in a range of interactive and kinaesthetic activities by the presence and support of several support staff. Thus, one child who could not walk or do active tasks was helped to pull brightly coloured materials through a tube, emphasising through signing the actions of pushing and pulling, and was able to demonstrate her understanding by changing her actions. In addition, communication skills and colour recognition were developed by continuous and repetitive commentary, with signing, by the teaching assistant. Meanwhile another teaching assistant worked with a child who was mobile but who required close monitoring, having epilepsy and ADHD among other special needs, to assist him to use a seesaw, ride a bike and roll on a large ball, again using the key vocabulary and being assessed through his actions and signs. The teacher worked with two other children with other special needs to help them use the seesaw, which they could not do without support. Yet another child, able to work with some independence, was pushing a pram, and being monitored and interacted with by whichever staff member she came towards.

Case Study 9.12 Use of space and detailed assessment

In another activity with the same group of children with Profound or Moderate Learning Difficulties, the class was divided into two groups by ability and moved into separate rooms to allow less distraction, and to provide smaller spaces for staff to supervise. The teacher mainly worked in one room with a teaching assistant, but also supervised the work in the adjoining room where two teaching assistants supported pupils. As a result these children, several of whom had mobility problems as well as short concentration spans and limited or no communication skills, were enabled to develop their mathematical skills in the area of data handling. They used playdough, tea sets, bags of varied objects and other resources to work on colour, counting, sorting and other related tasks, while also working continuously on their communication skills, following instructions and, where possible, signing or speaking key words. With these children, learning takes place in tiny increments and may consist of a recognisable, but momentary, attempt to reproduce a recognised sign such as 'more' or 'red'. It is only the close one-to-one work that not only allows the opportunities for these pupils to experience learning opportunities but also allows for their small and intermittent increments of learning to be observed and recorded. It is common policy also for a teaching assistant to take photographs of activities to capture children's engagement and achievement, not only for recording purposes but also to share with parents and carers.

In mainstream schools, the role of teaching assistants may differ somewhat, although Blatchford *et al.* (2009a: 60) found that 'TAs spent the majority of their time supporting low ability/SEN pupils, and rarely worked with high and middle ability pupils', and so much of the experience of Special School teaching assistants will be similar to that of teaching assistants in mainstream schools. Hughes adds that other aspects of the difference between the role of the teacher and the teaching assistant can have an impact on pupils' learning, as teaching assistants can be more relaxed in their interaction, and can act as 'valuable providers of help; promoting opportunities for collaborative work . . . and creating a secure setting for the pupils to reflect on what is being learned' (1997: 108), free from the whole-class management issues that may prevent the class teacher from providing this for all pupils.

Conclusion

Whether in a mainstream or Special School setting, there seem to be some criteria linked to success that might be pointers for all schools to consider when planning both the use of a creative curriculum and good practice in deployment of support staff. Key issues seem to be as follows.

- The need for close involvement of teaching assistants in planning, in shared approaches to achieving learning outcomes and in assessment of learning. The effective implementation of such involvement is identified as a key difficulty by Smith, Whitby and Sharp (2004): 'The main difficulty associated with working with teaching assistants was the lack of time teachers and teaching assistants had to prepare together.'
- Little progress seems to have been made in this area to date, as evidenced in the research cited earlier by Blatchford *et al.* and their concerns about teaching assistants' lack of 'preparedness' (2009a: 138). The fact that teaching assistants are typically part-time staff can aggravate the situation and they may find that they are present for parts of the initial planning but miss key elements because of their timetabled hours. A key finding from the Ofsted evaluation of the impact of workforce reform was that 'Collaborative planning between teachers and support staff, a shared understanding of what constituted good learning, and the direct involvement of support staff in assessing and recording pupils' progress led to more effective classroom support and intervention' (2010: 5).
- A positive perception of the value and status of support staff. We are now, thankfully, well distanced from Balshaw's (1999) description of the class teacher perception of adult support staff as a 'spy in the classroom'. In complete contrast, Blatchford *et al.* (2009a: 123) report: 'One of the most notable results from the study has been the positive effect of support staff on teachers', with reported positive impact on teacher workload and teachers being 'quite clear that their job satisfaction was positively affected by support staff' and two-thirds of teachers saying that 'support staff led to a decrease in stress'.
- The need for appropriate high-quality training for teaching assistants in relevant skills and subject knowledge. A further key finding from Blatchford *et al.* (2009a: 134) was that 'more often TAs' subject knowledge did not match that of teachers', and the teaching assistants' wider pedagogical role needed to be supported by training and continuing professional development.
- Teaching assistants' involvement in close analysis of pupil skills and needs, leading to good personalised learning with the information and processes shared among all staff. Blatchford *et al.* (2009a: 137) found that 'TAs tended to be more concerned with the completion of tasks rather than learning and understanding.' More opportunities for professional dialogue with the teacher as part of lesson preparation would enable the teaching assistant to be more aware of ways to develop pupils' understanding.
- Detailed curriculum mapping against activities in order both to identify opportunities for delivery and also to ensure clear understanding by all of exactly what is or can be delivered and how learning can be advanced.
- Detailed and highly informed summative assessment of progress by staff who know their pupils very well and are very clear about the opportunities offered by the lesson or series of lessons, including spotting incidental or unplanned learning opportunities.
- Clear success criteria for attainment and achievement, which feeds in to self and peer assessment of learning with assessment systems that allow for quick and on-the-spot recording of achievement, and continuous sharing of this with other colleagues to ensure progress is tracked.

- Explicit management of staff involvement with a realistic appraisal of cost effectiveness of effort involved in some thematic projects.
- Awareness of the impact of differences in contractual arrangements. Teaching assistants may have a range of diverse roles or job descriptions and different line managers – for example, they may act as classroom support, learning mentor, cover for planning, preparation and assessment (PPA) as an HLTA, midday supervisor or after-school club manager. This diversity in roles can militate against easy line management and clarity of priorities in supporting learning.
- Continuing changes in the school culture. Schools have now largely adapted to the workforce remodelling and will be changing to accommodate the new National Curriculum, while maintaining a positive approach to a creative and integrated curriculum, which may necessitate a review of roles and responsibilities between support and teaching staff.
- Training for teachers in working with teaching assistants. This was identified in Blatchford *et al.* (2009a: 133) as a contributory factor in problems in ensuring pupil attainment under teaching assistant support. They recommend that 'a substantial component of all teacher training courses should involve ways of working successfully with support staff', and stress the need to 'consider in a systematic way the management of TA deployment in relation to managerial, pedagogical and curriculum concerns'.

Special Schools may be able to address some of these management issues more easily as they tend to be facilitated by low pupil–adult ratios and by very small teaching groups. There may be more of a challenge in mainstream settings, but approaches that work should not be rejected out of hand just because they are difficult to deliver, or, indeed, adopted in situations where key success predictors cannot be met. On the other hand, they do identify some of the areas of potential challenge for the effective deployment of teaching assistants in the creative curriculum design, delivery and assessment. If, however, these issues are managed in a constructive and developmental way, the creative curriculum for the 21st century is more likely to meet Rose's view (2009), recognising that 'the new curriculum must be underpinned by an understanding of the distinct but interlocking ways in which children learn and develop'. This needs to be understood by all those involved in the delivery of that curriculum to ensure a holistic approach to advancing learning and utilising the skills of the whole school workforce through a well-managed approach and shared understandings.

References

Balshaw, M. (1999) *Help in the Classroom*. London: David Fulton.
Blatchford, P., Webster, R. and Russell, A. (2012) *Challenging the Role and Deployment of Teaching Assistants in Mainstream Schools: The Impact on Schools. Final Report on the Effective Deployment of Teaching Assistants* (EDTA) project. London: Institute of Education and Esmee Fairbairn Foundation. Available online at: http://www.teachingassistantresearch.co.uk/download/i/mark_dl/u/4012366993/4603695748/edtareport (accessed 18 May 2014).
Blatchford, P., Bassett, P., Brown, P., Koutsoubou, M., Martin, C., Russell, A. and Webber, R., with Rubie-Davies, C. (2009a) *Deployment and Impact of Support Staff in Schools: The impact of Support Staff in Schools (Results from Strand 2, Wave 2)*. London: Institute of Education DCSF Research Report DCSF RR148, Department for Children, Schools and Families.

Blatchford, P., Bassett, P., Brown, P., Martin, C., Russell, A. and Webber, R. (2009b) *Deployment and Impact of Support Staff in Schools: Characteristics, Working Conditions and Job Satisfaction of Support Staff in Schools (Strand 1, Waves 1–3 – 2004, 2006 and 2008)*. London: Institute of Education: DCSF Research Report DCSF RR154, Department for Children, Schools and Families.

Campbell, A. (2005) 'All different, all equal', in Campbell, A. and Fairbairn, G. (eds) *Working with Support in the Classroom*. London: Paul Chapman Publishing.

Daily Mail (2013) 'Army of teaching assistants faces the axe as Education Department attempts to save some of the £4 billion they cost each year'. *Daily Mail*, 3 June. Available online at: http://www.dailymail.co.uk/news/article-2334853/Army-teaching-assistants-faces-axe-Education-department-attempts-save-4billion-cost-year.html.

Department for Education (2013a) *School Workforce in England: November 2012*. SFR 15/2013 DfE. Available online at: https://www.gov.uk/government/publications/school-workforce-in-england-november-2012 (accessed 9 May 2014).

Department for Education (2013b) *Making Foreign Languages Compulsory at Key Stage 2*. Consultation Report: Overview, DfE. Available online at: http://dera.ioe.ac.uk/14904/9/mfl%20compulsory%20at%20ks2%20consultation%20report.pdf (accessed 17 March 2014).

Department for Education (2014) *School Workforce in England: November 2013*. SFR11/2014, DfE. Available online at: https://www.gov.uk/government/collections/statistics-school-workforce (accessed 9 May 2014).

Fox, P. & Avramidis, E. (2003) 'An evaluation of an outdoor education programme for students with emotional and behavioural difficulties'. *Emotional and Behavioural Difficulties* 8(4): 267–282.

Halliwell, M. (2003) *Supporting Children with Special Educational Needs* (2nd edn). London: David Fulton.

HLTA National Assessment Partnership Newsletter (2012) Available online at: http://www.hlta.org.uk (accessed 18 May 2014).

HMI (2002) *Teaching Assistants in Primary Schools: An Evaluation of the Quality and Impact of Their Work*. London: HMSO.

Hughes, M. (1997) 'Managing other adults in the classroom', in Craig, I. (ed.) *Managing Primary Classrooms*. London: Pitman Publishing.

Kerry, T. (2001) *Working with Support Staff*. Harlow: Pearson Education.

Mindham, C. (2004) 'Thinking across the curriculum', in Jones, R. and Wyse, D. (eds) *Creativity in the Primary Curriculum*. London: David Fulton.

Murray, J. (2009) 'Special people'. *Learning Support Journal* I (Autumn Term): 14–15.

Ofsted (2008) 'Learning outside the classroom'. Available online at: www.ofsted.gov.uk/publications/070219.

Ofsted (2010) 'Workforce reform in schools: has it made a difference? An evaluation of changes made to the school workforce 2003–2009'. Available online at: http://www.ofsted.gov.uk/resources/workforce-reform-schools-has-it-made-difference (accessed 18 May 2014).

Raising Standards and Tackling Workload: A National Agreement (2003) ATL, DfES, GMB, NAHT, NASUWT, NEOST, PAT, SHA, TGWU, UNISON, WAG. Available online at: http://webarchive.nationalarchives.gov.uk/20040722012358/http://www.teachernet.gov.uk/docbank/index.cfm?id=3479 (accessed 9 May 2014).

Rose, J. (2009) *Independent Review of the Primary Curriculum: Final Report* (Rose Review). London: DCSF.

Skates, E. (2013) 'Outside intervention'. *SEN Magazine* 63(March/April).

Smith, P., Whitby, K. and Sharp, C. (2004) *The Employment and Deployment of Teaching Assistants* (LGA Research Report 5/04). Slough: NFER.

Thorpe, L., Trewhitt, K. and Zuccollo, J. (2013) *Must do Better: Spending on Schools.* Reform Ideas No 5. Available online at: www.reform.co.uk/ . . . /must_do_better_spending_on_ schools (accessed 18 May 2014).

Walton, A. and Goddard, G. (2009) *Supporting Every Child: A Course Book for Foundation Degrees in Teaching and Supporting Learning.* Exeter: Learning Matters.

Wilson, R., Sharp, C., Shuayb, M., Kendall, L., Wade, P. and Easton, C. (2007) *Research into the Deployment and Impact of Support Staff Who Have Achieved HLTA Status.* Slough: NFER.

Internet source

BBC News, Education and Family, 8 July 2013. Available online at: http://www.bbc.co.uk/ news/education-23222068 (accessed 20 March 2014).

Part 5

Planning and assessing cross-curricular work

Chapter 10

Planning and preparation for cross-curricular learning and teaching

Judith Laurie

Introduction

This chapter asks why planning is at the heart of successful teaching and, by analysing feedback from educationalists, HMI and Ofsted on past cross-curricular approaches, suggests principles for more effective planning, especially in the medium and short term. It emphasises that schools, while following selected principles, should feel confident to use an appropriate planning model for their circumstances and children. Through a practical case study example, it illustrates how a medium-term plan may be devised. It also considers how a cross-curricular planning approach fits with the revised 2014 National Curriculum.

Background

Effective planning provides the foundation upon which high-quality teaching and learning can be built. Although teachers can often recall outstanding lessons that were taught 'off the cuff', in reality these are the exception not the rule. Most teachers will agree that equally vivid in their memories are the lessons that failed because of inadequate planning and preparation. Yet curriculum planning is the locus where a proactive and able teacher can come to excel, communicating 'content' in ways that are dynamic, creative and insightful – in short, fulfilling the highest ideals of the teaching profession.

Planning is the manifestation of a teacher's thinking about what (and how) she hopes children will achieve and learn by the end of the lesson, week or unit of work. Ideally, there will be a degree of collaboration with colleagues, which will result in planning that draws on a range of skills and expertise in different subjects. Certainly, Ofsted regards collaborative planning and good subject knowledge as positive features of outstanding teaching and learning (Ofsted 2002, 2009b, 2010). 'Planning is the process of thinking, consultation and developing ideas that leads to the production of plans which act as a guide for your lesson' (Hayes 1997: 54). Hayes's notion of planning as a process that involves consultation with others reminds us that this should, of course, include the children. Other steps in the process involve consideration of children's prior learning and achievements, and how to make the learning relevant, leading to a final plan, which is a 'guide' to what is going to happen in the classroom. The word 'guide' reminds us to adopt a flexible approach that will allow for the unexpected or changes in children's interests.

Whether for discrete subject teaching or integrated learning, effective planning is the key to success (Kerry 2010), and the overall features of effective planning apply to both approaches.

Implications of the 2014 revised National Curriculum

Much has been written about the effectiveness of a creative approach to designing and teaching the National Curriculum (NCSL 2004; Ofsted 2010; Craft *et al*. 2014), and the importance of a creative curriculum for raising standards (Ofsted 2010). When designing such a curriculum the importance of coherent planning is paramount to ensure that the outcomes are sufficiently challenging.

> Occasionally, teachers failed to grasp that creative learning was not simply a question of allowing pupils to follow their interests; **careful planning was needed for enquiry, debate, speculation, experimentation, review and presentation to be productive**.
>
> (Ofsted 2010: 6)

The revised National Curriculum (NC), it can be argued, has given the stamp of approval to creative, flexible and individualised planning by schools. This is an opportunity that teachers should grasp eagerly, since it provides the chance to gain satisfaction in the resultant enthusiasm of the pupils. This revised NC is widely regarded as a 'slimmed down' version of the statutory requirements for state-funded schools and one that encourages schools to take ownership of the curriculum for their pupils. Significantly, the National Curriculum document emphasises the importance of retaining a broad and balanced curriculum (DfE 2013: para. 2.1). This, it is to be hoped, lessens the danger that schools see the revised curriculum, primarily, as a way to reduce the demands of 'coverage' by planning a curriculum that teaches only the statutory elements and gives an even greater amount of teaching time to the discrete teaching of literacy and numeracy. Though this book argues against merely aggrandising content over cognition, it remains sensitive to the needs of curriculum to support quality content in both core and non-core subjects. Failure here would be of particular concern for the non-core subjects that, in the new curriculum, have greatly reduced Programmes of Study. However, we might take heart from the words of the National Curriculum document itself:

> The National Curriculum is just one element in the education of every child. There is time and space in the school day and in each week, term and year to range beyond the National Curriculum specifications. The National Curriculum provides an outline of core knowledge around which teachers can develop exciting and stimulating lessons . . . as part of the wider curriculum.

Furthermore, the argument for retaining appropriate amounts of time for the non-core subjects and a cross-curricular approach to planning is strengthened by the requirement to teach and apply basic numeracy and literacy skills in the context of studying other subjects (see an extended description of this in Chapter 6), as well as in discrete teaching sessions:

> Teachers should use every relevant subject to develop pupils' mathematical fluency.
>
> (DfE 2013: para. 5.1)

> Teachers should develop pupils' numeracy and mathematics reasoning in all subjects so that they understand and appreciate the importance of mathematics.
>
> (DfE 2013: para. 5.2)

Teachers should develop pupils' spoken language, reading, writing and vocabulary as integral aspects of the teaching of every subject.

(DfE 2013: para.6.1)

Even when referring to pupils in Year 1 who are still working below age-related expectations:

. . . these pupils should follow the Year 1 Programme of Study in terms of the books they listen to and discuss, so that they develop their vocabulary and understanding of grammar, **as well as their knowledge more generally across the curriculum**.

(DfE 2013: 19 – emphasis added)

Perhaps, therefore, we should regard the revised curriculum as an opportunity to ensure that each school is encouraged to design the most creative, exciting and relevant curriculum for their children. Certainly, Martin (2014: 14), writing for the Geographical Association, believes that it 'allows for flexibility to address local needs and interests', and Coulson (2014: 33) welcomes the reduced prescription, reasoning that this 'liberates schools to do it in the way they know best for their children' so long as they devise a curriculum with 'rigour and challenge'.

One note of caution, though: the 'slimming down' has inevitably meant that much content has been taken out, which, as noted previously, could result in an impoverished curriculum; it is vital that schools review the content to decide which aspects that are no longer statutory remain of key importance for their pupils. For example, teachers in Islington (www.islington.gov.uk/ . . . /(2014–01–17)-Briefing-Presentation-January-2) have been cautioned to avoid 'Anglo-centricism' by ensuring that extra materials from other cultures are included. Furthermore, the Islington consultative group regard the geography curriculum as 'dangerously UK-centric' and strongly recommend that, to reflect Islington pupils' cultural backgrounds, existing units of study focusing on continents other than Europe, North and South America should be retained.

Nonetheless, the benefits of providing an 'outline' national curriculum are taken further by Oates (2014), who argues that making a distinction between the National Curriculum and the School Curriculum is vital. He sees the distinction as one of 'content' (National Curriculum) and 'context' (School Curriculum). He argues that if the National Curriculum attempts to include both elements it will be too detailed and complex, and will require frequent change, resulting in it being 'exposed to inappropriate change driven by political or educational fad' (Oates 2014: 26). If something along these lines is what distinguishes individual schools from one another, here is a key area for the demonstration of excellence.

Regardless of the debate about whether the content of the new curriculum is too 'fact led' or 'Anglo-centric' (Islington 2013), the positive message is that, by reducing prescription, schools are encouraged to 'use their professional judgement and expertise to design the curriculum' (www.prospectsimprove.co.uk 2014). Anecdotal evidence from recent conversations with headteachers indicates that schools are currently deciding how to proceed in a situation where most have well-established and carefully designed schemes of work that they have been using to meet the requirements of the existing National Curriculum. Encouragingly, most are following advice from the National College for School Leadership (NCSL 2013) to regard this as an opportunity to review and develop existing curricula, rather than to sweep away schemes of work that are working well. The suggestion is to ask, 'How good is our current curriculum?' and to use the 'Hallmarks of an Outstanding

Curriculum' (NCSL 2013) as a starting point for identifying the strengths, areas for development and any gaps in meeting the 2014 statutory requirements. I shall return to this principle later when discussing the exemplar for planning (Table 10.1).

Nevertheless, whatever approach schools undertake the principles for effective planning remain the same.

What are the features of effective curriculum planning?

The answer to the question will be influenced by which type of planning is being discussed. It is commonly recognised that there are three main 'levels' of planning, as follows:

1   Long term: setting out learning for between one or two years or a whole Key Stage.
2   Medium term: setting out the learning for a term or half-term.
3   Short term: setting out the learning for a unit of work, normally between one and four weeks' duration. In addition, short term refers to planning for a specific lesson or session.

This chapter does not take further the individual features of these levels; this topic can be more fully explored in several sources (Jacques and Hyland 2003; Primary National Strategy 2004; Arthur, Grainger and Wray 2006; Briggs 2012). However, it is relevant to highlight the importance of achieving coherence between the levels, while avoiding repetition or overlap. Experience of working with student teachers shows that a common error in the early stages is to provide too much detail at medium term, much of which is then repeated in short-term planning. The golden rule is that each level of planning should not repeat information from the previous stage, but should provide detail *additional* to what has already been planned.

Focusing on which features will be present in effective planning at the medium and short term, authorities on education express notably similar views, and common features include:

- Clear objectives, related to the statutory curriculum
- Plans that focus on developing skills and concepts as well as knowledge
- Planning that takes account of children's prior learning
- Short-term planning that is informed by assessment for learning
- Planning that involves children in the process
- Planning that is flexible
- Planning that makes the learning relevant to children
- Strategies for inclusion and differentiation
- Activities well matched to objectives
- Opportunities for first-hand or investigative learning
- Links made between subjects.

This list, while not exhaustive, applies to planning equally for discrete subject teaching and for integrated learning through cross-curricular approaches. That said, there are specific challenges and excitements in planning for integrated learning upon which the remainder of this chapter will now focus; for it is in the interplay of challenge and creativity that new ideas and approaches are formed.

Issues related to successful planning for integrated learning

Integrated learning is a term used to refer to a range of learning experiences; here the context is cross-curricular learning, often referred to as thematic, project or topic approaches. In such approaches a number of different curriculum subjects are brought together to structure learning through a common 'topic'.

After the news of the Independent Review of Primary Education, led by Sir Jim Rose, began to filter into schools during 2008, older primary teachers were often of the view that his proposals were, at least in part, a return to pre-National Curriculum approaches to primary education when teaching through topic was common in most schools. However, Rose (DCFS 2009) emphasised that this was too simplistic a view. He was sharp in his response to the 'nothing new' opinion of the review and claimed that he was aiming for *quality* rather than *novelty*, and that, with regard to 'best practice', 'it would certainly be "new" if many more of our schools were as good as the best' (DCFS 2009: para. 18). It seems that there was a sense of frustration about effective pedagogy in schools and a key message that the curriculum should include 'challenging subject teaching alongside equally challenging cross-curricular studies' (Rose 2008: 4); this was remarkably similar to what had been said by Sir Jim Rose, and his colleagues Robin Alexander and Chris Woodhead, in 1992 (even though Woodhead later joined the 'disciplines' lobby):

> There is clear evidence to show that much topic work has led to fragmentary and superficial teaching and learning. There is also ample evidence to show that teaching focused on single subjects benefits primary pupils. We see a need both for more sharply focused and rigorously-planned topic work and for an increase in single subject teaching.
>
> (Alexander *et al.* 1992: 3.4)

The second major report of 2009 was the Cambridge Review led by Robin Alexander. While not in agreement with all of Rose's justifications for a cross-curricular approach, in particular using it to address aspects of curriculum overload, he recognised that integration is important, and suggested that 'schools think carefully about which aspects might be taught separately and which combined; which need to preserve disciplinary integrity; and which are amenable to thematic treatment' (Alexander 2009: 55). He was quite clear that a 'domain', his equivalent to Rose's 'areas of learning', had a thematic coherence and integrity, but was not 'an invitation to low-grade topic work' (2009: 43, 44).

Reflection

Having read to this point in the book, what are your beliefs about the relative values for pupils of discrete subject teaching and integrated learning? Have your beliefs changed?

Strengths and weaknesses of cross-curricular approaches

It seems reasonable to conclude that a cross-curricular approach should have a central place in primary teaching and learning (see Chapter 1 in this volume). It is widely accepted (Katz and Chard 2000; Dean 2001; Ofsted 2002, 2010; DfES 2004; Barnes 2007) that it has much to offer for successful teaching and learning, including:

- Coherence in learning between different subjects
- Making learning more relevant
- Building and reinforcing key concepts and skills
- Providing contexts for using and applying subject-specific skills and concepts.

At the same time there have been, over many years, identified weaknesses in topic or thematic teaching: effective planning requires professionals to identify and rectify pitfalls. As long ago as 1978, a survey by HMI recorded concerns that much topic or project teaching lacked progression in learning and resulted in superficial, fragmented and repetitive teaching, especially in subjects such as geography and history (HMI 1978); Barnes (2007: 179) referred to the danger of 'watering down' subject teaching; Alexander *et al.* (1992: 2) spoke of 'fragmented and superficial teaching and learning'; while Dean (2001: 155) was concerned about how well teachers could monitor children's learning or achieve continuity in the context of topic work.

These concerns of fragmented learning, lack of coherence, repetitive and superficial teaching will be used, in what follows, to consider how a more rigorous planning approach can support effective cross-curricular learning.

Fragmented learning or *lack of coherence* can be the result of selecting aspects of subjects somewhat randomly and bringing them into a topic for reasons that are not entirely related to children's learning. Criticisms have been made of planning for a topic that makes only tenuous or spurious links between subjects. Ofsted (2003: 18) identified that, although some of the most creative work seen in schools was interdisciplinary, simply making spurious cross-curricular links could be a barrier to creativity, especially if teachers had a lack of subject knowledge in the arts. Oates (2014: 25) describes two dimensions for 'curriculum coherence': the first relates to coherence between 'different elements of policy and arrangements', including, among others, curriculum content, assessment, inspection and accountability; the second refers to coherence through effective sequences for developing key concepts and knowledge. Teachers in school may not have significant influence on the first dimension but, assuming secure subject knowledge, will have an influence on the coherence of planning that provides sequential development of subject-related concepts, skills and knowledge.

Reflecting on my personal experience as a young teacher planning for topics in the 1970s, I am aware that I certainly made tenuous links between subjects. In some cases this was as a result of using the 'key word approach'. For example, a topic on the theme of water may lead to choices that happen to have the word 'water' in the title or involve water in some way. For example, choosing stories such as Charles Kingsley's *Water Babies*, John Burningham's 'Come Away From the Water, Shirley' or Noah's Ark; history work on how Victorians did their laundry or geography work on the water cycle; while Handel's 'Water Music' is chosen for listening and appraising. It should be said at once that there are meaningful links to be made between *some* of these aspects and, indeed, very good learning to come from studying all of them, although not necessarily in the context of a topic on water. The literature examples would make excellent contributions to children's literary experiences and may be too important to be left to chance inclusion in a topic. Selecting them merely because they have some relationship with water misses the true meaning of cross-curricular learning. It fails to support coherence in teaching history, geography, literacy or music through careful choice of subject content and key skills that are complementary and support learning in several subjects.

A strategy for a more successful starting point is to consider key questions such as 'What do we want children to gain from this work?' or 'What do we want the children to learn?' (Ofsted 2009b: para. 30). Furthermore, when these key questions have been answered, this helps to identify focused questions for enquiry-based learning, such as 'Why is water important in our lives?' The answers to such questions will begin to direct and guide the choices of what to include in the curriculum plan. Taking the importance of water as a specific question to be answered, we can see how some of the original choices may not advance the children's understanding of this concept. Although work about the Victorian laundry may well have a place here, perhaps there are other literature choices that can offer starting points for more pertinent discussion – for example, the Aboriginal legend of the water-holding frog 'Tiddalik', which, among other things, illustrates the effects of drought.

As well as seeking coherence across subjects, Pollard (2002: 199) noted that there should also be consideration of coherence *within* individual subjects in order to avoid *superficial* or '*watered down*' learning. He notes that coherence is 'only partially amenable to planning, for it derives its force from the sense, or otherwise, which the children make of the curriculum which is provided'. It seems reasonable to suggest that children can be helped to make sense of the curriculum if the teacher has a secure understanding of the subjects. However, an expectation that individual primary teachers can have in-depth expertise in all subjects of the statutory curriculum is unrealistic. Furthermore, what is meant by 'subject knowledge' and its relationship to effective teaching has been a matter of debate for many educationalists (e.g. Blenkin, Edwards and Kelly 1992; Alexander 2009). There is a particular concern about the difference between *mastery* of knowledge and simple knowledge of facts. Pollard (2002: Ch. 8) provides a useful overview of this debate.

Using the expertise of subject leaders who can support colleagues and monitor the coherence of planning for 'their' subject contributes to progression in learning and retains the integrity of individual subjects. The role of subject leaders has been one that Ofsted has repeatedly referred to in relation to effective planning and supporting teachers' subject knowledge (Ofsted 2002, 2009a). Most recently, in a report focusing on the particular demands that different subjects make on teachers' subject knowledge, Ofsted recommended that schools should develop access for teachers to 'an expert subject leader'. Recognising that it is unrealistic to expect that primary schools will have experts for all subjects, they encourage making links with other local schools, Leading Practitioners, and 'other' experts such as museum staff or members of the community (Ofsted 2009b). This is certainly an option that schools might actively consider to enhance the quality of their planning.

One aspect of teacher subject knowledge that may seem obvious but is key to success in planning is knowledge and understanding of the National Curriculum programmes of study and attainment targets. Being able to recognise where meaningful and coherent links can be made across individual subjects, and which transferable skills and concepts are relevant necessitates confidence in working from the National Curriculum documents. My work in Initial Teacher Training since 1995 has shown how much more difficult it has become to ensure that student teachers develop this familiarity. In many schools they are directed to teach from commercial schemes and internet sources that provide them with completed planning. Their inexperience means that they are not always confident to evaluate such plans for coherence or relate them to the programmes of study. Experienced teachers are likely to be able to make the links between the NC and the resources being used, but if ITT providers do not ensure that student teachers learn about the content of the statutory documents we may be educating teachers who will find it difficult to plan confidently and creatively for cross-curricular learning. The time has come to develop a new breed of teacher whose skills in curriculum development will equip pupils for the 2050s.

Reflection

How confident are you in your knowledge of National Curriculum programmes of study and the links between them? What do you need to do to gain in confidence?

Planning for coverage of the statutory curriculum content

In the first version of this chapter, I wrote about the challenge of 'covering' the extensive content included in the programmes of study of the 2007 National Curriculum. Potentially, if coverage were the driving force, the result was planning that achieved only *superficial* teaching and learning, and what Dadds (in Pollard 2002: 173) described as the 'hurry along' curriculum. In this case 'coverage' became a more dominant planning and teaching issue for teachers than learning itself (Kendall-Seatter 2005: 10). Equally important, within tightly prescriptive planning, is the possibility that the place of Assessment for Learning (AfL) is diminished and that there are reduced opportunities for children's interests to be drawn into the planning (Kendall-Seatter 2005: 12). In fact, an approach that focused entirely on 'covering' the National Curriculum content, disregarded the advice, such as that in *Excellence and Enjoyment* (DfES 2004: 17), to use the 'freedoms' available to them even within the statutory requirements. These included the freedom to decide which aspects to select for in-depth study and how long to spend on each subject. Much of the joy went out of teaching during this prescriptive era.

The 'slimming down' of content in the revised National Curriculum lessens the danger of planning that aims only for coverage; furthermore, even the reduced statutory content may be taught with varying degrees of depth. For example, when teaching the various periods of history it is not a requirement to allocate the same amount of study time to each period: 'the overview of the new curriculum makes it clear not all units have to be studied in the same depth . . . in planning teachers should combine overview and depth studies' (Taylor 2014).

A guide written for school leaders by the National College (NCSL 2004) drew on the work of 22 primary schools in England, all of which achieved high standards in the core subjects by teaching a rich and challenging curriculum. The advice encouraged schools to 'go for excellence through depth, by giving some aspects of the curriculum more emphasis than others'.

Such an approach is also valued by Nuffield Primary History (NPH), which quotes Marjorie Reeves, an Oxford historian who supports the notion of children learning with enthusiasm, as saying she would like pupils to sit down in 'a good rich patch of history and stay there for a satisfying amount of time' (Reeves 1980: 53). NPH goes on to emphasise the importance of avoiding fragmentation, not by giving equal time to all elements of the history curriculum but by making clear links (connecting threads) between each of the selected topics studied in depth (Nuffield Primary History, n.d.). They suggest that this can be achieved by 'planning a couple of lessons at the end of the year or key stage (and certainly at the end of Year 6) where you review and pull together the discrete units of history the children have studied'. (Chapter 14 of the current text goes a step further. 'Learning history' is not simply about 'content' and certainly not a divisive debate about 'which content?'. It is the understanding that the skills of learning and practising history can be accessed by pupils regardless of which period is studied, and that the skills transcend the individual gobbets of content.)

The Rose Review proposed further reduction in subject prescription and content in order to give schools more flexibility to select curriculum content according to local circumstances and resources. It emphasised the support of subject associations for reduced content and noted that those who 'champion' subjects 'acknowledge that forcing primary schools to teach too much curriculum content in the time available will lead to superficial treatment that is detrimental to their subject' (DCFS 2009: 1.15). The 2014 curriculum has met this recommendation and has a structure that includes: a National Curriculum setting out only essential knowledge; a 'basic' curriculum, which is also statutory, but may vary in content, such as a locally agreed syllabus for RE; and a 'local' curriculum that is determined fully by the school and local community. To maintain coherence, the local curriculum should, in some respects, enhance the National and basic curricula.

An interesting approach was explained to me in a primary school, which is regarded by Ofsted and local authority advisers as very successful, with outstanding features. The teachers' perceptions of planning are reported here as Case Study 10.1. This flexible planning exemplifies the way in which curriculum development can be stimulating as well as cognitively sound.

Case Study 10.1 Flexible planning

The teachers emphasise that their more flexible approach reflected the school's values and aim to provide a *broad and balanced* curriculum *relevant* to their children. They believe strongly that having tight, highly detailed pre-set topics taught repeatedly year after year adversely affects the possibility of making the curriculum relevant by responding to changes in the children's needs, as well as their interests (not to mention the teachers' interests and expertise!). Furthermore, they want the freedom to heed local opportunities such as, in their case, the building of a new airport close to the school. They are confident in taking the 'freedom' to decide which aspects of each subject will be covered in depth, thus avoiding the danger of 'superficial' teaching. Within a two-year cycle of broad topic headings different decisions are made, from one year to the next, about which aspects will be covered in depth. Self-evidently, in this more flexible approach there is a need to ensure that appropriate coverage of the statutory curriculum is achieved and that there is progression in the teaching of subject-related skills. In this particular school there is careful monitoring of medium-term planning by the subject leaders and senior staff so that, over the two-year cycle, they can ensure that all such matters are monitored.

A skills-based approach to planning

In contrast to planning that starts with subject content is an approach that places key transferable skills at the centre of planning. There is no doubt that the revised NC Programmes of Study continue to reflect the importance of such skills. One need only look at how strongly the development of communication skills is shown through the vocabulary of all subjects, with repeated references to discuss, 'explain', 'describe', 'communicate ideas', present information. Similarly, the skills related to investigative work such as asking questions, observing, predicting, researching, planning, inferring, comparing similarities and differences, classifying, interpreting are repeatedly used across programmes of study for science, geography, history, English and mathematics.

However, there are those, including Alexander (2009: 18), who dispute the view that children need a primarily skills-based curriculum rather than one focused on subject knowledge. He discusses at length the polarised views taken by some on this matter, and argues that 'setting them [skills versus subject knowledge] in opposition is foolish, unnecessary and epistemologically unsound'. He argues that we must define which skills are important, while also understanding that knowledge is far more than facts to be learned. He concludes that skills must 'complement knowing and understanding rather than supplant them' (2009: 18) and that educationalists must define what is meant by 'skills' or there is a danger that 'we shall carelessly lose not only knowledge and understanding, but also skill itself' (2009: 19).

It is clear that the revised National Curriculum, while promoting a range of key transferable and subject-related skills, also requires essential knowledge to be taught in all subjects. To achieve this balance of knowledge and skills, a thematic cross-curricular approach provides the ideal context for learning and will meet the expectations, described earlier, for core skills in English and mathematics, to be developed in all subjects. This is not to diminish the importance of planning time into the school day for some rigorous, discrete subject teaching; it is this combination of subject and thematic approaches that characterised the approaches of the high-achieving schools identified by Ofsted (2002, 2009). As pointed out by Pimley (n.d.) is also helpful to think about cross-curricular links in two ways. In one, children are enabled to apply aspects of learning from one subject in another. For example, the use of mathematical skills when learning to use a compass in geography, or calculating the results of a fair test in science; learning in both subjects will benefit. The second is when one subject (or in this case topic or theme) provides a context for developing learning in several subjects. This helps children see the links between subjects and also provides opportunities for following children's interests. This gives their learning more purpose and direction. It is upon this second type of cross-curricular learning that this chapter will now focus.

Suggested principles for planning integrated learning

In the light of the points discussed above, effective planning for 'rigorous' cross-curricular teaching and learning will result in curriculum coherence and a context for developing transferable and core subject skills in relevant and meaningful activities. Successful planning for cross-curricular work can be supported in the following ways:

- Include a limited number of subjects or parts of subjects, chosen because of meaningful links between them and how well they match the broad aims of the project.
- Consider having a lead subject (or two), which drive(s) the topic and provide(s) opportunities for in-depth study.
- Identify selected subject knowledge and transferable skills that will be the focus of particular attention for teaching and assessment.
- Begin with key questions related to the intended broad aims for the children's learning.
- Select specific questions, including those suggested by children, to help structure the choice of subject content and activities.
- Use the statutory curriculum programmes of study and attainment targets to inform the planning, but do not allow them to restrict the range of knowledge and skills.

> **Reflection**
>
> Which of the suggested principles do you feel could be more fully developed in your planning?

A possible model for planning integrated learning through topic

The threads and debates of this chapter are drawn together in what follows by use of an example of cross-curricular planning (Table 10.1). The example will be used to illustrate the principles articulated to this point, while also briefly addressing some additional issues that apply to all effective planning. These include:

- Relevance of teaching and learning
- Developing attitudes and dispositions
- Children's involvement in planning.

The example is not intended to suggest that all medium-term plans should be presented in this way; it offers only one model. However, it does attempt to show how some of the weaknesses identified by critics might be avoided through effective planning. The plan was originally designed for the first version of this chapter and so this update presented a good opportunity to trial the advice referred to earlier, that it is possible to review existing planning and adapt it for the new statutory requirements. This proved to be quite successful and with fairly minor changes to some aspects of content for geography, history and science, the main part of the project remains the same.

The plan is for a hypothetical school in an industrial town in Lancashire, and is for up to a term's study with a Year 3/4 class, although the planning could be adapted for a shorter period or for upper Key Stage 2. It has arisen from a long-term plan identifying broad themes linked to single subjects. For the term in question, the lead subject is geography, focused upon study of a locality in the United Kingdom and a country that is less economically developed. In this revised version, the history content has been increased: by selecting the specific Pennine village of Ribchester, study of the impact of the Roman invasion of Britain can be undertaken; this adaptation enables part of the history statutory content for Key Stage 2 to be taught.

The specific topic is 'Houses and Homes', which provides experience of study at a local, regional and international level. It is structured into three sections with, first, study in the local area, followed by study in another area of the north-west region that provides some contrast but is still close enough for fieldwork visits. Finally, there is a third section that focuses on houses and homes in a less economically developed country. This country could be in South America, helping meet the required locations of the statutory curriculum for geography or, to reflect the local population in many industrial Lancashire towns, may be from the Asian subcontinent. The time spent on each of the three sections may vary according to the teacher's decisions, influenced by the balance of other geography work over the whole year, and factors such as children's interests and pace of learning. In the context of the 2014 National Curriculum the first section may be shorter as it can draw on children's geography experiences in Key Stage 1 when they will have studied features of the local environment.

Table 10.1 Medium-term plan for a Y3/4 class

Overarching theme: Houses and Homes

Context: School in industrial town in NW England traditionally, from Industrial Revolution, many brick-built houses. Comparison with Pennine village, Ribchester, with many stone-built houses and evidence of a Roman settlement; comparison with homes in India or Brazil – rural/urban/rich/poor

Lead Subject: Geography

Main linked subjects: History, Science, Art, Computing, Mathematics, English

Key Question

In what ways and why are houses different?

Outcome: Display including art work, reference books made by children, graphs, tables, charts presenting key findings for other classes and parents to visit and see

Prior Learning: Work in Key Stage 1 on the human and physical geography of the local environment. Introduction to maps, atlases, simple fieldwork and observational skills.

What do we want the children to learn and get out of the topic? (Broad Aims) Also identifies the essential knowledge and skills to be assessed

- To understand that houses are different due to availability of materials, natural environment, climate and history, effects of economic activity
- To develop geographical skills – Geographical Enquiry (geographical vocabulary/questions, use secondary sources of information, express views about environments. Fieldwork Skills (sketching, photography, mapping, compass skills)
- To develop aspects of NC key transferable skills particularly: communication, reading and writing for information, application of number, IT
- To develop a range of transferable NC subject skills but particularly: use and interpret sources of evidence; classification, collect, present and interpret data, use books and IT to retrieve information, identify and comment on similarities and differences

NC Geography objectives	x-curricular links NC History, Science, Art, English, Mathematics, Computing objectives	Starting point questions	Exemplar activities
Geography **Locational knowledge** Locate the world's countries using maps concentrating on their environmental regions, key physical and human characteristics, countries and major cities.	**History** Local history study: a study of an aspect of history from a period beyond 1066 that is significant in the locality	**1st focus in local area** *This may be brief as it will draw on prior knowledge from key stage 1 work in local environment*	Walk in locality to identify, or recall from photographs, styles, ages, materials of houses; compare with different examples from other parts of town

Content	Questions	Activities
The Roman Empire and its impact on Britain **Science** **Working Scientifically** **Gathering, recording, classifying and presenting data in variety of ways to help in answering questions**	*What are houses like in our town/area of school? (style, materials, sizes)* *What are older houses like/built of and why?* *Are newer houses different? In what ways and why?*	Class survey of house types and features, building materials observed; record data in charts, graphs or tables Visit to building site or visit by architect/builder Investigations into house building including related traditional local building manufacture (opportunities for children's choices of focused study, e.g. brick-laying, brick-making, brick-bonds, joinery, window styles. . . .)
Reporting on findings from enquiries, including oral and written explanations, displays, or presentations of results and conclusions **Rocks** **Compare and group together different types of rocks on the basis of their appearance and simple physical properties**	*How are our houses heated and lit?* *How and why have houses changed over time in our area?* *What do the paintings of L. S. Lowry tell us about life in urban Lancashire?*	Interview local builder/older local residents Look at and discuss paintings of L. S. Lowry Paintings of local area exploring L. S. Lowry-style techniques
Place knowledge **Understand geographical similarities and differences through the study of human and physical geography** of a region of the United Kingdom and a region within South Asia **Human and Physical Geography** **Describe and understand key aspects of human geography, including:** types of settlement and land use, economic activity including trade links and the distribution of natural resources including energy, food, minerals and water **Art** **Aims to ensure that all pupils:** **Create sketchbooks to record their observations and use them to review and revisit ideas** Improve their mastery of art and design techniques, including drawing, painting and sculpture with a range of materials	*What painting techniques did Lowry use to convey atmosphere of industrial landscape?* **2nd focus in different part of the region** *What are houses like in the Pennine village?* *Why are there fewer brick-built houses?* *How are they built, heated, lit?*	Use Ordnance Survey maps to identify location and geographical features of Ribchester Introduce use of compass to identify direction of Ribchester from school Plan a field trip to Ribchester to investigate types of houses Investigate type of local stone (millstone grit) used to build houses in Ribchester Compare millstone grit with other types of rock used for building houses in other geographical areas in the UK

(continued)

Table 10.1 (continued)

NC Geography objectives	x-curricular links NC History, Science, Art, English, Mathematics, Computing objectives	Starting point questions	Exemplar activities
	Computing **Content** **Understand computer networks including the internet; how they can provide multiple services such as the worldwide web; and the opportunities they offer for communication and collaboration**	How and why are the houses different from our area? What are the most common types of houses and building materials in each area?	Compare similarities and differences of houses in home area and in Ribchester Investigate reasons for differences in building materials – i.e. stone instead of brick; visit to stone quarry
Geographical skills and fieldwork **Use maps, atlases, globes and digital/ computer mapping to locate countries and describe features studied**	Use search technologies effectively, appreciate how results are selected and ranked, and be discerning in evaluating digital content **Mathematics** **Number and place value**	Why did the Romans live in Ribchester? What evidence is there to show what Roman houses might have been like? What effect did the cotton industry have on homes in our town and in Ribchester?	Investigate why some new houses are still built of stone (environmental issues) Use sketchbook material as starting points for pencil drawings, painting or pastel work, 3D modelling, related to colour, pattern, texture, shape Investigate aspects of cotton industry in Lancashire, and effects on types and numbers of houses
Use the eight points of a compass, four-figure grid references, symbols and key (including the use of Ordnance Survey maps) to build their knowledge of the United Kingdom and the wider world	**Addition and subtraction** **Multiplication and division** Solve number problems **Measurement** Using Roman numerals Compare durations of events	**3rd focus in less economically developed country** What are houses like in India/ Brazil? How are they built, heated, lit?	Investigate the weavers' cottages in Ribchester Visit museum in Ribchester to see and hear about Roman history

Use fieldwork to observe, measure and record the human and physical features in the local area using a range of methods, including sketch maps, plans and graphs and digital technologies

Geometry
Describe positions on a 2D grid as coordinates in the first quadrant Y4
Statistics
Interpret and present data using bar charts, pictograms and tables Y3

Solve one-step and two-step problems Y3
Interpret and present discrete and continuous data using appropriate graphical methods, including bar charts and time graphs Y4

Solve comparison, sum and difference problems using information presented in bar charts, pictograms, tables and other graphs Y4
English
Spoken Language

Ask relevant questions to extend their understanding and knowledge
Articulate and justify answers, arguments and opinions give well-structured descriptions, explanations and narratives for different purposes, including for expressing feelings

How and why are the houses different from ones in our country?
Why do some people live in very poor conditions close to large cities? (Indian shanty towns or Brazilian favelas)

Use atlases and globes to locate India or Brazil
Make links by email and Skype with school in India or Brazil; share information on local areas and houses in particular
Use photographs to compare different types of homes in India or Brazil

Research types of house building, different from those found in UK
Introduce and discuss reasons for shanty towns and favelas
Present findings using graphical methods; interpret data from graphs, tables and charts
Use data from findings and statistics to calculate answers to mathematical problems

e.g. age of selected houses
calculate periods (decades/centuries) of intensive house building in selected areas
Take part in class discussion and feedback sessions throughout the project
Plan, prepare and carry out interviews with builders, residents and local historians
Use school and public libraries to retrieve relevant information books

(continued)

LINKS TO NC and Geography + History.

Table 10.1 (continued)

NC Geography objectives	x-curricular links NC History, Science, Art, English, Mathematics, Computing objectives	Starting point questions	Exemplar activities
	Use spoken language to develop understanding through speculating, hypothesising, imagining and exploring ideas		Use non-fiction books to learn information-retrieval reading skills
	Speak audibly and fluently with an increasing command of Standard English		Design, plan and produce non-fiction reference books to present findings
	Select and use appropriate registers for effective communication.		Write reports, explanations, accounts for the books and final display
	Reading		
	Comprehension		
	Retrieve and record information from non-fiction		
	Read books that are structured in different ways and read for a range of purposes		
	Asking questions to improve their understanding of a text		
	Identifying main ideas from more than one paragraph and summarising these		
	Identifying how language, structure, and presentation contribute to meaning		
	Participate in discussions about books both read to them and read themselves, taking turns and listening to others		

Writing

Composition

Writing for a range of real audiences and purposes

Making decisions about the form of writing appropriate to purpose and audience

Develop concepts and understanding of vocabulary, grammar and punctuation through applying knowledge in own speaking, reading and writing

Plan their writing

Drafting and writing

Evaluating and editing

Proofreading

Reading aloud own writing

Making decisions about subject knowledge, skills and concepts

As suggested, the plan begins with an overarching question: 'Why are houses different?' This provides a good starting point for the *Human and Physical Geography* section of the Key Stage 2 programme of study, in which children should be taught to describe and understand 'types of settlements and land use, economic activity including trade links . . . '. The question immediately begins to inform decisions about subject content and aims for the children's learning. It suggests that meaningful links can be made with history, while opportunities to study building materials inspire potential links with science and art.

This process could be approached in reverse, with broad aims for the topic being the starting point from which the key question(s) are identified. Thus, if the school long-term planning approach begins with key skills and concepts and, in a given term, the focus is on *Place Knowledge* and teaching children to *understand geographical similarities and differences* a different starting point question may arise.

The first column in Table 10.1 shows that not all elements of the geography POS have been included but, even so, there are a significant number. This demonstrates that, in most topics, it is possible to touch on many POS elements of both the lead subject and indeed related subjects, however, as noted earlier, choices can and should be made about which aspects will receive in-depth attention.

In this plan the emboldened objectives are those selected for most attention in teaching and assessment; those not in bold will be 'covered' but with a 'lighter touch', and may not be part of planned, focused assessments. Some objectives, especially those related to skills, for example, 'understand geographical similarities and differences' and 'use basic geographical vocabulary', will be included as 'ongoing' objectives in all geography topics, albeit with differences in the details. The focus of the study and the key question has influenced the choice of selected geography subject skills such as fieldwork and mapping skills.

The links with history, science and maths influenced the choice of cross-curricular, transferable skills such as collecting, recording and interpreting evidence, observation, classification, explaining similarities and differences, and recording findings using drawings, keys, bar charts and tables, all of which have links across these subjects.

The final point is that all choices should be made in the context of the school's long-term plan and feedback from subject leaders monitoring individual subjects. This will ensure that, over the year or Key Stage, children are receiving a broad and balanced curriculum, which meets, as a minimum, the requirements of the statutory curriculum.

Medium-term planning for a Year 3/4 class: overarching theme – Houses and Homes

Including mathematics and English in a cross-curricular approach

The example in Table 10.1 reflects common practice in schools, namely that the Foundation subjects are taught through topic, though Chapter 6 has also shown that interdisciplinary approaches are just as relevant to core subjects. Since the introduction of the National Literacy Strategy, the vast majority of schools allocate up to 50% of the school day, usually the morning sessions, to discrete English and Maths teaching. As previously noted, a balance of discrete and integrated teaching and learning is desirable, but it is vital that links are made to ensure that the core skills being taught discretely are applied to the real purposes and contexts that can be found in a carefully designed cross-curricular topic. This is achievable in two main ways; one might be called concurrent teaching. For example, a teacher may decide to teach the skills of report writing in literacy lessons in preparation for writing reports as part of the topic. Similarly, separate spelling, punctuation and grammar skills (SPAG) will have attention in discrete teaching time, but the children's understanding of how and why to use these skills to achieve effective written communication may best be illustrated when writing a letter to seek information for the topic or preparing a piece of writing as part of a presentation for parents.

The second way goes further in that teachers may decide to teach and assess some aspects of the core subjects entirely in the context of the topic. In Table 10.1 it can be seen that much of the statistics curriculum can be taught through the data-handling activities in the topic. The logic of this approach is that the learning and teaching are contextualised; data-handling activities must have data to handle, and why use random data that is selected only for the purpose of a teaching exercise when the data being collected as part of answering the topic question is meaningful and makes the mathematical learning purposeful?

Needless to say, a wide range of literacy and spoken communication skills will be used throughout a topic and, in this example, a focus on developing information retrieval and non-fiction reading and writing reflects the nature of the topic. The teacher will, of course, ensure a balance across the year of opportunities for different types of reading and writing. Here again, it is possible to teach aspects of the English curriculum entirely as part of the cross-curricular topic; furthermore, by doing so, the learning and teaching is linked to real audiences for writing and purposes for reading.

It is worth noting that cross-curricular topics provide opportunities for the assessment of many core and transferable skills in context; as noted by the Nuffield Foundation (2012: 13), 'for pupils to show their competence in "working scientifically" they need to be in situations where they are raising questions, planning investigations'. This principle of assessing children's skills in authentic contexts is valid for aspects of all subjects; furthermore, in integrated learning, observations of children in enquiry-based learning will enable the assessment of skills from across several subjects. (These issues are discussed in more detail in Chapter 11.)

A final point to note is that the medium-term plan does not identify specific learning objectives for lessons. The aims and subject objectives will need to be 'broken down' into smaller, more precise objectives at the short-term planning stage. For example, a geography-based objective such as mapping will need to be specified for more than one lesson; the lesson objective will identify which particular mapping features or skills will be focused upon. You can find detailed guidance on learning objectives and how to set them in Kerry (2002).

Reflection

What aspects of literacy or numeracy benefited, or might have benefited, from being taught or assessed as part of a topic you have taught or planned?

Moving from objectives to activities

It is common at the start of a topic for teachers to use a 'mind-mapping' approach for possible activities, ideally involving children in the activity. Such an activity might be the next step, using the key question as the prompt to trigger ideas pertinent to the topic. Completing a mind-map earlier in the process, using 'Houses and Homes' as the prompt, could result in an unmanageable range of possibilities. Even so, all mind-map suggestions should be evaluated and discussed to select the best options in relation to the broad aims, as well as those that have particular interest for the children.

It is from this process of mind-mapping that more focused starting-point questions and exemplar activities may be extracted and planned for. The precise details of study questions and activities will be refined in short-term planning. For example, knowledge of what is available in the local area of the school may lead to a particular focus on different styles of houses, while in another environment the ages of houses may be of particular interest. An activity to conduct a survey of differences in houses may include children's own houses, but a teacher who is aware of sensitive diversity issues may choose to 'depersonalise' this activity by carrying out a survey of houses observed during fieldwork.

Making the learning *relevant* to the children should begin at the medium-term planning stage and is related to making the learning *meaningful* for children. This picks up the need to scaffold learning, to begin from the children's own experiences and what is familiar. For the topic in the example, the starting point is houses in the local area. This will allow children to relate what they already know to new learning about houses and homes in other regions and countries. However, Barnes (2007: 186) asserts that planning for relevance is not only about selecting an 'entry point from everyday life'. He proposes the importance of 'the emotional setting of learning' in order to establish meaningful links by using shared or personal experiences to support relevant and meaningful learning. In the example (Table 10.1) the teacher may seek emotional relevance through aspects related to children's own homes, or experiences such as a child who has recently moved house, or by using literature or drama to engage children's emotional responses to aspects of the theme.

A danger when seeking relevance is that planning may remain too long within the immediate scope of children's personal experiences. Although children's experience is a good starting point, it is important for children 'to understand and know about phenomena distant from their own first hand experiences' (Katz and Chard 2000) – this theme is picked up again in Chapter 12. Ofsted (2009b: 18) recognises that a feature of planning that results in 'achieving excellence' is that topics start in familiar contexts but quickly move the learning on. This is particularly true in schools regarded as being in challenging circumstances, with children whose home experiences may be very limited. In these cases, providing opportunities for learning beyond the immediate environment is vital.

The concluding point to be gleaned from Table 10.1 is that *relevance* becomes very important when learning about houses in India, a more distant concept. As well as good choices of resources – for example, high-quality and recent photographic and internet sources – which are used well by the teacher, relevance must be achieved by comparisons with children's own homes to help them make sense of the learning. This key point is sometimes missed in topic work, when the study of India, Romans or Aztecs is focused only on researching and recording random, factual information, without opportunities to make the knowledge meaningful. A further danger to avoid is stereotyping; not all homes in India are poor, and the resources and information used should reflect a complete and accurate picture of the country.

Teachers always need to articulate and ensure achievement of the key concepts that underpin the planning. An appreciation of this in the present example can be gained through exploration of a key concept such as 'change over time' or, in a geography-led Houses and Homes topic, the effects of environmental, economic or climatic influences. Such conceptual understanding of differences and similarities will also provide vitally important opportunities for expanding relevance in learning by developing children's personal, social and citizenship values.

Short-term planning

The medium-term plan is deliberately not detailed or tightly linked to individual lessons in the topic. Some teachers would want to include other aspects at the medium-term planning stage, such as lists of resources, or suggestions for how differentiation and inclusion will be achieved. There is no problem about any of this, only a matter of what works best for individual schools or teachers. However, whatever is included should not take away the flexibility of the planning by including too much detail. Activities in the example medium-term plan (Table 10.1) are described only at a very general level to allow for further involvement of children in raising questions and selecting specific aspects of study. They are also only examples – some may be discarded as not relevant to the lines of enquiry, while new ones may emerge. This helps children to develop positive attitudes and dispositions to learning through ownership of work that is of interest to them; this was a key finding from the research conducted by Craft *et al.* (2014) into creative approaches to teaching and learning. Needless to say, teachers must monitor children's choices carefully, to ensure that they are part of a coherent learning experience overall.

Teachers unfamiliar with this way of working may wonder, when planning individual lessons within a cross-curricular topic, whether they should always aim to progress learning in more than one subject. There is not a simple yes or no answer to this question. Certainly the lesson may, like the topic, have a lead subject, and a good lesson plan will have one primary learning objective, which could be related to one subject area. It is common to have a secondary objective that highlights opportunities for a transferable skill such as synthesising information or group discussion. Alternatively, the primary objective might be related to a key concept such as 'change', and this could involve learning that includes both geographical and historical change. When planning at short term, teachers should constantly be alert to overall key concepts and skills, and include in the lesson teaching points pertinent to them. This approach has similarities to the one from Nuffield Primary History described earlier, whereby lessons are planned at the end of the year to make links between the various history study units. For short-term planning, this approach could be interpreted as planning specifically to make explicit links between subjects – for example, through teaching points or key questions used during the introduction or plenary of a lesson.

Above all, it is vital to bear in mind that children's learning should not be constrained by planning. Identifying and sharing with children clear learning objectives or intentions for a lesson is important, but teachers must expect some learning to occur outside the initial planning.

In general, the essential aspects for effective short-term planning, whether for weekly or daily lesson plans, include:

- Information on previous learning or experiences
- Specific questions and learning objectives – knowledge, concepts or skills

- Clearly articulated success criteria that support children's self-assessment
- Outline of any planned teacher assessments of key objectives, often related to focused work with small groups
- Teaching points, both subject-specific and cross-curricular
- Plans for what will be assessed and how
- Key questions, especially for the introduction and plenary, including some that are differentiated for the range of ability in the class
- Tasks and activities similarly differentiated
- Notes on organisation of the whole class, small groups and individuals
- Plans for roles of adults
- Resources
- Key vocabulary.

Reflection

How does the model in Table 10.1 compare with other medium-term and short-term planning approaches you have used?

Conclusion

It is indisputable that children's learning is supported by opportunities that cross subject boundaries. However, a cross-curricular approach will be effective only if the teacher's planning makes meaningful links across subjects and through experiences that allow the connections to make sense to children. Cross-curricular planning could be construed to be an advanced skill for teachers, requiring enhanced understanding and skill about classroom processes. But it is a skill replete with elements of creativity and invention that enthuse the professionalism of the teacher and the learning of the pupils.

Past and recent reports and initiatives, including the revised 2014 National Curriculum, have emphasised that schools should exercise flexibility in planning, and have the confidence and imagination to take ownership of the statutory curriculum by planning programmes that will meet the needs of their pupils. This will result in a range of different approaches to long-, medium- and short-term planning, rather than one model. However, as has been discussed in this chapter, effective cross-curricular planning needs to take heed of key principles that have arisen from previous criticisms of ineffective approaches to topic or thematic planning.

The examples in this chapter use history and geography as the lead subjects, but this should not suggest that the humanities should always be at the forefront (note, for example, Chapter 6). It is important, over time, to have the creative and expressive arts, English, mathematics, or science and technology as lead subjects in planning. Above all, over the whole primary phase, children should receive a broad and balanced experience of all subjects or areas of learning.

Progression in learning within discrete subjects or areas of learning does not need to be sacrificed within an integrated approach. Through planning, effective teachers ensure balance between activities that develop conceptual understanding of the subject and those that allow children to simply practise subject or transferable skills.

Finally, at this time of change, it is heartening to note that there is continued support from government and educationalists for cross-curricular approaches to learning. In schools where this approach has always been successfully in place, and for those who are in the process of developing planning for integrated learning, we can be confident that children will experience high-quality and coherent learning overall.

References

Alexander, R. (2009) *Towards a New Curriculum. Cambridge Primary Review Interim Report Part 2: The Future.* Cambridge: University of Cambridge.

Alexander, R., Rose, A. J. and Woodhead, C. (1992) *Curriculum Organisation and Classroom Practice in Primary Schools: A Discussion Paper.* London: DES.

Arthur, J., Grainger, T. and Wray, D. (2006) *Learning to Teach in the Primary School.* London: Routledge.

Barnes, J. (2007) *Cross-curricular Learning 3–14.* London: PCP.

Blenkin, G. M., Edwards, G. and Kelly, A.V. (1992) *Change and the Curriculum.* London: PCP.

Briggs, M. (2012) 'Planning', in Hansen, A. (ed.) *Primary Professional Studies* (2nd edn). Transforming Primary QTS Series. London: Learning Matters/Sage Publications Ltd.

Coulson, T. (2014) in Blatchford, R. (2013) *Taking Forward the Primary Curriculum: Applying the 2014 National Curriculum for KS1 and KS2.* Woodbridge: John Catt Educational Ltd.

Craft, A., Cremin, T., Hay, P. and Clack, J. (2014) Creative primary schools: developing and maintaining pedagogy for creativity. *Ethnography and Education* 9(1): 16–34. Available online at: http://oro.open.ac.uk/31491/3/Craft%20et%20al%20Creative%20Primary%20Schools%20%2012%20JULY%202013.pdf (accessed 25 May 2014).

DCFS (2009) *Independent Review of the Primary Curriculum: Final Report.* Available online at: www.teachernet.gov.uk/publications.

Dean, J. (2001) *Organising Learning in the Primary Classroom* (3rd edn). London: Routledge/Falmer.

DfE (2013) *The National Curriculum in England: Key Stages 1 and 2 Framework Document.*

DfES (2004) *Excellence and Enjoyment: A Strategy for Primary Schools.* Nottingham: DfES Publications.

Hansen, A. (ed.) (2012) *Primary Professional Studies* (2nd edn). London: Learning Matters/Sage Publications.

Hayes, D. (1997) *Success on Your Teaching Experience.* London: Hodder & Stoughton.

HMI (1978) *Primary Education in England: A Survey by HM Inspectors of Schools.* London: HM Stationery Office. Available online at: http://www.dg.dial.pipex.com/documents/hmi/7805.shtml (accessed 21 October 2009).

Jacques, K. and Hyland, R. (eds) (2003) *Professional Studies: Primary Phase* (2nd edn). Achieving QTS Series. Exeter: Learning Matters.

Katz, L. and Chard, S. (2000) *Engaging Children's Minds: The Project Approach.* Stamford, CN: Ablex.

Kendall-Seatter, S. (2005) *Reflective Reader: Primary Professional Studies.* Achieving QTS Series. Exeter: Learning Matters.

Kerry, T. (2002) *Learning Objectives, Task Setting and Differentiation.* Cheltenham: Nelson-Thornes.

Kerry, T. (2010) 'Plotting compelling lessons: framework for inspiring quality learning and teaching'. *Curriculum Briefing* 8(2): 10–15.

Martin, F. (2014) 'Interpreting and implementing the 2014 National Curriculum'. *Teaching Geography* 39(1): 14–15.

NCSL (2004) *Developing Creativity for Learning in the Primary School: A Practical Guide for School Leaders.* NCSL.

NCSL (2013) Available online at: http://apps.nationalcollege.org.uk/resources/modules/curriculum/Curriculum/Entries/2013/1/1_What_are_the_hallmarks_of_a_great_curriculum_framework.html (accessed 31 May 2014).

Nuffield Foundation (2012) *Developing Policy, Principles and Practice in Primary School Science.* Nuffield Foundation.

Nuffield Primary History (n.d.) Available online at: http://www.primaryhistory.org/leadinghistory/planning,270,SAR.html (accessed 30 September 2009).

Oates, T. (2014) 'Progress in science education? The revised National Curriculum for 2014'. *School Science Review* 95(352): 21–28.

Ofsted (2002) *The Curriculum in Successful Primary Schools.* Available online at: http://www.ofsted.gov.uk/Ofsted-home/Publications-and-research/Browse-all-by/Education/Key-stages-and-transition/Key-Stage-1/The-curriculum-in-successful-primary-schools (accessed 19 October 2009).

Ofsted (2003) *Expecting the Unexpected.* Available online at: http://www.ofsted.gov.uk/Ofsted-home/Publications-and-research/Browse-all-by/Education/Providers/Primary-schools/Expecting-the-unexpected (accessed 19 October 2009).

Ofsted (2009a) *Improving Primary Teachers' Subject Knowledge across the Curriculum.* Available online at: http://www.ofsted.gov.uk/Ofsted-home/Publications-and-research/Browse-all-by/Documents-by-type/Thematic-reports/Improving-primary-teachers-subject-knowledge-across-the-curriculum (accessed 26 October 2009).

Ofsted (2009b) *20 Outstanding Primary Schools Excelling against the Odds in Challenging Circumstances.* Available online at: http://www.ofsted.gov.uk/Ofsted-home/News/Press-and-media/2009/October/20-outstanding-primary-schools-excelling-against-the-odds-in-challenging-circumstances (accessed 19 October 2009).

Ofsted (2010) 'Learning: creative approaches that raise standards'. Available online at: http://www.ofsted.gov.uk/resources/learning-creative-approaches-raise-standards (accessed 25 May 2014).

Pimley, G. (n.d.) Available online at: http://www.teachprimary.com/learning_resources/view/making-cross-curricular-links (accessed 2 June 2014).

Pollard, A. (2002) *Reflective Teaching: Effective and Evidence-informed Professional Practice.* London: Continuum.

Primary National Strategy (PNS) (2004) *Excellence and Enjoyment: Learning and Teaching in the Primary Years. Planning and Assessment for Learning: Designing Opportunities for Learning. Professional Development Materials.* London: DfES. Available online at: http://nationalstrategies.standards.dcsf.gov.uk/node/88541.

Reeves, M. (1980) *Why History?* Nuffield Primary History. Available online at: http://www.primaryhistory.org/leading history/planning,270,SAR.html.

Rose (2008) *The Independent Review of the Primary Curriculum: Interim Report.* London: DCFS. Available online at: http://publications.teachernet.gov.uk.

Taylor, T. (2014) Available online at: http://www.imaginative-inquiry.co.uk/2013/07/the-new-primary-history-curriculum-whisper-it-is-really-good/ (accessed 31 June 2014).

Internet source

Ofsted (1999) *A Review of Primary Schools in England, 1994–1998.* Available online at: http://www.ofsted.gov.uk/Ofsted-home/Publications-and-research/Browse-all-by/Education/Key-stages-and-transition/Key-Stage-1/Primary-education-a-review-of-science-assessment.primary-schools-in-England-1994–98 (accessed 19 October 2009).

Chapter 11

Assessment for cross-curricular learning and teaching

Kathleen Taylor

Introduction

This chapter recognises that learning in primary schools is changing, and that assessment for learning techniques have to change in order to match these movements in educational thinking. Key concepts that teachers need to bring about effective assessment are considered: in particular, feedback and dialogue. The role of marking and its associated skills are discussed. The chapter then moves on to examine cross-curricular issues in assessment. A case study provides a practical example of assessment in its dynamic role, guiding learning. The chapter concludes that assessment works best when children adopt it as part of the integrated classroom experience.

Background

The purpose of this chapter is to consider how the integration of assessment 'for learning' works in a climate of changing practices and curriculum design in primary education.

Sternberg notes that, 'When students are taught in a way that fits how they think, they do better in school. Children with creative or practical abilities, who are almost never taught or assessed in a way that matches their pattern of abilities, may be at a disadvantage in course after course, year after year' (2006: 94). The idea of new 'freedoms' in primary education, advocated in the Excellence and Enjoyment initiative (2003), motivated schools to base their long-term planning to suit their ethos such that subject-based curriculum design began to be replaced by cross-curricular designs (DfES 2003: 16, 17). This decade has seen more schools taking up the freedoms to design their own curricula by gaining Academy status, and while state schools are required to provide the content of the new 2013 National Curriculum Programmes of Study, they are 'free to choose how they organise the school day' (DfE 2013: 5).

A topic- or thematic-based approach to teaching the curriculum is a common model, often covering Foundation subjects and science in the afternoons, while retaining English and mathematics teaching for the mornings. Another model used is 'topic weeks', where the whole week is given over to thematic teaching and learning. Cross-curricular organisation, such as through blocked and planned events as a structured part of the school year, or as part of routine activities, has been linked to creativity and creative teaching, as have well-organised cross-curricular links that allow scope for independent enquiry (Ofsted 2003: 11 13; Ofsted 2010: 8). Within the context of the 2013 National Curriculum, schools are continuing to develop long-term planning with a view to adopt a greater thematic cross-curricular approach, drawn from a wealth of experience gained through change.

Case Study 11.1 Key concepts as planning tools

A school leader for assessment explained how the school's curriculum was designed on the basis of key 'concepts', such as 'coordinates', 'time', 'shape' and 'measure', and 'inference', 'prediction', 'alternatives', etc. For example, inference is not limited to reading; rather it is a key concept where children use their past experiences to make judgements about what they see, which applies equally in science and other subjects, not only reading. She went on to explain that the school was not abandoning the principles that underpin innovative cross-curricular planning, rather its emphasis was on how it was planned, not by topic but by concepts. Using key concepts gave greater focus to assessment, which helped her and her team to 'know what to do now'. The teacher went on to say that planning in this way had developed pedagogy throughout the school, changing priority to assessment, and how to assess as part of teaching, not as an add-on.

Cross-curricular connections

Often, one finds teachers making cross-curricular connections within their medium- and short-term planning where a skill a child has learned in one subject can be reinforced and developed in another. For example, a suggested link for learning about coordinates is made in the 'Geometry: Position and direction' section of the Year 4 Programme of Study for maths (NC 2013), using coordinate-plotting ICT tools. Equally, 'Position and direction' objectives could be linked with 'Geographical skills for fieldwork', such as using grid references (DfE 2013: 112, 200). Enabling children to see the relevance of what they have learned in one subject by applying it to another is in itself motivating for the child and, importantly, helps the child to see relationships and make connections. The process resembles Bruner's spiral curriculum where curriculum design enables children to revisit their ideas, and build on knowledge and understanding, and at the same time allows them to practise previously learned skills (Bruner 1963: 52; see also Bruner's spiral curriculum, in Bruner 2006). In this way concepts are formed. The flexibility offered to schools, in the NC 2013, to introduce content earlier or later than set out in the Programme of Study further enhances Bruner's ideas of a spiral curriculum, and building and reflecting on learning.

Case Study 11.2 Developing cross-curricular work

A newly qualified teacher has been able to adopt a similar cross-curricular and creative approach in her medium-term plans, constructed collaboratively with other colleagues, and covering each half-term and her individual short-term weekly planning. She looks for links between subjects to make learning more relevant and exciting for the children. As part of her short-term planning for her Year 4 class, she had linked teaching about fractions in maths to teaching about notation in music – both elements from the medium-term plan relating to the Year 4 Programmes of Study. Music provided an opportunity for children to represent notes as fractions and use them to make connections between the length of a note, as well as using the language of whole, half, quarter and eighth notes correctly. In another short-term plan, she had linked data handling in mathematics to athletics and running races as part of practising for sports day in PE. In not wanting to take away teaching time from mathematics, she thought it 'a wonderful thing to combine the two', so planned a series of data-collecting activities outdoors (see Chapter 6). The teacher explained that assessment criteria linked to learning objectives for subject knowledge and skills for learning are clear in both long- and medium-term plans, giving her the confidence to make exciting and strong connections between subjects for developing children's conceptual understanding.

Reflection

Examine your short-term planning for opportunities where you could make exciting relevant connections between subjects. Ask how your long-term and medium-term planning supports you in making cross-curricular connections in your short-term plans.

Learning taxonomies and assessment for learning

Understanding the assessment criteria we use in schools is important to understanding actual practice and how to improve it. There are associations between the language used for assessment and fundamental principles of how we learn. The more the discourse for language to learn becomes part of teachers' spoken repertoire, the more focused the teaching for enabling children to improve. A teacher asking a child to *describe what* is happening – in, for instance, a science experiment – goes on to ask *why* one thing happens in *relation* to another, alerting the child to possible *connections* to deepen understanding and ultimately move the child towards providing a comprehensive *explanation*. The same 'language to learn' could equally be applied to making connections in a story. The discourse of how we learn crosses the curriculum, so when a teacher extends thinking in science by asking children to examine the *evidence* and *suggest* what might happen to heart rate if the independent variable were changed, such as type of exercise, the same happens in reading by asking children to *suggest* what might happen next in the story in light of what they have read (evidence) so far. Essentially the teacher, by using and modelling language that assists learning, is enabling the child to *extrapolate* – a skill that will assist them in learning across the curriculum.

Assessment criteria – whether devised by the school from the Programmes of Study in the 1989 NC or the later version in 1999, the 1998 National Numeracy and Literacy Frameworks and, more recently, in 2008 the Assessment for Learning Strategy (DCSF 2008) and the 2009 Assessing Pupil Progress (APP) for English, mathematics and science – draw upon the principles, and in particular the skills of how we learn. The assessment criteria of APP have been used to address the problem of relating overarching educational goals in the NC 1989/1999 Programmes of Study, and the same is being done in many schools for the NC 2013, to form assessment-focused long- and medium-term plans, to which the NQT refers. One of the advantages of cross-curricular planning is the way it moves teachers to contemplate the connections between overarching goals in the National Curriculum and discrete assessment criteria identified for lessons or a series of lessons. Beginning teachers sometimes find making the connection extremely difficult, but when they do it is as if a light has been switched on: suddenly they find a relevant context upon which to base anonymous learning objectives and outcomes, and develop a better sense of direction with the children. This is not to make light of the barriers that may be erected to adopting these kinds of approaches. For example, in schools in Malta moving to this model, Vella (2013) was right to note that:

> The constraints voiced by teachers were class size, students' motivation and ability and syllabus content, and that AfL is time consuming. Moreover, they also feel that not enough support is being given and they also lack training. Furthermore, teachers complained that they feel fatigued by the numerous innovations brought about by the current Reform in Education, including AfL. The teachers do however, desire, believe and request the necessary training so that formative assessment can be possible.

Fundamental to the Programmes of Study are taxonomies for learning, from which we form learning objectives and the related assessment criteria. Understanding this relationship helps embed within practice the ability (an advanced teaching skill) to assess as learning is happening so that teaching interventions are supportive and challenging for more learning to happen.

Benjamin Bloom, in the 1950s, devised a taxonomy of learning based on three overlapping learning domains: cognitive, affective and psychomotor. Each domain has within it a set of categories – the cognitive or 'thinking' domain contains the following six: knowledge, comprehension, application, analysis, synthesis and evaluation, ordered in degree of difficulty (see also Chapter 2). Anderson and Krathwohl revised the cognitive taxonomy to shift emphasis from a taxonomy as a measuring tool to one focused on cognitive processes (Krathwohl 2002: 213). Their focus places teaching at the centre of the assessment process, where it is used to progress children's learning, not only measure it. They devised new categories, which are: remember, understand, apply, analyse, evaluate and create, plus a subset of skills within each. The subset of skills from both taxonomies provided much of the skills for learning discourse that pervades the previous NC and current NC 2013. The same skills for learning are prevalent in the Development Matters for Early Years Foundation Stage document, running through the three elements that characterise effective early learning – 'playing and exploring', 'active learning' and 'critical thinking' – which link closely to Bloom's three learning domains. While the categories for learning are ordered in degree of difficulty, in practice skills for learning are iterative, working in relation to one another to deepen understanding, with the teacher providing the necessary inputs on content, and scaffolding language to enable the child to progress.

To further examine the iterative nature of learning and its significance to the way in which cross-curricular links can be made to enhance learning, the following scenario draws upon another taxonomy associated with reading comprehension.

Classification of comprehension skills was developed as long ago as 1968 by Barrett, in terms of literal comprehension, reorganisation including summarising, inferential comprehension, evaluation and appreciation. Beard, in his seminal work on reading, makes the point that the types of comprehension are not hierarchical; rather they should be used to open up possibilities for the teacher to ask more open-ended questions (Beard 1990: 147). For example, a teacher supporting a child reading from *Wind in the Willows*, complimented the child on *describing* Toad's glee at being reunited with his motor car, asking if there were any clues in the paragraph that might help *explain* why Toad *really* felt so happy. A further question posed by the teacher asked the child to *speculate* where it all might end. Rather than stop there, the teacher went on to ask questions about how the author had created hidden meaning (*inference*) drawing the child's attention to the subtle way in which verbs were used to capture Toad's defiance of authority and the obsession for motor cars at the root of Toad's glee. The teacher made the decision to teach to the higher-order skills involving the child in *appreciating* the writer's skill by drawing on examples by other authors the children had encountered, at the same time reinforcing, *recalling*, previously learned knowledge about the way language is used. Essentially it is an example of the teacher using questions drawing from the various types of comprehension and not limited to any one level.

The scenario makes clear the iterative process of learning and teaching that goes beyond teaching to a level. While categories from the various taxonomies are used hierarchically to measure attainment, research warns against teaching to the levels (Hull 1985; Drummond 2003; Hart *et al.* 2004; Wiliam 2011). A further important point is in recognising that the skills are not local to reading but transferable to other areas of the curriculum – for example, interpreting, appreciating and evaluating can apply to art, music and design, interpreting physical landscapes, evaluating contrasting arguments and interpretations from the past, etc. The skills are not bound by subject domain.

Promoting skills for learning across the curriculum was a key message in the previous NC (DfEE 1999: 20). Skills such as asking questions, observing and recording, collecting and classifying, making connections, were embedded in the NC Programmes of Study. Key Skills that help learners improve their learning and performance, and Thinking Skills associated with metacognition, learning how to learn, were also in the introduction to the NC (DfEE 1999: 20–22). Many of the same skills are embedded in the new NC 2013, and equally crucial in understanding the constructs for learning within the Aims and Programmes of Study. For example, while enquiry skills clearly underpin the 'working scientifically' section of the Science Programme of Study, skills associated with enquiry such as observe, explore, collect, classify, analyse, interpret, solve, reason, generate and evaluate, etc., permeate the Programmes of Study generally. Similarly, skills associated with communication, such as interpret, explain, infer and conjecture, cross the Programmes of Study. Recognising the way in which the 'discourse' of skills crosses the curriculum is important for planning but, most importantly, for teaching as it is in this context where children hear the language of skills and experience how they work. A teacher who models such discourse is in effect providing the language that enables the child to work equally well in various subject domains.

Often in the course of teaching a teacher will draw upon lower- and higher-order skills in a recursive way, like Bruner's spiral. In the example in Case Study 11.3, the teacher models the recursive nature of discourse for learning, in which assessment for learning is integral. In the exchanges that occur, the teacher assesses the children's thinking, providing the appropriate challenges to extend and deepen their understanding.

Case Study 11.3 Motorised eraser

The children in a Year 6 class are learning about electricity and magnetism through a series of science lessons linked to design and technology, where in entrepreneurial groups of four they have to *create* (synthesis) a motorised useful gadget. One group has made a motorised eraser. The teacher's first response was to admire it and ask 'How will you *assess its effectiveness*?' (evaluation). The children's response was to set up a series of tests using different papers, but they found that the motorised eraser alone could not provide the necessary pressure for rubbing out pencil marks. The teacher empathised with their dilemma, suggesting they *examine the relationships between each of the main components* (analysis) – the motor, the rubber and the paper – as there might be ways of strengthening, stiffening and reinforcing (D&T, Technical Knowledge – NC 2013). One of the children suggested the paper was too soft. In response the teacher suggested they *collect* and *organise* (synthesis) their ideas about why it would not work, and suggest possible *modifications* (synthesis) they could make. The teacher supported them through further dialogue, keeping questions open so that the children did the thinking.

The language of learning facilitates deeper understanding not only about the subject but about how to learn across the curriculum. The teacher in the case study is drawing upon knowledge about skills and knowledge about subjects to progress learning. Each example, the scenario and the case study, show the teacher seeking and interpreting what the children are saying and doing, making decisions about where they are in their learning, where they need to go and how best to get there (Assessment Reform Group 2002, in Harlen 2007: 16). The discourse acts as feedback, because it causes thinking about improving (Wiliam 2011: 120–127).

Reflection

Examine your school's medium-term assessment criteria. Are you able to make connections between the assessment criteria and how you use it for learning opportunities in the classroom?

Fisher talks about 'infusing' the language of thinking and learning into planning for teaching and classroom talk (Fisher 1998: 9). Think about the way you use language for learning in your interactions with children.

Assessment for learning

Vygotsky saw assessment, and what we would now refer to as assessment for learning, as a 'dynamic' process – not one that occurs only after having learned something, but as parallel with the learning (Drummond 2003: 136). Assessment for learning is about focusing not on what children have already learned, but rather on what children need to know and are about to learn, i.e. teaching in the 'zone of proximal development'. According to Drummond, a teacher who is 'enlightened by this form of assessment is in a good position to support each child's learning as it happens' (2003: 136). A common misconception in schools, reported in Ofsted's Annual Report 2012/2013, is the attention given to 'constant review of learning in lessons before sufficient learning has taken place' (Ofsted 2012/2013: 15). The teacher cross-examining pupils, and using searching questions to provoke deeper levels of understanding during task time epitomises 'outstanding' teaching (Ofsted 2012/2013: 16).

Research into classroom assessment, conducted by Black and Wiliam (1998), put children at the heart of assessment for learning, and as a consequence practices in assessment have indeed become much more *dynamic*, with greater emphasis being given to the child's role in assessment. This has led to the phrase 'assessment *as* learning' (Briggs *et al.* 2008) being used to describe assessment's integral role in the ongoing process of teaching and learning.

Involving children in assessment is crucial if assessment is to be meaningful to them. The strategy of children forming their own success criteria in relation to a learning objective is one way to ensure a sense of relevance for the child. It encapsulates what Black and Wiliam meant in the child being at the heart of assessment. In one school, children suggest success criteria as part of the taught lesson, collecting the criteria in a 'shopping trolley' drawn on the whiteboard. At the end of the lesson the children judge how relevant their success criteria are in relation to their learning. The most relevant is then used to scrutinise their learning and the teaching. From the discussions children organised in pairs or small groups feed back to the whole class with the next steps. Children are encouraged to make suggestions of ways forward, often resulting in their making cross-curricular links. For example, in a Y5 class learning about punctuation, children using their own success criteria decided they needed more practice using speech marks, suggesting they could write up the arguments for and against slavery, reporting on who said what, as part of their history project on the Romans. Involving children in the whole process of assessment for learning provides the children with the necessary opportunities to demonstrate their knowledge and understanding of what the words 'assessment for learning' mean in practice.

Planning is dynamic when it takes account of the day-to-day assessments made by the teacher and children, and provides opportunities the next day or in the near future for children to revisit areas of need. While some subject-specific needs might be met in the same subject, a subject domain should not restrict the needs of the child. Assessment should drive planning so that, when the teacher encounters a child struggling to understand, links with real-life situations or other areas of the curriculum are used to clarify understanding for the child. For example, in a Key Stage 1 maths lesson about measure it might be to remind the child of the relationship between standard units of measure that are difficult to understand out of context, i.e. 1,000 grams in a kilogram, 100 centimetres in a metre. The confusion for a child might be that in weight the name is given to the smaller unit, i.e. gram, whereas in measurement the name is given to the larger unit, i.e. metre. This could be explored by the teacher to help children remember the relationships in weight and in measurement, as would practice using the measures – for example, making biscuits in design and technology or measuring distances in geography. It is not sufficient to provide more of the same; rather make links across the curriculum where children can use and apply the measures for familiarity and understanding. Planning more opportunities for children to develop understanding of core subject principles through other subject areas, and based upon assessment of both common and unexpected misconceptions, provides the necessary practical and relevant experiences for gaining understanding.

Enquiry learning and working scientifically: making connections

Enquiry learning is a most meaningful way to link subjects. In many ways, 'working scientifically' sections in the science Programme of Study (NC 2013) exemplify an enquiry approach to learning using skills such as asking relevant questions, setting up simple practical enquiries, making systematic observations and accurate measurements, gathering and recording, classifying and presenting data, recording and reporting findings, using results to draw simple conclusions, using evidence to answer questions or to support their findings (NC 2013: Lower Key Stage 2 Programme of Study Working Scientifically). While closely associated with the science Programmes of Study, these skills pervade other subject Programmes of Study; the case study at the end of this section shows these skills in action across other subjects.

Enquiry, investigation and problem solving are not limited to science; rather they form the hub of how we go about learning, and for that reason are applicable to all subjects (see Chapter 14). A starting point for learning may well begin with a science focus – for example, investigating plants in the local environment (NC 2013 Programme of Study) – but invariably lead to questions about what grows where and why, providing strong links to geography, especially in geographical skills for fieldwork and human and physical geography sections of the NC 2013. Furthermore, skills in some subjects can enhance perception in another. For example, responding artistically (Art and Design) to what is seen, such as plants, rocks, animals in the natural environment (Science), deepens perception and causes the child to raise more questions (Pugh and Girod 2007: 19; Taylor and Woolley 2013: 9). Similarly, investigating lines of symmetry in maths enhances children's perception of symmetry in nature and its different forms, where symmetry occurs and why (Science).

Working scientifically exemplifies John Dewey's philosophy of education, which was a major influence in reforming educational practice in the early part of the 20th century and continues to influence education today. He believed the object of school was to 'arouse curiosity and investigation, to train the powers of observation and to instil a practical sense of the powers of enquiry', a philosophy that contributed to a shift away from only informing children in the subject to one where children were encouraged to investigate and make connections (Dewey, in Garforth 1966: 71; McDermott 1973: 498–499). Dewey commented on how much 'keener and more extensive' observations and ideas would be if formed through experience that required us to 'hunt for connections' (McDermott 1973: 499). Enquiry is all about seeking patterns, their similarities, differences and distinctions, and how the patterns connect one thing to another (Bateson 2002: 7).

Curiosity precedes enquiry and is integral to enquiry, which the NC 2013 promotes across subject domains. The 'high quality education' to which the NC 2013 aspires is about 'inspiring pupils' curiosity' referred to in a number of the 'Purpose of Study' sections. While children are naturally curious and open minded, 'working scientifically' is more demanding for both child and teacher in terms of asking questions, reflecting and re-forming them to see things in different ways, gathering evidence and clues, often through close observation and using these to suggest answers to the questions, generating and investigating ideas and ultimately testing the validity of such ideas. Teacher and child must draw upon their knowledge of science and other subjects to find explanations of their findings – all part of the enquiry process (Fisher 1995: 220–253). These skills provide a focus for assessment because they can be improved. Improving in the skills further motivates a child's curiosity to want to find out, make connections, identify relationships and solve problems.

The following case study is of an enquiry-based study generated in a Year 5/6 class. It shows the skills associated with working scientifically but not in science.

Case Study 11.4 Solving a storage problem

Several problems with storage were affecting the daily running of the classroom because of the time out needed to address the problems. The problems ranged from coats and clothing on the corridor floor, mix-ups with water bottles, missing children's workbooks, curled up corners of reading books . . . the list went on. The class teacher organised for pairs of children to take a problem, investigate and research it, and come up with possible ways to resolve it. The first step was for children to generate questions relating to their chosen problem. One pair of children investigating the coats on corridor floor problem generated several relevant questions such as:

- Are the same coats on the floor every day?
- Are the pegs too high for some children?
- Are the pegs too close together?
- Are the pegs curled enough to retain the coats?
- Are some coats longer than the distance from the peg to the floor?
- Have the coats all got loops?
- Are more things than coats hung on a peg?

The children worked out how to collect the data they needed to answer the questions, which involved various mathematical skills concerning data collection, including representation in graphs, charts, etc., and analysis. They were able to deduce the main causes for coats on the corridor floor and propose solutions. Sharing this information led the children into producing presentations (English and ICT) to their classmates. The solutions they suggested involved the children in making posters to remind children to keep their coats on pegs (Art and Design), designs for better pegs and stronger loops in coats (D&T).

Reflection

One of the main criticisms of cross-curricular design lies in the balance between the breadth of study and depth of study such that children are sufficiently empowered in the structures of the subject both in terms of skills and knowledge (Bruner 1963: 12).

The danger of multidisciplinary approaches is for subject knowledge to be covered too thinly. How would you ensure that an enquiry-based approach such as in the case study stimulated deep thinking in the various subjects?

Building opportunities for children to reflect on how they have learned in lessons is a way for them to evaluate how working scientifically has helped them learn something new, i.e. new knowledge. The next section looks at the role of reflection in more depth.

Assessment as the active agent in teaching and learning: feedback and dialogue

We can now take a closer look at the formative day-to-day assessment that lies at the heart of teaching, and that sits equally well in both subject-bound planning and cross-curricular planning. Assessment is not a passive process: it is active because of its integral role in the process of teaching such that the teacher's reflection on, and response to, children's learning involves interaction and intervention (Vella 2013). In this way, assessment for learning serves to reinforce, consolidate and extend learning. Black and Wiliam (1998) pointed to five specific features of assessment for learning that they saw as the most instrumental for improving achievement:

1   Positive feedback focusing on the quality of the child's work and advice about how to improve.
2   Children trained in self-assessment.
3   Opportunities for children to express their understanding designed into *any* piece of teaching, for this will initiate interaction whereby formative assessment aids learning.
4   Dialogue between children and teacher that is reflective, thoughtful, and focused to explore understanding.
5   Children given the opportunity and help to improve following feedback from tests and homework (Pollard 2002: 314–315).

These points are used to begin the discussion here because, when looked at as a whole, they form the basis of enabling practice for both teachers and children.

Implicit in the ethos of a good classroom is a teacher's and the children's shared appreciation of a positive approach and attitude to their work and efforts. Indeed Black and Wiliam (1998) make the point that 'entering a dialogue' with a child or children about a piece of work (the word 'work' here means any classroom task and is not confined to something which is written) should be from a 'positive' perspective by focusing on the 'qualities' of the work (Pollard 2002: 314). It is all too easy to lower a child's self-esteem with feedback that is negative or vague, or that appears positive but is in effect dismissive.

Black (1998) argues that 'vague and incomplete' feedback is an indication to the child that their work is poor, and that in time the child will come to believe success is unachievable (Black 1998: 133–134). He goes on to say that children's feelings about their work are 'key determiners' in whether they perceive themselves as good learners or weak. Indeed, what a child experiences in terms of feedback may well determine his or her success or failure. The idea of 'entering a dialogue' is key, as it rightly denies any dismissive responses by the teacher such as a glib 'that's fantastic', in preference to a response that gives the children the opportunity to explain why work is good and what the next steps might be. This sort of diagnostic feedback requires an open-ended questioning response by teachers where the emphasis is not on recalling information but about speculating and problem solving (Alexander 2008: 61).

Of course such dialogue takes time. For this reason, planning for such opportunities needs to be built in to lessons. For example, it is common practice for lessons to contain more than one plenary, referred to as mini-plenaries, which are strategically placed throughout the lesson to allow children to explore any difficulties they may be encountering and how to overcome and reflect on their learning for next steps. These types of plenary might involve peer and self-assessment, where one child explains the problems his/her partner is encountering in order for other children to help out. They also provide an opportunity for the teacher to assess and provide the teaching interventions necessary to resolve the problem and provide challenge to those who need it. A crucial aspect of such reflective tasks is for children to be clear about the purposes of their learning and the related criteria for assessment, so that they can relate them to their learning efforts and the efforts of others, as for peer assessment. In this way children come to know the conventions of dialogue and how to assess their work, because they see how it is done, learning from one another and practising the associated skills. Black and Wiliam (1998) refer to this as children being 'trained in self-assessment', and building self-assessment activities into classroom practice is one way of doing this (Black 1998: 130).

Dialogue is a word that has taken up greater significance in primary education in the 21st century because of renewed emphasis on its central role in learning (Mercer 1995, 2000; Alexander 2000, 2004, 2008; Primary National Strategy 2003). What is special about dialogue is that it involves a search, a journey with a quest, wherein the participants are all seeking to find knowledge and understanding. Dialogue is not loose, but guided by a teacher who actively encourages children to make connections, correct misconceptions and justify their views. It leads to deeper understanding and new knowledge, and brings about insights of oneself as a learner and teacher. Alexander's and Mercer's ideas, on dialogic teaching and discourse respectively, link well with assessment for learning because both require the teacher to be the 'reflective agent' who steers and directs the dialogue in a purposeful way and in light of what is being said (Pollard 2002: 312). The teacher simultaneously responds, interacts, reflects, initiates and leads, such that the reflections are active.

Black and Wiliam make a strong case for dialogue that is 'thoughtful, reflective, focused to evoke and explore understanding, and conducted so that pupils have the opportunity to think and express their ideas' (Black and Wiliam 1998: 12; Pollard 2002: 315). For the dialogue to remain focused on assessment for learning, both teacher and children need to know that their evaluations are based on known educational goals, including objectives that are part of a planned sequence of learning. If this does not happen, assessment becomes a limited exercise in opinion rather than one where the children have to explain and justify what they think. However, such reflective dialogue should not be designed only to see that objectives are being achieved. Undoubtedly, for some children this may be a hurdle in itself, but rather the dialogue can extend learning beyond the objectives. Dialogue that helps the child reflect will reinforce and consolidate learning as well as extend it. For this reason planning should take account of what teaching is involved in working below, within and beyond the expected levels of attainment to ensure the teacher is prepared to extend the dialogue to support learning beyond expectations (DfEE 1999: 17). The theme of support of learning beyond expectations is taken up also in Chapter 8.

Assessment for learning is the way to know the child so that the child's full potential to learn is realised. Socio-constructivist models of how 'knowledge is co-constructed' (Mercer 1995) suggest that learning can surpass levels of expectation through talk 'scaffolded' (Bruner, in Mercer 1995: 73) by the teacher that maximises the potential for learning, i.e. the zone of proximal development (Vygotsky 1978: 86, in Pollard 2002: 142).

Case Study 11.5 Scaffolded talk

In a Foundation Stage 2 class, children are using Julia Donaldson's book *The Snail and the Whale* as a basis for working across the curriculum. Painting and collage work, role play and drama, a collaboratively constructed story wall, small-world toys and outdoor play equipment are arranged to provide opportunities for the children to explore the adventures of the snail and the whale, and using their imagination, invent their own adventures. The rich experiences of the children spur them to want to write, and it is here where one sees on a daily basis the diagnostic scaffolded talk that supports and guides children to work at developmental levels above expectations. The teachers work to enable the children to meet and go beyond their educational goals in writing by listening to the children's ideas, supporting talk for children to express their ideas, focusing on writing skills linked to children's individual needs linked to phonics, pencil grip, letter formation, etc. Each child has a copy of the book to read and examine with adults and one another, and the story is retold regularly. The advantage of the cross-curricular medium-term plan means children can revisit the story in a variety of ways, each experience restimulating the imagination so that ideas for writing are not exhausted but rather generated.

Reflection

Think about how your classroom supports children to want to learn. How does painting and collage work support writing? Why is it important for the child to have their personal copy of the book? What teaching skills are involved in managing the complexity and demands of teaching through a cross-curricular approach in this Foundation Stage 2 classroom?

A difficulty for teachers, and especially new and beginning teachers, is the demand that socio-constructivist models place on their knowledge of practice and knowledge of the subject. Purposeful talk used for 'steering classroom talk with particular educational goals in view' and 'cumulative' talk where 'teachers and children build on their own and each other's ideas and chain them into coherent lines of thinking and enquiry' are relatively rare (Alexander 2004: 34). One of the most difficult aspects for those new to teaching to achieve is actively to pursue a line of enquiry with a single child, because it is high on demand about knowledge of pedagogy and knowledge of the subject; its very rarity means that beginning teachers may not have seen this modelled in the classroom.

One of the criticisms concerning cross-curricular activities is the danger of losing sight of educational goals pertaining specifically to knowledge of a subject. Furthermore, beginning teachers may not be entering a situation where the relationships with the children have been established; as the co-construction of knowledge lies heavily upon these relationships, this may pose another difficulty (Mercer 1995: 61). Nevertheless the contention of all the research cited here is that dialogue for learning should be given greater prominence in classroom practice.

While the argument here is for assessment for learning to be integral to dialogue and classroom talk, an attempt has been made to identify some of the difficulties for beginning teachers, especially in terms of knowledge about practice and the subject. In this context, however, a further point Black and Wiliam (1998) make regarding tests and homework is one worthy of further examination and one to which we turn in the next section.

Marking and feedback

Marking and the associated feedback on work and homework, unlike day-to-day assessment for learning, may not be tied tightly to the immediacy of classroom practice. Considering the child's work away from the classroom provides time for the teacher to think about what best to do next. Teachers in training, and newly qualified teachers, often gain much from marking children's work and designing feedback, because it is in this situation that there is time to think about the quality of the questions or instructions they set for the piece of work and, in doing so, they learn to modify what they ask in order to elicit more useful responses. Also, they are able to think carefully about what comments might best enhance learning and what implications their comments have in relation to providing opportunities to enable the children to put into practice their suggestions (see also Pollard 2002: 315). All teachers need time to reflect on what children's work tells them about the pupils' progress on the one hand, and about what it tells them about their own teaching on the other.

Marking is a reflective process and is one of the most strategic ways for a teacher to improve practice. It is like a dry run for assessment for learning in the classroom, whereby the implications of pursuing a line of enquiry with a child can be tried out at a distance. For the feedback comments to be of value, future planning needs to take on board the time needed for the child to address the feedback, and exactly how and where this will be achieved. This process may be cross-curricular in nature: thus a pupil may address issues and learning points in feedback about measurement in maths through geography or design technology. One example was of two students in training teaching place value, which was proving difficult and feedback directed within maths was working for only some of the children. Consequently, the two students designed several lessons on dance that required children to move relative to the decimal point, indicating the change and therefore the relevance of place value. Information gathered through marking, together with noteworthy insights collected through oral feedback during teaching, should form the basis of any necessary modifications on day-to-day planning, which may or may not influence only teaching in the subject but also through relevant opportunities in other subjects. In practice, the outcomes often take the form of annotations on lesson plans that show the modifications made to practice and the growth of the teacher as a reflective practitioner.

Case Study 11.6 Raising standards

Several years ago, when Alexander's work on dialogic teaching was introduced, the headteacher of one school incorporated it into the school's culture and strategic plan to raise standards. On his eight-year journey, so far the hardest element to achieve has been raising standards. He came to the understanding that standards are ultimately about the child, and posed three questions, which are now used in his school to drive teaching and learning:

- What motivates the child?
- What challenges the child?
- What is it that makes a child creative?

One of the ways in which these questions are answered centres around the dialogue that takes place as part of dialogic teaching, and dialogic feedback and marking established in the school. Feedback in the children's books is written during teaching time as well as in the usual way following a lesson. It invariably requires a response from the child. One of the teachers referred to the marking as 'scaffolded marking'. For example, for a child less likely to respond to her marking she provides options for the child to choose. For another child who finishes quickly she provides feedback where the child has to review the work for problems. Her comment was, 'You have four sentences beginning with "I"; what do you think?' The child responded, 'I think that I need to change them because it won't interest the reader.' For another child who was finding it difficult to write in paragraphs she asked the child to try to draw what a paragraph might look like, which the child did, showing a circle of arrows connecting the opening to the end with links in between.

Another example is of a child who has written at length about an experiment investigating why food mould is dangerous. The teacher's feedback picked out a 'super fact' qualified by 'So, if ice doesn't kill mould why do we freeze food?' To which the child wrote back, 'To freeze bacteria, then heat it up to kill them to prevent them inhabiting food.' Another child, having written about Hurricane Sandy, was asked as part of the teacher's marking, 'Is this worse than any human feature, for example a new airport being built?' The child's written response was, 'In my mind it would be the same because the hurricane destroys people's lives, and kills, but the airport causes the storm because pollution causes global warming and global warming causes extreme storms.'

Each book tells the story of the child's learning. The headteacher said, 'You can pick up a child's book in the school and know their story.' In the same way, like annotations on lesson plans, marking feedback also shows the growth of a teacher.

Reflection

How do you provide child–teacher dialogue in your feedback that gives the opportunity for the child to reflect and build upon what has been learned?

How does feedback on children's learning influence your day-to-day planning and lessons?

Consider the benefits and demands of both questions.

Cross-curricular contexts for learning and assessment for learning

In what follows we move to look at a context for learning that promotes cross-curricular learning, and where assessment for learning is integrated. Links are made between the more theoretical models from earlier in the chapter and practice drawn from classrooms. The following example of creating a Healthy Food School Shop, with an emphasis on Personal, Social, Health and Economic education, draws from several enterprise projects undertaken with children in school and student teachers in training. The original plans are adapted to the present purpose but the principle remains the same.

The needs of the children are paramount in learning through a cross-curricular project so that all pupils feel fully included and involved. For example, in one school with a proportion of children from an Asian culture, the class shop reflected their culture. Posters advertising the shop were written in various languages representative of the many cultures in the locality. In some school settings it is important to promote different cultures, and for those in Key Stage 2 learning a foreign language, a project such as this is an ideal setting for using the language in conversation, and developing accurate pronunciation and intonation (DfE 2013: 213). Overcoming potential barriers to learning for individuals and groups has to be given the highest priority when designing cross-curricular learning so that there are no barriers to every child achieving (DfE 2013: 8).

The project is appropriate for higher Key Stage 2 pupils but can easily be modified for other year groups including KS1. The medium-term plan for the enterprise should draw upon the KS2 Programmes of Study in a variety of subjects with a key focus on Design & Technology and Nutrition. Aspects of English, Spoken Language and Mathematics also feature strongly with some aspects of Science. PSHE facilitates various skills. For this project, social awareness, reflecting on learning and economic awareness form the three foci that form assessment questions for children, which are interchangeable across the curriculum. Student teachers working with similar projects provided reasons for conducting cross-curricular work of this nature, which are useful for contextualising the project within the Aims and Purposes of study in the National Curriculum 2013. These are as follows:

- Engagement of children in structured learning experiences leading to the development of a healthy shop for the class that will be economically viable and promote healthy eating.
- First-hand, real-life experiences through which pupils gain knowledge, skills and understanding in National Curriculum subjects that meet and exceed expectations.
- Assessment that is integral to planning and teaching where knowledge and skills learnt in one subject can be applied in others.
- Purpose and relevance to learning so that children are highly motivated and want to learn.

The enterprise involves children in:

- Meeting with the bank to organise funding and discuss money issues (the main source of funding was a starter sum as part of a government enterprise initiative with the bank; another way of raising money is to fund-raise for the project)
- Visiting a whole-food bakery, its mill and restaurant, to see what a healthy food shop looks like
- Conducting a healthy food survey in school to determine what would sell well
- Setting up a 'pantry' of ingredients for making the food
- Considering prices for buying ingredients
- Organising the working areas and arranging equipment
- Organising a site for the shop and equipping the shop
- Promoting the shop and healthy eating
- Working out ongoing costs.
- Practising skills to make the food, supply and run the shop
- Managing the shop
- Accounting.

Skills and subject content from the NC can be modified or emphasised depending upon the needs of the children in the class, and used to underpin the enterprise. Sharing with the children what skills and content are being emphasised is important for the integration of assessment for learning as this will help in their analysis of their own and one another's skills, knowledge and understanding, and attitudes as part of the reflective activities planned in to the lessons. Underpinning the enterprise with PSHE objectives supports the affective aspect of children's learning, i.e. their attitudes to learning, one of the domains of Bloom's taxonomy. Placing the assessment criteria in the form of child-friendly questions on cards that are then laminated provides a useful resource that could be used for reference throughout the enterprise, and help both children and teacher keep track of where they are going with the project in terms of learning. The lesson plans are devised from the medium-term plan, which sets out the matrix of objectives from the Programmes of Study and the associated assessment criteria in relation to the sequence of contextualised activities.

The task (below) is one of several that make up the enterprise project. It aims to address skills, knowledge, and understanding and attitudes across the curriculum for Year 5 and 6 children. Assessment activities for the children are built in so that children can reflect upon their learning and identify their learning needs for the project to move forward. The organisation for the task is for all the children in four or five groups to engage in the task over the period of four days and in preparation for the presentations on the fifth day. A group representing the managers (from another class) taste the produce as it is made, write a comment on the quality – in terms of presentation, how it looks, how it tastes – and identify what distinguishes one group's produce from another group's for reference at the presentations. The organisation for making the food determines the timetable for the other parts of the task to take place. It should all take place within a week. The taught sessions that accompany the task are in parentheses.

As part of the organisation for the task, children's assessment of their own and one another's learning is built in. For example, one group makes wholemeal bread while another group observes and assesses using child-friendly sets of questions to help them. Table 11.1 shows skills and subject content from the NC Programmes of Study, which in itself can be adapted so that children can use them as part of their observations and assessments. The NC references are included here, but these need not be part of the information given to the children. Similarly the questions can be used by the groups involved and the managers to help judge the presentations, and are adapted from the Programmes of Study pertinent to the presentation task. Debriefing time and plenaries provide crucial opportunities for the groups to reflect on their observations, discuss the skills they have used, the knowledge they have gained, their attitudes to the various elements of the task, the insights they might have gained into themselves as learners, and what implications there are for their development as learners. Often a group will add to or modify the original questions aligned to 'children's assessment criteria' in order to convey meaning more clearly.

The task for children

As a result of a survey conducted in school, mini wholemeal bread buns were found to be one of the popular choices of foods for morning break time; the managers of the healthy food shop have decided to buy in their bread on a daily basis. The optimum number of bread buns needed per day calculated from survey figures is 28.

You are invited to tender for the contract to supply the healthy food shop with 28 mini wholemeal bread buns per day, Monday to Friday. Your task is to:

Table 11.1 Using assessment criteria

Skills and subject knowledge for the task National Curriculum 2013 Programmes of Study	Children's assessment criteria
English: spoken language 1–6 Listen and respond appropriately to adults and their peers	• Were the group members able to ensure everyone was listened to and how did they do this?
• Maintain attention and participate actively in collaborative conversations, staying on topic and responding to comments • Gain, maintain and monitor the interests of the listeners	• What did you see happening that encouraged people to join in? • Was communication always verbal or did you notice other means of communication such as facial expression or gesture, and what effect did this have?
English: Programme of Study Y5 & Y6	• How were the main ideas clearly conveyed? • How did the organisational features of the text grab the attention of the audience?
• Select appropriate form of writing for a presentation • Use organisational and presentational devices • Perform the presentation using appropriate intonation, volume and movement so that meaning is clear	• What changes would you suggest to improve the writing? • Were there elements of the presentation that were provocative? How did the presenters draw these aspects to your attention?
Mathematics: programme of study Y5 & Y6 Number: addition and subtraction (Y5)	• Were there elements you would have included? If so why? • What did the group need to know to work out costings for the supply of mini wholemeal bread buns to the shop?
• Add and subtract numbers mentally with increasingly large numbers • Solve addition and subtraction multi-step problems in context deciding which operations to use and why • Use rounding to check answers to calculations and determine, in the context of a problem, levels of accuracy	• How did they identify problems and re-solve them? • How did they check for accuracy? • What were the different ways in which the group solved problems about the cost and quantities of ingredients?
Number: addition, subtraction, multiplication and division (Y6)	• What problems did the group encounter when calculating? What would you do to help and what would you do differently?
• Perform mental calculations, including with mixed operations and large numbers • Solve problems involving addition, subtraction, multiplication and division • Use estimation to check answers to calculations and determine, in the context of a problem levels of accuracy	• How did the group refine preparation, cooking and cleaning-away skills to make the process more efficient? • How did the group ensure the process was hygienic? • How did the group make their bread buns distinctive?
Design & Technology: Aims (KS2)	• What sources of ICT did the group draw upon and in what way were they useful?
• Understand and apply the principles of nutrition and learn how to cook • Prepare and cook using a range of cooking techniques	• Why did the group use ICT to support their presentation? • What ICT innovations enhanced the presentation? • How did the group promote healthy eating?

(continued)

Table 11.1 (continued)

Skills and subject knowledge for the task National Curriculum 2013 Programmes of Study	Children's assessment criteria
Computing: Aims (KS2) • Responsible, competent, confident and creative users of information and communication technology Personal, Social, Health and Economic education Social awareness: Contribute to group tasks and discussions Be aware of other people's needs Cooperate with others Appreciate the experience of others Benefit from what others say and do Personal reflection and improving own learning and performance: Reflect and critically evaluate your work and what you have learned With the support of others, identify ways to improve your learning Solve problems: Identify and understand a problem Plan ways to solve it Monitor the solution and review the situation	• How did the group decide who does what? • How did the group make decisions and how was agreement reached? • How did they help one another? • What problems did the group experience and how did they overcome these? • Were you clear about the purposes of the task in terms of what it helped you to learn? • Can you identify aspects of the task where you felt you learned the most? • What obstacles hindered your learning and how did you overcome them? • How did the group find out about and decide on a recipe for the bread? • How did the group resolve problems such as cost versus health? • Did the group examine solutions to problems and why was this important?

- Decide a company name and logo (group work)
- Consider how to meet the requirements of supplying the shop with 28 mini wholemeal bread buns per day (maths and design/technology taught sessions and group work)
- Design and cost the mini wholemeal bread buns (design/technology and maths taught sessions and group work/ICT)
- Make a sample of mini wholemeal bread buns for tasting (supervised group work)
- Put in writing your costings and, at the presentation, hand them to the healthy food shop managers; you will need to consider the profit you need to make to ensure you can remain in business (maths, teacher-led sessions and group work)
- Prepare a three-minute presentation to the managers of the healthy food shop trialling the mini wholemeal bread buns (ICT/English speaking and listening, writing and drama).

Presentations

The presentation that forms one of the outcomes of this task is the cumulative result of the peer assessment and debriefing activities integral to the project; it provides a further means by which the children can make explicit learning that is implicit. For this reason it is a very useful assessment tool. Barnes (2007: 224) makes a distinction between presentation and performance, where presentation is defined as work in progress. The presentation in this project, while it forms an end-point in terms of the tender, occurs relatively early in the project and is one of several presentations for a real-life purpose that can be built in – for example, presentations that address the cost versus health issues. The questions for the managers, like the questions used to assess spoken language and skills in ICT elsewhere in the project (Table 11.1), ensure that the assessment of presentations remains focused and relevant and is yet another means of educating children in assessment for learning (see Table 11.1).

The value of such a project is the high level of motivation it stirs in the children, and the exciting and joyful learning environment highly motivated children create. The assessment for learning built in to the project is there to serve the child first and foremost. Children come to see that criteria for assessment, whether as statements or questions, or both, are there to help them understand why they are learning what they are learning and, importantly, how to move their learning forward. The cycle of learning the task follows is very much aligned to Kolb's cycle of experiential learning, where learning is rooted in first-hand 'concrete experiences' that are 'observed and reflected upon' and lead to the 'abstract conceptualisation', or how we think about things, all of which is achieved by being actively involved, which Kolb calls 'active experimentation' (http://www.business-balls.com/kolblearningstyles.htm).

Conclusion

Children gaining familiarity with the language of assessment by engaging in assessment for learning activities as part of a meaningful project are more able to pose further questions that help modify or even redefine the original problem and thereby analyse solutions more thoroughly. Sternberg (2007) suggests that in the process of redefining a problem is a 'willingness to grow' and a willingness 'to persevere in face of obstacles'.

Assessment for learning pushes the boundaries of conventional forms of teaching. So, too, do adventurous contexts for learning across the curriculum. Together these elements set the tone for exciting and adventurous classrooms. Their combination leaves room for much future research into their dynamics and interrelationships.

References

Alexander, R. (2000) *Culture and Pedagogy: International Comparisons in Primary Education.* Oxford: Blackwell.

Alexander, R. (2004) *Towards Dialogic Teaching: Rethinking Classroom Talk* (3rd edn). York: Dialogos.

Alexander, R. (2008) *Essays in Pedagogy.* London: Routledge.

Assessment Reform Group (ARG) (2002) *Assessment for Learning: 10 Principles: Research-based Principles to Guide Classroom Practice.* Cambridge: Cambridge Institute of Education Assessment Reform Group.

Barnes, J. (2007) *Cross-curricular Learning 3–14.* London: PCP.

Bateson, G. (2002) *Mind and Nature: A Necessary Unity.* Cresskill, NJ: Hampton Press, Inc.

Beard, R. (1990) *Developing Reading 3–13* (2nd edn). London: Hodder & Stoughton.

Black, P. (1998) *Testing: Friend or Foe? Theory and Practice of Assessment and Testing.* London: Falmer Press.

Black, P. and Wiliam, D. (1998) *Inside the Black Box: Raising Standards Through Classroom Assessment*. London: King's College.

Briggs, M., Woodfield, A., Martin, C. and Swatton, P. (2008) *Assessment for Learning and Teaching in Primary Schools* (2nd edn). Exeter: Learning Matters.

Bruner, J. (1963) *The Process of Education*. New York: Vintage Books.

Bruner, J. (2006) *Jerome Bruner's Constructivist Model and the Spiral Curriculum for Teaching and Learning*. Available online at: http://www.archive.today/www.gtce.org.uk/tla/rft/bruner0506 (accessed 10 June 2014).

DCSF (2008) *The Assessment for Learning Strategy*. National Strategies, QCA/Chartered Institute of Educational Assessors. Nottingham: DCSF. Available online at: https://www.education.gov.uk/publications/ . . . /DCSF-00341–2008.pdf (accessed 10 June 2014).

DfE (2013) *The National Curriculum in England: Framework Document*. Crown Copyright.

DfEE (1999) *The Review of the National Curriculum in England: The Consultation Materials*. London: DfEE.

DfEE and QCA (1999) *The National Curriculum: Handbook for Primary Teachers in England. Key Stages 1 and 2*. London: DfEE/QCA.

DfES (2003) *Excellence and Enjoyment: A Strategy for Primary Schools*. London: DfES.

Drummond, M. (2003) *Assessing Children's Learning* (2nd edn). London: David Fulton.

ESRC (2009) *Assessment in Schools. Fit for Purpose? A Commentary by the Teaching and Learning Research Programme*. London: ESRC, TLRP. Available online at: http://www.tlrp.org/pub/documents/assessment.pdf (accessed 10 June 2014).

Fisher, R. (1995) *Teaching Children to Think*. Cheltenham: Stanley Thornes (Publishers) Ltd.

Fisher, R. (1998) 'Thinking about thinking: developing meta-cognition in children'. *Early Childhood Development and Care* 141: 1–15.

Garforth, F. W. (1966) *John Dewey Selected Educational Writings*. London: Heinemann.

Harlen, W. (2007) *Assessment of Learning*. London: Sage Publications.

Hart, S., Dixon, A., Drummond, M. J. and McIntyre, D. (2004) *Learning without Limits*. Maidenhead: Open University Press.

Hull, R. (1985) *The Language Gap. How Classroom Dialogue Fails*. London: Methuen.

Krathwohl, D. R. (2002) 'A revision of Bloom's taxonomy: an overview'. *Theory Into Practice* 41(4): 213–218.

McDermott, J. J. (1973) *The Philosophy of John Dewey*. London and Chicago: University of Chicago Press.

Mercer, N. (1995) *The Guided Construction of Knowledge: Talk Amongst Teachers and Learners*. Clevedon: Multilingual Matters.

Mercer, N. (2000) *Words and Minds: How We Use Language to Think Together*. London: Routledge.

Ofsted (2003) *Expecting the Unexpected*. Available online at: http://www.ofsted.gov.uk/resources/expecting-unexpected-Ofsted (accessed 4th June 2014).

Ofsted (2010) *Learning: Creative Approaches That Raise Standards*. Available online at: http://www.ofsted.gov.uk/resources/learning-creative-approaches-raise-standards (accessed 30 May 2014).

Ofsted (2012/2013) *The Report of Her Majesty's Chief Inspector of Education, Children's Services and Skills*. Available online at: http://www.ofsted.gov.uk/resources/ofsted-annual-report-201213-schools (accessed 30 May 2014).

Pollard, A. (2002) *Reflective Teaching: Effective and Evidence-informed Professional Practice*. London: Continuum.

Primary National Strategy (2003) *Speaking, Listening, Learning: Working With Children in Key Stages 1 and 2*. London: QCA/DfES.

Pugh, K. J. and Girod, M. (2007) 'Science, art and experience: constructing a science pedagogy from Dewey's aesthetics'. *Journal of Science Teacher Education* 18: 9–27.

Sternberg, R. (2006) 'The nature of creativity'. *Creativity Research Journal* 18(1): 87–98.

Sternberg, R. (2007) *Creating Creative Thinkers for a Changing World*. Cambridge Assessment Conference, October. Cambridge: University of Cambridge.

Taylor, K. and Woolley, R. (2013) *Values and Vision in Primary Education*. Maidenhead: Open University Press.

Vella, G. (2013) 'Developing an assessment for learning policy document in two primary schools of a school network'. MSc thesis, University of Leicester.

Vygotsky, L. S. (1978) *Mind and Society: The Development of Higher Psychological Processes*. Cambridge, MA: Harvard University Press.

Wiliam, D. (2011) *Embedded Formative Assessment*. Bloomington, IN: Solution Tree Press.

Internet sources

DCSF (2009) *Getting to Grips with Assessing Pupils' Progress*. National Strategies, QCA/Chartered Institute of Educational Assessors. Nottingham: DCSF. Available online at: https://www.education.gov.uk/publications/standard/ . . . /DCSF-00129–200 . . . (accessed 10 June 2014).

http://www.businessballs.com/kolblearningstyles.htm

Part 6

Some specific techniques for cross-curricular teaching and learning

Chapter 12

Using a range of media in cross-curricular teaching

Trevor Kerry

Introduction

This chapter looks at the increasingly creative use of a variety of presentational media, through which individual children or groups can access learning and, importantly, express their learning outcomes in ways that cohere with the integrative approaches advocated in this text. It covers such topics as ICT, video presentation, photography, videoconferencing, role play and dramatic productions, and media reporting. Examples are drawn from the world of schools and classrooms, and analysed for their practicality and effectiveness as learning tools.

Background

There is no intention here to claim that the days of the exercise book are numbered or that children producing work orally in the form of answers to the teacher are undertaking an outmoded activity. But the fact remains that, just as a variety of approaches keeps teachers' lessons fresh and stimulating, so utilising and encouraging a variety of responses from pupils by employing a range of media provides most effectively for individualising learning and meeting preferred learning styles. This chapter accords with the work of Bazalgette (2010), who suggests that children of primary age need to broaden their experiences of different kinds of media, and in the process sharpen their awareness of analysis and criticality in relation to the material that is presented to them. She points out the creative potential of media-based learning and its roles in imaginative thinking and decision making, and argues to extend these approaches beyond supporting traditional subject-based teaching. Semenderiadis and Martidou (2009: 66) make a powerful and logical case for bringing the same approaches even to nursery classes, and summarise this as follows:

> The interdisciplinary approach, as a way of selecting and organizing knowledge, must and should promote the connections between different subject matters, helping students gain a more holistic approach to knowledge, by relating, composing, and generalising it . . . In this context, audio-visual media play a significant role in the education process, particularly when used extensively by both teacher and children. Audio-visual media provide children with many stimuli, due to their nature (sounds, images). They enrich the learning environment, nurturing explorations, experiments and discoveries, and encourage children to develop their speech and express their thoughts.

Further, we argue here that cross-curricular thinking is most pertinently encapsulated using appropriate media – whatever these happen to be. We use examples to support the view that innovative lessons often lead to innovative presentations by pupils of what they have learned and that, through that process, learning is better anchored in the pupil's consciousness. A brief example will suffice to move us into the debates.

An art lesson lends itself well to pupils exploring a number of different media. Most of us would not expect art to be constrained by a single approach or interpretation – unless, of course, the intention of a specific lesson was simply to teach a designated skill such as modelling clay or drawing an object from life. So, in the case study that follows, what the teacher sets is the theme; what the pupils do is to interpret the task as they see fit.

Case Study 12.1 Pattern

The teacher wants the pupils to explore the concept of pattern. She provides them with some ideas from everyday life as stimulus: paving stones, a roll of wallpaper, the natural patterns of lichen on the school wall, the shape of the soil moved by the plough on a distant field that is visible through the classroom window.

They discuss the essential nature of pattern. That it is repetitive. That it makes shapes. That sometimes the shapes it makes break up the outlines – e.g. the camouflage pattern on Tony's jacket. That it can be bold or subtle. That it can deceive the eye.

When they have explored the idea, the teacher suggests they begin to think about the medium in which they might best express the idea of pattern. She says they can work alone or in small groups of up to four.

The task is the same however they choose to work: to create or discover patterns and bring the outcomes to the next lesson to show everyone else. Then they will show their patterns, explain them to their peers, and tell everyone why they chose the medium they did in order to demonstrate their chosen patterns. Here are some of the outcomes.

- Sharon and Tracey decided to make their own patterns. They wanted to make their own wallpaper, so they got a roll of plain paper and traced out some designs on it, which they then coloured in.
- Tony liked the camouflage pattern on his jacket so he made a three-dimensional model of a jungle and put some of the toy zoo animals (tigers, leopards) in it to demonstrate how they disappear from sight because of the patterns on their coats.
- Janet and John took out a digital camera and looked round the school site for potential patterns. They came back with photographs of the hopscotch court, the concentric rings of the tennis target, the loops in the goal nets and the diamond shapes of the wire round the school field.
- Niall took a scraperboard and etched out the patterns in a feather he had found.
- Rick and Ally got excited by natural things, and made models of ladybirds and butterflies with mirror-image wings using folded paper and mirrors.
- Jo and Sandra face-painted a panda face on Kelly, trying to capture the slightly lopsided pattern of panda markings.

- A group of four took the video camera and ran it round the outside of the school building looking at the patterns made by building bricks when they are laid, the patterns of flower heads in the school garden, and the cracking of paint on an old wooden shed.
- Rodney, who is averse to some of the more practical aspects of art and prefers reading, took the view that words make patterns, for example in poetry. So he made up a poem:

> Bumble bee
> Mumble bee
> Rumble bee
> Buzz
> Honey bee
> Money bee
> Sunny bee
> ZZZZZZ

The next week the pupils presented their findings and they discovered: patterns are everywhere in the built environment and in nature; patterns often have a purpose (strength in a wall, safety in camouflage); patterns can be made by sound, not just visually; patterns come in all shapes, sizes and colours; patterns may soothe or deceive our looking. The teacher thought that next week they might look for patterns, and create some, in sound, in music, in words – even in mathematics.

This example – fictitious as it stands but based on several different lessons – makes a number of important points about children's learning and how teachers can promote it.

First, a child has to be 'ready' to learn something before he or she can do so. This phenomenon has been well documented over the years (Bourne 1994: 216–217; www. offordcentre.com/readiness). The built-in choices that the teacher has allowed here take account of different levels of readiness. Thus Sharon and Tracey's response to the task is rather dependent on the teacher's ideas in the introduction to the lesson; but Rodney has provided a completely different kind of response, which is both in a different medium and at a very different cognitive level. Vygotsky (1978) noted that children progress through learning by building one idea upon another – what he labels 'scaffolding'. In this lesson the teacher has laid a foundation that scaffolds to the next level in at least two ways. First, in the report-back lesson they learn from one another, and then she takes back some control in opening up the concept of pattern (e.g. through mathematics).

The structure of the learning here is also interesting because it takes account of preferred learning style (Jarvis 2005: 80–93) and the idea that children may have predispositions to some kinds of learning rather than others, which have to be coaxed into life. They have begun, though, to reflect on their own learning through their discoveries and applications of patterns, so there is a metacognitive element at work here (Kerry and Wilding 2004: 248–253; Blakey & Spence 2008, online at www.education.com/Reference/article/ Ref_Dev_Metacognition). Yet one can sense in the responses to the task a degree of self-motivation and self-direction, which marks this out as effective learning (Nutbrown 2002: 56). Much of the good work has been achieved through the coalescence of several key factors: choice, the use of the child's environment (Ratcliffe and Grace 2003: 144), cross-curricular connections (Bowring-Carr and West-Burnham 1997: 69), and the perceived value of each person's contribution (Stoll, Fink and Earl 2003: 48).

In the rest of the chapter we will go on to look at the way in which a variety of presentational forms can promote children's enthusiasm for learning, and at some real examples of learning that concentrate on personal experience.

First-hand experience

It has long been established that children learn better by doing than by being told (Fisher 1991: 11). This view is supported by an article in the web journal of State University, USA, which points out that audio-visual media can become interventionist at various stages in the learning process: as a stimulus for thought, as a source for information and as a medium for the presentation of pupil outcomes (http://education.stateuniversity.com/pages/2495/Technology-in-SCHOOL.html). In the spirit of this approach the chapter turns now to look at the genesis of a first-hand learning experience.

At Beatrix Potter School in London, we trace out the process by which an idea for such a learning experience came about. The work was featured on the BBC's *Breakfast* programme over several days and what follows in Case Study 12.2 is an insight into how the events took shape in the mind of the headteacher. The passage is a mind-map and not a chronological account of what happened; and that approach is retained in order to demonstrate that some planning of this kind is serendipitous rather than formally structured. Nevertheless, the account contains classic features of integrative planning.

Case Study 12.2 The evacuation project: headteacher Steph Neale reflects

When does one hit upon a unique idea for an educational theme? The National Curriculum brought a sense of order to teaching, but over the years was often seen as a straitjacket that teachers rarely escaped from. Yet, as a result of a logbook documenting a school's evacuation, teachers leapt out from the straitjacket and created a day of stunning experiential learning that has yet further to develop.

In a chance conversation about our school log, we suddenly realised we had an event that was pivotal in this nation's history: the evacuation of children from cities and towns across the UK in 1939. We had used this log for the Year 5 Second World War topic with the new Wandsworth Museum, through the good offices of Andrew Lynch and assisted by a set of people who strongly believed that history is better taught from seeing and experiencing it.

Our initial intention was to draw up a plan, think of resources and look for sources of visits, and so on – a conventional approach. But this did not grab the imagination. Better, could we not try to find some of the original names in the log and locate the people? OK – how do you locate people from some seventy years ago? In practice, it's fairly straightforward; we used various societies, local knowledge and press releases. Word of mouth also spread news of a sort of reunion.

Children were charged with part of the task. Some eight evacuees appeared with their unique stories, and all holding various photos and original documents. As head, I thought: why not recreate what happened, get the kids dressed and evacuate them locally? Nice and simple. But nothing is ever that simple. One Y2 pupil asked me, after an assembly about the log, why could we not go and see where our children went. So Andrew discovered the local history society of Shamley Green – the place to which our evacuees had been sent – and suddenly our idea took on a wholly different direction.

Our aim had always been to capture on the web the voices of the evacuees, the children's thoughts on how they would feel, and to surround this with activities: a 'dig for victory' garden, building an air raid shelter, singing air raid practice songs. We would use a range of devices to capture the ideas and set up an online resource for all.

Now, suddenly, I thought: we could hire a train, maybe a steam train, ride it as in 1939 and play as the children did on the green while being billeted.

Unique hands-on live experience looked good. At Shamley Green teachers and children met Michael Harding and the Shamley Historical Society; artefacts, billeting knowledge and photos came out, and suddenly there were real people who had been there as kids in 1939. It was a moment of sheer pleasure: that one could envisage our children talking to people who left our school and the people they were billeted with.

I discovered that hiring a real and very large steam train was actually easy. Railtrack came on board to fit in the train on the timetables and suddenly we had an evacuation train. We started reading to the children extracts from the 1938 log about the first preparations for evacuation. The children were fascinated by the realisation they were sitting in the same rooms as the children of 1938.

We were also very fortunate to discover Joy Gardiner, who had the original letter to parents from 1938 (as well as her letters home from 1939 onwards as a seven year old). From this, the children at Key Stage 2 researched the evacuation procedures using the 1938–39 log as a source. They prepared their own letters for parents as though informing them of events. Research highlighted the scale of the undertaking in London alone. Teachers prepared the children using a range of resources from the period. Various companies and the Imperial War Museum all have superb copies of original documents, books and posters. Teachers explained what happened and, using extracts from the school log, explained how the head had organised events. As we approached the summer break we had children from Year 1 upwards well versed in the period.

Year 1 had thought about their toys in the suitcase and at Year 6 how they would feel, as the oldest, leaving their parents, surrounded by younger children. There are a whole range of accounts and sources on the web about children and their reactions and feelings during evacuation. Year 5 were charged with discovering these and selecting the most appropriate for each class.

For the parents, we sent home the original letter to them about their roles in the forthcoming evacuation and how they were to prepare the children. We also sent home images on how we might dress the children. We revisited Shamley Green, with the date now booked as 29 September. They had moved forward preparations from their end, and the village green was ours, courtesy of Waverley Council. The whole village wanted to join in, and many ex-combatants and families who had housed the evacuees were talking to Michael at the Historical Society.

It was very clear that this event had really struck a chord with the village. They wanted to show the children where the London children had been billeted and where, sadly, one young boy had been killed. We became aware that people wanted children to comprehend how important the past and this event were to many: we now had a whole range of people able to tell their experiences as local children receiving these London children, as service personnel at Shamley Green, and as participants of the period.

Such an opportunity for present children to go where our children of 1939 had been, and to meet the very people who had been there, is unique and offers an experience of real history: the children themselves are making their own history. They began to get an idea about how the war affected real people's lives. Meeting people personally involved and handling objects from the period of time was very important. The preparation and lead-up activities taught in the classroom were equally important, giving context in order to help children to understand things happening on the day.

The atmosphere at Shamley Green, and inclusion of historic vehicles and tents, added to the children's understanding of 1940s Britain. Children took digital cameras, flip videos and a set of handhelds. Photos recorded every event and more. Digital cameras are very forgiving, and out of some 800 images on the average data card the children could create a montage of the day with a degree of professionalism. Flip videos allowed the children to record conversations with evacuees, veterans who had served in the Second World War, and to collect the thoughts of the re-enactors and period vehicle owners.

The older children plotted on GPS the location of the billets, and plan to link them to original photos of the period and photos of the sites today. All will be placed on open access to anyone interested in the resource. The video pieces will go towards a compilation video of the day.

But the learning did not stop there. Now a 'People's Voice' activity will follow. Wandsworth Museum will teach the children oral history skills and then the children will interview the evacuees and the people of Shamley Green over the next year. The ultimate goal is a unique online resource about this period of UK history.

What other experiences added to the impact of the event?

Empathy is something that comes with maturity, but those who were able to do so were definitely thinking of the experiences of the children who had been evacuated. For some of the younger children the experience was powerful; it was hard for them to draw the line and know where the re-enactment ended. But certainly some children were able to get under the skin of the event. The re-evacuation (especially the Blitz experience) has helped to give depth to the children's responses of how it might have felt to have been living then (activities that allowed children to document their feelings after the event have helped teachers to see evidence of this).

A Year 5 teacher thought that her class would get restless on the guided walk around the billets, perhaps finding it was too long; but she was surprised to see in the letters they wrote afterwards that many considered it to be one of the highlights of their day. The fact that staff were relaxed, and that older children were given responsibility for younger children, helped them to feel important and has helped the school community to bond.

Some of the younger children had been scared in the run-up to the event, and they had had a few crying episodes, but all were enthusiastic when it came to the day. As well as being relevant for the children currently studying the Second World War, the experience has unexpectedly acted as a point of reference to many other areas of learning. For example, a Year 1 child asked the teacher if the toys they were looking at (in their Toys in the Past module) were from before or after the Second World War. Again, it has been beneficial for cross-curricular learning and feelings of self-esteem, bonding individuals together within and outside school.

The work has fulfilled many of the themes and aims in our PSHE curriculum. It has also helped people to engage with the community and talk about things in school within their home environments and feel proud of their achievements. Community involvement is probably the most valuable thing to come out of the event for the school, and the extent of this was unexpected. The people who came out to wave the children off made them feel extremely special and part of something important. It was something that the parents could be involved with, which was valuable. This project brought the whole community together including ex-parents and pupils (all ages). It was the unexpected things (television, newspapers, people making a fuss, feedback from external parties, teachers dressing up with them) that helped the children to feel proud they were part of something special to many people, and of something unique.

We intend that much more will emerge as we gradually develop the resources we have put together. Year 6 will perform the play *The Evacuees*; songs of the period are being learned by the choir. Creative writing using the experience of the day is showing surprising talent and innovation in a whole range of children. Without any doubt, the impact of the day and the preparation has re-energised the staff, and given parents a view of the curriculum they did not expect. Parents have described how focused the children were on getting the day right, their real pleasure in looking up information that had real purpose and meaning to their studies and understanding.

Teachers were motivated and can see how to adapt the principles here to other areas. Obviously they cannot create an evacuation but they realise the value of innovation and excitement, a word that falls a little flat in the National Curriculum.

This case study about the birth of an exciting learning experience is interesting, not least for its spontaneity. There are other curriculum approaches, too, that lend themselves to work that breaks out of the straitjackets that Neale referred to above. To some of these we now turn our attention.

Video presentation and photography

Visual literacy is a cross-curricular skill and a life skill of the highest order. No less a person than the highly respected American film director Martin Scorsese (Scorsese 2013) championed this cause recently – presumably, as someone who puts a lot into creating images for the public, he should understand more than most the importance of people's ability to then deconstruct and interpret those images. He pleads for children to understand the difference between images that 'are just telling them something' and those that 'engage their humanity and their intelligence'.

We are all bombarded daily with images: they are not random. They attract our attention, draw on our sympathy, and are intended to persuade our thinking, bend our understanding of events, try to create needs in us (such as the need to purchase), and alter our moods. Images relate (of course) to global events, but they permeate even the most trivial activities of our lives. Our ability to absorb images, filter them, edit them, interpret them, evaluate them – all this has to be rapid, even instantaneous.

Yet some people have no visual literacy skill – a skill every bit as real and objective as numerical skill, reading skill or writing skill. If one picture is indeed worth a thousand words – or even only a hundred – then visual literacy is a skill of paramount importance.

Whether the image is moving or still, the issue is the same. It is about the toolbox that we bring in our minds – the tools with which we deconstruct the images we see, and piece together not just the messages they purport to convey but the underlying themes we are meant to construe from them: even the underlying, subliminal propaganda of imagery.

Equipping children with the skills that relate to visual literacy is almost (one might argue on the basis of sound evidence) more important than most of what else they learn in school. In the days of i-players, mobile phone imagery, computer screens, fantasy computer games, digital cameras and constant media pressures (such as rolling news), can it be doubted that this is *the* central life skill for the 21st century?

Yet it has nothing to do with subject learning. It is not art. It is not even photography. It may include those things, but it transcends them. It embraces all knowledge, and it demands of the viewer a breadth of vision in the interpretation that is incredibly demanding.

From time to time, considerable claims are made for the impact of visual literacy activities. Thus the United Kingdom Literacy Association (Bearne and Grainger 2004) claimed 'an improvement in writing and attitudes to writing by boys. If boys' writing is a concern in a school then the school should consider developing these aspects to support its improvement.' The DfES (2005) demonstrated that, by the end of a project involving visual literacy approaches to writing, boys 'were more able to express ideas about the process of writing and effective writing behaviours and indicated that they saw themselves as much more in control of their own writing'. But it is not just boys who need visual literacy skills.

A useful website might be: http://www.teachingexpertise.com/articles/visual-literacy-3961. It is suggested here that using visual literacy skills could affect writing by pupils in the following ways:

- Increased quantity
- Increased quality
- Wider vocabulary
- Greater use of imagery
- Increased fluency
- More adventurous approaches
- Improved attitudes
- Improved motivation.

Kinds of visual stimulus material include the following:

- Looking at and discussing still pictures
- Film and television images
- Hidden images
- Media such as advertising
- Picture dictionaries
- Linking pictures and sound
- Charts and diagrams.

These are useful points, but could be applied across a range of learning and not simply to literacy. In what follows, the Reflection panel is used to raise your awareness of your own visual literacy as well as that of your pupils.

Reflection

Try some of these visual literacy ideas to test your own awareness.

Perspective

Take a digital camera with a zoom lens. Stand in your school or the school's road. Shoot six pictures, the first one wide angle, then progressively zooming to telephoto, ending with maximum zoom. Now examine the pictures. How does perspective change your perception (or your pupils' perception) of the scene?

Editing (subconsciously?)

In the previous task, why did you choose to look in the direction you chose? What would you have seen in the opposite direction, and how would the view have altered your perception of the location?

Catching the eye

I wrote two texts, both on education. One was presented by the designer with a dark-blue cover showing an 'old master' painting in rather sombre hues. The other had a yellow cover with a child's monochrome drawing on it. Which book ran to fourteen impressions?

Manipulating your pictures

Shoot with a digital camera any picture, but preferably one with fairly simple, strong lines (such as a headshot, a picture of a bridge or a striking building). Upload the picture to your computer and manipulate it using a program such as Photoshop Elements. You can turn the colour shot monochrome; you can play with the different levels of saturation; or you can use the filter options, for example to create a watercolour effect. Which images are most striking and why? What does it tell you about matching 'mode' to subject matter?

Interpreting what you see (activity using Figure 12.1)

Choose a striking portrait and give each pupil a copy. Ask them (without consulting) to write down twenty words that describe the face. Compare the results. To what extent do they overlap and differ? (This is a good task for developing vocabulary, too.) Figure 12.1 shows some starter pictures that might help you to embark on this process.

Bamford (2003) talks about visual syntax, which involves some of the elements we have looked at in the Reflection above. These include the following.

- *Scale*: images can distort relative size and importance.
- *Motion*: blurring an image can create an enhanced impression of speed.
- *Shape*: 'real' objects can be turned into abstract ideas.
- *Arrangement and juxtaposing*: clashes of position (soft toy holding sharp knife) can jar the senses or challenge our understandings.
- *Manipulation*: manipulating an image also manipulates its meaning.
- *Use of foreground or background*: try shooting two objects (e.g. a 'no parking' cone and a parked car) first with one item in the foreground then the other. How does the result change the meaning of the image?
- *Tone*: soft tones (gold, sepia) imply tranquillity, nostalgia, comfort; hard tones (red, black) are disturbing and jarring.

Figure 12.1 What do faces tell us?

Pupils in the 21st century need very highly developed visual skills. Whenever they look at an image they have to ask themselves, almost consciously, a number of questions about it. They have to be aware of how they are interpreting the image. They need to know that images are often designed to have social impact, and that means to manipulate our understanding of the topic (simply put, a shot of a dead pheasant may mean cruel sport to some and good eating to others). We, and our pupils, have to ask ourselves about who owns the ideas behind the images we see; and whether we are evaluating them adequately so as not to be subjected to propaganda. Visual learning can extend understanding; but only once we have learned the rules of visual literacy. In the same way we can use and create images to support the messages we want to convey – to persuade, inform, cajole. These processes disguise moral dilemmas – those dilemmas are a part of the learning process and should be teased out and deconstructed.

A couple of years ago I was fortunate enough to have one of my photographs selected for the shortlist of prize contenders in an international competition. The image was duly printed in a book of winning pictures (O'Brien 2007). Photographers were asked to contribute a short insight into imagery, and this was mine: photography is a window into the soul; it illuminates the observer and the observed. Therein lies its ambiguity: how much of an image is what we see? How much of it is what we were intended to see? What do our answers tell us about us? But also, what do they tell us about the creator of the image? Some people are said to walk around with their eyes shut. They don't. They see what the rest of us see, but they lack the visual literacy to interpret its significance. In today's world they are, potentially, victims. For example, try the exercise in Figure 12.2.

Other media

Having looked in some depth at the issues that underpin visual literacy (though there is, of course, much more that could be said – the topic deserves a book to itself), we move on in this chapter to examine some other approaches that might be used with pupils or that pupils might use. In so doing, it would be useful to bear in mind the broad principles that

(a)

(b)

(c)

Figure 12.2 Seeing: (a) Benign landscape; (b) Cascade; (c) Under my wing. How much of an image is what we see? How much of it is what we were intended to see? What do our answers tell us about us? But also, what do they tell us about the creator of the image? To what extent do the titles given to images condition the way we feel about them?

this chapter has established so far, in particular about criticality, and about the ability of these media to be used both as means to promote learning and as means to express what has been learned. In such a short chapter these issues can be dealt with using only broad brushstrokes, and the reader is urged to follow up each as its potential seems relevant to his or her work.

Video conferencing

Increasingly, schools are gaining access to their own or other people's videoconferencing facilities. Videoconferencing works much like a video-phone: during a conversation it is possible for groups to see one another and to see what each is doing. An obvious use of this kind of facility is for groups at a considerable distance to share learning: it is perfectly possible for classes to communicate across countries. Though the site is American, some useful ideas and principles appear on http://www/kn/att.com/vidconf/ideas.html.

The issue with all technology is, how far is it merely a gimmick, or to what extent can it become a genuine learning tool? Videoconferencing allows the users to transport themselves with some immediacy into the situation of the other party. A class in metropolitan Birmingham can share experience with a group on the Cumbrian fells. A class in Nigeria or Eastern Europe can have very personal contact with classes in Hemel Hempstead or Harrogate.

Thus learning through videoconferencing can provide rich experience that comes close to first-hand experience, whether in cross-curricular or narrower fields. Its success, like so much else in teaching, depends on good planning and preparation. Access to facilities is often time limited, and teachers need to know how to extract the best usage out of the time available.

Videoconferencing has another important use. It can allow two groups in quite different places to share, and participate in, exemplary lessons. It may allow a class to be taught by someone with a specific skill or interest to which they would not otherwise have access. The National Portrait Gallery offers videoconferencing sessions to schools (see http://www.npg.org.uk/learning/schools/primary-schools/videoconferencing.php); these provide expert information and discussion quite literally 'to your door'. But the potential for this kind of usage is massive.

Videoconferencing is likely – like most technologies – to become more widely available. As it does so its potential will be limited only by the imagination of the users. As an educational tool it will provide the opportunity for making the world smaller and for opening pupils' horizons. It allows for two-way communication in which learning can take place, and through which young people can communicate their understandings to others.

Drama and production

Most teachers will need little persuasion that drama, in one form or another, has a powerful learning potential. Of course, we are all familiar with the 'school production', and much learning takes place as a result of it (subject matter, and skills like confidence). Similarly, role play is often used to help pupils get inside the skin of a topic, to deal with the affective issues in a lesson. These processes are commonplace.

What is being argued here is that, at times, a response to a classroom task might best be expressed in drama rather than – for example – in a piece of writing or an artefact. The case for drama in this sense is well put by the Curriculum online website whose (somewhat unwieldy) web address appears at the end of this chapter. This site claims that:

Drama requires impersonation, personification and role-play involvement. It is an ideal methodology for the teaching of history, as:

- The involvement of children in role-playing means they will empathise with characters in the past and come to defend their actions against the arguments of others;
- Drama aims to re-create human experience. The pupil-actor is personally affected by the experience and this motivates him/her to know and understand more;
- Drama militates against a simplistic approach to a topic. All points of view are articulated so that situations are no longer viewed in 'black or white' terms.

Of course, it is not just history that benefits from this cross-curricular approach. Subjects across the whole curriculum can be illuminated by drama. Teachers can download a model drama policy from the Arts on the Move website, which can be adapted to individual school needs: http://www.artsonthemove.co.uk/education/primary/primary.php. For the present purpose, the section to emphasise in this document relates to its concern for cross-curricular links:

There are strong links to other subjects including English, history, music, PE, PSHE and Citizenship, geography, art and religious education. Drama methods can be used within these subjects to explore a variety of roles, topics, feelings, situations and facts.

Specific aspects of all subjects can be explored using drama, such as character motivation, scenes and situations, roles, emotions, pivotal moments, debates, decisions and personal choices, and reactions or responses.

The points made about drama and role play may apply equally to other forms of classroom talk, such as debates, discussions and presentations. These, too, can be used both as tasks set by the teacher or as means chosen by pupils as ways to express their knowledge.

Media reporting

One obvious way of communicating, in today's world, is through the media. This may be the radio or television interview, or it may be through newspaper and magazine articles. Learning can often be made more immediate by imagining that the class is 'present' at an event (at Henry VIII's court or in the shelters during the Second World War, for example). Interviewing can also be a means to investigate a topic, on the model of the 'World at One' interviews with politicians. Newspapers and magazines present both visual (see above) and written versions of events in the local area or on the national scene. Using the techniques can have a number of learning outcomes:

- Alerting pupils to bias in reporting
- Helping them with speaking and listening skills
- Teaching them the skills of asking insightful questions
- Promoting confidence on both sides of the microphone
- And many others.

A very practical application of these skills is in the School Council, where pupils can use the democratic process of representation to elect their members, make a case, argue a point and bring about incremental change in what happens in their school. Guidance on School Councils is available on http://www.innovation-unit.co.uk/about-us/publications/new-resources-for-primary-school-councils.html. This source has some good materials presented for young people in cartoon format.

An example of pupils acting as media reporters was included in Kerry (2002: 68–75). The task described there (producing a class newspaper) is timeless, but the major learning point of the exercise was not about the means of production, or the content, or about writing skill. It was about time: the need to work to deadlines, to work within the team, to achieve the end product within the allotted parameters. That approach mirrors life, and is thus valuable learning across the curriculum in every sphere of learning. The BBC (BBC News School Report) does a good job in encouraging pupils to act as reporters of news, and while some of this work is carried out in secondary contexts the principles are easily reapplied into the primary sector (http://www/bbc.co.uk/school report 25259600).

Information and communications technology

The penultimate section in this collection of media activities for pupils relates to the use of ICT. There are plenty of people with specialist expertise in the hardware and software of ICT, but this section is concerned not with these aspects but the principles for the use of ICT, especially access to the web, by all teachers and pupils. Effective ICT use requires teachers to harness the potential in ways that enhance pupils' learning and internet usage, and – just as importantly – not to use the technology in ways that subvert learning. Making connections between ICT and integrated learning approaches is considered important in this context.

IT media now change at a breathtaking rate, and the recent proliferation of mobile/camera phones, smartphones and tablets are symptomatic of this. These developments are sufficiently significant that it is clear that they are changing our society in a variety of ways. A few examples will suffice:

- Media outlets/TV companies increasingly rely on opportunistic passers-by at some major event to provide immediate images for the rolling news.
- Satnav provides a whole new perspective on maps, geography and outdoor pursuits.
- Instant communication, wherever and whenever we are, via phones and tablets, will change our pupils' concepts of work and employment.
- Apps can provide information within the palm of the hand on everything from the serial number and destination of a plane flying overhead to tomorrow's weather as a result of a couple of flicks of the finger.

These media present us with both opportunities and dilemmas, and it is to some of these, as they affect the education process, that attention is now directed.

Leu *et al.* (2008) are anxious to emphasise that today's is the first generation of students to be global publishers (because they can share their work online), and that in the process they develop social skills through IT collaboration – even though they will never meet their collaborators. These students see 'school as a global communications centre'. Braham (n.d.) argues that we live in an increasingly fact-based society, to which technology gives pupils a key. Lankshear and Knobel (2011: 255) were advised by the profession that blogging, photo sharing and other IT skills would aid teachers in understanding how new literacies could be integrated into classroom learning.

But what should we make of the statement that the internet gives everyone – primary pupils and adults – access to immeasurable quantities of information (data, content)? These data leave open some important debates, only some of which can be dealt with, albeit cursorily, here:

- How valuable (authentic, reliable) are these data?
- What are the implications for curriculum of all these data?
- How do these data advantage cross-curricular approaches to learning?
- What do these quantities of data tell us about the nature of knowledge itself (epistemology)?
- Are there implications embedded in the data or in our answers to these questions about how children should be exposed to all this information?

Data

- We have seen the exponential growth in data (in philosophical terms there may be distinctions between information and data, but in common parlance the words are used interchangeably, which is the policy adopted here). Teachers often refer to pupils accessing these data as being engaged in 'research'. Research is a term best left for finding new things and breaking new ground. What the web does for most people most of the time is to provide a simple means of access to existing information. The web can be an excellent means of initial data/information collection.
- Data collection is only a stage – in thinking terms, a fairly low-order operation – in the process of learning. Pupils should be encouraged to avoid bad habits. Data that are merely cut-and-pasted have no life in the minds of the pupils; the information is not theirs, it is someone else's. The stitching together of unabsorbed snippets of data should be discouraged. There are also question marks about whether this found material is consistently reliable and authentic (see below).
- Data collection gives access to a world of thought that involves: sifting, comparing, contrasting, following new leads, checking contradictions, analysing, synthesising, making judgements and evaluating. These are higher-order thinking tasks. The web is best used to feed these higher-order operations, not to replace them. These are critical operations in learning the skill of discernment between reliable and less reliable sources.
- All web searches should be set against the clearly stated objectives for that lesson or learning activity, and should involve the higher-order processes identified above.
- At best, classroom tasks should be so structured that the web is used as a tool, not as an end in itself – except for the brief period where access skills are being learned.

Curriculum

The sheer volume of data available via the internet raises questions about the nature of content, information and data in the curriculum. There are those who believe that 'knowing' or memorising information is an important part of 'education'. There are immediate *non sequiturs* in this position. What is worth memorising? Who decides what is worth memorising? What is the importance of memorisation and regurgitation when there is instant access to the information anyway?

These are teasing but probably unanswerable questions. If I momentarily forget the dates of accession and death of Henry VIII, this represents no tragedy or failure of knowing. If I don't understand the contextual relationship of the reign of Henry VIII to that of Elizabeth I, this could be more of a problem in having a grasp of Tudor history. In another field, 9 x 45 is the work of a moment on the calculator facility; but not having some vague notion of the correct answer could be fatal if I press the wrong key and come up with an answer of 333. So clearly memory is useful, and so is broad understanding, whether of history or numbers; but where to draw the line about what knowledge is absolutely necessary is ambiguous.

Politicians, of course, think that they should draw the lines of what is worth 'knowing'. But it is at least arguable that this approach is flawed. What politicians are often obsessed by is finding ways to 'score' things, to use these scores to demonstrate 'progress', and thus to claim superiority over their predecessors in office. These concerns are political, and are spurious to education. They call into question assessment procedures and their proper values. (This issue is pursued further in Chapter 14.)

But the deeper problem is about epistemology: what is the relationship between 'knowing something' and what we have called elsewhere (Chapter 2) 'deep knowledge' – which includes understanding, appreciation, context and potential application, in fact a whole range of cerebral activities that have very little to do with (but that go far beyond) 'knowing' in the limited, shorthand sense of memorising decontextualised 'facts'.

These are not dilemmas with instant and cleanly soluble answers, but they are incredibly important to our understanding of the educative process and what happens in classrooms (at every level of education). They would be well to be in every teacher's consciousness, rather than resorting to the ill-defined rhetoric of public educational debate. We would do well, for example, to recall that much that passes for 'fact' is actually interpretation at best, and opinion at worst. In accessing web-based data pupils need to learn to make these distinctions.

Cross-curricular approaches

There can be little doubt that the information garnered via the world wide web is not, for the most part, filtered through the colander of conventional subject dimensions; and that the quantity of data on any given topic almost ensures that many different approaches will be adopted across the sources, often within an individual source. For the most part, then, web-based data are not predicated on subject boundaries. This simple fact makes it imperative that there is an interchange of understanding generated here between the student and the data: first, that the form of the data discovered in response to any individual query is likely to come in formats that support integrated knowledge; and that the student may need to respond (compile, sift, edit, evaluate) those data in a way that takes on board their essential cross-curricular and integrative nature.

Epistemology

The way that pupils receive knowledge in a classroom is dependent, at least in part, on the view that their teachers hold about the nature of knowledge: epistemology. This text has argued throughout that knowledge requires integration to be fully useful. By contrast, some politicians hold up the school systems of areas such as Singapore as superior to our own – mainly on the grounds that pupils are taught to memorise 'facts', to reproduce those facts in tests, and to do this in ways that are generally decontextualised from anything but subject disciplines. It comes as no surprise, then, that a study by Chai (2010) of Singaporean teachers' epistemological beliefs found that his studied teachers 'were more knowledge transmissionist in orientation. Results also implied that the relationship between epistemic beliefs and pedagogical beliefs seemed to be mediated by teachers' awareness of students' readiness and what they perceived as their priorities in the school context.'

Chai felt, as a result of this study, that it was

> . . . important to change the context in which teachers operate if the ICT-supported reform efforts are to take root . . . A more conducive environment jointly created by the policy makers and school leaders has to be in place . . . Teachers may choose to adopt traditional teaching approach that works well for examinations and tests. It is the hope of the researcher that this article illustrates the complex interplay between teachers' beliefs and their teaching context, from the teachers' point of view.

Though the study was a small-scale, in-depth case study, it bears out what is known of such education systems, and the myths of their 'success'.

Teaching and learning

Beyond the use of the web for data collection, inspections suggest that:

> Almost all children respond to ICT in a positive way and are motivated by the inclusion of ICT-related activities during lessons; they are particularly motivated by the whole-class aspect of ICT in learning and teaching, where, for example, a data projector or an IWB is used, leading to good discussion and high levels of engagement. In a small number of the schools, the children take ownership of ICT initiatives, such as updating the scrolling display in the school foyer, or older children mentoring younger classes in the use of ICT. Children's involvement and interest are promoted where there is good integration of experiences using ICT into real learning situations and where use is made of the local area.

Where there is a whole-school culture of using ICT to enhance the children's learning across the curriculum, there are many examples of the thoughtful use of applications where the children's ICT experiences are planned and are appropriately challenging (http://www. etini.gov.uk/information_and_communication_ technology_in_primary_schools.pdf).

Many sources note that the commonest uses of ICT are for word processing, and there is nothing wrong with using it for this purpose. But, once more, such a use reduces the computer simply to the status of a tool. To raise its value above this, it is important to have applications that make demands at higher-order levels of thinking: solving design problems, writing stories, producing leaflets, and so on. To help teachers and pupils with the process of becoming discerning about internet sources, the Canadian Department for Education has produced two useful checklists, which are reproduced here as Tables 12.1 and 12.2.

Table 12.1 Website evaluation guide

Credibility
- Is the site appropriate for your students?
- Is there a creation/last-updated date on the site?
- Has the website been updated?
- Do dates make a difference to the credibility of the information?
- Who is the author?
- Is the author's education or position listed?
- Can the author be contacted?
- What is the purpose of the website – informational? persuasive? solicitation? entertainment?
- Where does the information come from? Is it a reliable source?
- Is there a bibliography? Are correct citations made?

Information
- Is the information at a comfortable reading level for the student?
- Is there any misinformation on the site?
- Does the information appear to be valid?
- Is the same or similar information found on other websites?
- Do links provide relevant information?
- Is the information current?
- Are language conventions (e.g. spelling, grammar) used correctly?

Website design
- Is the website attractive? Is it well laid out?
- Are there appropriate graphics on the webpage? Do they support the information?
- Is the information organised?
- Is there a site map to organise information?
- Is the site easy to navigate?
- Are links to other sites active?

Bias
- What is the purpose of this site?
- Does the author have a particular point of view? If so, is the author critical of the opposite point of view?
- Are opinions expressed? Does the information seem one-sided? Is there a hidden message?
- Are there examples of racial, cultural, faith or gender stereotyping in information, illustrations or graphics?
- Are all people and cultures respected?
- Is the information factual with references and links?

The problem of gaming

A specific subset of ICT activity is gaming. All the same kinds of issues that relate to the use of IT-based learning apply equally to video-games and gaming, but concerns might be deemed to rise in number and severity. Lacasa, Martinez and Mendez (2008: 103) claimed that video-games complement the use of other, written or audio-visual, methods in primary classrooms. Sceptics might argue that, while pupils warm to methods familiar to them in out-of-school and social contexts, this 'if you can't beat them, join them' mentality is fuelling a problem inherent in many video-games: the substitution of fantasy for reality.

Table 12.2 Think literacy: cross-curricular approaches grades 7–12

Student Resource
Checklist for Evaluating Websites
Answer 'Yes', 'No' or '?' to the following statements.

- The information in the website seems to be correct and can be found on other websites and in print materials.
- If there are pictures on the page, the pictures seem to be original and not edited.
- The information on this site helps me to answer my research question.
- The website has information that is up to date.
- The author of the website is identified and can be contacted.
- There are no examples of stereotyping (racial, cultural, faith or gender) found on the website.
- All people and cultures that are represented are depicted respectfully.
- The site is relatively free of bias.
- The information on the website is factual, and not an opinion expressed by the author.
- If a point of view has been expressed, the opposite point of view has also been presented in an impartial way.
- The website is attractive, well organised and has eye-catching visuals.
- Words are spelled correctly and the grammar is correct.
- All of the hyperlinks are working, well chosen and well organised.
- The website is easy to navigate and the home page can always be accessed.

If you have answered 'Yes', to all of the statements, this website may be useful to you.
If you have answered 'No', to any of the statements, you need to consider whether this website will be of use to you.
If you have a '?', you should discuss the statement with a teacher or group member.

- What is the best part of this website?
- What would be the best way to find this website in the future?
- How could this website be improved?
- Describe how you might help a friend find similar information more quickly.

Source: THINK LITERACY cross-curricular approaches grades 7–12 available online at: www.edu.gov.on.ca/eng/studentsuccess/thinkliteracy/files/thinkenglish10–12.pdf

Young people (our primary pupils) and even those up to young adulthood are now being exposed to a bewildering variety of games of varying degrees of fantasy, from *Pokémon*, through *Football Manager* to a plethora of survival games with sci-fi, violent and conflict-driven content. While not all primary pupils will be involved in the undesirable end of this spectrum, commercial pressure and, in unfortunate cases, unsuitable parenting, predispose them to potential dangers.

The problem is neatly illustrated by putting a phrase such as 'effects of gaming on children' into a computer search engine. When this was done while composing this chapter the first page of references brought up: an attempt to take a balanced view based on some rather dated research; a piece that claimed deleterious effects; an article on the positive learning outcomes derived from children gaming; and a story from a national newspaper claiming that video-games can alter children's brains. So what are the arguments, and to what extent is it possible to establish any 'facts'?

Gentile *et al.* (2004), looking at teenaged gamers, conclude boys played for more hours than girls but that all those who played tended to become more aggressive, to confront teachers more, and to lower school achievements. However, Gentile – turned now from academic to journalist – later listed the benefits in gaming (www.pedsforparents.com/articles/2791.shtml) in self-care for asthmatics; and there may be gains in motor skills and visual attention. On the face of it, a more promising study emanated from Glasgow University, involving 11,000 children (Parkes *et al.* 2013). This found no adverse effects on behaviour, attention or emotional issues in primary-aged children. However, some caution has to be exercised in that the data were dependent on parental reporting rather than independent observation. The study did not explore important psychological dimensions such as whether children confuse fantasy with reality more readily as a result of extensive gaming. At best one can say that the jury is still out on this dilemma, and teachers should approach with caution.

Certainly, some of the more extreme reactions to children and gaming seem to have little foundation in reality (even though there *is* a lack of research on the fantasy/reality divide). It was not so long ago (Robbins 2010) that debate surrounded the sacking of neuroscientist Baroness Susan Greenfield from the Royal Institution after a string of claims about the evils of the internet, including the apparent assertion that children's brains may be harmed by the use of social websites, caused vicious controversy because of its lack of scientific evidence.

An ethical approach to informational technology

All of the above suggest that it is opportune to remind oneself that there need to be guidelines for the use and application of IT in educational settings. IT has massive potential for expanding informational and social horizons, for accessing second-hand experience, for acquiring and practising specific skills. In itself it is value neutral. But it has dangers – some obvious, some darker in their implications. What is needed is an informed and ethical approach to its use – a point well made by Rikowski (2006). Much of her article relates to contexts beyond the primary school, but it is worth pulling out a number of points that do apply even at this stage of education. These concern the following:

- *Behaviour of individual pupils*: when using email or other communications media, the rules of truth, manners and personal respect apply just as they do in the classroom, the playground or the dining room.
- *Confidentiality*: passwords and other personal information should be safeguarded.
- *Plagiarism and the use of sources by pupils*: merely copying material is stealing or plagiarism, and good habits in this regard are best inculcated from an early age.
- *Teacher IT behaviour*: full professional confidentiality and behaviour are appropriate online at all times, just as they are in the face-to-face world of personal relationships.

Information technology-based teaching is in its infancy, even though it seems to be progressing at a staggering rate. This was, in part, the outcome of a longitudinal study in Norway by Ilomäki (2008). She concluded that there were 'true changes in teaching practices'. In one element of her investigation she found that 'many teachers adopted student-centred and collaborative, inquiry-oriented teaching practices that are believed to promote meaningful learning'. In another section of the research 'the practices supported students' authentic activities, independent work, knowledge building, and students' responsibility'. But she noted that this was dependent on 'teachers with good ICT-related technical, organisational and management skills as well as interest in pedagogical use of ICT conducted student and knowledge-centred activities at classroom level'. Teachers in both studies were involved in 'boundary crossing', and had opportunities to negotiate new meanings through collaboration which resulted in 'pedagogical innovation'. Such innovations were fulfilled regularly through large- and small-scale 'integrative learning projects'. It seems likely that a similar study here would find much the same, though it is speculative to generalise across cultures.

Summary

It seems reasonable to conclude that using a computer as a tool for learning is no different from other approaches to classroom teaching: its effectiveness depends on the quality of the task it is intended the pupils should achieve through its use. The more practical, realistic and embedded these tasks are in the thinking skills that delineate high-quality learning, the more value the work will have – a thought that leads appropriately into a consideration of problem solving as a learning tool. However, what seems clear is the positive relationship between ICT and integrated approaches to knowledge.

Real-life problem solving

An increasingly common mode of working in primary schools is, quite rightly, the attempt to encourage pupils to solve real problems, and problems on their own scale that mirror the real world. In Case Study 12.3 we see one such problem at work. The benefits of such first-hand, experiential learning are self-evident in the text that follows. Taking a more theoretical stance, what research suggests is that the values of problem solving lie in improving cognitive demand, helping pupils to develop models through which to solve problems, and the application of problem-solving models to real-life situations (Wallace, Berry and Cave 2008). A useful recent (2012) source can be found at http://oer.edu.cam.ac.uk/wiki/Problem-Solving_in_Primary_Education/Document, which identifies these processes in problem solving in so far as pupils can:

- Understand the concept of cause and effect
- Apply prior learning to a problem
- Recognise and can talk (or otherwise communicate) about a problem
- Consider a range of possible solutions
- Ask questions, and select and record information relevant to the problem
- Plan the steps and strategies they will use
- Predict possible effects of different solutions or modifications
- Respond to a problem or task using trial and error
- Use a cycle of trial, error and improvement
- Review what has been done and recognise the outcome (i.e. that the problem has been solved or a different course of action is needed).

Case Study 12.3 Themed week on money

The curriculum was suspended for the week before the autumn half-term and replaced by a money 'themed week' (see Chapter 8).

The short-term learning objectives (i.e. one half-day) for the mixed-age class of Year 4 and Year 5 pupils were clearly articulated – today, Wednesday, was a 'food sampling day' where, for comparison, the children sampled a series of expensive products and cheaper 'own store' brands. The tasting was blind. On Thursday, the medium-term objective was to bake scones in preparation for the long-term objective of selling the scones at the Friday local farmers' market.

The children had earlier had a 'The Price is Right' assembly where the whole school had been involved. The assembly was based on the television programme, *The Price is Right*; each child was given a number on entering the hall, and different contestants were called up for different games. The first game was 'Contestants' Row' where four children had to guess the price of an object – for example, a mobile phone. After the price was revealed, the child whose guess was the closest got to play that round's pricing game. For each round the children had a series of objects and they had to guess the price of the object; in one game the children were required to match the correct prices to the correct object. The children who were in the audience could help the contestant by shouting out the price they thought was closest to the actual price.

The 'food sampling day' linked to this assembly in that children were given the opportunity to sample various products in order to assess the quality of the products on offer compared to the price. The children sampled jelly babies, kiwi fruit, chocolate, pizza, sponge cake, cheese, jelly beans and, lastly, scones. One of each pair of products was Asda economy own brand, the other was a branded item, such as Galaxy chocolate or a more expensive Asda own product.

A small piece of each of the two foods was tasted – the children were asked to consider which they preferred and why; which they thought was the cheaper product; whether, once the products had been identified, the more expensive food merited the difference in price between the two products; whether they thought the ingredients in one product might be more healthy than in the other.

But it was not all 'taste and enjoy' – for example, the children had to compute mentally the difference between the two prices, and were not able just to say 'I like (a) better than (b)'; valid reasons for making the decision had to be explained. Questions were distributed around the class with the children eager to contribute.

With the tasting nearly at an end, the class teacher explained that the last items to be tasted, some scones, were to act as the bridge between that day's tasting and the following day's activity.

A conventional lesson followed the tasting, immediately after break, which set the scene for further activity: group work to decide which ingredients to purchase for the practical lesson on Thursday. The teacher outlined the practicalities of the scone-baking session the following day, and the children's attendance at the local farmers' market to try to sell the resulting produce.

The links between the three activities were explained to the children: in their conventional lesson they had to weigh up the merits of whether to purchase, for example, the expensive flour or the 'smart price' flour. They were steered into thinking that one might yield more profit than the other and, in the context of 'money week', profit might be the important criterion.

Once the children had tasted the foods, they were split into small groups so that they could decide which flavour scones they would make to sell at the farmers' market and what 'standard' ingredients they wanted to purchase. The children decided to buy a mixture of more expensive and cheaper ingredients. They thought carefully about what they had learned and which ones would affect the quality of the final product. The children decided we could buy 'smart price' flour, sugar and currants, but that we should buy more expensive eggs and cheese because of what they had tasted earlier on in the session.

The children enjoyed making their scones the next day, and when we visited the farmers' market on the Friday all of the produce that had been made by the whole school was sold. We came back to school with a profit of £39.94 overall. Only two children from each class were able to attend the farmers' market, so on their return to school they shared with the rest of the class what they had done, and what they had learned. The bread and fairy cakes made by children in other classes sold the most quickly, and we could have made a larger profit had we used all of the ingredients that had been bought, but this was hindered by time limitations. Further discussions of what we achieved and what we learned will be discussed at Enterprise Club, and we plan to carry out a similar event at the Nativity on North Hykeham Green in December.

Conclusion

What this chapter has aimed to do has been to open teachers' eyes to the rich and varied methods they might employ not simply to present learning in an innovative, exciting and stimulating way, but to gather feedback about learning from pupils. In the process we are helping to promote the kind of integrative knowledge that is needed in developing life skills, enterprise skills and the kinds of skills that will be needed for pupils to become economically self-sustaining citizens. The bonus is that these approaches can lead to learning that is genuinely imaginative and dynamic. Heppell (2011) urges us to persevere; and it is a message that resonates in a UK education system that sometimes feels unreasonably constrained by government directives. He notes:

> It has been all too tempting to see ourselves in the manner of a pedagogic proletariat, shackled by systems, with little control over our destiny, and aspiring simply to move on up in respectability and esteem. To focus on that parochial fight would be to betray the opportunity presented and to selfishly abandon the millions who might be helped. If Media Education has a manifesto then surely it should be headlined by a wish to push within all our institutions for ambitious change, to overturn moribund models of practice, to challenge ossified pedagogy, to be the engine of change, to apply what we know.

Every lesson can be, or can incorporate, learning through and from the media, either in the presentation of material by teachers or in pupils' responses to it; and media learning is frequently, and almost by definition, cross-curricular. Though there are challenges here, there are also dynamic opportunities.

References

Bamford, A. (2003) *The Visual Literacy White Paper*. Sydney: Adobe Systems.

Bazalgette, C. (2010) *Teaching Media in Primary Schools*. London: Sage.

Bearne, E. and Grainger, T. (2004) 'Research in progress – raising boys' achievements in writing: joint PNS/UKLA pilot research project'. *Literacy* 38(3): 156–158.

Bourne, J. (1994) *Thinking Through Primary Practice*. London: Routledge/Open University Press.

Bowring-Carr, C. and West-Burnham, J. (1997) *Effective Learning in Schools*. London: Pitman.

Chai, C. S. (2010) 'Teachers' epistemic beliefs and their pedagogical beliefs: a qualitative case study among Singaporean teachers in the context of ICT-supported reforms'. *Turkish Online Journal of Educational Technology* 9(4), 1280139.

Department for Education and Skills (2005) *Raising Boys' Achievement*. London: HMSO.

Fisher, R. (1991) *Teaching Juniors*. Oxford: Blackwell.

Gentile, D. A., Lynch, P., Lindder, J. and Walsh, D. (2004) 'The effects of violent video game habits on adolescent hostility, aggressive behaviour and school practice'. *Journal of Adolescence* 27: 5–22.

Heppell, S. (2011) 'Because we can, surely we should?' Available online at: http://www.manifestoformediaeducation.co.uk/2011/02/stephen-heppell.

Ilomäki, L. (2008) *The Effects of ICT on School: Teachers' and Pupils' Perspectives*. Turku: University of Turku, Department of Teacher Education.

Jarvis, M. (2005) *The Psychology of Effective Learning and Teaching*. Cheltenham: Nelson-Thornes.

Kerry, T. (2002) *Learning Objectives, Task Setting and Differentiation*. Cheltenham: Nelson-Thornes.

Kerry, T. and Wilding, M. (2004) *Effective Classroom Teacher*. London: Pearson.

Lacasa, P., Martinez, R. and Mendez, L. (2008) 'Developing new literacies using commercial videogames as educational tools'. *Linguistics and Education* 19.

Lankshear, C. and Knobel, M. (2011) *New Literacies: Everyday Practices and Classroom Learning*. New York: Open University Press/McGraw-Hill.

Leu, D. J. Jr, Caro, J., Costek, C., Hartman, D. K., Henry, L. A. and Reinking, D. (2008) 'Research on instruction and assessment of the new literacies on on-line reading comprehension', in Block, C. C., Parkes, A., Sweeting, H., Wight, D. and Henderson, M. (eds) (2013) 'Do television and electronic games predict children's psychosocial adjustment? Longitudinal research using the UK Millenium Cohort Study'. Available online at: http://adc.bmj.com/content/early/2013/02/21/archdischild-2011–301508.full.

Nutbrown, C. (2002) *Research Studies in Early Childhood Education*. Stoke-on-Trent: Trentham Books.

O'Brien, B. (2007) *The World's Greatest Black and White Photography No. 1*. London: The Spider Awards.

Parkes, A., Sweeting, H., Wight, D. and Henderson, M. (2013) 'Do television and electronic games predict children's psychological adjustment? Longitudinal research using the UK Millenium Cohort Study'. Available online at: http://adc.bmj.com/content/early/2013/02/21/archdischild-2011–301598.full.

Ratcliffe, M. and Grace, M. (2003) *Science Education for Citizenship*. Maidenhead: Open University.

Rikowski, R. (2006) 'Teaching ethical issues in information technology: how and when'. *Information for Social Change* 23.

Robbins, M. (2010) 'Susan Greenfield's sacking: now the Royal Institution can focus on science'. *Guardian: Notes & Theories*, 11 January.

Scorsese, M. (2013) 'Persistence of vision: reading the language of cinema'. Jefferson Lecture in the Humanities. Washington: Kennedy Centre, April.

Semenderiadis, T. and Martidou, R. (2009) 'Using audiovisual media in nursery school, within the framework of an interdisciplinary approach'. *Synergies Sud-Est européen* 2: 65–76.

Stoll, L., Fink, D. and Earl, L. (2003) *It's About Learning and It's About Time*. London: Routledge Falmer.

Vygotsky, L. (1978) *Mind in Society*. Cambridge, MA: Harvard University Press.

Wallace, B., Berry, A. and Cave, D. (2008) *Teaching Problem-solving and Thinking Skills through Science*. London: Routledge.

Internet sources

http://education.stateuniversity.com/pages/2495/Technology-in-SCHOOL.html

http://oer.edu.cam.ac.uk/wiki/Problem-Solving_in_Primary_Education/Document

http://www.artsonthemove.co.uk/education/primary/primary.php

http://www/bbc.co.uk/schoolreport25259600

http://www.curriculumonline.ie/en/Primary_School_Curriculum/Social_Environ-mental_and_Scientific_Education_SESE_/History/History_Teacher_Guidelines/Approaches_and_methodologies/Drama_and_role-play/

http://www.etini.gov.uk/information_and_communication_technology_in_primary_schools.pdf

http://www.innovation-unit.co.uk/about-us/publications/new-resources-for-primary-school-councils.html

http://www/kn/att.com/vidconf/ideas.html

http://www.manifestoformediaeducation.co.uk/2011/02/stephen-heppell

http://www.npg.org.uk/learning/schools/primary-schools/videoconferencing.php

http://www.teachingexpertise.com/articles/visual-literacy-3961

https://patherfile.unm.edu/edu/braham/www/brhampdfs/48_technologyandepistemology.pdf

www.education.com/Reference/article/Ref_Dev_Metacognition

www.edu.gov.on.ca/eng/studentsuccess/thinkliteracy/files/thinkenglish10–12.pdf

www.offordcentre.com/readiness

www.pedsforparents.com/articles/2791.shtml

Other useful sources

www.MirandaNet.ac.uk – a community of education professionals with opportunities for exchanging and developing ideas

www.schoolstech.org.uk – an interactive site that encourages views about teaching with technology, though perhaps one that is less independent of government than MirandaNet

The BBC's *Click* programme, usually shown on BBC1 and BBC2, and accessed also via www.bbc.co.uk/Click – a good source of up-to-date information about IT developments and potential future directions.

Chapter 13

Planning effective team teaching for cross-curricular learning

Peter Harrod and Trevor Kerry

Introduction

This chapter looks at team teaching as a way of organising pupils' learning. It suggests that team teaching may be used for all or part of a child's learning experience, but that it is especially suited to periods where learning is presented as cross-curricular. The chapter examines some definitions of team teaching; various models that can be applied to it; its advantages as a means of organisation, and its limitations. The chapter also emphasises that team teaching is an advanced teaching skill that demands proper preparation and appropriate staff training. The chapter sets out advice and examples for those who want to try their hand at working in this collaborative way.

Background

A chapter about team teaching is especially appropriate in a book about integrated approaches to curriculum. It is a simple logic: cross-curricular knowledge is broader than subject-based knowledge, so teams of two or more teachers are likely to have wider and more varied perspectives on offer to support the basic philosophy and approach of integration. When we embarked upon revising this book, it was suggested to us that this theme, and that of Chapter 12 (using a range of media) had the feel of being in some sense incidental to the main theme of cross-curricular approaches. Nothing could be further from the truth. Integrated approaches require teachers to re-examine their pedagogy and teaching methodologies, in addition to reappraising their overall philosophy of education (as we suggest in Chapters 1 and 2). The example that follows encapsulates this insight with respect to team teaching, and highlights the dangers of failing to do so.

It is easy to make unwarranted assumptions about teachers and teaching: e.g. that teachers can teach, and therefore they can adapt their teaching style appropriately to any kind of external circumstance and can work in it without training.

The fallacy of this assumption struck home some years ago during a study of a new primary school space (Kerry and Wilding 2004: 259–280). The space was an open-plan building, well equipped and carpeted, in what had been a former swimming pool. The newly refurbished room could hold three classes at once, but was occupied by two teachers and two parallel groups. It opened directly into the playground and the school field. The researchers were asked to investigate why this expensive and attractive space was not delivering a learning benefit to the pupils after a year of operation.

This is not the place to rehearse the story of this research. Suffice it to say that we looked at the cognitive levels of learning (see Chapter 2); at pupils' time-on-task; at the classroom organisation and its suitability for the location, with special attention paid to the use of group, individual and whole-class work; at behaviour and the kinds of deviance in evidence when pupils were not occupied with their work; and at how pupils of high, middle and lower levels of ability operated within the lessons. We also listened to and collected evidence from pupils, teachers, the headteacher and the governors who had raised funds for the rebuilding.

Our conclusions were quite damning in terms of the quality of the learning experience (though the teachers involved were highly competent, experienced and dedicated professionals). We found that, while behaviour of pupils was good (so the scene was set for effective learning), there was little cognitively extended task demand, work was rarely differentiated other than by outcome, opportunities to cater for the most and least able were lost, and pupil voice was nowhere in evidence. A space that should have been in itself a dynamic learning area was not 'owned' by anyone, and was therefore sterile and unstimulating. Social relations were good all round, but lessons were often unfocused, as far as we could discern, and there were overt signs of boredom from the pupils.

What was patently obvious was that two teachers vying with each other to teach two independently planned lessons (of which one might require children to be active and quite noisy, and one static and quiet) in a single space produced neither rational teaching nor effective learning. If frustration was running high among staff, it was worse for the pupils. Our report to the governing body made this clear. A précis of this, but generalised to fit more diverse situations, gives the flavour:

> The move to the advanced skill of team teaching and the more effective use of support personnel would be helpful, but would imply a degree of collaborative forward planning on the part of teachers, so that they consulted with one another in advance on what would be taught when, by whom, and in what circumstances. This would not preclude pupils being allocated to 'tutor groups' for organisational and pastoral purposes. It would allow the teachers to bring their individual strengths to curriculum and lesson planning, and to the delivery of individual areas of learning. It would open up more potential for problem-solving approaches by pupils. This in turn would provide for a better approach to differentiation in lessons, which are currently orientated towards whole-class work; even where pupils are organised into groups they currently tackle identical tasks. Above all, the staff involved in this team teaching need to be trained in the appropriate skills. Consideration should be given to any courses that might be available and to opportunities that they might have to visit team teaching in action in other schools. The benefits of team teaching should be communicated to all stakeholders, not least parents and governors.

Reflection

Have you tried team teaching? If so, what did you find were its strengths and weaknesses?

If not, what are the factors that most attract you to it, or put you off?

In this chapter our intention is to analyse the prerequisites, the caveats and the benefits that relate to team working by teachers. In so doing, we are not advocating that every school or every lesson should be based on this model. We are arguing, however, that the model has strengths that can be exploited for pupils' benefit in all schools and by all teachers in appropriate circumstances. What is clear, from the example above, is that the model cannot work without a proper understanding of its philosophy and practice, and it is to this that we turn our attention.

Team teaching: historical roots and present definition

The origins of 'team teaching' are succinctly reported in Freeman (1969). There seemed little doubt to him that team teaching originated in the USA in the early years of the 20th century, through projects such as the Dalton Plan. However, UK interest in the concept dates back to the 1950s, inspired by initiatives in the USA culminating in the publication of Trump's (1959) 'Images of the future', in which Trump predicted that the school of the future would include activities of one hundred or more pupils under the supervision of one or more teachers, and would follow many different patterns. Such a scheme has echoes of the 'Monitorial' system in England. Freeman suggests that team teaching had its roots in the availability of 'modern' audio-visual equipment, including teaching machines, CCTV, overhead projectors and similar devices. As we saw in the previous chapter, this list would have now to be moderated or augmented to include both hardware (cameras, phones, PCs, whiteboards, etc.), their related software approaches, and the understandings needed by teachers and pupils to approach these in critical ways. It is also worth saying that, while audio-visual approaches facilitate team teaching, they do not require it.

Given the different guises in which team teaching appears, it is hardly surprising that there are several different definitions. Indeed, Taylor (1974: 7) argues that it is not possible to offer a complete or exact description of team teaching, since it must be regarded as having an 'evolving and fluid character'. Her study of team teaching experiments in ten junior schools found that there was considerable variety of aims and arrangements, but that the one common factor was that the staff were teaching together, sharing the same group of children and the responsibility for their learning (1974: 120).

Freeman himself cites Shaplin and Olds' (1964) definition, following a survey of various schemes, as 'instructional organisation in which two or more teachers are given responsibility, working together, for all or a significant part of the instruction of the same group of pupils'. Loeser (2008) offers a similar definition, describing team teaching as the practice of including two or more teachers of equal status in a classroom to provide instruction to one group of students. (Whether the teachers need to be of 'equal status' is of course arguable: asymmetrical relationships may have positive advantages for both parties – see the section on teaching assistants in Chapter 9.) Buckley (2000: 5) refers to a definition by Bair and Woodward (1964), in which team teaching is seen as lying 'in the essential spirit of cooperative planning, constant collaboration, close unity, unrestrained communication, and sincere sharing'. Scicluna (2013), however, prefers Buckley's own (2000: 4) definition:

> A group of instructors working purposefully, regularly and co-operatively to help a group of students learn. As a team, the teachers work together in setting goals for a course, designing a syllabus, preparing individual lesson plans, actually teaching students together and evaluating the results.

Warwick (1971: 10), in a study of team teaching in secondary schools, points to two different schools of thought that envisage team teaching either as an economic and relatively democratic way of organising and administering a school or as a philosophy of education that emphasises a reorientation of the curriculum to meet more fully the needs of both teachers and pupils. In the latter case, it takes as its starting point the needs of the children, and questions the notion that the requirements of either teacher or pupil are best served by an arbitrary subject division, with each one working in isolation from the others (1971: 12). In giving an overview of team teaching in elementary schools in Nevada as a situation in which two teachers share approximately thirty students in the same room all day, Anderson (in Northern Nevada Writing Project 1996: 3–9) suggests that it is 'obvious that team teaching can look very different from level to level and class to class'. The tentative conclusion is that the best definition of team teaching is a broad one: two or more teachers coming together for a common purpose to help enhance their teaching and their students' learning. It may, on occasion, be even simpler than that: the 'spontaneous cooperation of two like-minded teachers who decided to put their classes together and plan and record together' (O'Neill and Worrall n.d.).

Reflection

If learning is organised using a teaching team, how might team teaching best be used to meet the needs of individual children?

It is clear that, whatever the precise origins or even the exact definition, the concept rests on certain assumptions and philosophies that are broadly recognised by writers. We have tried to draw these together in Table 13.1, along with some of the disadvantages of the method in Table 13.2 – for its advantages do not amount to a panacea. The tables are a composite of material culled from our cited sources, but also from our own experiences as teachers and as teacher trainers.

Team teaching: a practical and research perspective

So far, our consideration of team teaching has – for the sake of simplicity – assumed that it is a single phenomenon, but this is some way from the truth. For example, Goetz (2000) draws out half a dozen models from her own work and the work of Maroney (1995), and of Robinson and Schaible (1995). The labels are hers:

- *Traditional*: one teacher provides instruction, while the other constructs a concept map on an OHP or computer to support her colleague.
- *Collaborative*: several teachers devise the content as a discussion in the presence of the learners, so that the construction itself becomes a learning process.
- *Complementary/supportive*: one teacher teaches while the other looks after follow-up activities or provides study skill support.
- *Parallel*: the class is divided into two small groups and each teacher teaches identical material, using the situation for more individualised support.

Table 13.1 Principles and assumptions of a team-teaching approach

Team teaching (with a fellow teacher/s or teaching assistants) allows (in no particular order of importance):

From a teacher's perspective
Reduction of teacher stress
Teachers to share the time and work of planning
More creative and imaginative approaches through joint planning
Teachers to collaborate on curriculum development projects
Teachers to share and/or contrast teaching philosophies
A movement away from teacher autonomy into shared responsibility for learning
Opportunities for teachers to grow professionally by learning from the practice of others
Experience by teachers of different but complementary teaching styles
Opportunities for teachers to operate in a cooperative learning environment
A model of good practice to less experienced teachers and/or Trainees/NQTs
Teachers to be freed up for planning activities without disturbing lessons

From a pupil's perspective
Sharing expertise in a cross-curricular topic-centred approach
A model in which cross-curricular understandings are seen to produce improved outcomes
Matching preferred learning styles with teaching styles more effectively and flexibly
Providing pupils with more effective learning outcomes
Offering a model of good practice to pupils in terms of co-operation, teamwork, positive
   interaction, and collaborative effort
Learning for pupils which is more closely personalised
Improved opportunities for pupils' social learning
Sharper focus on pedagogic skills
Experience by pupils of different but complementary teaching styles
Introduction of a positive competitive edge to teaching and learning, including sharper learning
   objectives and success criteria leading to better pupil performance
More varied opportunities to differentiate having shared some basic knowledge
Generating respect for differences among teachers

From a management perspective
Reduction in teacher–pupil ratios
More effective pastoral care and behaviour management of pupils
Team members to refine organisation and management skills
More meaningful and reliable formative assessment data
Weaker teachers to be supported
Using Higher Level Teaching Assistants to provide models of good practice to others
Opportunities emerge to show collective support for whole-school policies
Willingness to embrace the symbiotic nature of the teacher–pupil relationship
Emergencies/unforeseen events to be better catered for
The advantages of team working identified in business (e.g. heightened morale and commitment) to
   rub off in a school situation

- *Differentiated split class*: each teacher teaches the same topic but the class is divided, e.g. into more able and less able learners, the content being appropriately differentiated for the groups.
- *Monitoring*: one teacher teaches, the other monitors behaviour or checks understanding of individuals.

Table 13.2 Possible disadvantages of team teaching

From a teacher perspective

Interpersonal problems/problems of relationships within the team
Possible incompatibility of teaching styles
Need for sensitivity by management in realising team memberships
Need to have willing participants
Need for an agreed division of labour
The loss of teacher autonomy
Fear of poor performance in front of peers
Logistical factors, such as findings opportunities to share planning time

From the student's perspective

Some students may be confused by conflicting opinions
Some students just want to be 'told the facts'
Preparation for lessons can be more demanding
The system allows pupils more readily to compare teachers (Jang 2006)

From a management perspective

Team teaching requires an upfront investment of time in training, etc.
Team working may be a complicating factor in interviewing and appointing staff
Resistance from senior management, governors, parents

Team teaching (Igawa 2009) is only one of a number of descriptors attached to this way of working. Friend and Cook (2010) and Hurley (2012) prefer the term co-teaching, while Sandholtz (2000) opts for the rather more cumbersome cooperative teaching. Wadkins, Miller and Wozniak (2004), reported by Scicluna (2013), invent labels for three apparent models of this approach, as follows.

1   The *Collaborative model*: where typically two or more teachers are in the classroom during lesson time. Since only one teacher can speak at a time, there may be minor differences in the time allotted to each team member. Particular topics are divided among instructors depending on each teacher's particular strengths. For this reason, it is best to have teachers who can complement one another in their areas of expertise.
2   The *Tag-team teaching model* or *Turn-teaching*: where each teacher takes the lead in different aspects of the lesson and handles them single-handedly. Team-teachers take turns being responsible for in-class teaching time and operate on their own in the classroom.
3   The *Coordinator model*: where the 'team' in this model consists of a single coordinator who invites specialists to give a one-time presentation of specific material that fits in the scheme of the course.

Blanchard (2006) tried – perhaps too hard – to produce a comprehensive definition. He muddied the waters between philosophical, procedural and outcome issues. Based on the acronym PERFORM, he argues for:

• Purpose and values enshrined in team teaching to be identified
• Empowering of teachers to use this approach
• Relationships and communication structures to be in place

- Flexibility to be paramount on the part of those involved
- Optimal productivity to be achieved as a result
- Recognition to be given of the worth of the endeavour and those involved in it
- Morale being enhanced as a result.

In England, the respected and well-published educationist Joan Dean (Dean 1970: 6) supported a view that team teaching is a broad church of definitions: the only thing they have in common is that the various forms work with groups of children and/or teachers rather than on the principle of one teacher one class. At around the same time, the National Foundation for Educational Research (NFER), in a report on the subject (Taylor 1974), offered the view that the move to this approach was an Americanism (presumably a pejorative term!) adopted by English teachers merely to 'get on the bandwagon' of innovation; and it took the line that it was related to architectural trends towards open-plan schools. None of these assumptions is entirely necessary, or indeed accurate, as a judgement on the method rather than its context. Our own view is that *an innovation or methodology is justifiable only in so far as it brings learning gains*, and this chapter argues for learning gains through team teaching without committing itself to a view that team approaches should represent the only, or the full-time, diet of children in schools.

The Northern Nevada Writing Project (NNWP 1996) looked into team teaching and found it was the shared moments that were the great positive in team teaching: the working environment became more humane and, importantly, interactions increased. Learning and teaching styles could be matched more easily. Teachers believed that the curriculum had been enhanced through the increased skill range of the staff, and there was more activity – better hands-on approaches in the classroom and more visits out of it. Benefits were not only to the children but also to staff, who were more prepared to take risks in an atmosphere of collaboration and shared responsibility. That is not to say that all ran smoothly in team contexts: the participants suffered from territorial disputes, failures of communication, the need to sustain initial enthusiasms and commitments to joint activity, and the resentments that are inevitable if the decision to team teach is management imposed.

In a brief and tantalising study of two secondary school teachers in Taiwan, Jang (2006) compared team and traditional approaches. Two teachers taught four classes for twelve weeks, two in the traditional way and two using team teaching. When results from the classes were compared, those taught using team methods were higher than those taught traditionally. Furthermore, the students tended to prefer the team teaching organisation. However, he notes that team teaching did not win the support of the school administration, which set out actively to impede their planning. This is a salutary case of management making decisions based not on educational but on ideological principles.

The NNWP results were mirrored in the more recent work, albeit small scale, by Scicluna (2013). She found that teachers said their preparation was easier – although the preparation opportunities for all team members did need to be coordinated. Teachers felt they could play to their strengths; and the fact that others might compensate for their individual weakness in knowledge in a particular area provides them with increased confidence and less stress. However, the teachers in her study did meet some resistance from some members of senior management (though not the headteacher). The headteacher identified a (perceived) improvement in pupil outcomes and performance, though no data were produced to support this view.

> **Reflection**
>
> Why might a senior management team in a school look less than favourably on a move towards team teaching?

In the UK, Dewhurst and Tamburrini (1978) had undertaken studies in 71 infant and junior schools. As a result they had identified five models of team teaching that seemed to emerge from practice at the time. These were as follows:

1   *The Assignment Model*: teachers work cooperatively, and pupils engage in activities either individually or in small groups. Tasks are either self-chosen or individually assigned by teachers. Each teacher usually takes responsibility for one aspect of the curriculum, although the approach is not subject dominated.
2   *The Rotation Model*: groups (home or class based) are timetabled to move in turn from one designated area to another for different curriculum activities, with a balance over a day or a week, etc. Teachers tend to remain in one activity area.
3   *The Setting Model*: the basics are taught in sets according to ability in maths and language, while project activities (afternoons) are planned cooperatively by teachers ('skills and frills').
4   *The Half-day Model*: similar to the model above, but without 'setting', the basics being taught in mixed-ability classes.
5   *The Occasional Model*: work on a special project for a limited period, with teachers sharing particular interests and expertise.

Dewhurst saw these organisational methods as serving one or more of three core purposes: they depended on a child-centred philosophy of education with individualisation at its heart; they espoused a knowledge-based philosophy of integration as a means of presenting subject matter; or they were economic, being designed to maximise staff, expertise and space. These summary points are each of considerable significance.

It appears from the more modern literature that team teaching is more openly practised and appreciated overseas than in the more traditional (some might say, public school influenced) UK. We have noted Jang's (2006) Taiwanese study above. Scicluna's (2013) work was Malta-based. Beamish, Bryer and Davies (2005), working in Australia, concluded that team teaching had positive benefits both for those with learning difficulties, and for the gifted and talented pupils in classes. They noted that teachers became less proprietorial about classes ('our' children not 'your' children). They grew to enjoy one another as co-workers. In Ireland, Ó'Murchú (2011: Abstract), working in secondary settings, expressed his support even more strongly. Following a longitudinal study, he concluded:

> Research to date on team teaching has been too focused on outcomes over short time-frames, and not focused enough on the process that is team teaching. As a consequence team teaching has been under-used, under-valued, under-theorized and generally not well understood . . . Conclusions from this study have implications for the triad of research, practice and policy development.

The reader will have noted that, while we have striven to give up-to-date references for team teaching, some of the material appears relatively dated. This is because, while team teaching was recommended as long ago as the Plowden Report (1967) as an organisational method for learning that was worthy of exploration, the Plowden backlash of the 1980s (*pace* the National Curriculum under a Conservative administration), and the continued dominance of the teaching profession by ultra-traditional Ofsted leaders such as Chris Woodhead under New Labour, effectively spelled its death knell for a time as a widely adopted mode of working. As was indicated in the Foreword, there was a potential resurgence in integrated approaches in the period around 2011, but this was largely negated by Secretary of State Gove's recent and very traditional approach and pursuit of the subject-teaching chimera. So perhaps this is a good moment to see the effects this situation has had on team teaching in action and on the management of team teaching in schools by comparing our original Case Study (13.1) from the first edition of this text with a follow-up visit a short time ago (Case Study 13.2).

Case Study 13.1 Team teaching at Priory Witham Academy School

Although team teaching has not been widespread in the UK since the 1970s, one school that has bucked the trend is the Priory Witham Academy School (Infant and Nursery Section, formerly Moorlands Infant School) in Lincoln. Its whole-school approach has evolved over the last twelve years or so, and has been the subject of a 'mini' case study by the present authors. In common with the case studies reported in Freeman (1969: 82), the participating teachers were sent an interview schedule questionnaire in advance of the interview itself, outlining issues and questions judged to be relevant to the study. These questions were based on earlier studies by Close, Rudd and Plimmer (1974: 116) and NNWP (1996: 96), allowing for some comparative analysis. Teachers were given the opportunity to respond both individually and as a group. The results may be conveniently examined in three broad areas: principles and philosophy; principles into practice; and advantages, limitations and outcomes.

The main principles underlying the approach were as follows:

- A whole-school approach, led by the headteacher
- Team planning
- Group collaboration and participation
- All teachers involved in the same activity
- Group and/or class rotations
- Assessments and profiling by all teachers to ensure reliability
- Involvement of teaching assistants and, where available, parent helpers
- Practice never remains static; it is continuously evolving.

The approach, while having a common ethos and shared objectives, was variable according to the age phase and subject matter. In the Early Years Foundation Stage, for example, the whole-team approach and cross-curricular nature of the work lent itself naturally to a team teaching culture, and this provided a basis for adoption in modified form in Key Stage 1. As one teacher reported, it is perhaps easier to implement in the early years, as the children are used to moving around the class from one activity to another, and to having access to all areas at all times. There was a general consensus that this stage was perhaps more conducive to team teaching. In Key Stage 1 the approach had evolved over time through afternoon topic-based work. Typically there were three teachers and six assistants in the early years, whereas in Key Stage 1 there were two teachers and four main assistants. In both cases, however, flexibility was the watchword.

Three examples of how the principles worked in practice were a week with an art focus, science-based days and a book week. During such projects, there would be a whole-school rotation, with Reception children working together with Year 2 pupils. Staff would provide leads from their own interests and expertise. It was felt that team teaching is less applicable in mathematics, because of the nature of the subject, and the need for step-by-step learning. By contrast, staff were highly enthusiastic about how it operated in literacy, where good results had been achieved. For example in phonics sessions, consistency of approach resulted from all teachers planning together and being involved in the shared delivery of the sessions. Moreover, the opportunity to be able to observe the children more closely led to more reliable formative assessments, with more focused target setting. Applying Dewhurst and Tamburrini's (1978) model, the approach would seem to be a mixture of the 'assignment', 'rotation' and 'occasional' models.

Many advantages of the school's approach to team teaching were identified and shared enthusiastically. These included:

- The value to the children of different teaching styles and strategies
- The opportunity for children to approach different teachers and assistants
- Sharing ideas during planning, teaching and evaluation
- Preparing and sharing resources; reducing the workload
- Easier and more reliable assessments, including profiling and target setting
- Teachers' knowledge of a greater range of children, so that their abilities and levels were more easily identified, and their needs addressed to enhance differentiation and personalised learning
- Behaviour management as a shared responsibility, and different strategies available
- Subject knowledge and staff interests and expertise, for example through subject coordinators, shared to the benefit of both children and colleagues
- Teachers' own professional development of skills, knowledge and understanding enhanced by observing colleagues at work
- Greater safety and security for the children
- The social and emotional skills of the children developed
- The culture of shared enterprise and responsibility presenting a good role model for the children's own social development.

In addition to the advantages of the approach, some limitations and constraints were identified and discussed, as follows:

- There were some logistical problems involving timetabling, and the match between different individual class timetables.
- It was pointed out that a weak teacher *could* have a negative effect on the approach, but that there were no weak teachers at the school!
- There needs to be mutual respect among teachers and assistants; clashes can occur, but need to be addressed professionally, through discussion leading to resolution. The focus should be on practice and not personalities.
- There has to be give and take; compromise is sometimes inevitable.

- There could be some potential problems with children with special needs, including insecure children who need the security of one identified teacher. This needs to be approached sensitively, with gradual integration into a team teaching environment.
- The approach needs to evolve continuously through trial and error, and the need to train and accommodate new members of staff. There is a need for constant review, particularly when allocating staff to teams for the forthcoming academic year, bearing in mind personalities, and a balance of strengths and experience.
- New staff need time and support to adapt to the approach. One experienced teacher described how she had moved from another school and needed a period of adjustment, supported by colleagues. An NQT described how much he had learned from more experienced teachers, for example in developing a range of behaviour management strategies. A trainee following a Graduate Teacher Programme in the school also reported that he had clearly benefited from team teaching, lending credence to O'Neill and Worrall's (undated) finding that students in teacher training are helped and supported through such an apprenticeship approach.

The results of this study are remarkably comparable to those reported in similar studies in the 1960s and 1970s, and discussed elsewhere in this chapter.

Two general conclusions may be drawn from this 'mini' case study. It is certainly clear that team teaching could be, and was, successful even within the relative straitjacket of the National Curriculum of the time, when there is leadership, conviction and a collaborative ethos with the willingness to make it work. As Freeman (1969: 88) reported, such a system cannot work without teamwork and dedication. It is equally clear that the present trend towards a more integrated cross-curricular approach to teaching and learning will facilitate and encourage those schools wishing to embrace a team teaching philosophy and pedagogy. Moreover this study, albeit small scale, confirms that team teaching is a dynamic, flexible and organic process that, while varying in style and purpose from one school to another, is essentially an approach that allows teachers to pool their energies and expertise for the benefit of the children. The Priory Witham Academy School (Nursery and Infant Section), as portrayed in our original case study, presents a blueprint for this process, and a shining example of good practice. So what happened to this mode of learning between 2011 and 2014? The story continues in Case Study 13.2.

Case Study 13.2 Priory Witham Academy revisited

Three years is a long time in education, and there have been many reforms under the present administration that have exerted external constraints on every educational institution. As far as the Priory Witham Academy is concerned, these changes have included the gradual transition from a traditional infant school to a 0–18 comprehensive academy, and the move to a new purpose-built campus from the former pre-war buildings, now demolished. Some new members of staff, including a headteacher of the primary section following the retirement of the former head, have been appointed. In several ways, however, government policy has allowed the Academy greater freedom to plan and manage its own affairs. All academies are to some extent free of local government control and influence, and are supposedly less accountable to central government than the more traditional state schools.

Philosophically, the primary section of the Academy remains totally committed to the principles, practices and advantages of a collaborative team-teaching approach outlined in the original case study. Within the structure of the Academy, this has been facilitated by the appointment of highly qualified, experienced curriculum leaders, who are passionate about sharing their skills, and who act as models for high-quality teaching and learning. This is particularly noticeable in the training of new staff, and the continued professional development of teachers, teaching assistants and other adults working in the Academy. The Graduate Teacher Programme and the new School Direct policy, with teachers being trained on the job, have each contributed to the success of these initiatives.

As I found on a recent visit, the Academy has been on a 'journey' for the last three years, as the institution adapted to its new buildings, it greater size and its status as a 3–11 academy. It struck me very strongly as I left the building, feeling energised and inspired by my visit, that the primary section of the Prior Witham Academy has retained that 'leadership, conviction and collaborative ethos' that was so tangibly evident in the earlier case study. That this has happened despite the monumental changes that have taken place in such a small period of time is a great tribute to the management of the institution as a whole, but in particular to the dedication, commitment and passion of its staff, and their willingness to collaborate to make their vision a reality. As such, it provides a beacon to those institutions facing similar changes and challenges, and acts as an inspiration to their own aspirations.

Reflection

Consider Case Studies 13.1 and 13.2. What are the similarities and differences between them? From this, and from your experience, suggest what effects political/policy decision making might have on the learning organisation of schools? To what extent and in what ways are these effects likely to be (a) positive or (b) negative?

Pulling together the key factors

Whatever else one concludes about them, these two cases show an enduring commitment to a way of learning that many teachers value and that is effective for many pupils. As suggested in the Case Study 13.2, one of the very best assessments of team teaching, clear sighted about both its pros and its cons, is by Buckley (2000), albeit conducted with older students. Many of the points made by Buckley are contiguous with those made elsewhere in this chapter and by other writers, but some of the issues to which he draws attention are particularly pertinent. For us, this statement, for example:

> Teamwork improves the quality of scholarship and teaching as various experts in the same field or different fields approach the same topic from different angles and areas of expertise: theory and practice, past and present, different gender or ethnic backgrounds. Teacher strengths are combined. Teacher weaknesses are remedied. Teachers complement one another's expertise.
>
> (Buckley 2000: 11)

It is hard to gainsay this common-sense assessment. It accords with our own experience. In one situation in which we taught, a humanities and social studies curriculum was devised by an English specialist, a geographer, and a specialist in social and religious studies. We brought both male and female perspectives to the issues. We had particular individual interests: film, poetry, the links between arts and science, outdoor activities, survey work, photography. Each of us had a circle of acquaintances we could bring in for 'live' specialist inputs. We could free one another up to undertake detailed planning. The impact of the curriculum was 'more than the sum of its parts', and a parallel group, taught in conventional ways, even went so far as to lobby the headteacher to be allowed the same kind of experience.

Buckley also explodes myths. He challenges the view that all children learn at the same rate: one of the inevitable pillars of whole-class traditional teaching. He, rightly, notes that lesson lengths are not efficient just because they are all the same (in the system described in the last paragraph we opted for whole days, half days, double and single lessons across the working week – these gave maximum flexibility). He challenges the myths of class size; in fact, some activities are best conducted with small groups, some can take place perfectly appropriately with very large ones. He points to the limitations of self-contained classrooms, but is really hinting that the kind of one-teacher-one-classroom mentality is outmoded: we have argued elsewhere that for too long English education has been bedevilled by the 'fine and private place' mentality of classroom organisation. If you are wondering about the allusion, it comes from a 17th-century poem and refers to the grave. Buckley challenges the boring diet that many pupils endure, of endless regurgitation (see Chapter 2) – the graveyard of learning.

But he is not concerned solely with teachers: Buckley also looks at team teaching from the pupil perspective:

> The clash of teacher viewpoints, changes of voice and rhythm, and alternation of different styles and personalities are stimulating and exciting. This gets and keeps attention and prevents boredom . . . The teachers model critical thinking for students: they debate, disagree with premises or conclusions, raise new questions, point out consequences. The contrast of viewpoint encourages more class participation and independent thinking.
>
> (Buckley 2000: 13)

All this is true. It urges us to make one more point: team teaching brings closer the ideal that teachers and learners are in fact all engaged in the process of learning. MacBeath (2005) identifies four critical factors in integrated learning in schools: collaborative learning; internal networking; the proliferation of informal conversation; and 'a constant simmering of ideas'. Scicluna (2013) sums this up neatly as 'the dynamic interplay of multiple minds and personalities'.

Curriculum reform on a periodic basis is in everyone's interest; and continual review and evaluation is a professional bottom line. But simply establishing (even less, imposing) new content, however that is conceived, is not enough; pedagogy and content have to proceed hand in glove. So we come to our conclusion, which is a quotation from O'Neill and Worrall (n.d.):

> Team teaching is essentially a flexible system, and can be used in whatever ways a team of teachers think is best for themselves and their children. We commend team teaching unreservedly to teachers and everyone else concerned with practice, theory, and policy-making in education.

References

Bair, M. and Woodward, R. G. (1964) *Team Teaching in Action*. Boston: Houghton Mifflin.

Beamish, W., Bryer, F. and Davies, M. (n.d.) 'Co-teaching in Queensland primary schools', in Bartlett, B., Bryer, F. and Roebuck, D. (eds) *Stimulating the 'Action', as Participants in Participatory Research*, Vol. 1. Brisbane, Australia: School of Cognition, Language, and Special Education, Griffith University: 65–80.

Blanchard, K. (2006) *Ignite! Newsletter*, Vol. 11. Ken Blanchard Companies. Available online at: http://www.kenblanchard.com/Leading-Research/Ignite-Newsletter/Ignite!-Newsletter-Archive/Vol11–2006 (accessed 3 July 2013).

Buckley, F. (2000) *Team Teaching: What, How and Why?* Thousand Oaks, CA: Sage Publications, Inc.

Close, J., Rudd, W. G. A. and Plimmer, F. (1974) *Team Teaching Experiments*. Windsor: NFER.

Dean, J. (1970) 'Team teaching'. *New Era* 53: 6.

Dewhurst, J. and Tamburrini, J. (1978) 'Team teaching in primary schools'. *Education 3–13* 6(2): 19–24.

Freeman, J. (1969) *Team Teaching in Britain*. London: Ward Lock Educational.

Friend, M. and Cook, L. (2010) Co-teaching: an illustration of the complexity of collaboration in special education. *Journal of Educational and Psychological Consultation* 20: 9–27.

Goetz, K. (2000) 'Perspectives on team teaching'. *Egallery* 1(4). Available online at: http://www.ucalgary.ca/~egallery (accessed 31 March 2009).

Hurley, S. (2012) 'Co-planning/co-teaching: a rich opportunity for breaking down the walls of our classrooms in perspectives'. Available online at: http://teachingoutloud.org/2012/06/21/co-planningco-teaching-a-rich-opportunity-for-breaking-down-the-walls-of-our-classrooms/ (accessed 7 July 2013).

Igawa, K. (2009) 'EFL teachers' views on team-teaching: in the case of Japanese secondary school teachers'. *Shitennoji University Bulletin* 47: 145–172.

Jang, S.-J. (2006) 'Research on the effects of team teaching upon two secondary school teachers'. *Educational Research* 48(2): 177–194.

Kerry, T. and Wilding, M. (2004) *Effective Classroom Teacher*. London: Pearson.

Loeser, J. (2008) 'Team teaching'. EBSCOHOST website, Research Starters, Education, Team Teaching.

MacBeath, J. (2005) 'Supporting innovative pedagogies: the role of school leadership'. Paper presented for the ESRC Seminar IV: Enactments of Professionalism: Classrooms and Pedagogies. Kings College London, 5 July. Available online at: www.tlrp.org/themes/seminar/gewirtz/ . . . /paper%20-%20macbeath.doc (accessed 25 June 2013).

Maroney, S. (1995) 'Team teaching'. Available online at: http://www.wiu.edu/users/mfsam1/TeamTchg.html.

Northern Nevada Writing Project (1996) *Team Teaching: The Northern Nevada Writing Project Teacher–Researcher Group*. York, ME: Stenhouse Publishers.

Ó'Murchú, C. P. (2011) 'Team teaching for inclusive learning: purposes, practices and perceptions of a team teaching initiative in Irish post-primary schools'. PhD thesis, University of Cork.

O'Neill, M. and Worrall, M. (n.d. – probably 1972) *Team Teaching in a Primary School*. Newcastle University: Institute of Education.

Plowden Report (1967) *Children and Their Primary Schools*. London: HMSO.

Robinson, B. and Schaible, R. (1995) 'Collaborative teaching: reaping the benefits'. *College Teaching* 43(2): 57–60.

Sandholtz, J. H. (2000) 'Interdisciplinary team teaching as a form of professional development' *Teacher Education Quarterly* 27(3): 39–54.

Scicluna, E. V. (2013) 'The quest for school achievement and performance: a study of the effects of team teaching upon a group of Year 4 teachers at St Christopher's Primary School'. Paper submitted in part-fulfilment of the regulations for the degree of MSc in Education Leadership, Leicester.

Shaplin, J. T. and Olds, H. F. (1964) *Team Teaching*. New York: Harper & Row.

Taylor, M. (1974) *Team Teaching Experiments*. Windsor: NFER.

Trump, J. L. (1959) *Images of the Future*. Santa Monica, CA: Rand Corporation.

Wadkins, T., Miller, R. L. and Wozniak, W. (2004) *Team Teaching Models*. UNK/CTE. Compendium of Teaching Resources and Ideas, University of Nebraska, Kearney, NE. Available online at: http://www.unk.edu/uploadedFiles/academics/cte/compendium.pdf (accessed 6 May 2013).

Warwick, D. (1971) *Team Teaching*. London: University of London Press.

Internet source

www.teachingexpertise.com

Part 7

Drawing together the threads of cross-curricular thinking

Chapter 14

Questioning the supremacy of disciplines

Some conclusions and recommendations

Trevor Kerry

Introduction

This chapter returns to the theme of the relationship between disciplines and cross-curricular working. It examines the claimed supremacy of disciplines as a way into knowledge. Using the example of history it deconstructs these claims and identifies that disciplines and cross-disciplinary working are each essential to proper understanding. It encourages teachers to take a more informed and determined stance in using cross-curricular methods in their professional work.

Background

What, it is to be hoped, this text has provided has been a justification in sound theoretical terms of an approach to learning and teaching through cross-curricular understandings, some consideration of teaching methods using this approach, and some advice on how to refine one's teaching skills to bring out the best in pupils during cross-curricular lessons. The chapters have spoken for themselves, and the messages from them do not need reiteration here. It has not been claimed (we would not be so arrogant) that this methodology is the 'only', the 'best' or the 'foremost' – only that it is legitimate and valuable, and has specific advantages in the context of children's learning and teachers' teaching.

However, what is perhaps worth revisiting is the old objection that underpins this book: that disciplines rule, and that integrated approaches are somehow inferior. While Chapter 1 provided a sound basis for the refutation of this view, the issue continues to rear its head in both society at large ('When I were a lad, we learnt it like this . . . '), and in politics ('We need to get back to basics . . . '). The controversy, asserted in most instances with power and determination, if not with overwhelming evidence, makes teachers nervous about adopting other approaches.

The fact is that the notion of disciplines has gone unchallenged for too long. Disciplines are not the watertight, surefire, reliable, eternal entities that they claim to be. They are subject to change, debate and contention. So, this final chapter opens up the can of worms that is reliance on disciplines, and interrogates one of them (in the first instance) to see how much integrity there is in the claim that disciplines have a validity that transcends integration, and an internal consistency that makes them somehow more 'reliable' than other approaches to accessing understanding.

The problem of history

Most of us engage with history not just because we are part of it, but out of genuine interest and a desire to know. Family history, military history, Roman history, local history – even our current obsession with antiques and television programmes about antiques – are guided by a sense of history that seems to be common to human consciousness. We seem compelled to find out who we are, our place in the drama of the past that has led us to the present, who the other actors are and what we share (or don't share) with them, and how events have shaped us.

Most of us will, at some time, have searched some record or other – what historians call primary sources; we will have obtained a birth certificate, browsed a photograph album, clambered over ruined walls, penetrated a Bronze Age barrow or visited a National Trust building. Though we may not be fully aware of it, this process provides us with hands-on experience: we can touch, see, empathise with, even smell, the related artefacts. People talk about becoming part of history; this is close to what they mean.

Furthermore, most of us will have studied history at school. People of my generation were generally taught *facts*, i.e. timelines of kings and queens with their dates, commonly held views of why key historical events took place (Henry VIII separated from the Church of Rome to gain a divorce, for example); received wisdom about national and cultural achievements of our country (such as the philanthropy of the Victorians in the countries of the Empire).

In recent decades history teaching in schools moved away from this towards a more 'hands on' and empathetic or experiential approach aimed more at understanding and empathy with historical situations than with the *facts* of history. They may have even been encouraged to look for evidence, such as punishments meted out to slaves on Victorian plantations: which might have meant, for example, tempering a view of Victorian high-mindedness, noted above as part of the received wisdom, with views about why they condoned slavery.

In 2013 the then Secretary of State Michael Gove determined that this latter approach to history had moved us away from the *facts*, and that we all needed to take a step backwards to the 1950s and learn history in sequence, with the *facts* etched sequentially into our brains, and examined and assessed for school pupils by their ability to rehearse them. It is an assertion he repeated on Radio 4 in 2014.

While all of this is common experience, it remains problematic; and the problems can be illustrated in two quite interesting but separate ways.

In the first way, let us think about something that happened yesterday (it was yesterday to this writing, though it will not be yesterday to your reading). This happening was a visit by a group of aeronautical enthusiasts to RAF Mildenhall, an air force base owned by Britain but used by the American military. Three of them chose to write down their experience in journals, and here are the three accounts:

> *Anthony's account*: The sun shone on our visit to Mildenhall; two kinds of rare aircraft were present on the base and we were able to secure photographs of them from the control tower. The B1 bomber was parked immediately below us, and from our elevated position we could read its tail-code and watch the operatives preparing it for whatever its next mission might prove to be. The Osprey aircraft, a kind of hybrid helicopter/conventional aircraft with rotating propellers blades, were a 'first'.

Jane's account: On the way down from the control tower (eight floors up) to lunch the lift came to a sudden halt between floors and we had to await rescue. Being trapped in a lift is one of my recurring nightmares and here it was happening in reality.

Jo's account: The highlight of the day was a visit to a tanker aircraft which undertakes refuelling duties in respect of other aircraft, thus extending their range and capability to deliver their respective missions. We took turns to lie in the boom operator's compartment under the tail of the plane and watch simulations of how the refuelling probe operated.

Now, were it to be suggested to you that you should try to reconstruct the 'history' of this visit from the extant narratives, you might be tempted simply to add together the individual events that each writer describes and try to piece them into a sequential narrative – what is popularly known as a piece of history.

But, if these narratives were part of an historian's attempt to reconstruct the visit to Mildenhall (and they are 'history' in that sense), they would present problems. These are just some of the problems they would present:

- How do we know the sequence of events that the narratives purport to recount?
- What other events happened about which none of the writers provides information?
- How many other people participated? If there were others, where are their accounts and what do they say?
- Who exactly, and how many, are the 'we' all the writers refer to?
- Were all the experiences common to all the members of this group referred to as 'we'?
- Did all the participants recognise the 'rare' aircraft?
- Did all the participants photograph them?
- Were Antony's identifications of the 'rare' aircraft accurate – and how do we know whether they were or not?
- Is Anthony's opening sentence a meteorological fact or a metaphor for a good aeronautical experience?
- Were the Osprey aircraft a 'first' for him (the first time he had seen them), a first (in that sense for everyone in the party), their first ever appearance at Mildenhall, or all of those things?
- Jane's account may have meant that she missed other events during the visit, but we don't know whether she did or not.
- Jane's account is clearly one that had a psychological effect on her because of her pre-existing fear; so how did that colour her judgement of other activities during the visit? Why does she record none? Why does she fail to record any?
- Was Jo's account an additional or an alternative activity to the control tower visit?
- Is each writer simply presenting (in their private record) a personal perception of the most formative experience they had during a multifaceted visit?

The questions go on, and are not easily answered or answerable. And this is just the beginning: what about the omissions from the story?

- What else happened? Who else was there? What were the perspectives of the hosts rather than those of the visitors?

- Could we find out? How?
- Would other facets (if there were some) of the visit put a different complexion on the event?

Reconstructing this visit, then, would seem to be neither possible nor – in so far as we can make some guesses at the answers to the questions above and make some sense of the three narratives – capable of providing a reader or the researcher with a secure reality or 'truth' about the event. Yet this brief scenario precisely mirrors the attempt that historians make to reconstruct a 'history' from sources.

When they embark on the process, the task is made even harder by another factor endemic to the historian him/herself. We can examine this in a further metaphor. The metaphor is of a photographer taking an image of a view. Like the person recording an event (the record may be contemporary but in hindsight becomes 'history'), the photographer is intending to record what is in front of him/her. So he presses the shutter and immediately creates 'history'. Look at the picture in Figure 14.1 for the result.

However, like the accounts of the visit to Mildenhall, the picture in Figure 14.1, which is of the Eildon Hills in the Scottish Borders, raises more questions than it answers.

First of all, the photographer chooses a viewpoint, but in doing so inevitably edits in or out of the picture some elements of the whole scene. There may have been animals in the foreground for example, but if there were, we can't see them. Had he moved slightly to the right he might have revealed a power cable running to a pylon, but he chose to eliminate this. With today's digital technology he might have added workers in the fields who were not actually there at that time – and thus created a more Marxist feel to the shot. But how do we know that they were not there, and the photographer has actually eliminated them?

Then the weather at the time when the picture was taken was fine: how different the view might have been in mist, rain, frost or snow – yet these are all realities of this view at one time or another.

Figure 14.1 Interpretation

The time of shooting was early in the morning, the low light providing some modelling to the hills; yet noon or sunset would have shown a different facet of the same hills.

The print is in monochrome, though the original was in colour.

It was early summer, but would look different in spring, autumn or winter, even though the viewpoint is the same and the hills are still the Eildons.

Computer technology has allowed for increases in contrast compared with the original shot; for the clouds to be enhanced; for the tones of the grass, the sky and buildings to be adjusted to please the eye and create increased impact.

The photographer's selections before, during and after the exposure equate to the way in which the narratives of history are compiled, with perspectives, philosophies and ideologies used like the adjustment tools on Photoshop to create a specific view of the subject.

We have not even begun to explore the motive that sits behind the picture, which might have been for a family album, as an entry to a photographic competition or to try to imitate the style of the great photographer Ansel Adams. The same phenomenon – motive – may lie behind the narrative of an historical event, imparting a Marxist, a Christian, a Humanist or some other perspective through the more, or less, conscious whim or intention of the writer.

And so we have to come to the crunch question for history: what is truth? From time to time, government directives and those with similar views clearly believe that it is possible to use historical records/narratives/evidence to construct something called Truth with a capital T. But we have rehearsed some of the dangers of assuming that we can do this from extant evidence or even that the process can ever be feasible. Indeed, we have to ask: is there such a thing as historical truth? How might we move closer to it, if it does exist? And how might we explore whether it does exist or not? Because one thing is clear: teaching a *version* of history as if it were Truth, as the former Secretary of State for Education Michael Gove would have had us do, is at best misleading, and at worst corrupting because it robs us of our judgement.

So begins the debate about history and the role of the historian. It is a real debate for all of us – at least, for all of us who believe that we are products (in some measure) of our culture and environment. We cannot just dismiss the issue as the fevered ramblings of academics and fail to address it. Thus two opposing schools of thought in the debate about history have to concern us.

The first is what might be labelled 'traditionalist'. It says that events really happened back then, that people recorded them, that (using appropriate evidence) we can reconstruct those 'realities' (at least to some degree, depending on passage of time and the quality of the data), and that we can therefore build a picture of the past that bears some relationship to objective truth – or what actually happened.

At the other end of this philosophical continuum (because that is what it is) are the 'postmodernists'. They concentrate on those records, mostly the textual records or narratives of past events. Since, they claim, all records pass through the interpretative processes of the writer, these records present us merely with the subjective creations of the recorders. This applies, they say, whether the narratives are those of Herodotus or Arthur C. Clarke. They are interpretive not objective accounts, akin, in the way they should be regarded, to literary creations. The language of recording is used to build a picture created by the individual historian; and no historical accounts can be held to be reliable or a reflection of anything that can be securely labelled as 'reality'. History, then, can never be viewed as an account of what really happened.

Now, clearly, to take the second view is to question whether history can ever produce an accurate or detached version of whatever events took place back then; it leaves us unable to distinguish fact from fiction – or, at best, unable to distinguish the reliable from the unreliable. Yet, clearly, an objector to the traditional view might claim that all historical reconstruction (i.e. the writings of historians) is indeed suspect in so far as there is a need to distinguish 'what happened' from 'the interpretation of what happened' – which is challenging. It is not so much that history is lies, damned lies and statistics, but that it is untruth, perceived truth and interpreted truth. If history is to have a future as a respected discipline, then there has to be a resolution of this dichotomy. If we are to understand ourselves in the context of the past there has to be some notion of how this riddle can be answered.

That was the very dilemma that I felt when I began to write a historical book: *Of Roseates and Rectories: The Birding Biography of the Revd Francis Linley Blathwayt* (Kerry 2005). Blathwayt was a leftover from the age of the great Victorian parson-naturalists, and had both an interesting narrative and a set of recorded achievements in ornithology. In undertaking the task of recording Blathwayt's life and significance to birding, my account had to resolve the dilemma identified above between history as *fact* and history as postmodernist *creation*. This practical problem set me on the path of thinking through the dilemma; and the rest of this chapter tracks my thought process through this Gordian knot. What follows in the rest of the book is an attempt to apply my solution to a part of Blathwayt's history in a more rigorous way than I did then; the purpose being to establish not the detail about Francis Blathwayt but the principles on which discovering that *reality* (or something closer to it) might be based.

Questions raised by the study of history

The previous section raised the fundamental problem of understanding history: is it possible to reach back into the past and reconstruct it free from contamination by interpretation and interpreters? Or, to put it another way, is historical 'truth' (even more so, Truth) merely a chimera? The questions raised here have to be seen as open questions. The answers, as we have seen, are not wholly straightforward. But the time has come to explore, in a little more detail, elements of that potential interpretation that might cloud our understandings. To do this four additional questions have to be addressed.

1. Is history a separate epistemology?

Those who believe that knowledge can be divided into major areas (variously labelled, for example, as chemistry, theology, psychology, and so on) also tend to maintain that each of these 'disciplines' has its own way of understanding the world – its own epistemology. Indeed, circuitously or tautologously, the definition of a discipline usually includes the statement that it is delineated, at least in part, by its own 'disciplines'.

This argument is open to some question, but if we were to accept it at face value, what we would be saying here would be: history has its own methods of working that are distinctive to it and to its understanding, and are not shared by other disciplines, e.g. theology, chemistry. History can, then, only be judged by its own disciplines. These disciplines include an unravelling of the past by means of an examination of the evidence about the past as revealed in (usually written) formats.

Of course, having done this, the intrepid historian then goes on to produce his/her own account of the events studied, usually by a further written construction, which itself then adds to the 'evidence base' about the topic scrutinised – *which suffers from all the same issues*. This leads us to another question:

2. How significant is the narrative form in history writing?

Now, of course, we are back into the deep waters of interpretation – but, worse, the narrative form itself is regarded by some as the main source of the epistemology of history. In other words, when we look at historical documents, we are looking at artefacts that should not be judged by some criteria of history-as-a-discipline, but by the criteria that attach to the interpretation of narrative, i.e. literary criticism. History, in this view, ceases to be its own discipline and becomes, at best, the servant of another discipline: literary criticism. This dichotomy of view about the nature of history attracts labels for the exponents of each view.

The empiricist view is that a historical narrative emerges in naturalistic form from raw data; that the story is related explicitly, impersonally and transparently. There is a relation between history as it is lived (the past) and history as it is written (narrative).

By contrast, the postmodernists or deconstructionists claim that written history comes from a plot – invented as much as found by the historian. Such writing employs four 'tropes': metaphor, metonymy, synecdoche and irony. These have to be understood, and their effects cut through, as part of the attempt to understand the past. But the process is always at best partial. Thus, there is no objective certainty in the past, i.e. correspondence of evidence with Truth: all writing, it is suggested, is ideologically contaminated. By the same token, the more the quantity of written history, the less historians agree about it. So written history is never fixed (or reliable in any ultimate sense). Such an insight – disturbing to many – leads us on to ask:

3. What, then, is the character/function of historical evidence?

Since most historical evidence comes in the form of written records, if the postmodernists are right it is contaminated at source and interpreted further thereafter. The implications of this line of thinking are explored further below under what we have called 'perspectives on history'. But, similarly, we must ask about people studying history today:

4. What is the role of the historian?

The scientific or empirical historian believes that he/she is working back through the evidence to uncover the truest possible nature of what happened in the past, and he/she may also assume that data are connected by a universal explanation. It is this explanation towards which 'scientific' history steers. But an objector will proclaim that, in fact, history is a series of unique events, causes and consequences that cannot be compartmentalised or characterised in this way. If (most) history is literature, it follows that the historian is a narrator, and that begs questions of selection, motivation and objectivity (as indeed, we have hinted above). So if history has an epistemology peculiar to itself, it is as 'the narrative interpretation and explanation of human agency and intention' – which is a long way from the traditional view of history as the journey into the past for the reconstruction of a near-reality.

To sum up, then: history may not be as objective or reliable as it has sometimes been portrayed; the source of its unreliability is set in its narrative forms; and as guardians and perpetrators of the narratives of history, historians can never be more than the interpreters of the past. Let us assume for the moment that this is a fair assessment of what is labelled as history in the contemporary world; then let us pursue some of the interpretations that have found most favour, or most prominence, over recent decades.

Perspectives in history and historiography

What has been said to date provides a backdrop to the problems both of writing history and of studying it. If it is true – and to some extent it has to be – that all written records (and these account for the bulk of our historical sources) carry a form of bias in terms of the narrator's view, then it follows that almost all historiography must be deemed to adopt a 'perspective' on events. The job of the would-be scientific or empirical historian becomes the peeling away of those lenses used by the narrators and the perspectives offered by the individual historian. What follows looks at some length at the variety of perspectives that one can trace (and the list is far from exhaustive), and briefly at the key points relating to each of the perspectives identified.

1. History from the perspective of the state

A traditional approach to historiography has been the political stance, of history from the perspective of the state. Some would argue that this was substantially the stance of the would-be empiricists: archived materials of states and governments, and those involved intimately with them, offered the best chance (on this view) of a scientific approach to reconstructing events into a kind of 'reality'. There was, in the 19th century, a belief that the affairs of nations and the tide of government provided a better chance for the reconstructing of a sound and objective account of the past than did the study of individuals and their roles within these global actions. They saw history as building the big picture of the future by tracing the passage of the past. But while they developed sound approaches to contextualising sources and comparing different accounts of events, historians of the period in the UK nonetheless failed to realise that the past had within it seeds of future disintegration rather than development. The history that was developed had a very English (as opposed to British) bias, was tied to a Whig philosophy, and excluded social groupings such as women or ethnic minorities. The history they constructed, especially through published papers, helped to place the subject on the curriculum of schools and to develop it as a university discipline; but there lay within this community of historians a cadre of thinkers who would later challenge the accepted perspective as too narrow and exclusive.

2. Marxist history: the class struggle

The lens chosen by this group of academics is that characterised by a view that the class struggle is the key historical agency. It is hard to determine whether Marxists applied their Marxism to history, or whether historians applied their history to Marxism (or both), but from the middle of the 19th century this overall approach was adopted both by Marx himself and by his adherents. Sometimes the process was fired by organisations with a particular motive of their own – such as the Workers' Educational Association. Sometimes the impetus was more individual in nature, involving writers like Hobsbawm, whose works have become widely known both by professional and amateur historians. Big-picture Marxism also gave way in the 20th century to micro-studies of individual lives viewed through those same historical agencies; and the principles of the class struggle were read back into the more distant past as well as being applied to recently unfolding events. However, just because the perspective bears a common label, one should not expect all those writing under it to share an identical view. Differences exist between Eastern and Western historical writers; and some later authors grew disillusioned with the narrowness of the Marxist perspective alone. Nor were all the Marxist writers people whom the public would see as 'typical' Marxists, forging their historical accounts in the white heat of class oppression: notably, writers like Rodney Hilton, who was a product of Manchester Grammar School and Oxford University.

3. History and gender: the role of women reassessed

One of the disillusionments of Marxist historians was the realisation that, in pursuing class history, they had neglected the issue of gender. From the 1960s, probably as a backlash from two world wars and the employment of women associated with these, there was a determination (mainly, but not wholly, among women) to 'rewrite history' in gender/ feminist terms. The enthusiasm for this was occasionally almost messianic, as this quotation from Renaissance historian Joan Kelly signals:

> The change I went through was kaleidoscopic. I had not read a new book. I did not stumble on a new archive. No fresh piece of information was added to everything I knew. But I knew now that the entire picture I had held of the Renaissance was partial, distorted, limited, and deeply flawed.

However, a case can be made that women's history in the 20th century did not reshape historiography. What it did was to shift the perspectives both in global terms (such as suffrage) and personal terms (the contributions of notable women), and place those elements into a better contextual whole. What women's history, and the history of women, may have done is provide clearer understandings of the constraints and social expectations that limited women's involvements in history, especially before the 1900s; and to that extent it may have added a political dimension to more recent historiography towards an understanding of gender's role in world events.

4. History and ethnicity

Similar in principle, but more recent, is the perspective on historiography caused by a consciousness of ethnicity. Perhaps originating in the USA, history from the ethnic perspective began to surface forcibly in the 1970s. Underlying the movement is the perceived need by historical writers to establish their own roots in the past and use them as a lens through which to view both past and unfolding events. Differences of ethnicity can often be subtle – embracing not merely 'race' but the tribe. Ethnicity cannot always be divorced from religious cultures; and religious identities in particular can have powerful and even violent expression. But the issue has been complicated by both immigration and the effects of globalisation. For example, the children of Hong Kong colonial immigrants to the UK may 'look' Chinese to the indigenous population but may claim that their Britishness embraces much more than a designation on a passport: it is what they know and what they are.

Summary

These perspectives on history and historiography have alerted the reader to alternative ways of looking at the world. When these become part of historiography, then the reader has to deconstruct that historical narrative in order to understand it better. What is neglected in the process is any notion of 'history' as some gold standard of reliable and uncontroversial truth. With that goes the view that learning chunks of it as if it were fact is a relatively questionable process: better to learn the skills with which to interrogate it. So history is not a monolithic phenomenon standing against corruption by integrated approaches that involve an understanding of historical events and historical methods for interpreting them. But, if the argument is pursued a little further, we find that history as a discrete discipline is itself a questionable notion. It can, in practice, be appreciated only through other disciplines.

History in relation to other academic disciplines

Economic history

Contrary to opinion in some circles, disciplines – even the discipline of history – do not exist or evolve in a vacuum.

From about the 1880s, and vigorously in the early decades of the 20th century, some historians became aware of the enormous contribution to historical understanding made by economics. Thus James E. Thorold Rogers was early in the field to assert that, rather than seeing history primarily as an account of the actions of princes and statesmen, it should be viewed against more quantitative sources, thus adopting 'the wise habit of developing inferences from evidence'. This rejection of the view of history through the lens of 'high politics' was necessary because the questions being asked of historians by society were now of a different hue. At root, issues such as employment, commerce and industrial development could be seen to be drivers of history. This economic movement was accordingly provided with respectability by being recognised in the universities, initially in the USA and soon in the UK; and inevitably, as a result, in publications in journals such as the *Economic History Review*.

The development of this historical perspective was fuelled, too, by the circumstances of the times. Late 19th- and early 20th-century concerns reflected the social ferment and agitation of the moment, and – doubtless – the rise of ideologies such as that epitomised by the labour movement. While forged in the white heat of contemporary thinking, these ideas were easily read back into the historical past. This was the territory of tenants and landlords, of factory workers and owners, of social and monetary divisions. Here was another – somewhat different – way of looking at social divisions, which also fuelled Marxism. Even an apparently innocuous topic such as the history of a village, viewed from this perspective, saw its focus shift. This particular perspective had begun to give a place in the historical narrative to the 'common man' and to recognise the importance of every individual to the developments in the past that had led to the present, which historians now had to explain.

History and sociology

These two disciplines have what many consider to be the strongest overlaps of any of history's interconnections across academia. Both are devoted to the study of humans operating within society, and to the operation of society. There are some differences, of course. History tends to deal with past events (but plenty of sociologists have taken their subject matter from the past, too). Historians may be held to be interested in 'events', whereas sociologists look for patterns of behaviour (but, as we have seen, historians also look for patterns in their data). Sociologists often claim to represent a 'science' (though some schools of sociology prefer more qualitative approaches, which it could be argued are more akin to the narratives of history). So the distinctions are, at least, blurred around the edges. Clearly, schools of historical thought such as Marxism, have their roots in explaining society. Some would argue that as the two disciplines emerged during the 19th century, sociology became less historical and history became less rooted in sociological method. Certainly, though, the two subjects developed along parallel paths: with their own academic departments and exponents, their own journals, their own learned societies, and so on. Perhaps the move towards establishing its status as a 'science' on the part of sociologists was the most significant key to separation of the two disciplines; and exponents of sociology such as Durkheim who claimed to deal in 'social facts' and a move in the 20th century towards quantitative sociology were probably factors in the eventual (partial) separation.

Of course, a divorce was not entirely practical. Just as sociologists had studied family, class, religion, deviance and urbanisation, so a new class of historians found the same topics important for the discipline of history. 'Top-down history' (explaining events from the perspective of high politics, for example) could be studied through manuscript evidence; 'history from below' (perceptions from the common man) did not leave such a record and needed new sources of data. In the 1960s and 1970s the distinctions between history and sociology became increasingly blurred. However, both disciplines continued to change and evolve individually; and historians of the late 20th century found the increasing use of ethnomethodology and phenomenology in sociological research unacceptable. History today may still contain elements of those approaches, but the traditionalists retain a good deal of sway in the way that history is thought of by the general public.

Clearly, history and sociology share a subject matter, and a range of concerns. They may share some methodologies and reject others as belonging to 'the other side'. Perhaps, in the end, their approaches can be thought of as a continuum along which there are both overlaps and distinctions.

History and anthropology

As with sociology, Geertz talks about the 'blurring of the genres' between history and anthropology. Bernard Cohen felt that the major distinction between the two was that historians dealt with social events in time, anthropologists in space. But maybe the passage of time has shown this to be too simplistic. Anthropology came into its own in the postcolonial age, when peoples in Asia and Africa needed to find identity separated from their colonial pasts. There was a hunt among both groups for the 'culture' of the peoples studied, and an increasing interest from historians in the history of everyday life. In seeking that culture anthropologists often expounded the histories of the people studied, and studied their evolution over time. Thus there is a considerable overlap in the two approaches, which may be difficult to distinguish. One suggestion is that anthropologists are more bound by theory than are some historians; they emphasise the need to explain change, not merely to describe it. Yet even that distinction does not hold true for all practitioners or for all studies.

So how might one sum up the difference between anthropology and history? As an experiment you might try putting the anthropology of fashion into a search engine. This entry came up for me (by Professor Marie Leshkowich from College of the Holy Cross, Worcester, Massachusetts):

> *Course Description*: Clothing is among the most visible and meaningful ways in which we express our identities. At the same time, our clothes are material items produced and consumed through an ever-expanding global fashion industry. This course will explore the various social, cultural, economic, political, and personal meanings associated with fashion and consumption. Combining anthropological and historical methods, we will focus on such questions as:
>
> What role does fashion play in the construction of identity?
>
> Why are fashion and consumption seen as feminine concerns?
>
> What role has clothing played in political and cultural resistance movements?
>
> How is clothing used to differentiate people, in both positive and negative ways?
>
> What are the historical origins of consumer societies?
>
> How has consumer capitalism become a global phenomenon? With what consequences?
>
> Readings will include social theory about fashion and consumption (Bourdieu, Barthes, and Veblen) and ethnographies focusing on such topics as Muslim fashion in Indonesia and Britain, Japanese haute couture, used clothing in Zambia, punks in Britain, American feminists' critiques of the fashion and beauty industry, and the global popularity of blue jeans. Particular attention will be paid to the relationship between consumption of fashion and gender, race, ethnicity, and class.

Then try the same process using the words 'history of fashion'. This reveals (using only the key sites that occur on the first page of Google or similar) various lists that are characterised by dates or era (e.g. Greek, Roman, WW2); within each date division is a description of major garments worn by males and females; some attempt is made to link some of the style trends to circumstance (e.g. availability or shortage of specific materials, geographical location, access to technologies and so on). While the two approaches will cover similar issues and garments, the reader will rapidly be aware of the different emphases in the two perspectives; perhaps with a tendency to greater leaning to description, sequence and information in the historical lens, and greater theorisation in the anthropological.

Summary

Even this brief discussion has indicated that other 'disciplines', while having some distinctive features, cannot be isolated from history as a legitimate mode of exploration; nor can history be satisfactorily disentangled from other disciplines when we come to study the past. This interdependence is, in the end, true of knowledge as a whole. The myth of the ring-fenced discipline – capable of definition, isolation and exclusivity – unsullied by the contaminants of integrated understandings is just that: a myth. But the story doesn't end there, as we shall see.

The emergence of history through cultural media

Amateur history: alternative ways of doing history

It is not just history that cannot exist in some ivory tower of exclusivity, it is also historians. The explosion of TV programmes and publications about historical research (typically family history) sends a clear signal that history is not confined to what historians like to call 'the academy' – i.e. people who are paid to 'do' history as professionals and/or academics. In fact, in principle at least, the distinction is illusory. Even Rubinstein has to admit that 'the intellectual format of questions addressed by family historians is similar to those addressed by academic historians'. However, it is significant to Rubinstein's argument that he selects family history as the example. It enables him to suggest that, once the family tree has been identified, the project is at an end. By contrast, for the academic historian, life goes on, he argues – usually deconstructively. The professional's task, he says, is never completed because he/she recognises the layers of interpretation that he/she needs to bring to unravel the problem studied. The professional studies more complicated topics. Professional historians identify shades of evidence.

This argument is somewhat disingenuous. For one thing, choosing family history (admittedly a widespread interest) may well limit the degree to which an understanding of deconstructive history is necessary. But, as was demonstrated when I undertook my Blathwayt study, things are not that simple. I constructed the family tree, and used records to put together 'a biography' – I was a family historian (of the family of another). But other issues complicated the topic after parts of it had been published. The Blathwayt family provided new evidence, which amended some conclusions. Rivalries among birders threw up different constructions of birding events in Blathwayt's life. New evidence came to light from the press. Amended and expanded papers had to be written to correct or augment previous conclusions; and so on. But I am not a professional historian. I know of others who delve into the past who are as diligent, or more diligent, than I am. Should their 'amateur' (= unpaid) history be differently viewed from 'professional' (paid, employed) history? If they follow the same diligence, principles, exactitude, etc., then the answer has to be 'No.' In both cases it is either history or it is not history – in both cases it can be good history or bad history, balanced history or biased history. Each case is judged on its merits, not on who does it. Remember the *Hitler Diaries* (McArthur 2008)?

Equally open to condemnation is the suggestion that amateurs usually have less knowledge of their subject matter. Indeed, the reverse is often the case. Keen amateurs (in any field) tend to soak up information about their chosen topic wherever they can glean it. Professionals tend to be trained through examinations and theses, which (because of their highly focused concerns) can have a very limiting effect on their overall knowledge of (and even interest in!) the wider field.

Nonetheless, it could be argued that some forms of historical data are more accessible to 'amateurs' than others; and it is to some of these that we must cast our eyes, and ask what contribution these forms of historical data make to the perspectives on history we have discussed earlier.

History, popular culture and emerging sources

Popular culture might be delineated as any culture shared by a society, or (in more élitist vein) the culture of 'ordinary' people. There is certainly a growing tendency for historians (and other academics, such as sociologists) to look at issues such as football or other forms of sport; and history itself is full of quaint and curious customs whose origins may make a suitable study: Morris dancing is a widespread example. Popular music of various genres is now a respectable field of study. Media such as television, photography or advertising also lend themselves to historical research. The list is limited only by imagination, in reality. Topics like these tend to be seen as 'less academic' by some, and thus more trivial. This is not an appropriate debate at this point. In so far as the study of such topics, from a historical perspective, adds to our appreciation of history, then they are valid areas for research – but they should not be labelled as 'amateur' concerns, as compared with the 'serious' history of professionals since plenty of professionals engage in them. Indeed, it might be more useful to think of these topics as themes that permeate (part of) our history – themes that can be isolated and subjected to separate study within, say, our national history but not independent of it. Indeed, there are examples in the UK of reputable universities offering master's degrees and doctorates (i.e. professional qualifications) in exactly these fields, and whose graduates are no more likely to be well versed in 'traditional' historical knowledge than are keen amateurs volunteering for the National Trust or who study aspects of the Second World War – probably less so.

There are other themes, or sources of information, that have come into their own in historical work of recent generations; these will be reviewed briefly for their distinctive contributions. Family history has been mentioned, and while it is true to say that it has become something of a popular hobby and may have limitations compared to the bigger sweeps investigated by 'professional' historians, it is nonetheless a valid and valuable aspect of history. Each 'little' story contributes to a bigger picture and a wider understanding of the development of society as we know it. Thus, the medal collector who assiduously traces the history of the decorated hero is filling out the whole picture of the war; and at best it is sound and legitimate history, even if narrow in scope. Conceivably, it may even add something original to knowledge – the same criterion as is required of a doctorate.

Professional historians are more concerned, perhaps, about film and its relationship to history. But there are points to make here. If film is defined as archive material (e.g. a new discovery of old films depicting life in 19th-century Bradford factories) then it becomes evidence in the same way that a manuscript would become evidence. There is a greater issue for historians when it comes to, say, a commercial film loosely built to tell the tale of events surrounding the Russian Revolution or the killing of the Romanovs. These commercial films are events seen through the lens of (i.e. interpreted by) the director, the writer and the cast – and are no different in principle to the writings of historical novelists. But, then, we must also return to the points made earlier. If it is claimed that depictions of events in written records (whatever they are – even formal documents), are subject to interpretation before the historian gets his/her hands on them, then it follows that, for films, both archive and commercial forms are corrupted (even if in different ways and to different extents because of different motivations). In both cases the historian must deconstruct them – but that is true for every other form of evidence, too.

Increasingly one sees small books of often self-published or locally published history relating to localities such as villages or streets. This kind of local history is valuable in the same way that family history is valuable – as a small cog in the big wheel of more global events. That said, each source has to be judged on its merits – for what it deconstructs successfully and what it accepts uncritically. But since that is ever the historian's dilemma one might conclude: there's nothing new there, then.

Finally, in this summary, there is history of an increasingly popular kind, which is based on the 'living voice' – narratives, often recorded or video-recorded, of older people speaking about events that happened earlier in their own lives. Typical of these might be someone describing memories of the Blitz, or reliving their time in the village school of sixty years ago. The impetus from these histories is to capture them before their owners depart this mortal world. Once more, they are often fascinating in their immediacy, albeit limited in scope. They help to throw individual light on bigger pictures. But they are as subject to the need for checking and deconstruction as are the tales of Herodotus.

Summary

History, then, comes in many guises, but all of them are subject to the same caveats. Programmes like *Time Team*, arguably, make people careless about how they handle data. It is a caricature (but not an excessive one) to say that sometimes two bricks, a fraction of what was once a pot, and three vertebrae result in a fully reconstructed manor house with a representation of a woman in a kitchen area – as if the computer generation were 'truth'. It may well be – and no one would question the skills of the archaeologists, the integrity of the historians who back the programme, its value as 'good television' – but the reconstruction remains heavily inferred truth.

So where do we want to get to from here?

What stands out of this discussion for an amateur historian like me may be summarised as follows:

> In the best of all worlds, it would be good to have some evidence about any given historical situation – situation X – which could be considered or shown to be as reliable as possible. Dates probably come into this category. Some artefacts may do so.

Sources are almost certainly tainted if truth is defined in terms of Truth. But sources can be subject to deconstruction; and some elements that match across sources can probably be relied upon.

Deconstruction itself has to be not just thorough, but carried through in the double awareness of what the then-writers brought to the record, and what the now-interpreters would like to bring to the record of situation X: those insights should be fully explicated in any further addition to the written corpus about that event.

But there is more, and something about which too little is said: context. To understand, for example, the events, feelings, emotions, hopes, aspirations, intellectual understandings, politics (and so on) that surround situation X is to get closer to the skin of it. Any situation X studied by amateur or professional historians should be placed in the macro-picture as well as the micro.

This insight implies that the same situation should be studied and written about using a range of interdisciplinary skills. We need to accept that, in history and in all disciplines, specialism/specialist can have both positive and negative connotations: it can imply narrow, tunnelled and biased as easily as it can suggest expert, detailed and authoritative.

Conclusion

What has emerged from this discussion of history and historiography are, perhaps, some confused and confusing conflicts of approach, alongside some particular philosophies that rest on a view of what history is and what it should be. History is certainly not simple: it is not about our ability to construct Truth in any absolute form. It may be about unpicking the layers of past events to get at some truths – things that happened, when, and, to some extent, how they happened. But beyond that, any attempt to try to answer the question of why they happened takes the reader into realms of interpretation, speculation and theory; and even uncovering the sources demands highly developed awareness and a skill in the process of deconstruction, literary or ideological.

What is clear is that history as a discipline is not fixed and immutable – it is subject to change through fashion or increased understanding. The materials that form its subject matter shift over time in relative importance, not least because of new insights and discoveries. The story that history constructs is not absolute. Each society manufactures the history it wants or deserves. Even the tools that history uses are not unique to itself. History as a 'discipline' is not alone in suffering these problems.

Above all, what is most revealed by this discussion is the lunacy of the date-and-facts school of history beloved of 'let's get back to basics' politicians who would have us believe that our past can be faithfully reconstructed into a single, accurate narrative, subjected to rote learning, and our appreciation of it tested against standard measures. Whatever the tortuousness of deciding what history is, it has to be better than the simplistic adherence to the dates-and-facts delusion.

Beyond history

Maybe, at this point, someone who pursued history as a specialism might be thinking, 'Why are they picking on me?' Well, this text certainly is not. Everything that has been said here – *everything* – has been said by professional historians themselves, of one philosophical persuasion or another, about history. But it is not just history. The suggestion here is that each of the traditional disciplines could be subjected to the same scrutiny, with results that might hold similar import. There is not time to argue this case fully here, but a few observations are worthwhile.

It seems likely that Descartes was on to something when he examined the question of disciplines:

> Perhaps we can correctly infer that, while physics, astronomy, medicine and other disciplines that study composites are dubious, disciplines like arithmetic and geometry, which deal only with completely simple and universal things without regard to whether they exist in the world, are somehow certain and indubitable. For whether we are awake or asleep two plus three is always five, and the square never has more than four sides.

The website Let's Talk Science (http://www. letstalkscience.ca/about-us/why-science) makes an unequivocal claim on interdisciplinary approaches:

The world is not fragmented into discrete subjects and science is not isolated from everything else in our lives – it crosses into all subjects.

Of geography, Dunbar (2001) claims:

Geography is a holistic and integrative university discipline that bridges the natural and social sciences. It is rare for a subject to make integration a priority and to do so successfully.

Golding (2009) suggested that:

There are various important but complex problems, phenomena and concepts that resist understanding or resolution when approached from single disciplines. Climate change and world poverty are clear examples . . . Carolan (2008) shows that the debate surrounding genetically modified organisms involves a tangle of factual, moral and epistemic issues that require multiple disciplines to unravel . . . While disciplinary depth is essential for investigating these complex issues, they also require what Howard Gardner called 'a synthesizing mind' (2006, p. 3) . . . The implication is that we must educate for both disciplinary and interdisciplinary expertise.

This is neatly illustrated by the latest ornithological tome (Birkhead, Wimpenny and Montgomeri 2014). In the first chapter alone – which is a comprehensive review of birds in the fossil record and the early studies in bird flight – the authors make the point that bird flight is hugely more complicated than human (aircraft) flight. As well as palaeontology, they suggest that photography, aeronautics and physiology, combined with wind tunnel experiments, electromyographs and computer modelling, are all required to expand our understanding of this everyday phenomenon. No one could, realistically, doubt that, while the individual disciplines used to unravel this mystery are important, they do not, alone and of themselves, have the capacity to solve this problem which is 'more complex than we once thought' (2014: 36).

Aberdeen University in 2014 advertised its master's course in Languages and Linguistics, while promoting the discipline as a catch-all, in this expansive and over-blown way:

This is really a discipline [note this word – *ed.*] for people who want to learn about different societies around the world through the language and culture. Even linguistics, which takes a much more scientific approach, consists of people with brains the size of the planet using them to analyse in microscopic detail the means by which humanity has evolved its multifarious systems of communication. What you can do with the results of your study is incredibly varied, from working as a critic on the *Times Literary Supplement* to studying endangered species in Outer Mongolia. If you can speak a foreign language, and have the get up and go to travel, the world is, as they say, your oyster.

Then we should return to where we started in Chapter 1, to the 'discipline' of physics, which, according to Study Portals (2014 – online at http://www.mastersportal.eu/disciplines/38/physics.html), we now discover to be defined thus:

The achievements of the field of physics also influence other sciences like mathematics, philosophy, geology or engineering. This discipline is very complex and wide, with a commonly-accepted division into: physics of condensed matter, atomics, molecular physics and optics, high energy physics and astrophysics.

So even this, one of the oldest of all the disciplines, now wants to take its place in an integrated context – albeit, implicitly, as a guide and leader among subjects perhaps, rather than as a follower. A plethora of highly acclaimed universities have attached their endorsement in the form of advertising for their own courses. But the truth is, one might equally have added theology in the list of allied subjects, since much speculation in physics is mirrored also by a subject many would not even label a science.

The move by disciplines, it would appear, is no longer to deny the value of integration but to claim some primary role in discovering and exploiting it! Those cited are just a few of many examples.

Finally

The tenor of this chapter has been simple. Disciplines are not a form of 'superior knowledge', as their more traditional exponents would have us believe; nor should teachers using a cross-curricular approach feel like second cousins to the 'big boys' who are teaching 'real subjects'. Disciplines are just tools, along with many others, in organising and understanding our world and its problems. The map of intellectual understanding may have to be redrawn – however long it takes. In another place I suggested that, in just a couple of generations, many teachers – drunk on the notion of 'facts' – had diminished themselves from the village intellectual into the king-pin of the pub quiz team. This book demonstrates that I would adhere to that notion. 'Knowing' who won the cup final 76 years ago or the colour a pop star had dyed their hair when they had their last number one hit can be construed as 'facts' in so far as they are demonstrably accurate pieces of information with 'correct' answers. They contribute, however, nothing to real 'knowledge', nothing at all to understanding, they make no connections between fragments of information, contribute even less to developing wisdom and do not signal 'intelligence' on the part of the knower. As the chroniclers of Charles Rennie MacIntosh (McKean and Baxter n.d.: 15) record of the artist, he hit a target when he reflected:

> I find I have a great deal to learn – or unlearn. I seem to know far too much and this knowledge obscures the really significant facts.

References

Birkhead, T., Wimpenny, J. and Montgomerie, B. (2014) *Ten Thousand Birds: Ornithology Since Darwin*. Princeton and Oxford: Princeton University Press.
Carolan, M. (2008) 'The multi-dimensionality of environmental problems: the GMO controversy and the limits of scientific materialism'. *Environmental Values* 17: 67–82.
Dunbar, G. S. (2001) *Geography: Discipline, Profession and Subject Since 1870: An International Survey*. New York and London: The GeoJournal Library.
Gardner, H. (2006) *Five Minds for the Future*. Boston, MA: Harvard Business School.
Golding, C. (2009) 'Integrating the disciplines: successful interdisciplinary subjects'. Paper for the Centre for the Study of Higher Education Melbourne, Australia: University of Melbourne.

Kerry, T. (2005) *Of Roseates and Rectories: The Birding Biography of the Revd Francis Blathwayt.* Lincoln: PintailTKC.

McArthur, B. (2008) 'Hitler Diaries scandal: we'd printed the scoop of the century and then turned it to dust'. *Telegraph*, 25 April.

McKean, J. and Baxter, C. (n.d.) *Charles Rennie MacIntosh: Architect, Artist, Icon.* Broxburn, Scotland: Lomond.

Further reading

For those wanting to explore in more detail the nature of history, the following texts may be helpful:

Jenkins, K. (1995) *On 'What is History?'*, London: Routledge.

Labert, P. and Schofield, P. (2004) *Making History: An Introduction to the History and Practice of a Discipline.* London: Routledge.

Lemon, M. C. (2003) *Philosophy of History.* London: Routledge.

Munslow, A. (1997) *Deconstructing History.* London: Routledge.

Internet sources

http://www.findamasters.com/advice/subjectguides/discipline.aspx?did-7
http://www.letstalkscience.ca/about-us/why-science
http://oregonstate.eds/instruct/ph1302/distance/descartes/comment4.html

Index